Illustration 1. A seal found at Tell en-Nasbeh in North Israel (eighth century B.C.E.) (see McCown 1947, pl. 63) by Lauren R. Sneed. Diana Edelman interprets it as representing two men flanking a tree of life = wisdom (2006, 149-53). They appear to be magically imbibing wisdom.

The Social World of the Sages

The Social World of the Sages

An Introduction to Israelite and Jewish Wisdom Literature

Mark R. Sneed

Fortress Press
Minneapolis

THE SOCIAL WORLD OF THE SAGES

An Introduction to the Israelite and Jewish Wisdom Literature

Cover image: Illustration of a seal found at Tell en-Nasbeh in North Israel ©
Lauren R. Sneed

Cover design: Alisha Lofgren

Library of Congress Cataloging-in-Publication Data

Print ISBN: 978-1-4514-7036-9

eBook ISBN: 978-1-4514-7987-4

The paper used in this publication meets the minimum requirements of American
National Standard for Information Sciences — Permanence of Paper for Printed
Library Materials, ANSI Z329.48-1984.

Manufactured in the U.S.A.

This book was produced using PressBooks.com, and PDF rendering was done by
PrinceXML.

Contents

Acknowledgements and Dedication

I would like to acknowledge the Chair of the Bible Department at Lubbock Christian University, Charles Stephenson, and my Dean, Jesse Long, Jr., for creating a partial sabbatical for me during the fall of 2014, so that I might put the finishing touches to the book. I would also like to thank the LCU library for helping me retrieve sources when this was difficult. Special thanks go to Michael Martin who introduced me to genre criticism. Thanks go to Neil Elliott who accepted this project and Lisa Gruenisen for helping make the manuscript better. I also want to thank my wife, Arlene, for putting up with many long hours at the computer at our home and away at the office, while writing this book. Without her patience and support, this book would have never been written. I dedicate this book to my parents, Ronald C. and Joanne Sneed, who always pushed me to do the best I could do academically or otherwise when I was young.

Maps, Illustrations, Figures and Sidebars

Maps

Map 1: The Ancient Near East

Map 2: Topography of Syro-Palestine

Map 3: Syro-Palestine in the Late Bronze Age

Illustrations

All illustrations By Lauren R. Sneed

Illustration 1 (cover): Seal found at Tell en-Nasbeh

Illustration 2: Ea

Illustration 3: Thoth

Illustration 4: Maat

Illustration 5: Israelite Cosmology

Illustration 6: El

Illustration 7: Cuneiform Tablet

Figures

Sidebars

Abbreviations

CBQ	*Catholic Biblical Quarterly*
JBL	*Journal of Biblical Literature*
JSOT	*Journal for the Study of the Old Testament*
SBL	Society of Biblical Literature
WP	Western Periphery (of Mesopotamia)

1

The Nature of Wisdom and Its Practitioners

Who were the Hebrew sages and what did they do? This is a simple enough question, but it is not easy to answer. Unlike the prophets and priests, the category of sages does not designate a homogenous group of people with clearly defined boundaries. In fact, there were many types of sages who served in ancient Israel. Part of the problem is that the feature that defines and unites this group, wisdom, is an ability shared by the masses at large. And so there is wisdom of a very general sort but also a technical version of it. In other words, all Israelites could develop wisdom and be wise, but only certain segments of Israelite society could rightly be called sages, and these of various categories.

Of course, Israelite priests were not all of the same category. The Aaronide or Zadokite priests came to dominate the Levites, who did the menial tasks, like cleaning up after a sacrifice. The Levites became essentially second-class priests. But, generally, one could have probably more easily identified a priest than a sage: by their clothing, their locale, and their vocational skills. Priests are usually defined as cultic or ritual experts. Israelite priests conducted important rituals either at local holy shrines or at the Temple in Jerusalem. They were experts in dealing with the problem of sin and impurity: how to remove it through sacrifices, rites, and observing various laws. They were also experts at soliciting divine knowledge through the mysterious Urim and Thummim, a priestly casting of lots—a form of divination (e.g., 1 Sam. 28:6). Priests were often also teachers, especially the Levites, and served as judges (Neh. 8:7-8).

Israelite prophets were also not without their distinctions. Prophets specialized as mediums who communicated God's will to the people. There were professional court prophets like Nathan and Isaiah, and there were rustic, amateur prophets like Amos. There may have been even what scholars call cultic prophets, who worked at holy shrines or served at the Temple, perhaps even involved with musical production at these sites—e.g., Habakkuk 3 constitutes a hymn that contains musical notations! Prophets sometimes distinguished themselves by their dress (Elijah's hairy mantle [2 Kgs. 1:8]) and bizarre behavior (Isaiah walked around naked for three years [Isa. 20:2-3]).

Identifying the Israelite sages would have been a more difficult endeavor. They received no divine calling like the prophets, neither did they customarily employ any divinatory techniques to discern God's will, as did the priests (except for mantic sages, which will be discussed later). They were not cultic specialists or musicians, nor usually conduits through whom God spoke directly. Their extraordinary skill resided elsewhere: in their heads. Wisdom was the skill or ability they excelled in. So, in what did wisdom consist? What is it exactly?

Defining Wisdom

Before we talk about the special types of wisdom the various sages employed, we must focus on Israelite wisdom in the most general sense. Basically, wisdom is an ability, gift, or skill. In a nutshell it is intelligence, especially high cognitive ability. Of course, from a biological perspective, intelligence is an important adaptive skill and ability that all species share. But humans are exceptional in this category. While we do not have the largest brains, we have the largest ones among primates and our brains have an extraordinary number of neurons. Humans may not be "red in tooth and claw," but we do have these wonderful brains that have enabled our species to prevail and become dominant on the earth. No wonder we call ourselves homo sapiens, "intelligent being." It is appropriate that the word *sapiens* is the Latin word that means "wise" and the word from which our word "sage" comes. Our high intelligence gives us an advantage over other species, but, also, within our own species, intelligence can be a critical ability that enables us as individuals or groups to survive or become dominant.

Types of Wisdom

Amateur Wisdom

The Hebrew word for "wisdom" is *chokmah* and the adjective "wise" is *chakam*. It denotes what might be called amateur or common, non-technical wisdom translated as "cleverness" or "cunning." A "wise" woman saves her city by persuading Joab, David's military commander, to not destroy it (2 Sam. 20:15-22). Like Spock in Star Trek, she convinces Joab that it is better or more logical to slay the one rather than the many of her city. It would be pointless to kill so many innocent people. She then throws the head of the culprit (Sheba) Joab wants over the wall of the city, and he withdraws.

Sidebar 1: Hebrew Transliteration

Like many other ancient alphabetic Semitic languages (Ugaritic, Aramaic, etc.), written Hebrew did not originally include vowels. Vowel indicators, called vowel points, were not added to Hebrew until the Middle Ages by the rabbis. The rabbis had been pronouncing the Hebrew for centuries without these markings under the consonants. The lack of vowel points is partly due to the fact that no Hebrew words began with vowels, unlike the ancient Greek language, which needed vowels at the beginning of some of its words, such as its negative particle *ou*. The Israelite scribes simply memorized the vowel sounds and eventually used certain consonants to function doubly as consonants and vowels, like the *waw*, pronounced *o* as a vowel but the *vee* sound as a consonant. The root of a Hebrew word refers to the three identifying consonants that formed most Hebrew words, without the vowels. It is also the simplest form of the word. From this root, all the nouns, adjectives, adverbs, and verbs can be formed, by adding prefixes and suffixes to the root. For example, the word for "wise" is *ch* + *k* + *m*, with only the consonants, but when you add the vowels it becomes *chakam*. If you turn it into a noun, "wisdom," it becomes *chokmah* = *ch* + *k* + *m* + *h*, plus the vowels. I use the simplest form of Hebrew translation in this book, without indicating the various technical nuances of word formation and sound.

Abigail demonstrates this kind of wisdom when she uses her wits to save her family from slaughter by David, whom her husband Nabal, nickname meaning "fool," had insulted (1 Sam. 25). She quickly meets David and provides him and his men with gifts, is very deferential, and convinces him that what he is about to do is very unjust. At the beginning of the story, she is described as *tovah sekel*—literally "good of insight" (v. 3). And at the end, David pronounces, "Blessed is your discretion!" (*ta'am*)[1] (v. 33), because she had kept him from shedding innocent blood.

Divine Wisdom

A more specialized but fundamental form is divine wisdom because the source of wisdom ultimately goes back to the deities. The gods of the ancient Near East often claimed to be wise in addition to other characteristics like powerful, just, immortal, and majestic. The head of the Canaanite pantheon, El, is called "wise" and "old" (Müller 1980, 366), characteristics usually found together. When the other Canaanite gods are praised, El is usually the comparison. In Mesopotamia, the god Enki/Ea is the god of wisdom and magic who counsels the other gods.[2] Marduk, the great god of the Babylonians, is also described as very wise. Similarly, in Egypt, the god of wisdom is Thoth, who is depicted with the head of an ibis or baboon, and is also the god of the scribes. Thoth is usually depicted holding a wand in one hand, which represents power, and an ankh symbol in the other, which represents life. Thoth was married to Maat, whose headdress held a feather, so light it would not cause the scales of judgment to tilt

---

1. Translations of the Hebrew Scriptures are my own, unless otherwise indicated.
2. Bob Becking (1996, 34–54) argues that Yahweh assumes the role of Ea in 2 Kings 4:31–37 by exorcizing the Shunemite woman's son at the bequest of Elisha.

falsely. Maat thus represented justice, order, balance, and truth. She is the great theme of the Egyptian wisdom literature.

Illustration 2. Ea.

The gods in fact were often thought to have brought wisdom to humans, much like Prometheus with his gift of fire. In Mesopotamian lore, Ea was responsible for the creation of humans, which he sired. Ea also imparted his wisdom to seven divine sages, who in turn passed on knowledge and culture to humans before the flood. These were followed by four semi-divine sages, some of them kings, until finally Mesopotamian scribal teachers transmitted this knowledge to their students. To get around the obvious problem of transmitting culture and knowledge from before the flood to after it, one version of the Epic of Gilgamesh has the Babylonian "Noah," Utnapishtim, a.k.a. Atrahsis (= "extremely wise"), bury the instructions for human culture in Sippar, where they could be found after the flood. A Babylonian text, "The Instructions of Shuruppak," claims to be part of that instruction. The genealogy of Cain (Gen. 4:17-24) partly parallels these explanations. Cain's descendants are the bearers of culture and civilization (city-builders, tent-dwellers, musicians, and smiths) to the antediluvian world. And the personification of wisdom, Woman Wisdom, created before the creation of the world, in Proverbs 8 functions in the same way, as a bearer of culture. In fact, one could call her the Hebrew Prometheus!

Of course, the Israelites also claimed that the Lord was very wise: "With him are wisdom and strength; he has advice and discernment" (Job 12:13). Compare the doxology in Rev. 7:12: "Amen! Blessing and glory and *wisdom* and thanksgiving and honor and power and might be to our God forever and ever! Amen" (*NRSV*). That there are seven attributes reinforces the perfection of the deity. In Isaiah 40, there is a comparison of God with the idols and gods of the nations that combines many of these elements: his power, might, glory, and his superior knowledge (vv. 10-31).

Illustration 3. Thoth

Figure 1: Timeline of the Ancient Near East		
Mesopotamia and Palestine	Egypt	Israel
Early Bronze Age or **EBA** (3500–2100 B.C.E.)	Old Kingdom (2650–2135 B.C.E.)	
Middle Bronze Age or **MBA** (2100–1550 B.C.E.)	First Intermediate Period (2135–2040 B.C.E.)	
	Middle Kingdom (2040–1650 B.C.E.)	
	Second Intermediate Period (1650–1550 B.C.E.)	
Late Bronze Age or **LBA** (1550–1200 B.C.E.)	New Kingdom (1550–1080 B.C.E.)	
		Iron Age I (1200–1000 B.C.E.)
		Iron Age II (1000–587 B.C.E.)
		Neo–Babylonian Period (587–539 B.C.E.)
		Persian Period (539–332 B.C.E.)
		Ptolemaic Period (332–198 B.C.E.)
		Seleucid Period (198–140 B.C.E.)
		Hasmonean Dynasty (140–37 B.C.E.)

Illustration 4. Maat

Though the book Proverbs assumes that one can study the many aphorisms in the book and attain wisdom through hard work and effort (Prov. 1:2-6, 8, 23-25), it simultaneously depicts God as the ultimate source of wisdom:

> For the Lord gives wisdom,
> from his mouth is knowledge and understanding.
> And he will store up for the upright success,
> and protection for those who walk in integrity (Prov. 2:6-7).
>
> For wisdom will come into your heart,
> and knowledge will be pleasant to your soul (Prov. 2:10).

All wisdom ultimately goes back to him, and, thus, has divine origins. This fits with the depiction of Woman Wisdom as the source of all wisdom, who represents God (Prov. 8:22-31). Thus, the whole world is saturated with wisdom and reflects its designs and orderliness.

Royal Wisdom

As the gods, so go the kings. They claimed to have great wisdom in addition to their power, justice, and majesty. Of course, Solomon humbly asks for wisdom to govern the Israelites as their king instead of wealth, honor, long life, and power over his enemies (1 Kgs. 3). Because of this, God gives Solomon all of them. A king could use his power alone (his army) to force his people to submit, but this is much less effective and more costly than for him to be wise and beneficent to them as well. The people are more likely to follow the king who is persuasive and wise than one who rules with an iron fist alone. This is what Max Weber, a father of sociology, called "legitimacy," that a ruler desires those he rules to view it as legitimate (1978, 31; see Swedberg 2005, 147-49). Yet Solomon's wisdom went beyond legal and political astuteness. He is depicted as a true polymath and having great literary abilities, such as the skill to compose 3000 proverbs and 1005 songs (1 Kgs. 5:9-12), as well as having encyclopedic knowledge (v. 13), similar to the Egyptian onomastica, or catalogs of things according to their kind.

Sidebar 2: Egyptian Onomostica

The Egyptian onomastica were catalogs of things arranged according to their kind. The "Onomastica of Amenope" begins: "Beginning of the teaching for clearing the mind, for instruction of the ignorant and for learning all things that exist: what Ptah created, what Thoth copied down, heaven with its affairs, earth and what is in it, what the mountains belch forth, what is watered by the flood, all things upon which Re has

---

> shone, all that is grown on the back of earth, excogitated by the scribe of the sacred books in the House of Life, Amenope, son of Amenope." The list begins: "[S]ky, sun, moon, star, Orion, the Great Bear, . . . storm, tempest, dawn, darkness, light, shadow, sunlight, rays of the sun, storm-cloud, dew, snow, rainstorm . . ." Here is another section of the list: "[G]od, goddess, male spirit, female spirit, king, queen, king's wife, king's mother, king's child, crown-prince, vizier, sole friend, eldest king's son, great overseer of the army, the courtiers . . ." (Gardiner 1947, 2, 5-6, 13-21).

Azitawadda, king of Danuna, near Ugarit, Syria (720 B.C.E.), boasts that the vassal kings he controlled chose him because of his righteousness, wisdom, and graciousness (Müller 1980, 366). In ancient Egypt, the tomb autobiographies of Pharaohs and noblemen often include boastings of being wise. Also, the Egyptian official Sinuhe (twentieth century B.C.E.) describes the new king as "lord of wisdom" (Müller 1980, 369). Thutmose III (fifteenth century B.C.E.) calls himself "shrewd in wisdom." The Assyrian king Ashurbanipal (seventh century B.C.E.) states that he comprehends the wisdom of Nabû, god of the scribes (Sweet 1990, 55).

Professional or Technical Wisdom

There is also a technical type of wisdom that involves high skill or expertise in some trade or field of study or practice. Hiram of Tyre was hired by Solomon to do the bronze work on the Temple because of his unusual expertise in the artisan craft (1 Kgs. 7:13-45). A woman from Tekoa is described as "wise" (2 Sam. 14:2), and, because of her superb theatrical talents, she convinced David to allow his son Absalom to return from exile. Solomon is famous for demonstrating his judicial "wisdom" by determining the real mother of the living baby in the story of the two prostitutes (1 Kgs. 3). This event immediately follows his reception of wisdom from God in a dream (1 Kgs. 3:12). A person who is described as "knowledgeable about (painful) worms" found on a clay tablet from Uruk in Babylonia (fourth-second centuries B.C.E.) is probably a dentist (Müller 1980, 366-67).

Mantic Wisdom and Magic

In Akkadian, the language of the Babylonians, "wisdom" is often used to describe a special type of technical expertise: the art of divination. Daniel purportedly was trained as a mantic sage in Babylonia. The Babylonian king took from the Jewish exiles "young men among whom there was no blemish and handsome and wise concerning all wisdom (chokmah) and knowledgeable and intelligent and who were able to stand in the king's court and in order to teach them the literature and language of the Babylonians" (Dan. 1:4). This literature would have been the vast omen literature studied by diviners, those who observed the stars and other signs like the entrails of animals to determine what the future held. Though Daniel was trained broadly in this lore, his expertise was in the interpretation of dreams (oneiromancy), which ability he received from God (Dan. 2:28). Joseph was an expert in this particular type of divination as well. Both Daniel and Joseph outdo their pagan colleagues and competitors. In Isa. 44:24-28, God contrasts his power and the authenticity of his prophets with Babylon and its mediums; he is a God "who frustrates the omens of oracle priests, and makes a mockery of diviners; who turns back the wise, and makes their knowledge foolishness." Again, in Isa. 47:10 there is a polemic against Babylon and its diviners, astrologers, charmers, and sorcerers.

Related to mantic wisdom is magical wisdom. Psalm 58:5 refers to the "cunning enchanter" or snake charmer (see Müller 1980, 378). More famously, Pharaoh summons the "wise men and the sorcerers" to turn their rods into serpents as Aaron did (Exod. 7:11). Magic was an important component of Egyptian and Mesopotamian religion and politics. It was less so in Israel, at least officially. The ordeal for the wife suspected of adultery (Num. 5:11-31), though, smacks of magic and is similar to Mesopotamian practices, as will be seen.

Sidebar 3: Omen Wisdom

Mesopotamians had two types of divination: inspired, where a deity reveals the future to a person in a dream or vision. The other type was deductive divination, where the gods reveal the future through signs in nature. A horse mounting an ox means a reduction in the numbers of livestock. A person losing his seal (form of identity) means his son will disappear. Here is an astrological example: "If the Moon, on rising, is partly dimmed, the right point of its crescent broken off, but the other sharp and perfectly discernible—the country's economic activity will stagnate for three years" (Bottéro 2001, 192).

Political Wisdom

Political advice was a highly desired commodity among the Israelite elite. A poor but wise man in a besieged city was able to deliver the city due to his expertise in military strategy (Eccles. 9:13-16). The political advice of Ahithophel, David's counselor, is described as "according to a man who asked concerning the word of God" (2 Sam. 16:23). David's nephew, Jonadab, is described as a "very wise man" (*chakam me'od*) (2 Sam. 13:3), who advises his cousin, Amnon, on how he might trap his beautiful half-sister Tamar, Absalom's full sister, to rape her with impunity. However, the advice eventually backfires when Amnon later dies at the hands of Absalom for this treachery.

Rhetorical Wisdom

A special type of wisdom might be called expertise in rhetoric. When a lyre-player is sought for king Saul to soothe the evil spirit God had sent upon him, one of his officers recommended David and described him as "one who knows how to play an instrument, is very strong, a man of war, knowledgeable in speech, handsome, and the Lord is with him" (1 Sam. 16:18). The Hebrew phrase literally is "one skillful (root *byn*, a synonym of *chakam*) in speech," which means David was an effective speaker and negotiator. David demonstrated his talent in speech by turning the table on the Philistine giant Goliath (1 Sam. 17:41-51). He literally takes Goliath's rhetorical flourish and turns it against him, using Goliath's very words, and, then, delivers what he has just promised!

The importance of the art of rhetoric is especially emphasized in the book of Proverbs, where many aphorisms abound that promote the value of gracious speech:

Death and life are in the hand of the tongue,
and the one who loves it, will eat its fruit (18:21).
Like a honeycomb are pleasant words,
sweet to the soul and health to the bones (16:24).

The Egyptian text, the "Tale of the Eloquent Peasant," was apparently composed to instruct young scribes in the importance of persuasive speech. The story tells of a poor farmer who is able to convince the Pharaoh and his noblemen to side in his favor against a high steward who had wronged him.

Literary or Aesthetic Wisdom

The last category of wisdom involves literary finesse and subtlety. The prologue to Proverbs refers to their ascertainment as one of the aims of the book: "to understand an aphorism and figure, the words of the wise and their riddles" (1:6). This signifies that comprehending wisdom literature is not always straightforward and that training is necessary. It also indicates that it is not just the content of wisdom that is important but also its medium, the package it is placed in. A later chapter will be devoted to examining the high artistic quality of the wisdom literature and its genres.

The Semantic Domain of Wisdom

In America, one often hears someone distinguish between knowledge and wisdom: "Being wise doesn't mean just knowing facts. It means knowing how to use them." That notion is true for ancient Israel and the rest of the ancient Near East as well. The French phrase "savoir-faire" is apt here: "know-how." In the Hebrew Bible, words for "wisdom" and for "being wise" are frequently paired with nouns for "knowledge," "understanding," "instruction," and "advice," and verbs like "to know," "to instruct," "to prescribe" and "to advise" (see Müller 1980, 371-72). In Hebrew, the root *chkm* ("to be wise") is synonymous with *byn* (to understand) and *yd'* ("to know"). The Hebrew wisdom literature naturally likes to cluster these synonyms:

> Should the wise (root *chkm*) answer with windy knowledge (root *yd'*)
> and fill themselves with the east wind? (Job 15:2).
> For the Lord gives wisdom (root *chkm*);
> from his mouth come knowledge (root *yd'*)
> and understanding (root *byn*)[ ] (Prov. 2:6).

Wisdom is often connected with "instruction." In Prov. 21:11 "become wise" is in parallel "to obtain knowledge":

> In the punishment of a scoffer the simple become wise (root *chkm*),
> and in the instruction of the wise they obtain knowledge (root *yd'*).

Root *chkm* is semantically related to root *zaqen* ("to be old") and root *tsdq* ("to be righteous") (Müller 1980, 372). In Job 32:9, the young whippersnapper Elihu tries to challenge the normative assumption that age and wisdom belong together: "It is not the aged that are wise, nor the old that understand justice." To El it is said, "[T]he gray of your beard has truly instructed you" (Müller 1980, 366). "Wisdom" and "righteous" (or the notion of piety) also appear together frequently:

> Give to the wise and he will become wiser still,
> make the righteous knowledgeable
> and he will increase learning (Prov. 9:9).
> The fear of the Lord is the beginning of knowledge;
> but wisdom and discipline fools despise (Prov. 1:7).

The last verse cited is usually considered the motto for the book of Proverbs. Fearing God in the Hebrew Bible, but especially in the wisdom literature, means being pious, i.e., being righteous. This does not mean that wisdom and righteousness are totally synonymous. We have already seen that wisdom can be used for good or bad, and the term sometimes implies simply a skill or expertise that is morally neutral. However, it does point to the fact that wisdom often has a moral dimension, especially when referring to a wise lifestyle. This also means that wisdom always assumes a religious perspective. It would be anachronistic to speak of some sort of secular knowledge or wisdom existing in the ancient world. All ancient peoples were religious, to one degree or another, in the ancient Near East. There were no true atheists, though there were plenty of dissidents and the unorthodox. This is one of the things that distinguishes the modern intellect and science from ancient ways of knowing, which are always morally and religiously based. From an ancient standpoint, a person who is truly wise would adopt a pious lifestyle. Most ancient peoples thought that being faithful to one's deity would be repaid with long life and prosperity—obviously a wise choice!

For ancient peoples, including Israel, the "heart" (*leb*) was the seat of wisdom, instead of the head (see Müller 1980, 372). The wise are often called "wise of heart" (e.g., Job 9:4; Prov. 10:8; 16:21). God provides a wise and discerning heart to Solomon (1 Kgs. 3:12). In 1 Kgs. 4:29, "wisdom" is equated with "breadth of heart." The fool, contrarily, is "without heart" (*chesar leb*).

Antonyms of "wise" (*chakam*) include *kesel* ("stupid"), *'evil* ("foolish"), *sakhal* ("foolish"), *nabal*, and *lets* ("babbler" or "scoffer") (see Müller 1980, 372). The wise and the fool are often juxtaposed in the book of Proverbs, which serves to clarify the distinctive characteristics of these categories of people: "The wise store up knowledge, but the mouth of the fool means destruction nearby" (10:14).

Two Broad Kinds of Wisdom

We have examined wisdom as a skill or ability that people either had naturally or had attained it with instruction and developed it with practice. However, there is another type of wisdom that is perhaps the dominant kind in the wisdom literature. It is less a particular skill or gift and more a lifestyle. Often when the wisdom writers in the Hebrew Bible refer to "the wise" or "the righteous" or "the fool" or "the wicked," they are referring to a lifestyle that reflects a certain moral disposition rather than a specific talent:

> The wise of heart will heed commandments,
> but foolish lips will be ruined (Prov. 10:8)
> The righteous are delivered from need,
> but the wicked will enter it instead (11:8).

Compare this with Eccles. 8:1 and 8:5:

> Who is like the *wise* and who knows
> the interpretation of a matter? (v. 1).
> One who keeps the command will avoid an evil matter,
> time and sentence the heart of the *wise* knows (v. 5).

Scott C. Jones (2006, 211–28) makes the case that this section is about the liabilities of mantic wisdom (e.g., Daniel's skills) in the context of the court. This means that the type of wisdom being referred to here is very technical and, thus, not available to the general public and only an option for specialists.

The German term *Lebenskunst* ("the art of living") appropriately captures the nuance of lifestyle wisdom. Again, this type of wisdom does not necessarily refer to a superior kind of intellect or gift but is a kind of wisdom that anyone could practice; it is, thus, potentially universal and democratic. The wise lifestyle would fit what we today would call being a conformist, someone who abides by the norms and mores of society, i.e., a good citizen. The fool, however, would be what we would call a deviant: a gang member, criminal, trouble-maker, etc.; one who does not play by the rules. The wise conformist would do his/her duty to the larger public, whether village or city, but he would also wisely look out for the interest of his immediate family, defend their honor, and only bring prestige to their reputation. Scripture does not clearly differentiate between wisdom (or folly) as a lifestyle and as a gift or talent, and they often overlap. As we shall see, scribes could do both simultaneously!

Who Were the Sages?

Now that we have broadly defined what wisdom is (a skill and a lifestyle) and shown some of the different ways the concept has been used in the Hebrew Bible and ancient Near East, it is now time to identify the sages. Again, as said in the beginning, there was no one clearly defined group that was described as sages (*chakemim* or "wise ones") in ancient Israel, unlike for the priests and prophets. This is chiefly so because the concept of wisdom, having so many different nuances and usages, could be applied to a greater number of types of individuals and groups. In other words, there would have been a lot more possible ways of being wise for an Israelite than for being priestly or prophetic.

While any Israelites could have lived a wise lifestyle, not all Israelites would have been considered sages. All of the latter would have to be specially qualified and assume a particular role, many having exceptional gifts, abilities, and/or expertise in particular crafts, skills, and types of knowledge. There were certainly professional sages in ancient Israel who would have had to undergo special training and education, and who, as a group, formed a type of vocational guild. But there were amateur sages as well, who trained themselves or had special innate abilities or assumed certain roles in Israelite society. We will also consider what could be called ad hoc sages, persons who temporarily or periodically assume the role of sage as an advisor or counselor but whose primary occupation was not as a sage. We now briefly provide an overview of the various types of sages that served in ancient Israelite society.

Parents as Sages

The most basic and even archetypal role of sage in ancient Israel would have been the parents, both father and mother. While no one in ancient times would have particularly referred to parents as sages in the ancient world, the label fits because of their important role as educators or teachers of children. This resonates with the Hebrew linguistic connection of wisdom and instruction. One of the most significant functions of a sage in the ancient Near East was that of teacher or educator. Parents, of course, are the quintessential teachers who passed on their life experiences, skills, and wisdom to their children in order to enable them to be productive members of the family and citizens in the broader world. They also taught them skills, both technical and general, that would enable them to be successful in their lives and vocations. So, it makes sense to begin with parents in order to fully understand the role of sage in ancient Israel. In other words, wisdom begins in the home.

The voice of the parents is especially significant for the wisdom literature of the Hebrew Bible. In both the book of Proverbs (e.g., 1:8 and throughout chapters 1-9) and Ecclesiastes (12:12), the vocative "my son" is used to address the intended audience. Most scholars agree that this usage is metaphorical and employed as a personal address to a student by his teacher. But it is more than that in Proverbs 1-9. Here the voice of the parents, which also includes the maternal voice (1:8b; 6:20b), is used rhetorically to persuade the student to obtain wisdom and understanding. The narrator's voice, thus, draws on the authority of the parent, an especially powerful and attractive appeal to a young audience. The connection between wisdom and parents is also found in 23:22-23:

> Listen to your father who begot you,
> and do not despise your mother because she is old.
> Buy the truth and sell it not,
> wisdom, instruction, and understanding.

The voice of the mother is also found in Prov. 31:1-9. It is the queen mother who gives advice to her young son about the dangers of alcohol and seductive women—which sounds strikingly modern!

That the wisdom writers feel it appropriate to connect parents with the type of wisdom they offer further legitimates referring to parents as actual sages, though not in the strict sense. Grandparents would have also assumed this role, but this leads to the next category of sage.

Elders as Sages

Another significant kind of sage would be elders. We have already seen that in the ancient Near East being old or having grey hair was connected with wisdom. As persons aged in the ancient world, their honor or prestige increased correlatively, and they were valued for their wisdom and knowledge that had accrued over a lifetime. Younger persons would go to the elders for advice and counsel. The most basic kind of elder was the village or city elder. The village or city elder would have been at least the head of his extended or nuclear family (bet 'av) and most likely one of the wealthier members of the village or town.

Village/city elders had three main functions in ancient Israel (see Willis 2001, 11-31, 61-67). First, elders were peacemakers, serving to adjudicate conflicts among members and within families. Elders were chosen by the community based on their prestige and renown for impartiality and for placing the interests of the village community above their own. A person who was hot-headed or unsociable or that displayed undue favoritism would not have been selected. Their older age, numerous life experiences, and accumulated wisdom enabled them to serve effectively. Second, elders served as representatives for their village or city in the larger clan and tribal gatherings and festivals and in judicial cases that involved more than one clan, as in a homicide. Being wise would certainly aid in this significant endeavor. Third, they served as judges in the city or village they lived in.

The "wise" friends of Job are portrayed as village or city elders who have come to comfort one of their own. Apparently the calamities that afflicted Job and his family and his reaction to them had created a disruption within the community that had to be rectified. Eliphaz says of his colleagues:

> Both the old and aged are among us,
> older than your father (Job 15:10).
> I will declare to you and listen to me!
> And what I have seen and will recount it.
> What the wise have reported,
> they have not hidden it from their fathers (vv. 17-18).

They apparently came to convince Job of the error of his way and help him move past the disasters; they came to stabilize matters and bring harmony again to the community. These friends are quite effective rhetorically as they debate with Job. The ambiance of the debate between Job and his friends smacks of a legal setting at the gate of a city or town, where court cases were adjudicated. Elders were frequently judges in the cities. Archaeologists have discovered benches in the city gates, where court cases may have been held.

There were also what might be called royal elders who served as the king's servants and advisors (2 Sam. 12:17). A verse from Jeremiah that refers to enemies of the prophet, when compared with one from Ezekiel, seems to indirectly identify these particular sages:

> And they said, "Come and let us scheme concerning Jeremiah plans, for instruction will not perish from the priest, nor counsel from the wise, nor the word from the prophet" (Jer. 18:18).

> [T]hey will seek a vision from the prophet; instruction will perish from the priest, and counsel from *the elders* (Ezek. 7:26).

A last type of elder would be national or tribal elders. These would be city elders from the most prestigious families who would represent regions and would meet regularly. For example, David gives war spoils to "the elders of Judah" (1 Sam. 30:26).

Judges as Sages

Judges in ancient Israel were certainly a type of sage. We have just considered elders as judges, but there were also judges who were governmental officials. Already discussed is the example of the judicial wisdom of Solomon in 1 Kgs. 3, who has assumed the typical royal role of what we would call a Supreme Court justice. In the appointment of judges in Deut. 1:9-18 (cf. Exod. 18:13-27), Moses cannot serve as judge for all the people, so he commands the people to choose from each of the tribes individuals who are "wise and understanding and who know how to judge you" (Deut. 1:13). These would have also been considered elders of their clans.

Kings as Sages

The king also assumed the role of sage. In ancient Mesopotamia, the kings demonstrated their great wisdom and piety in building temples for their favorite gods. In inscriptions, the Babylonian king Nebuchadnezzar (sixth century B.C.E.) commemorates the building of temples, while employing epithets for himself that denote his great wisdom (Sweet 1990, 56-57). And the Assyrian king Ashurbanipal (seventh century) even claims to have studied to become a scribe and sage, leaning the secret lore of the diviners (Sweet 1990, 55). Again, we have already mentioned Solomon and the account of his reception of great wisdom (1 Kgs. 3). Its close proximity to his building of the Temple (1 Kgs. 5-6) is no coincidence! In the Hebrew Bible, he is in fact depicted as the quintessential sage, a sort of Socrates for the Jews. It is no surprise that to him is ascribed the authorship of the book of Proverbs (1:1; 10:1), though other authors are cited as well in the book (e.g., the oracle of Agur [30:1-14]). Similarly, Hezekiah is said to have commanded his officials to collect the proverbs of Solomon (Prov. 25:1). In Ecclesiastes, the author assumes the role of Solomon in the first two chapters in order to conduct an experiment to test what value the efforts and strivings of humans really are. Also, the Wisdom of Solomon purports to be from the hand of Solomon, though written in the first century B.C.E. In Egypt, some of the instructions, a type of wisdom literature, are purported to have been written by kings ("Instruction of King Amenemhet I," "Instruction for Merikare"). We have also seen that Solomon's father, David, is also described as wise. Interestingly, in the Qumran literature (11QPsa 27:2-5), it is David, not Solomon who is acclaimed for his wisdom and sapiential writings: 3,600 psalms and 4,050 songs (see Perdue 2008, 380). The kings of Israel and other ancient Near Eastern nations were expected to be paragons of virtue, power, and especially wisdom.

Courtiers as Sages

Closely connected to the wise king are his courtiers, i.e., advisors and counselors at the king's court, who qualify, of course, as sages. Courtiers were also often scribes (treated next) but not always. Ahithophel was David's courtier, but there is no mention of his serving as a scribe (1 Chron. 27:33), whereas Jonathan, David's uncle, is described as his counselor and as "a man of understanding and a scribe" (1 Chron. 27:32). Nathan, though his primary role was that of prophet, certainly functions as a courtier or consultant to David. Ahiqar, described as a wise scribe, is purported to have served under King Esarhaddon (seventh century) of Assyria and wrote an instruction for his successor. In the book of Proverbs, there are a few admonitions that are rather courtly. Here is an example:

> Do not boast before the king,
> and do not stand in the place of the great.
> For it is better that one say to you, "Come up,"
> than you be humbled before a nobleman
> who sees your eyes (25:6-7).

Similarly, in Ecclesiastes, there is a courtly saying:

> I say that you keep the edict of the king
> and because of the matter of your oath to God.
> Do not hasten from before him.
> Do not remain in an evil matter
> for all which he desires he will do.
> For the word of the king is supreme,
> and who can say to him,
> "What are you doing?" (8:2-4).

Both passages from Proverbs and Ecclesiastes assume that the hearer might find himself standing before a king, a necessity for serving as a courtier. But, again, not all sages were courtiers.

Mantic Sages and Magicians

Again, Daniel and his three friends functioned as mantic sages for the Babylonians, with oneiromancy as their area of expertise. The group of mantic sages that composed the book of Daniel refer to themselves as the *maskilim* ("wise ones") (11:33, 35; 12:3, 10) and appear to be a persecuted sect. In the Qumran text 4QInstruction, the related title *mebin* ("understanding one") is used for an apocalyptic group that studied mysteries. In Dan. 2:2, the "enchanters" are exorcists (Redditt 1999, 52). Exorcists would be a type of magical sage (Acts 19:13), and the Babylonians were experts of the craft.

Sidebar 4: An Exorcist Ritual
The ancient Mesopotamians believed demons caused illness. To cure an individual, an exorcist or magician was called upon to drive them out. In a typical ritual, the exorcist presents the illness and recalls its origins (from demons). He then describes the wretched state of the victim. Next the supernatural nature of the cure is emphasized. The exorcist then rubs loaves of bread on the victim who spits on any crumbs that fall. These items soak up the illness/demon. The loaves are left for rodents to eat, who subsequently take on the illness/demon. A final invocation is made, "May the divine healer Gula, who is able to restore the dying to life, make him

whole again by the touch of her hand? And you,
compassionate Marduk, utter the formula that will free him
from his trouble, so that he is completely out of danger!"
(Bottéro 2001, 170-71)

Wise Scribes

The final type of sage and the one we will be most interested in is the
scribe. As the English word indicates, a scribe is one who inscribes,
copies, or writes. The Hebrew word for scribe, *sopher*, means most
concretely "one who counts." The very first scribes worked in the
first civilization of humankind: Sumer, in lower Mesopotamia
(southern Iraq) (fourth-third millennia B.C.E.). As the human
population began to swell in ancient Sumer, it was necessary for
the early rulers to control and organize the population. This meant
that administrators were necessary, and the development of writing
was key to organizing irrigation (of the Tigris and Euphrates rivers)
and building projects. The only way to centralize these endeavors
and to have enough resources was through a robust administration
that surveyed the land, collected taxes, and kept records. Voila! The
scribe was born! The first scribes were accountants, and writing,
including mathematics and numbers, was created in conjunction
with scribalism. From accountants and record-keepers, scribes
quickly rose to become scholars and authors in their own right.
Scribes were very important throughout the ancient Near East. They
were responsible for not only composing religious texts but also for
preserving them. Our Bible exists today mainly thanks to scribes.

The connection between scribes and wisdom is tight and natural. Ben Sira (second century B.C.E.) most clearly reveals this connection:

> The wisdom of the scribe depends
> on the opportunity of leisure; only the one
> who has little business can become wise.
> How different the one who devotes himself
> to the study of the law of the Most High!
> He seeks out the wisdom of all the ancients,
> and is concerned with prophesies;
> he preserves the saying of the famous
> and penetrates the subtleties of parables;
> he seeks out the hidden meaning of proverbs
> and is at home with the obscurities of parables.
> He serves among the great
> and appears before rulers;
> he travels in foreign lands
> and learns what is good and evil in the human lot
> (38:24, 38:34-39:4; *NRSV*).

But even as far back as Jeremiah (sixth century B.C.E.), the connection between scribes and wisdom was also natural:

> How can you say,
> "We are *wise* and the instruction of the Lord is with us"?
> Therefore, behold, the false stylus of the scribes has made it a lie.
> The wise are ashamed and dismayed, and are captured.
> Behold, they have rejected the word of the Lord and what wisdom do
> they have? (8:8-9).

The narrator of the book of Ecclesiastes specifically identifies the Teacher (*Qohelet* in Hebrew) as a sage (12:9) (*haya Qohelet chakam*; literally "the Teacher was wise"). Also, the description of his special skills in the same verse utilizes technical terms for scribal activities: "weighing and searching and arranging many aphorisms" (see Fishbane 1988, 29-32). The Teacher also refers to other sages, no doubt scribes who differed with him: "And I saw all the work of God, indeed humans cannot comprehend the work that is done under the sun on account of the fact that humans toil to seek it but do not find it. And also though the wise claim to know, they are not able to find it out" (Eccles. 8:17).

Not all scribes were perhaps called wise, only the most talented ones. These would have been Israelite scholars, ones that Ben Sira described, who pondered parables and proverbs and prophecies, and no doubt composed their own texts. These are the wise referred to in the superscriptions in Proverbs: "the words of the wise" (22:17; 24:23). Scribes might serve as courtiers sometimes, but not always. This explains to a great degree why Proverbs is not overly courtly. Adjacent to these wise scribes or scholars would have been scribes who held high administrative posts in Jerusalem (e.g., "chief scribe" [2 Kgs. 22; Jer. 36:10]). A lower rung of scribes would have served in administrative districts, while others officiated in towns and villages, as copiers, notaries, and judges. It is the wise scribes that this book is primarily interested in, and the rest of the book will now focus on them and the wisdom literature of the Hebrew Bible, the literature these scribes composed.

2

The World and Worldview of the Wise

An Anthropological Approach

You will not understand the Israelite wisdom literature if you do not know at least the basics of the broader Israelite culture. Culture is the unique way humans have adapted to their environment, versus animals that rely largely on instinct (see Haviland 2002, 32-53). Each particular culture creatively responds to its environment in order to promote the wellbeing of its citizens and to organize social behavior so that the society can flourish and the needs of its individuals can be met. A society's culture serves to create rules and customs that enable life to become predictable for its members. A culture must deal with major problems that face every family and individual like reproduction, education, medicine, sexuality, subsistence, social conflict, and death. A particular culture must also balance the needs of the individual over against those of society at large. A culture that does not enable its people to function adequately and maintain a relatively happy existence will experience crises where people act out and possibly revolt.

Every culture has social, ideological, technological, environmental, and economic components. The wisdom literature focuses on the social and ideological, particularly morality and values, though the economic sphere is always just below the surface. However, technological and environmental issues are alluded to as well.

Geography and Climate of Ancient Palestine

The land settled by ancient Israel was very tiny, about the size of New Jersey. Israel resided in the larger territory of Palestine, which is approximately the size of New Hampshire or Vermont (Matthews 2001, 12). Palestine was the land bridge between Egypt and the Fertile Crescent. The Fertile Crescent refers to the non-desert strip of land that ran from the Persian Gulf in Mesopotamia ("between the rivers"), or the land of modern Iraq, up northwest into lower Turkey and Syria, and then southwest down to the Sinai Peninsula in Egypt. This strip was wide in Mesopotamia and Syria but then narrows considerably in Palestine.

Two factors insured the fertility of this area: flat lands and the abundance of water (Aharoni et al. 1993, 12). The richest part is in Mesopotamia where the great rivers, the Tigris and Euphrates, flowed. Because of the richness of this region and its water supply, the first civilization emerged in the lower section of it in what was called Sumer in the late fourth and early third millennia B.C.E. Here writing was first produced, which originally began as numbers used in keeping inventories of tax receipts. The Sumerians were the first to irrigate the rivers in a centralized way and, thus, spawned the first urban society with its own sophisticated administration.

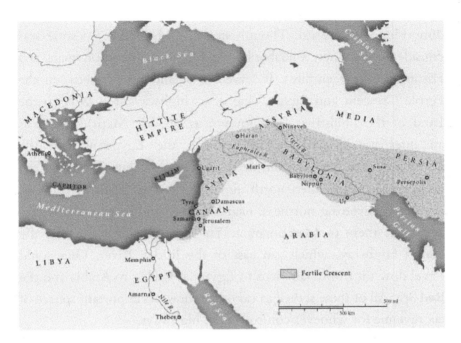

Map 1: The Ancient Near East

Though Egypt is not part of the Fertile Crescent, it was also very lush and fertile. Again, this was due to the same two factors: flat land and plenty of water. The Nile River, which got its water from the mountains of Ethiopia, ensured that Egypt would always have water even if other nations did not. Again, irrigation was big impetus for the rapid development and prosperity of Egypt. Writing developed here shortly after it did in Sumer. Also, Egypt was naturally isolated, and this helped preserve its static character as a culture that changed only very slowly.

Within the Fertile Crescent, however, the territory of Syria and Palestine was smaller and poorer (see Aharoni et al. 1993, 12). Their rivers did not allow passage in boats, and the riverbeds were so deep that water could not be used for irrigation. The land also is not flat, with limited plains. Rain mainly fell in one season, with the amount

33

diminishing southward. Though smaller and poorer, Palestine was considered extremely valuable by the Egyptian, Mesopotamian, and Hittite (Turkey) empires. It served as a land bridge between the Fertile Crescent and Egypt. One of its highways, the Way to the Land of the Philistines (also known as the Via Maris), served as an international trade route between the Egyptians and the Mesopotamians (see Aharoni et al. 1993, 16). It ran east along the coast of Sinai and then north along the coastal plain of Canaan, eventually diverting northeast near Megiddo and then to Damascus, and from there to Mesopotamia. The other major route was the King's Highway, which ran east of the Jordan River. One could travel down it from Damascus to Egypt, as well as to Arabia and the Red Sea. All of these served as caravan routes, an important source of tax revenue for whoever controlled the highways.

Palestine was known for its olive and grape production, which were staples of the ancient Mediterranean world. Olive trees do not grow in either Egypt or Mesopotamia because a certain chill is necessary for them to mature (see Stager and King 2001, 95-98). Olive oil was used in cooking, medicine, perfumes, moisturizers, fuel for lamps, a base for cosmetics, and in ritual contexts. Except for some oases, grapes do not grow well in Egypt (see Stager and King 2001, 98-101). In Mesopotamia, they grow only in the north. Wine was the staple beverage of ancient Israel, since water was often contaminated. Grapes ripen in June-July, and harvest occurs in August-September.

The Feast of Booths or Tabernacles (*Sukkot*) in September or October, earlier known as the Feast of Ingathering, refers to the autumnal feast that celebrated the last harvest, which including the grape harvest. The name "Booths" refers to the practice of living in the huts during the seven-day festival. It is interesting that the book of Ecclesiastes, part of the Five Megilloth (scrolls) or festival scrolls, is read today during this festival. Particularly significant for this tradition are the seven refrains in Ecclesiastes (2:24; 3:12-13, 22; 5:18-20; 8:15; 9:7-10; 11:7-10) that advise the enjoyment of life, known as a "carpe diem" ethic: "Come, eat your bread with gladness and drink your wine with a good heart for God has already approved of your action" (9:7). The book, thus, seems to legitimate the rowdy festivities of *Sukkot*.

The terrain of ancient Israel was quite varied due to the drastic differences in elevation and climatic conditions (Aharoni et al. 1993, 14). The land is split into two main parts along a deep rift or fault that extends from Syria to the Red Sea and then the northeast coast of Africa. The west side of this area in Palestine is the Cisjordan, whereas the east side is Transjordan. Ancient Israel was situated between the Mediterranean Sea and the Arabian Desert, and both influenced its character. Westerly winds brought the life-giving rains, while the easterly winds dried the land. The higher and more northern the location, the wetter it was. The southern section of ancient Israel was arid and is part of a desert zone that runs across the globe. As for elevation, one can go from Mt. Hermon in the far north at 9232 feet to -1300 feet at the Dead Sea, the lowest place on earth.

The land of Israel is sometimes referred to as the land "flowing with milk and honey" (e.g., Exod. 33:3; Num. 13:27). This most likely refers to a dessert of yogurt and either bee honey or honey made from grapes or dates. The land might have been agriculturally abundant but only with hard work (see Deist 2000, 123-24). Numbers 13:32 is less idyllic: "A land that devours its inhabitants." The well-watered and easily tended lush garden of Eden in Gen. 2-3 is a utopian inversion of the harsh land Israel had to work "by the sweat of [his] brow" (3:19) (see Deist 2000, 156-57).

There are four major geographic regions in ancient Israel: the Negev (south), the Shephelah (lowlands), the hill-country, and the steppe or wilderness (Josh. 15:21, 33, 48, 61) (see Aharoni et al.

1993, 14). The breadbasket for the Israelites was the Shephelah or lowlands or foothills between the coastal plain and hill-country. The archenemy of Israel, the Philistines, was constantly trying to control this region. The land of ancient Israel actually consists of 17 distinct geomorphic regions, none of which has the same climactic or geological conditions (see Hopkins 1985, 56-72). This diversity complicated the ability of farmers to rely on one particular method for producing the necessary food for their families (see Hopkins 1985, 72-75). Instead, farmers had to diversify farming strategies because of the different ecologies of the various regions. As a result, farmers could not rely on just grains or even vegetables. They also grew orchards and vineyards, while simultaneously being pastoralists, especially of sheep and goats, which could be described as walking surplus calories (see Hopkins 1985, 245-50)! This condition also meant that the various villages and cities were dependent on each other; none was absolutely self-sufficient. Thus, pressure was exerted to form alliances and cooperation, at least among neighbors.

In general, dry, warm summers contrasted with wet, cool winters (see Hopkins 1985, 79; Stager and King 2000, 86-87). Summer lasted from May-June through September, when there was little rain. Winter lasted from mid-October through March, with most of Palestine's rain occurring November through February. Rain was so important to the Israelites that they had several words for it like "rain (in general)" *matar*, "early rain" *yoreh* and "later rain" *malqosh*, and "winter rain" *geshem* (see Stager and King 2000, 86-87). In Prov. 16:15, *malqosh* is used: "In the light of the king's face is life, and his favor is like a cloud of later rain." While the early rain in autumn softened the ground for plowing, the later rain in April provided the necessary moisture for the cereal harvest to be successful. In the same way, the king's favor brings blessing and prosperity to the one who elicits it.

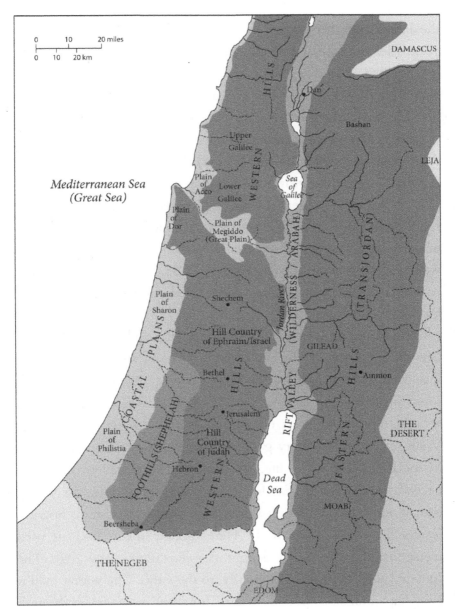

Map 2: Topography of Syro-Palestine

The average annual rainfall is 550 mm in Jerusalem today, which is equivalent to the rainfall in London (Hopkins 1985, 86). However, the difference is that the rain in London is distributed throughout the year, whereas in Jerusalem 79 percent of the rain falls from December to February. The mean temperature in Jerusalem in the winter is 49.5°F and 77°F during the summer. Though the summers were hot, by mid-afternoon the sea breeze would finally reach the hill-country and provide a nice cooling effect and aid in winnowing during the harvest (Hopkins 1985, 81). Complicating all this is the fact that three or four years out of every ten drought occurs (Hopkins 1985, 87). On the other extreme, high intensity rains would often result in flash floods (Hopkins 1985, 86). In the hill-country, terraces, made of stones, were constructed to prevent the runoff of surplus water and prevent erosion (see Hopkins 1985, 173-86, 208-09). Their construction and maintenance necessitated cooperation among the locals.

Other water sources include natural springs and man-made wells, dew, which forms in the dry summer months, rock-hewn cisterns that were often plastered to be made waterproof, and underground reservoirs (see Hopkins 1985, 94-99). Water was so essential in such an arid region that it is often used as a metaphor in the Bible. Wells were the customary gathering place of the village, the center of social and economic life. Women were expected to draw the necessary water for the day for the home. In Prov. 5:15, the young man is admonished, "Drink water from your own cistern, flowing waters from your own well." Here "water," like "food" is used metaphorically for sexual delight (see Fox 2000, 199-209). The "cistern" and "well" refer, obviously, to the vulva. The young man is being encouraged to slake his "thirst" for erotic engagement through his wife alone and not a stranger. The dangers of adultery in the ancient world were more pronounced than in our own. A cuckolded husband had the right to retaliate with impunity.

Another example of the high estimation of water is Prov. 21:1: "Like canals of water is the heart of the king in the hand of the Lord; wherever he wills, he directs it." The verse emphasizes both the sovereignty of God, even over the king, and also God's life-giving blessings, as water is directed through human-made channels to parched ground (Waltke 2005, 167-68). This refers to water runoff that could be directed to needed crops.

The first rain came in September or October just after the Feast of Booths, which softened the ground so farmers could sow with a scratch plow, often holding an iron tip (see Rainey and Notley 2006, 41-42). The hill-country soil was shallow and rocky, so such a plow was sufficient. A second plowing covered the seed. Because of the particular climactic pattern, farmers could stagger their crops. In fact, there was no time during the year where there was not some type of farming activity occurring. The main sowing was from November through December, with late sowing in January. By March grass is cut for fodder. In April, the "latter rain" swells the grain up for harvest. Also, the differences in the maturation in grains helped stagger harvest times. Barley matures faster than wheat, as indicated by the Gezer calendar (tenth century B.C.E.):

> August and September to pick olives,
> October to sow barley,
> December and January to weed,
> February to cut flax,
> March to harvest barley,
> April to harvest wheat and to pay tithes,
> May and June to prune vines,
> July to pick the fruit of summer
> (Matthews and Benjamin 2006, 156).

This calendar may have been composed as a school exercise for novice scribes. The nonconformist in Israelite society, the sloth, does not attune himself to the seasons and times for planting and finds himself in peril: "In winter, the sloth does not plow, but he will desire in the harvest but find nothing" (Prov. 20:4). This proverb teaches the same truth as Aesop's fable "The Grasshopper and the Ants." The fool, however, is a little different. He is contrasted to the ant, "She prepares her bread in the summer; she brings in her food at the harvest" (Prov. 6:8). The fool knows that one must sow first to receive the harvest. However, his mistake is that he does not "prepare" after the sowing, which includes "plowing the field, maintaining irrigation systems, weeding, and treating pests and disease" (Heim 2013, 151). In other words, he is a minimalist, who "cuts corners" (Heim 2013, 151).

Israelite Society

The Family

The most basic social institution of Israelite society was the family. An institution is a way or tradition that develops in a society to deal with a fundamental need or problem. Of course, the family is a universal institution that has been in existence since the dawn of humanity (see Haviland 2002, 242-67). The particular configuration of the family, however, has differed geographically and throughout time. The family serves primarily reproductive purposes for the male and female couple, but then more broadly, the larger community. It also serves as the locus of socialization or education of children so that they might contribute to the larger society. The family in ancient Israel was called the *bet 'av* or "house of the father." In early Israel and in the smaller cities and villages this was usually the extended family. This meant a patriarch and his wife, up to four children, with only two making it to adulthood (the life expectancy of an Israelite male was 40; 30 for a female because of labor and delivery complications [Meyers 1997, 18-19, 28]), his widowed mother, the wives and children of his sons, any unmarried children, perhaps slaves, clients or people dependent on the patriarch, and sometimes even clerics (see Judges 17-18) (see Stager and King 2001, 12-19, 36-43). The average Israelite family was between 7-15 persons. A large family was necessary for the Israelite peasants, who needed many members to work the land and tend the flocks.

Israelites males usually married later in life than females, who married shortly after puberty (see Meyers 1997, 28; Stager and King 2001, 53). This meant that husbands usually died before their wives and is why widows, who had no male heirs to protect them, receive such concern in the Hebrew Bible. A formula frequently appears in the Hebrew Bible that warns the Israelites to care for the poor, widows, orphans, aliens, and sometimes Levites (e.g., Ps. 94:6; Deut. 10:18; see Sneed 1999, 498-507). Males often returned to their father's home with their new brides (patrilocality).

Marriages were primarily an economic arrangement between two families and not a romantic affair. Usually the groom did not even see the bride until the day of the wedding (see Stager and King 2001, 54). Romance and then love developed later as the relationship matured. The book of Proverbs commends finding a wife, particularly a good one: "A home and wealth are an inheritance from fathers, but a prudent wife is from the Lord" (19:14; cf. 18:22). The nagging or "sour" wife, however, was to be avoided at all cost: "Better to dwell in the corner of the rooftop than to live in the same house with a contentious woman" (21:9).

The Israelites usually practiced endogamy, the marriage of a close relative within the clan (see Stager and King 2001, 38; Haviland 2002, 223-24; Meyers 1997, 18). Endogamy served to strengthen the bonds within the village or vicinity, which was necessary in the precarious conditions the early Israelites faced (Hopkins 1985,

257). It also served to create a tighter group identity within the clan (Faust 2012, 241), and kept land from falling into the hands of non-Israelites (Kessler 2008, 236). The Israelite preference for walled villages indicates a kinship structure based on endogamy (Faust 2012, 241). A classic example of endogamy is Jacob, who was sent off by his father Isaac to his maternal uncle to find a wife (Gen. 28:5). Exogamy or the marriage outside the clan or nation was practiced sometimes by the elite to form alliances with other nations, as Solomon did when he married the daughter of Pharaoh (1 Kgs. 3:1).

The Israelite houses were pillared and often had four rooms (see Stager and King 2001, 28-35). Two rows of pillars usually divided the house into three rooms, with a broad fourth room at the rear of the house. The two side rooms often had stone-paved floors, while the middle room was dirt or plastered. The stone floor of the two side rooms and the stone pillars indicate that animals like the famous "fatted calf" were kept tied to the pillars in these rooms, with the cobbled floor serving as drainage for urine. The central room often had an oven for baking. Israelite houses were usually two stories. A courtyard outside the house often had an additional oven. Small windows allowed smoke to escape.

The family resided on the second floor, while the stable animals and slaves occupied the lower level. During the winter, heat from the animals would drift upward to warm the family, as well as the smells! During the summer, members could sleep on the roof since it was cooler. The roof was usually plastered to inhibit leaking, which was not always successful: "Like a leaking roof continually dripping on the day of a cloudburst is a contentious wife" (Prov. 27:15). The patriarch and his wife would dwell in the main house, while sons, with their families, would dwell in additional rooms attached to this structure. Archaeologically, extended families lived in the countryside, while in the larger cities nuclear families were the norm (Faust 2012, 160).

The next societal level was the clan or *mishpachah*, which consisted of either all the families in a small village or related families in a subdivision of a city or region. That the clan, not individuals, owned the land is indicated by three factors. First, if a woman's husband died before any males were born, then one of his unmarried brothers was expected to marry her and the first male born would carry on the name of the deceased husband (known as the levirate law) and inherit his property (patrilineage). Second, if one had to sell one's property because of debt, then a more financially established kinsman (*goel* or "kinsman redeemer") was expected to pay the debt so that the property would remain within the clan (Lev. 25:48-49). Third, every fifty years, the year of Jubilee (Lev. 25:8-13), all property that had been "sold" for debt was automatically transferred back to the original owners. Thus, technically all land was possessed by the clan in perpetuity and could never be sold, at least not permanently.

Clans would meet regularly for feasts and holidays. For example, David told Jonathan to make excuse for him not eating one day at the table of king Saul because he was going to the annual clan festival of the New Moon in Bethlehem (1 Sam. 20:5-6). The ancestors of the clan were thought to participate in the festivities and food, a form of ancestor worship (see Stager and King 2001, 376; Blenkinsopp 1997, 71, 78-82).

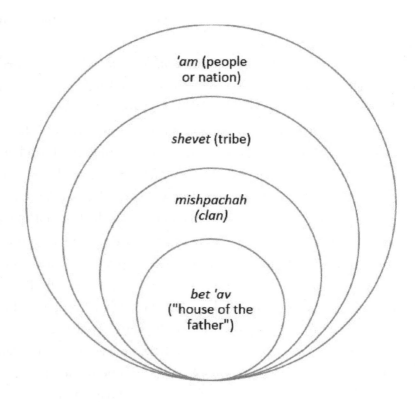

'am (people
or nation)

shevet (tribe)

mishpachah
(clan)

bet 'av
("house of the
father")

Figure 2: Clan

In contrast to the *bet 'av*, the clan was more stable and served as the risk spreading strategy of the rural Israelites and the main mechanism of reciprocity (giving and receiving necessary items) (Hopkins 1985, 256-61). In times of drought, a clan could pool its resources and households could obtain necessary food stuffs and other resources within the clan. The clan was also the organization that enabled terrace building and maintenance, which was absolutely essential for Israelite survival in the highlands. Of all the social organizations of ancient Israel, the clan was probably the most important for the survival of the Israelites, especially in rural areas (Hopkins 1985, 260-61).

Tribe and Nation

The next societal level was the tribe. The members of a tribe were more distantly related, often with the relationship being fictive. What was important is that a tribe's members claimed to have a common ancestor. The tribe was important for crisis management, especially threat from foreigners (Hopkins 1985, 260). This is reflected in the book of Judges, where a tribe or a group of tribes would unite to fight a common enemy, like the Philistines or Midianites. The famous "twelve tribes" of Israel is fictive because the number of tribes fluctuates according the source (see Noll 2013, 7-10). Sometimes the list includes Levi (Deut. 27:12-13), and sometimes it does not (Num. 1:5-15). Judges 5 only lists 10 tribes.

The highest societal level would be the Israelites as a people or nation. The first extra-biblical reference to the Israelites is in the thirteenth century when Pharaoh Merneptah (1224-1214 B.C.E.) refers to conquering a people called "Israel." Archaeologically, the Israelites emerge as a recognizable people in the highlands of Canaan around 1200 B.C.E. During the period described in the book of Judges (twelfth through eleventh centuries), the Israelites are depicted as a nation of allied tribes. Only with the emergence of the monarchy did the Israelites become an independent state. Two states emerged in the ninth century with Judah in the south and North Israel above. The Northern Kingdom was destroyed by the Assyrians in 722 B.C.E. and became a colony under them. Many of its elite citizens (king and royal family, high officials, scribes, skilled craftsmen) were exiled to Assyria, and foreign peoples were relocated to North Israel's territory. Thus, after the Assyrians conquered North Israel, it never was a state again. Judah remained a state until it was destroyed by the Neo-Babylonians in 587 B.C.E. Again, the elite were exiled, while the peasants were left behind with new leadership, Gedaliah, as governor [2 Kgs. 25:22]), who was loyal to the Babylonians.

From the time the Babylonians conquered Judah onward, except for a brief century of relative independence during the Hasmonean Dynasty (140-37 B.C.E.), the Jews lived as a colony under several imperial powers: Babylonia, Persia, the Greece (the Ptolemies and the Seleucids), and finally Rome. Previous to this time, both Judah and North Israel sometimes had been made vassal states under more powerful states (e.g. the Egyptians, the Syrians, and North Israel subjugating Judah).

Economy of Ancient Israel

During its earliest period Israel had a subsistence economy. Farmers grew enough crops and raised adequate herds to survive. Any surplus foods were preserved and placed in pots and in grain pits. Or herds were allowed to multiply beyond what was necessary. Both of these strategies were meant for unexpected emergencies like droughts and plagues, not for aggrandizing the household. However, over time some families and clans would accumulate surpluses of flocks and crops, becoming richer, while other families and clans became poorer. This eventually led to the emergence of social classes.

The economy of a subsistence society contains both reciprocal and redistributive elements, but mainly the former (see Haviland 2002, 192-94). The household itself constitutes a miniature redistributive system where any surplus goods brought into the household (center) were then redistributed to members as needed (periphery) (see Liverani 2001, 6). On a larger level, the early Israelite subsistence society was a reciprocal system because it was not geared toward creating surpluses but producing enough goods as necessary for the survival of the family and clan. Necessary items that could not be grown or made were acquired through trade. In trading, equality was assumed to exist between the negotiators, though in reality there is never complete parity (Liverani 2001, 7).

Reciprocity

One of the most important facets of the Israelite economy was reciprocity. It was the customary means by which Israelite individuals and communities had access to necessary and luxury goods and services. Three types of reciprocity are operative in subsistence societies (see Deist 2000, 165-69). The first is generalized reciprocity. It involves goods of roughly equal value being exchanged between households and individuals. No calculation of value is involved, nor is the time of repayment specified. This type of exchange allows households to exchange any surplus items they have for items they lack and provides a type of social security for times of crisis. Generalized reciprocity involves exchanges between kin and close friends.

The second is balanced reciprocity, which is a more sporadic type of gift-giving. It places responsibility on the recipient to respond with a gift of equal value or risk damaging the relationship. Gift-giving was very important in the Israelite society and was a way to maintain and extend relationships that could benefit an individual and family, a glue that made everyone dependent on everyone else. It also affected one's status in society. Balanced reciprocity is represented in Prov. 18:16: "A gift will make opportunity for a person, and it will lead him before the great." The sages wouldn't have considered this a bribe because it was used for noble purposes. Here the end justifies the means. However, the sages condemn bribes that pervert justice:

"The wicked will take out a bribe from the pocket to distort the ways of justice" (17:23). This type of reciprocity occurs among family, friends, even strangers. Both generalized and balanced reciprocity serve as a type of social security or protection in times of crisis. Families who received benefits could return the favor to others when they were able.

The third type is negative reciprocity. This type involves the attempt to get the better of the deal, as in a market situation. It occurs among non-kin. Guile and deception are often involved here, and there is pride in outsmarting a customer. The book of Proverbs condemns this type of reciprocity among Israelites: "Different scales for weight, different measures for grain; both are an abomination to the Lord" (20:10). Israelite merchants apparently used different scales and containers depending on whether they were buying or selling. Negative reciprocity is also involved when the Israelites charged interest on loans made to foreigners, but not their fellow Israelites (Deut. 23:20).

The Monarchy and Redistributive Economy

With the development of the monarchy, a new redistributive system emerged that overlay the reciprocal economy that continued to operate. The king needed a standing army, administrators, advisors, royal land, and taxes in order to run the new state. The king also needed to build monumental architecture and establish military posts to protect the land. This meant that the earlier subsistence economy would not suffice. Farmers and pastoralists would have to produce more, and the surplus would go to the crown. "Cash crops" like olives and grapes, from which could be made oil and wine and could be exported, became more enticing for farmers. But the more these they grew, the less space they could devote to the formerly diverse crops necessary for nutritional needs. They then had to trade for these items. All of these factors served to push the small peasants into debt because they could not manage feeding their families and simultaneously paying the exorbitant royal tribute.

Also, with this development, under the direction of the powerful priesthood, the newly built Temple became a bank of sorts because the tithes had to be sent to this central location, which served as the main redistribution center. How much more than the tithe the Israelites had to pay we do not know, but it was most likely more. The surplus is sent to the center and then parceled out again as dictated by a central administration (see Haviland 2002, 197). With this system, the ruling class lives in luxury, but some of these goods are redistributed to others, like retainers (the people who directly serve the elite, like the military, cooks, and servants) and the masses, when needed, as in a drought.

Also with this system, social stratification becomes more pronounced and social classes emerge, with "haves" at the top and "have nots" at the bottom. Peasants often found themselves among the latter, especially if there was a catastrophe like drought or locust plague, resulting in their inability to pay the tribute. They often had to resort to borrowing credit from wealthy urban creditors in order to survive. Eventually, however, their debt became so extreme that they had to sell their own children or spouses into debt slavery in order to pay it off, as indicted in Nehemiah 5. Nehemiah, serving as governor of Judah, forces the urban patricians to forgive this debt and allow the people to have a fresh start (see Gottwald 1999, 1-19). Debtors might even have to sell their land, unless a kinsman could bail them out (known as a "Kinsman Redeemer").

While the monarchy brought many advantages to the common Israelites, like security, aid in times of catastrophe, and a sense of national pride, it also cost them much. Samuel warns the people what they can expect:

> This will be the legal claim of the king who will rule over you. He will take your sons, and set them upon his chariot and his horses. They will run before his chariot. And he will appoint leaders of thousands and of fifties, and they will do his plowing and his harvesting and make his military and chariot implements. And he will take your daughters to be perfumers and cooks and bakers. And he will take your best fields and vineyards and your olive groves and give them to his officials. And he will take a tenth from your seed and your vineyards, and he will give this to his high officials and servants. And he will take your best male and female servants, your unmarried sons, and your donkeys and make them do his work. He will take a tenth of your sheep, and you will be his slaves. And you will cry out on that day because of your king whom you chose for yourself, but the Lord will not answer you on that day. (1 Sam. 8:11-18)

The Israelite monarchy formed what can be called a patrimonial kingdom, the type found in the ancient Near East (see Stager and King 2001, 4-5, 201-58). The ideology of this polity is basically co-opted from the *bet 'av*. Kinship terms are used to describe the monarchy. In fact, the Israelites did not have a word for "palace," and so words like "house of the king" or "house" are used. The lack of vocabulary points to the fact that the household was the fundamental symbol for ancient Israel on familial, royal, and divine levels (Stager and King 2001, 202). The king assumes the role of "father" over the nation. His relationship with his officials is literally as a father or patron. And, of course, he is "father" to the masses. The king was expected to care for and protect the most vulnerable of society, as a father. King Lemuel's mother advises him, "Open your mouth for the dumb, and for the cause of those who are passing away. Open your mouth, judge rightly, and plead the cause of the poor and needy" (Prov. 31:8-9). As a father, the king could even be appealed to in order to override customary law (2 Sam. 14:4-21) (see Bellafontaine

1997, 206-31). Similarly, in *The Godfather*, a man approaches the godfather to obtain justice for his daughter when the legal system (police) had failed him.

Saul, the first king of Israel, had a tiny administration, with only one official, Abner, the commander of his host, who was simultaneously his nephew (1 Sam. 14:50). The rest of his "administration" consisted of his sons (1 Sam. 31:2), serving in the army as leaders. David's administration is larger than Saul's and extends beyond his family (see Kessler 2008, 79-83). In 2 Sam. 8:16-18 (cf. 20:23-26) we find the following offices: Joab (commander in chief); Jehoshophat (secretary or chancellor); Zadok and Achimilek (chief priests); Seraiah (high ranking scribe); Benaiah (captain of the mercenaries). The sons of David were priests, which, of course, violates the later Pentateuchal legislation that sanctions only Levites as priests. Seals have been found that refer to the owner as *'eved hamelek*, "servant of the king," who were not relatives of the king (see Kessler 2008, 81).

With Solomon, dropping the mercenary overseer, a chief palace official and 13 other officials overseen by a senior official are added to this list, including "the king's friend" (1 Kgs. 4:1-19; see Deist 2000, 171-72). The latter was an important position, which involved serving as confidant and political advisor to the king (see Deist 2000, 274). Hushai served in this role and helped David during the coup d'état of Absalom, functioning as a spy for David and giving erroneous advice to Absalom to foil his plans. The 13 officials served as tax collectors in 12 newly established districts, each supplying food for the palace one month out the year (Deist 2000, 172). A thirteenth minister was needed because a thirteenth month would occur every few years since the calendar was based on lunar months. Of course, this would have led the other tribes to resent Judah. Also, as the speech from Samuel indicates, Solomon used press gangs and corvée or forced labor on construction projects like the Temple, palace, and military forts. The press gangs were manned by Canaanites, while the corvée was applied to Israelites (Rainey and Notley 2006, 167).

Various terms used for storehouses are found in the Hebrew Bible (e.g., *bet 'asufim* "house of stores" [1 Chron. 26:15]; *'otsar* "storehouse" [2 Kgs. 20:13]; *bet hakeli* "house of implements" [2 Kgs. 20:13]), including store cities (1 Kgs. 9:19; 2 Chron. 17:12). This suggests a well-organized redistributive economy (Deist 2000, 172-83). It also points to how foolish King Hezekiah was for showing the Babylonians *all* his storehouses (2 Kgs. 20:12-18)! Seals have been found that say *lamelek* "belonging to the king," as in the ostracon (piece of pottery) from Tell Qasile (eighth century B.C.E.; see Ahituv 2008, 154), referring to oil that belonged to the king, perhaps meant to be shipped and kept in a storehouse. Megiddo was probably one of the store cities in North Israel.

That the burden of taxation was very great, especially on the masses, is indicated in the division of the united kingdom into two states. After Solomon's death, the people, especially the northern tribes, complain to Rehoboam, Solomon's successor, about the tax burden and want it lightened: "Your father made our yoke difficult, but now lighten the difficult labor of your father and the heavy yoke he placed on us and we will serve you" (1 Kgs. 12:4). Rehoboam then consults with the wise elders who had advised his father. They advise him, "If today you would be a servant to this people and would serve them, then you will answer them and say to them pleasing words. Then they will be your servants forever" (v. 7). However, Rehoboam did not listen to their advice and instead consulted his younger courtiers, who advised him to tell the people, "My little finger is fatter than the loins of my father!" (v. 10). This is a euphemism that Rehoboam is figuratively better "endowed" than his father (see Bodner 2012, 67-68). They further advise him to tell the people,

"And now my father heavily burdened you with a heavy yoke, but I will increase your yoke; my father chastised you with whips, but I will chastise you with scorpions!" (1 Kgs. 11). After this message is delivered by Rehoboam, the northerners, under the leadership of Jeroboam, a former high official of Solomon, separate from Judah and form their own northern state.

During the colonial periods, the economic system changed to some extent, and the tax burden was most likely greater than during the monarchic period. Instead of a king, there were governors (e.g., Nehemiah; Zerubbabel). But more significantly, the priesthood became in effect the governing class. The high priest was for all practical purposes the new king of the Jews. Josephus even refers to this polity as a theocracy (*Ag. Ap.* 2.165), though a better term is "hierocracy," rule by priests. In a colonial situation, what often happens is the imperial powers collude with the indigenous elite, who are allowed to govern their own people as long as the tribute was paid to the empire (see Lenski 1984, 244). In return, the elite get to share in the tribute collection. In other words, not only were the imperial powers taking a substantial part of the surplus, but the Judean elite got a cut as well! So, in addition to the tithe, there were more taxes. For instance, during the Ptolemaic period there were a plethora of small taxes levied on the common people in addition to the tribute required: poll, guild, bath, trade, salt, trade, and animal taxes (see Sneed 2012, 91-98). The indigenous elite were often relieved from such taxes. The Ptolemaic kings also mostly likely had royal land in Judah.

Leveling Mechanisms

Mitigating the negative effects of a redistributive system, the upper class in ancient Israel would have been expected to share its wealth with the less fortunate. In Papua New Guinea, the "Big Men" or chiefs receive gifts from those under them only in order to give them away in lavish feats and thereby attain honor—a prestige economy (see Haviland 2002, 198-202). The redistributive system here sends surplus to the top, but then it trickles back down. The giving away of the wealth is an example of a leveling mechanism (see Haviland 2002, 190-91). In ancient Israel, the redistribution was not quite that leveling, but pressure was placed on the wealthy to be charitable and spread their wealth out, at least to a greater extent than is expected of our modern wealthy in the West! And laws were in place that helped prevent Israelites from starving, like the requirement that farmers leave the edges of their fields un-harvested so that the poor could glean them (Lev. 23:22). And archaeologically there may have been "homeless shelters" near the city gates in ancient Israel that provided basic accommodations and food for the most vulnerable (see Faust 2012, 100-109).

In the story of David and Nabal (1 Sam. 25), Nabal, a wealthy and powerful nobleman, was expected to share some of his wealth with David and his men during the sheep shearing celebration, especially since they never touched any of Nabal's possessions when they passed through his property. Nabal not only refused but also insulted David and his men. Thus, Nabal, "the fool," is shamed for his miserliness by God striking him down. On the other hand, the generosity of Abigail, Nabal's wife, earned her prestige, the label of "wise," and the hand of marriage with David!

The Ancient Israelite Worldview

Non-Scientific View of the Cosmos

The sages of ancient Israel shared the same worldview as the rest of Israelites. The ancient Israelites did not hold a scientific view of the world. They viewed the earth as the center of the universe, with the sun, stars, and planets rotating around it: a geocentric view of the solar system instead of the heliocentric one we hold today, where the sun stands still and the planets revolve around it. Like the Egyptians, the Israelites believed the sun traveled across the sky during the day and then traveled beneath the earth in the Underworld during the night to arise again the next morning and then repeat the cycle. Ecclesiastes 1:5 assumes this perspective: "The sun rises and it travels; to its place it returns. There it is rises (again)." While the Mesopotamians and the Egyptians viewed the sun, planets, and stars as divinities, the Israelites viewed them as entities that served the Hebrew God and had a particular function within the cosmos: "to rule the day and to rule the night" (Gen. 1:18).

Like the Babylonians, the Israelites believed the solar bodies moved along respective tracks located in a giant inverted "bowl" or dome that covered the earth, called the "firmament" in the *King James Version*. This canopy divided the celestial waters above it from the terrestrial waters beneath it. The celestial waters made the sky appear blue, like the terrestrial waters, the oceans and lakes. Rain, snow, and hail came from windows or gates in the firmament that opened and allowed them to fall from the celestial realm to the earth below. In his appearance in the whirlwind, God asks Job, "Have you entered into the chambers of snow or seen the chambers of hail, which I have restrained until a time of distress, for a day of battle and war" (Job 38:22-23)?

The Israelites, like the Mesopotamians, believed the world was flat and surrounded by water on all sides and beneath. The waters beneath the earth were the source of springs and wells, and could spring forth violently and flood the earth as in the days of Noah. Both the celestial and terrestrial waters created this great flood: "All the springs of the great deep broke forth, and the windows of the heavens were opened" (Gen. 6:11). The earth was held up by great pillars or foundations: "Where were you when I laid the foundations of the earth? Report if you have understanding. Who set its measurements, if you know? Or who extended upon it a measuring line? Upon what were its pedestals sunk? Or who laid its corner stone . . . ?" (Job 38:4-6); "Who causes the earth to totter from its place so that its pillars will shake?" (9:6).

Beneath the earth was Sheol, which means "pit" or "the Underworld" in Hebrew. Sheol was no heaven and hell where afterlife justice was delivered as depicted in the New Testament. Rather it was a mysterious and dark place where the nature of afterlife existence could not be determined by mortals: "If Sheol and Abaddon ("place of destruction") lie exposed before the Lord; how much more so the hearts of humans!" (Prov. 15:11). Job's description of it is also dark and dreary: "If I must wait for Sheol as my home, in darkness, spread out my bed, to the pit say, 'You're my father,' 'My mother and my sister,' to the maggot. Where then is my hope? My hope, who will see it? Will it descend to the bars of Sheol? Shall we descend together into the dust?" (17:13-16). One "slept with (his/her) fathers" (e.g., 2 Sam. 7:10) in the Underworld, but activities like praising God (Ps. 6:6) were out of the question. So are memories and emotions; the dead know nothing! (Eccles. 9:5-6).

Illustration 5. Israelite Cosmology

One could, however, preserve afterlife existence in Sheol by offering food to the dead (see Stager and King 2001, 379-80). Though this practice is condemned in Deut. 26:13-14, it was probably a frequent occurrence, especially in the countryside, where the official policies of Judah were less influential. In ancient Mesopotamia, pipes were actually installed above tombs so that beer could be offered directly to the dead for their sustenance. In the Canaanite tale of Danel, a king needs a son as heir, one who will have the responsibility for his father's postmortem care. Danel prays to Baal, who appeals to El so that his request might be fulfilled:

Raise up a son for his household.
Establish an heir in his palace.
Give Danil a son to erect a stela for the divine patrons of his ancestors,
to build a shrine for the household of Danil in their sanctuary.

Give Danil a son to burn incense for him,
to chant beside his grave.

....

To eat a sacrificial meal for him in the sanctuary of Baal,
to consume his portion in the House of El . . .
(Matthews and Benjamin 2006, 71-72).

In the wisdom tradition, only the Wisdom of Solomon (1:12-16) and
the Dead Sea Scroll wisdom literature (4Q418 69 ii 7) embrace the
notion of life after death, both reflecting Greek influence. The author
of Ecclesiastes entertains the possibility of such a concept in 3:21, but
he is too skeptical to embrace it.

Religious View of Causality

Like other ancient Near Eastern people, the Israelites resisted the idea
that the world was somehow irrational or chaotic or that random
events occurred. Rather, they held that the world was orderly, an
order imposed on continually threatening chaos and evil, associated
with demons and unjust deities. This is indicated subtly in Gen. 1:1,
where God begins his creative act by placing order on a watery chaos.
Throughout the first creation account (1:1-2:4a), God must carefully
divide and separate what were originally chaotic, mixed elements (the
union of the celestial and terrestrial waters) and, thus, sequentially
impose order on disorder. This is similar to other creation accounts
where a major deity fights and defeats a deity that represents chaos,
darkness, and evil. Baal defeats the sea monster Yam and the god
of death Mot; Marduk, the Babylonian Zeus, defeats the dragoness
Tiamat (depicted as multi-headed) and creates part of the world with
her body. Similarly, the Lord fights and defeats sea monsters (Pss.
74:13-14; 89:10; Isa. 27:1; 51:9; Job 26:12-13).

The human species seems to be wired to obsessively pursue signs of order in the world. Where this is hard to find, we impose it in creative ways. Part of the success of the human species is the ability of our ancestors to be able to empathize with others and "get into their heads" (see McCauley 2011, 76-82, 162-221; Wilson 2012, 225-54; Kahneman 2011, 71-78). In other words, they were experts at determining the intentions of other human beings. Also, their ability to organize and cooperate with each other so that they could hunt other species and fight off predators ensured their success and gave us remarkable advantages.

Our ability to read the intentions of others also created faulty ways of thinking. Humans often apply human agency onto non-human entities, like animals and plants (fables). Proverbs 6:6-8 describes ants in human terms:

> Go to the ant, consider its ways and be wise!
> They have no leader, or official or ruler.
> Yet they prepare their food in the summer.
> They gather in the harvest their nourishment.

The analogy here is faulty on two fronts. There are no "lazy" or "industrious" ants; ants act on instinct and not culture, which is the distinctive way humans have adapted for survival. Second, ants are not "wise." Individually, in fact, they are stupid. What gives them their intelligence is their collective "brain," formed when each ant follows some basic rules that benefit the colony as a whole (Miller 2007). Ants, thus, have what is called "hive intelligence."

The Israelites also project agency on naturalistic events like thunder and lightning, and even drought. In Jer. 3:3, God speaks of climactic punishment of Judah for her whoring after other gods: "the spring rain will be withheld, and the late rain will not be." The ancients did not understand thunder and lightning from a scientific standpoint, and so they saw these powerful and mysterious wonders as direct acts of God: "The voice of your thunder was in the whirlwind; the lightning illuminated the world. The land trembled and shook" (Ps. 77:18). Whatever was mysterious in the world was demystified by attributing divine agency to it. Thunder and lightning become instruments of God. For the ancients, there were no events or happenings that were random or coincidental. Just as human agency involves purpose, so all events and phenomena had an underlying function.

Doctrine of Retribution

In the same way, the Israelites perceived that persons who made wise decisions, lived good moral and pious lives, and worked hard seemed to fare better than deviants who did not play by society's rules and attempted to cheat others. Many proverbs in the wisdom literature express this connection:

> The wise woman builds up her house,
> while a foolish woman tears it down with her own hands (Prov. 14:1).

> The Lord does not let the righteous go hungry,
> but the desire of the wicked he will push away (10:3).

> A slack hand makes poverty,
> but a diligent hand will make one rich (10:4).

The connection of moral lifestyle and fortune is what scholars refer to as the doctrine of retribution. One's lifestyle and actions are rewarded by divine favor or disfavor. This doctrine implies that one's morality has cosmic repercussions and consequences. The fool does not just injure himself and others; he violates the cosmic and moral order. Retribution must occur for order to be restored. In fact, German scholars often view this connection of morality and fate as a built-in cosmic mechanism that does not need God to maintain it, though he installed it (a kind of deistic notion or karma): *Tun-Ergehen-Zusammenhang* or "action-consequence connection." The doctrine is a primitive notion of causality that has the advantage of explaining the fates of most persons.[1]

But exceptions to the doctrine could be explained as well, as in the story of Job, the most righteous person on earth, who experiences terrible calamities. The Israelites will not see such anomalies as simply random, mysterious events. Rather, they desperately attempted to make sense of them in one way or the other. Typically, fortune and misfortune were ascribed to moral fault on the part of the victims. The friends of Job blame him for some sin he had not repented of. The frame narrative of the book of Job (chs. 1-2, 42) explains it as a test rather than punishment. But note that Job is eventually blessed for passing the test at the end of the story (42:10-17). Thus, the connection between moral behavior and consequences is preserved.

The doctrine of retribution is also a form of reciprocity. God perceived of the Israelites as his "children," a fictive kin notion. Thus, the many "gifts" and blessings he extended to Israel would be perceived as within a family relationship, thus, generalized reciprocity. God gives many more gifts than the Israelites can ever return. But the Israelites do "pay God back" with loyalty and regular sacrifices. If an Israelite is loyal and obedient to God or "wise" and "righteous," then he will reciprocate with blessings and longevity. However, if an Israelite is disloyal and disobedient, like the "fool" or "slothful" or "wicked," then God reciprocates with curses and disaster. This shows that reciprocity was a fundamental and integral core concept within the Israelite worldview.

---

1. Timothy Sandoval's claim that the incentive of wealth connected with wisdom is always used metaphorically, and not literally, to emphasize the value of wisdom is a case of special pleading (2006). See review by J. A. Loader (2006).

Official and Popular Religion

The official Israelite position was the belief in only one God, Yahweh. However, the masses, including many elite, worshipped Yahweh but also other deities like Baal and Asherah. The strong monotheism of the official position in the Hebrew Bible seems at odds with the rest of the ancient Near Eastern peoples, who were polytheistic, the belief in numerous gods. However, during the late Bronze Age and into the Iron Age, in Syro-Palestine henotheism became popular ("heno" means "one" in Greek), where one believes in many gods but one becomes dominant (see Smith 1990, 1-79; Noll 2013, 182-214). Among the Canaanites, Baal and his consort Anat or Ashteroth—a form of Ishtar, the Babylonian goddess of fertility—became the dominant pair of deities. Baal becomes the patron deity, replacing El, originally the head of the Canaanite pantheon. El is depicted as being old, with a grey beard, and sitting on a throne. His consort was Asherah. Likewise, Chemosh became supreme among the Moabites. Similarly, scholars theorize that originally El may have been the primary god of the Israelites (see Smith 1990, 7; Cross 1997, 1-76). Note that the name "Israel" contains his name. Eventually, he lost out to Yahweh, originally perhaps a Bedouin warrior deity who dwelt in a moveable tent ("tabernacle") (cf. Cross 1997, 91-111).

Illustration 6. El

Yahweh's chief competitor was Baal, who was the god of the thunderstorm, like Zeus, and fertility. He brought the rains and virility among the flocks. Scholars theorize that Israelites were attracted to him because Yahweh originally was a warrior deity and not a fertility god (cf. Smith 1990, 41-79). The Israelites were basically hedging their bets, worshipping the great warrior god Yahweh, but then ensuring their crops grew by sacrifices to Baal—what we would call supplemental insurance! Over time, Yahweh absorbed many of the features of El and Baal, even assuming Baal's stereotypical description of "riding in the clouds": the Lord "who makes the clouds his chariot, traveling upon the wings of the wind" (Ps. 104:3b).

Thus, the strong monotheism of Israelite faith represents a development in the direction of the dominant henotheism of the time and region. True monotheism has strengths and weaknesses.

Positively, it promotes high ethical standards since there are no morally ambivalent minor deities to become enamored with and no adulterous affairs and bickering among the gods. However, this is also a liability in that the one God becomes less human and less approachable because of his moral perfection. But a chief weakness is that with the belief in only one God, evil cannot be blamed on a demon or wicked god. Because of this, monotheism is especially vulnerable to the problem of theodicy or evil. A theodicy ("-dicy" from the Greek verb *dikaio* ["to justify"] and "theo-" from *theos* ["God"]) is an attempt to justify a deity who has created a world filled with evil and calamity. With only one God, you cannot blame disaster on another deity! Polytheism has the advantage of doing just that.

Note that Yahweh does not have a consort, at least officially. This may reflect the fact that Israelite women were not perceived as being as valuable as males. This patriarchal perspective is common in societies that practice intensive agriculture, where female activities are often largely confined to the household (see Haviland 2002, 366). Religion among the Israelite masses, however, apparently included the perspective that Yahweh had a wife, Asherah (El's consort!). A drawing on some pithoi (large pots) at Kuntillet ʿAjrud possibly depicts Yahweh, Asherah, and Bes, an Egyptian god that protects children (see Aḥituv 2008, 313-29). Writing on it refers to "Yahweh and his Asherah." Scholars disagree about whether this is the name of a female goddess or a symbol representing her (see Smith 1990, 80-114). Nevertheless, it points to the fact that the common and especially rural people expected Yahweh to have a wife and worshipped both him and his consort. Archaeologists have also discovered numerous feminine figurines in Israelite tombs that may represent fertility goddesses, no doubt common people compensating for a solely masculine deity.

Magic and Divination

While the official religious policy was to repress magic as much as possible, it probably was common among the masses. Magic is usually distinguished from religious practice by the notion of manipulating a deity with a technique or talisman. Instead of manipulation, religious practice involves appealing to and persuading the deity(ies) with prayers and sacrifices. However, the boundary between magic and religion is actually very blurred (see Haviland 2002, 377-78).

Max Weber speculates that the early Israelites were just as magically oriented as the other ancient Near Eastern peoples but that over time their religion become more rationalized and systematized than that of the other peoples (1976, 90-225, 235). An example would be in comparing the use of blood in ritual in Mesopotamia and Israel. The Mesopotamians applied blood on objects like door posts and foundation stones to drive away the demons of the Underworld or applied it to the body to heal epilepsy, while Israel (and the Hittites) used it to remove metaphysical evil (impurity, sin, etc.) and applied it to objects to purify them (see Feder 2011, 120-21).

Still even the official Israelite polity had vestiges of magic. The ordeal of a woman accused of adultery (Num. 5:11-31) is actually quite magical in form (see de Tarragon 1995, 2078). The ordeal is an old custom used in trials when there was not enough evidence to render a verdict and is a type of divination. Here a husband is suspicious ("spirit of jealousy" coming from a demon) that his wife has committed adultery, her pregnancy becoming visible. To restore his honor and the innocence of the woman, a bizarre ritual is followed. Dust from the sanctuary is placed in pure water and a curse is written on a scroll and then washed off into the water, which the woman is made to drink. If the woman does not get sick from drinking the water, she is innocent; if she does and aborts the fetus, she is guilty. The dust from the sanctuary mixed with the water "binds the litigant to the divinity, who is obliged to bring about a judgment" (de Tarragon 1995, 2078). This is similar to a Mari (northern Mesopotamia) prophetic letter that mentions gods drinking a concoction of dirt from the city gate and water and swearing an oath, promising not to harm the "brickwork" of a certain Mari official (see Sparks 2005, 204).

That the masses practiced magic is indicated by the silver amulet with a version of the priestly blessing (Num. 6:24-26) inscribed on it found at Ketef Hinnom (seventh century B.C.E.) (see Aḥituv 2008, 49-55). Another manifestation of magic is the cross-cultural phenomenon of the evil eye (Elliott 1991, 147-59). The wisdom literature alludes to it: "A man with an evil eye is hasty for wealth and does not know that want will come upon him" (Prov. 28:22; cf. 23:6; Sir. 14:8; 31:13). From an anthropological perspective, an evil eye is the greedy person who envies what someone else has. The possessor of the evil eye is caused to glare at the envied person, and, consequently, the stare places a curse on the unfortunate victim. The victim would suffer some loss or disease, perhaps even death. Because of this phenomenon, most persons refrained from conspicuously displaying their wealth for fear of the evil eye—another leveling mechanism. Our proverb shows that the one with the evil eye can suffer calamity as well.

The wisdom writers appear to also have been interested in divination and in predicting the future as well. There will be more on this later.

3

Scribalism in Egypt and Mesopotamia

As was discussed in the introductory chapter, the scribe could be a kind of sage in ancient Israel, though certainly not the only type. In this chapter, we want to profile the scribes in their broader ancient Near Eastern context, particularly in Mesopotamia and Egypt. We will investigate the various roles scribes served, the type of training they received, and literature they studied.

Mesopotamian Scribalism

The very first writing can be dated to 3100 B.C.E. in the city of Uruk in Sumer (Michalowski 1995, 2281). It was economic and administrative in nature. The earliest documentation concerns ration lists and the allocation of goods (consumable or real estate) and records about the conscription of workers for various tasks (Visicato 2000, 7). Tablets found at Early Dynastic Ur (2900-2700 B.C.E.) include lists on cereals (11 percent), lands (23 percent), allocation of grain products (bread, flour, and beer) (27 percent), personnel (6 percent), other matters (wood, metal, hides, reeds, etc.) (3 percent), and texts whose subject matter cannot be determined (23 percent). Approximately nine or so generations after the invention of writing what we would call literature was created; it served aesthetic and moral and not just economic functions (Michalowski 1995, 2279).

Scribal Roles

The Sumerian word for scribe *dubsar* means "tablet writer" (Pearce 1995, 2272; cf. *tiphsar* in Hebrew: "official"). This, of course, reflects the material on which he wrote. Scribes wrote on clay tablets when they were still wet. The first writing system was cuneiform, which consisted of wedge shaped markings that were applied by the scribe with a reed, which served as a pen. Cuneiform was not an alphabetic script but consisted of hundreds of pictograms, like hieroglyphs. It later developed into signs that represented syllables. This meant that learning this system was arduous for scribes and took many years.

Sidebar 5: Mesopotamian Scribal Titles

- deaf writer (probably a copyist)
- female scribe
- field scribe, land-registrar, geometer
- inscriber of stone
- judge's scribe
- mathematician

- military scribe

- scribe for laborer groups

- scribe of the property of the temple of Anu

- scribe of the *naditu* (cloistered) women

- scribe of (the omen series) *Enūma Anu Enlil* (an astrologer)

(Pearce 1995, 2272)

Many types of scribes existed in the early Mesopotamian world, but what united them all was the use of cuneiform writing in their respective roles (Pearce 1995, 2272-73). Scribes were involved in every facet of Mesopotamian life where writing was employed: 70 percent administrative, 20 percent private, and 10 percent "scientific." As private individuals, scribes recorded business transactions, composed contracts, functioned as notaries, and served as witnesses as a third-party but also as witnesses in their own transactions. While scribes earned compensation for these scribal activities, they often accrued more income from the sale and rent of real estate, accumulation and trading in shares held in temple offerings, and in providing loans. Merchants often hired scribes for sending letters and keeping business records. They also served as businessmen in entrepreneurial firms.

Illustration 7. Cuneiform Tablet

In addition to engaging in private practice, whether fulltime or free-lance, some scribes worked in the palace (Pearce 1995, 2273-74). Palace scribes served a variety of administrative roles, including archiving important texts and records, tax collecting, supervising laborers, and managing public buildings like granaries. Scribes also served as secretaries to kings, in charge of all royal communication. Palace scribes were also often real scholars, especially in the first millennium B.C.E., who specialized in haruspicy (expertise in interpreting the entrails of sacrificed animals as omens), astrology, exorcism, medicine, and the performance of hymns to appease angry gods who might be punishing the people with famine or plague.

Scribes also served as translators (Pearce 1995, 2274). This was necessitated by the Mesopotamian kings expanding their reach into other regions. International activity in Egypt, Mesopotamia, and the Hittite Empire during the middle and late second millennium B.C.E. necessitated the skill of scribes who could translate cuneiform into Egyptian. At the Egyptian capital Armana (the capitol of Pharaoh Akhnaten, father of king Tut), non-Egyptian scribes learned Egyptian.

Also, during the Old Babylonian period, scribes spoke the contemporary language Akkadian, but had to learn Sumerian during their education. This is because the best literature and educative texts were in Sumerian. Also a form of elitism is connected with this practice. Scribes who knew Sumerian could communicate amongst themselves without the larger populace understanding them. This is similar to our recent history when learning Greek and Latin were prerequisites for someone becoming a leader in society. Those who could not become proficient where excluded from the significant social circles—a bit of academic hazing!

Scribes also worked in temples, though not as officiants who performed rituals (Pearce 1995, 2274). They largely functioned as administrators and bureaucrats. They were responsible for managing incoming goods like grain, fish, wool, and silver. They traveled a lot and purchased grain for the temple. They aided archivists in classifying tablets according to categories. They helped persons in preparing tablets as votive (relating to vows) offerings to the gods. In the late first millennium, scribes aided priests in keeping records of astronomical observations in order to predict the future.

Illustration 8. Mesopotamian Scribes

Most scribes spent the majority of their time composing mundane business documents. However, some scholars stand out as real scholars, as already mentioned (Pearce 1995, 2274-75). Cuneiform scholars were scribes who, having mastered the basic scribal curriculum, received advanced training that allowed them to specialize in one or more areas. These scribes collected tablets for personal, family, and royal libraries. Those who became proficient in a particular genre or discipline often composed unique texts that were copied over and over again by later scribes. For example, Saggil-kinam-ubbib was the author of the "The Babylonian Theodicy," a wisdom text that is similar to the book of Job. He composed it in the form of an acrostic where the first cuneiform sign that begins each successive stanza of the poem spells out "I, Saggil-kinam-ubbib, the incantation priest, am adorant of the god and the king"! The scribal teacher was called an *ummānu* in Akkadian and denoted a master or one proficient in a particular discipline. This term was applied to diviners and exorcists, astronomers and astrologists, and physicians who attended to members of the court. The king regularly consulted such experts and asked their advice, especially diviners who could predict what his next political move should be. Astronomers and astrologers made up the largest percentage of scribal scholars.

Curriculum

The scribal school was known as the *edubba* or "tablet house" (Pearce 1995, 2270). Two levels of instruction are indicated (Pearce 1995, 2265). The most basic level was training as copyists. The scribes acquired basic literacy and numeracy that would enable them to serve the business community, whether public or private. The second level was reserved for more talented students who became proficient in advanced bodies of knowledge like science, literature, and religion. These became true scholars and were responsible for preserving the cultural heritage of Mesopotamia.

Four major areas of study formed the curriculum: language (including vocabulary and grammar), literature, mathematics (and surveying), and music (Pearce 1995, 2270). In the early stages, the teacher or assistant would write the day's lesson on one side of a tablet, and the student would copy this on the other side. At first this consisted of the student learning how to impress the clay with the stylus and form cuneiform marks, then individual signs and words. The tablets at this rudimentary stage show crude signs and only short connective passages, like proverbs or aphorisms.

Language skills were developed through the copying of lists: signs, vocabularies, syllabaries, and grammar. These lexical lists were organized by theme, like professions or geographical names, or by the shape of the cuneiform signs (Michalowski 1995, 2281). The lists reflect a drive to classify and to apply order to the cosmos as known to the Mesopotamians (Bottéro 1995, 2300).

Students became proficient in writing letters and business contracts by copying practice letters and model contracts (Pearce 1995, 2271). Mastery of a particular discipline was achieved by the copying of technical vocabulary, as well as by grouping words according to subject matter. Advanced training also included learning priestly and administrative vocabulary, stelae (inscribed erected stones) preparation, and copying legal codes and court proceedings.

Mathematics was the third area of instruction (Pearce 1995, 2271). Based on exercises on tablets, students were trained in multiplication, reciprocals, squares, square roots, algebra, geometry, and surveying. Texts have been found that contain problems to be worked out for training scribes for a variety of administrative roles. Even the Assyrian king Assurbanipal bragged of his mathematical skills gained in scribal training: "I can unravel complicated reciprocals and products that do not have a solution (in the problem)" (Nemat-Nejat 1995, 253). Scribal students also learned metrology, the science of weights and measurements.

In the fourth curricular area, students entering temple service were trained in music (Pearce 1995, 2271). They mastered several instruments and learned Sumerian technical terms equivalent to antiphon, recital, and finale. This prepared scribes to fulfill the role of chief singer of lamentations/dirges. Ordinary performers were probably illiterate.

Sidebar 6: Sequence of Mesopotamian Curriculum

First grade: proverbs, exempla, fables, short didactic pieces

Second grade: "school texts" (texts that focus on the subject of schools), longer didactic pieces, debates

Third grade: hymns, odes, performative texts

Fourth grade: major hymnic, lyric or "historical texts" (possibly also performative)

Fifth grade: major narrative poems about heroes or gods; reflective poems (Vanstiphout 1999, 83)

Literature Emerges!

The very first imaginative writing or what we might call literature emerged during the Early Dynastic period (around 2500 B.C.E.) (Michalwoski 1995, 2281). One text tells of a legendary king, and some are magical charms against disease. Most of these texts, however, were mythological and treat the topic of the gods or were hymns to them. During this period, the area was politically fragmented with various dialects spoken. But since scribes knew

Sumerian, this helped them communicate between themselves and strengthened the camaraderie of the guild.

Around 2300 B.C.E. Mesopotamia was united under the rule of the city of Akkad (from which comes the word "Akkadian" language comes) (Michalowski 1995, 2282). King Sargon established an empire and centralized the region. This necessitated a new propaganda apparatus, and, so, scribes were now trained and controlled by the state. Trained scribes were sent out to run the local districts. After the fall of Sargon's empire, Ur emerged as the dominant city with five successive kings, including the famous Shulgi (2122-2004 B.C.E.). Some songs and poems about the court and temples were created during this period.

Sumerian Literature

The widest variety of Sumerian literature is found in the Old Babylonian period during the eighteenth century B.C.E., when Sumerian was a dead language (Michalowski 1995, 2282-83). Most of the texts we have come from Southern Babylonia. Here "schools" may have been no more than a scribal father who taught his sons and neighborhood kids at his home, and these schools were not controlled by the state, unlike in the north (Michalowski 1995, 2283).

Court Literature

One of the most important types of literature used in the schools was court literature (Michalowski 1995, 2284). This tradition and perhaps much of this literature stem back to the time of Shulgi, during the Ur III period. He was one of the few Mesopotamian kings who claimed to be able to read and write: "Since I was a child I (studied in) the school, I learned the scribal art from the tablets of Sumer and Akkad, (and) among the children no one could write a tablet like I could!" (Michalwoski 1995, 2284). Shulgi and his successors were the first to understand the importance of using Sumerian literature for political propaganda.

The court literature includes numerous royal hymns but also the famous debates or dialogues between animals or objects, which may have been performed at the court of Ur (Micahlowski 1995, 2284). Other genres include love songs of King Shu-Sin, the *Curse of Agade*, which bemoans the fall of the earlier state and was composed during Ur III times, and the "law code" of Ur-Namma. This "code" was not really a legal code but rather an abstract demonstration of royal wisdom and justice. Such codes were usually inscribed on monuments for people to see.

The heroic tales of legendary kings of the Early Dynastic period, like Gilgamesh of Uruk, may have been composed during the Ur III period (Michalowski 1995, 2284). Shulgi, in fact, frequently compares himself to Gilgamesh. Gilgamesh was half divine, and Shulgi himself claimed divinity. Descent from a god helped legitimate Shulgi's kingship.

Historical texts were also studied, like the "Sumerian King List," which lists kings that lived before and after the great flood (Michalowski 1995, 2284). The antediluvian kings lived for incredible spans of time (64,000 years! cf. Methuselah 969 years [Gen. 5:27]). Also, literary biographies of ancient kings were studied, which treated the themes of kingship and human destiny. The poem "The Ballad of Heroes of Old" is an example and is quite pessimistic (see Alster 2005, 265-322). It looks back to the days of the ancient kings nostalgically but realizes that things have changed. It advises a carpe diem ethic of enjoying life as much as possible, including drinking beer. Connected with this pessimistic theme are other works like "Nothing is of Value," which also advocates a carpe diem perspective.

These have been classified as wisdom texts (e.g., Alster 2005, 265-322).

Figure 3: "Sumerian King List": Antedeluvian Kings		
City	King	Years of Reign
Eridu	A-lulim	28,800
	Alalgar	36,000
Bad-tibira	En-men-lu-Anna	43,200
	En-men-gal	28,800
	Dumuzi	36,000
Larak	En-sipa-zi-Anna	28,800
Sippar	En-men-dur-Anna	21,000
Shuruppak	Ubar-Tutu	18,600

(Configured from Pritchard 1969, 265)

Figure 4: Postdeluvian Kings		
City	King	Years of Reign
Kish	Ga . . . ur	1,200
	?	960
	Pala-kinatim	900
	Nangish-lishma	?
	Bahina	?
	. . . um	840
	Kalibum	960
	Qalumum	840
	Zuqaqip	900

	Atab	600
	Mashdad	840
	Arwi'um	720
	Etana	1,560
	Balih	400
	En-me-nunna	600
	Melam-Kishi	900
	Bar-sal-nunna	1,200
	Samug	305
	Ilku'	900
	Ilta-sadum	1,200
	En-men-barage-si	900
	Aka	629
Eanna	Mes-kiag-gasher	324
	En-me-kar	420
	Lugal-banda	1,200
	Dumuzi	100
	Gilgamesh	126
	Ur-Nungal	30
	Utul-kalamma	15
	Laba[h . . .]ir	9
	En-nun-dara-Anna	8
	?	36
	Melam-Anna	6
	Lugal-i-tun	36
Ur	Mes-Anne-pada	80
	Mes-kiag-Nanna	36

	Elulu	25
	Balulu	36

Hymnic Literature

The life of a Mesopotamian king was filled with ceremony and ritual, and hymns were composed for these occasions (Micahlowski 1995, 2284-85). Shulgi was celebrated with 24 hymns. These royal hymns were related to hymns to the gods. Many of these hymns in fact involve the king or someone on behalf of the king addressing the deity. Also, hymns devoted to temples and their deities are found.

Sumerian love poetry was also popular. While Greek love poetry is always in the form of a monologue, in the ancient Near East two or more voices are preferred, and the songs are more like dramas (Westenholz 1995, 2472). Sumerian love poetry consists of three categories: deities who are portrayed as lovers, Sumerian kings who unite with consorts or goddesses, and non-royal, human lovers. In the first category, the most significant are songs devoted to the doomed love affair between Inanna (Ishtar in Akkadian) and Dumuzi (or Tammuz), whose death was mourned by Judahite women [Ezek. 8:14]). Dumuzi was a shepherd god of fertility and Inanna, goddess of love and war, was his consort. Their marriage and separation (Dumuzi's confinement to the Underworld) symbolized the agricultural cycle of rebirth and dying of the spring/summer and then fall/winter.

A rather graphic example is "Prosperity in the Palace," in which Inanna compares her genitals to various kinds of landscape. She asks who will plow it for her and, of course, Dumuzi volunteers:

"The vulva it is . . . ,

. . . .

It is fallow land, in the plain . . . ,
It is a *field*, which the *uz*-bird . . the *uz*-bird,
It is a *high field*, my . . . ,
As for me, my vulva is a . . . hillock,—*for me*,
I, the maid, who will be its plower?
My vulva is . . . wet ground *for me*,
I, the queen, who will station there the ox?"
"Lady, the king will plow it for you,
Dumuzi, the king, will plow it for you."
"Plow my vulva, my sweetheart" (Pritchard 1969, 643).

The second category belongs to the "sacred marriage" texts which describe the mystical union of the Sumerian king and the goddess Inanna. Its recitation and performance occurred during the New Year holiday and signified the renewal of the harmony of the natural world and determined the fates of the king and his people (Westenholz 1995, 2274).

Mythmaking

Narrative poems about the deities were also composed. These can be classified as myths, and they treat the problem of order and chaos in the cosmos (Michalowski 1995, 2285-86). These texts usually begin with order having been disturbed in the universe or not yet fully present as in "Enki and the World Order." This story describes the creation of the cosmos and its supervision assigned to various deities. Several etiological texts exist that explain why things are as they are, such as "Inanna and the Numun-Plant," which describes where fire came from, and "How Grain Came to Sumer."

THE SOCIAL WORLD OF THE SAGES

Each city had its own patron god, who dwelt in a central shrine. These gods would literally travel as idols to visit other gods in other cities. Accounts of these visits are depicted in stories like "Enki's Journey to Nippur."

While court literature extolled the virtues of the kingship and state, other texts demonstrate the limits of these institutions. A poem about the death of king Ur-Nammu, the "Curse of Age," and "Lamentation over the Destruction of Sumer and Ur" all point to the limitations of royal power.

Other Genres

Short stories, proverb collections, and collections of older letters that may have served as models for young scribes are also found (Michalowski 1995, 2286-87). The Sumerian letters eventually morphed into a new genre: letter-prayers. These were prayers to gods or kings deposited in front of statues.

One of the most popular and oldest proverb collections is represented by "The Instructions of Shuruppak." Shuruppak is the name of a Mesopotamian city and the author refers to himself as "the man from Shuruppak" (Alster 2005, 31-33). He was an antediluvian sage who passed on his wisdom to his son Zisudra, also known in Akkadian as Utnapishtim or Atraḫasis, a.k.a. the Babylonian Noah. The wise sayings are purportedly intended to educate him in the role of ruler of Shurupak, though the proverbs themselves do not address such matters specifically. Some of the proverbs are even critical of the kingship. Here are a few of the proverbs:

> Don't act as a guarantor; that man will have a hold on you (Alster 2005, 60).

Stand aside from quarrels; when facing an insult, go around it on another road! (61).

Don't have sexual intercourse with your slave girl; she will neglect you (66).

The "honey-mouth" gathers sweet herbs (75).

The boaster reached (out for) his (empty) leather bag (75).

Sleeping, the fool loses something (76).

Don't buy a prostitute; she is a mouth with sharpened teeth! (83)

As mentioned earlier, debate poems were popular (Michalowski 1995, 2287). These involved debates between animals, plants, or objects about who is of superior value. For example, in the "Disputation between the Hoe and the Plow," a sage argues that the unattractive, muddy hoe builds dams and all sorts of things, while the plow is valuable for crops. But the plow takes 4 men and 6 oxen to work and often breaks down. The victor is the lowly hoe (Kramer 1990, 34). In the "Disputation between Silver and Mighty Copper," copper is proclaimed victor because it is used for so many implements, while silver is just for decoration (Kramer 1990, 35). Note that the unlikely candidate in the debates seems to always win. In the "Disputation between Summer and Winter," winter wins because it supplies all the water that summer will eventually use to help make the land fertile (Kramer 1990, 35). These debate poems especially resonate with a major concern in the book of Proverbs: the assessment of values.

Related to the debate are fables, which often involve dialogue. In "The Fox and Enlil as Merchant," a fox tries to outsmart one of the major Sumerian gods, Enlil, who is disguised as a merchant (Alster 2005, 346). The fox (and a dog) tried to smuggle some goods past an inspection point downstream from Nippur. Enlil was smart enough to detect the attempt and tried to stop him. The fox flees but when caught blames the dog! In "The Elephant and the Wren," the elephant brags that no animal can compare to him, to which the wren responds that he is equal to the elephant (Alster 2005, 366). In the Akkadian version, we find out that the bird demonstrates this by pointing out that he defecates just like the elephant, i.e., proportionately!

Another important genre were incantation or magical charms (Michalowski 1995, 2287). These were used in rituals and also served in school exercises to demonstrate literary qualities.

After the Old Babylonian period, Sumerian literature consisted of lexical texts, incantations, prayers, ritual compositions, and a small number of myths (Michalowski 1995, 2288). However, the Ur III tradition, with its royal hymns, epics, and historical texts, was not continued.

Akkadian Literature

Akkadian literature did not really emerge until the Old Babylonian period, around the eighteenth century B.C.E. (Bottéro 1995, 2294-95). Much of the Sumerian literature was translated into Akkadian, the contemporary language of the scribes. This was done to provide the scribes sources for ideas, genres, and literary expressions. Genres and themes that were not continued include the accounts of visits between gods, the divine character of the kings, the city lamentations (now that city-states had ceased), and the "King List." The latter was replaced by epic narratives about kings.

Narrative and Liturgical Texts

New genres and works appeared in Akkadian (Bottéro 1995, 2296). In contrast to the narrower perspective of Sumerian literature, the Babylonians produced works of broad synthesis. These include "Atraḥasis" (or "wise one"), who is the "Babylonian Noah," and concerns the great flood sent by the gods to destroy humanity. The story is filled with etiologies. For example, it explains the purpose of humans offering sacrifices: to provide "food" for the gods. In the story humans stop offering sacrifices to force the hand of the gods. In return, the gods send plagues and famine to motivate the people to work for them. It also explains why humans were created in the first place: to do the labor of the world, like dredging the canals of Mesopotamia, so that the lesser warrior gods would not have to. It also explains why some women were celibate and infertile: a sort of population control so that great numbers of humans would not disturb the gods.

Another example is the "Enuma Elish," ("when above"—the words that begin the account), which has been called the "Babylonian Genesis." It is a creation account that explains the birth of the cosmos and creation of humans as a result of a battle between the god of Babylon, Marduk, and a hideous dragoness Tiamat (depicted as multi-headed), who represents chaos and evil. Marduk wins the battle and becomes the chief god of the Babylonian pantheon. The battle began because the newer generation of gods were disturbing the creator deity Apsu with their noise. Ea, the god of wisdom, stops Apsu from slaying these divine warriors by killing him and thereby slaying Tiamat's husband. After the battle, Tiamat's body is used by Marduk to create the sky and earth. Also, Marduk assigns certain gods to serve as constellations to mark seasons, and the moon is directed to measure the months. The blood of Tiamat's new husband, Kingu, is used to make humans, who will now do the work of the warrior gods. The story also served as propaganda for the preeminence of the city of Babylon.

Illustration 9. Tiamat versus Marduk

Another classic, the "Epic of Gilgamesh," recounts the tale of the semi-divine Gilgamesh, king of Uruk. Gilgamesh has become a tyrant to the citizens of Uruk, and so the gods create for him a wild and hairy man, Enkidu, to preoccupy him. Enkidu and Gilgamesh end up offending the gods for bad behavior and Enkidu is stricken with a disease and dies. After mourning his friend, Gilgamesh becomes obsessed with the quest for eternal life. As he sets out on his journey to find it, he stops at a tavern and expresses his desire to a divine barmaid. She advises him to forget his pursuit because the gods have kept immortal life for themselves and commends to him a carpe diem ethic strikingly similar to Eccles. 9:7-9:

> Let your belly be full,
> make merry day and night.
> Turn each day into a feast of rejoicing,
> dance and play day and night.
> Put on fresh garments,
> wash your hair and body in water.
> Play with your children,
> take pleasure in your wife
> (Matthews and Benjamin 2006, 26).

Gilgamesh refuses to listen and continues to the great sage Utnapishtim, the Babylonian Noah = Atraḥasis. Because he and his wife escaped the fate of the other humans by a great flood, they were granted immortality. Utnaphishtim tells Gilgamesh about the plant of life, which Gilgamesh retrieves from the bottom of the sea. However, he loses it subsequently to a snake while napping on the shore. This resonates with the Sumerian Tale of Adapa, a wise man who is offered eternal life because of his unexpected ability to control the wind of a storm but refuses it at the advice of Ea. Both of these stories are etiologies explaining why humans, who share features of the divine, are yet mortal. At the end of the story, Gilgamesh goes back to Uruk and is content that he has made a name for himself and built such a grand city. Here is the Mesopotamian conception of "immortality" through great deeds and renown.

Peculiar to Akkadian are also compositions about the gods and their worship appearing in a long liturgical style (Bottéro 1995, 2296-97). Works were dedicated to Ishtar (goddess of love and war), Marduk, Nabû (god of the scribes), and Shamash (the sun god and god of justice).

Reflective Wisdom Literature

Dialogues and monologues about the problem of evil were popular (Bottéro 1995, 2297). These were probably written because the inherited mythology did not adequately treat these themes. Examples are "Dialogue of a Man with His God," "In Praise of the Lord of Wisdom," and the "Babylonian Theodicy." In the latter, a man debates his suffering friend concerning why he is suffering so terribly when he is God-fearing. The work is quite strikingly similar to the book of Job. Also, in this category is the "Dialogue of Pessimism," in which a master and slave debate whether they should do various activities, one of which is for both of them to commit suicide, which they do not follow through on. None of these literary dialogues appear to seriously challenge the notion of divine retribution or justice. Rather, they serve to relativize this teaching and emphasize the limitations of human cognition: one cannot completely comprehend the ways of the gods (van der Toorn 1991, 59-75).

Court Literature

Literature about rulers was composed, such as annals and chronicles (Bottéro 1995, 2297-98). The latter were loosely based on the "Sumerian King List," and they placed in chronological order the successive reigns of significant kings. Kings also praised themselves, such as in the introduction to the "Code of Hammurabi," and there were fictive biographies and autobiographies like "The Birth of Sargon," whose birth story strikingly resembles that of Moses.

Literature about Conduct and Experience

In distinction from political, religious, and historical literature, compositions about conduct and experience were produced (Bottéro 1995, 2298). In addition to collections of proverbs, instructions, fables and disputations, satirical and witty tales are found like "The Poor Man of Nippur." This tale is about a poor man who is treated unjustly by the mayor of Nippur but ends up outwitting him three times in revenge and becoming rich as a result (see Foster 1995, 2466). Love songs were also popular.

The literature of exorcism became especially prevalent during the Akkadian period. Ancient Mesopotamians believed that illness and misfortune was cause by demons who had to be exorcised in order to restore health or prosperity. Here we enter the realm of magic where rituals of exorcists were used to ward off demons. The Israelites had similar notions.

Divination Literature and Knowledge about Knowledge

Another genre not found in the Sumerian corpus is divination literature (Bottéro 1995, 2299). This literature is based on observation of events and happenings and the seeming consequences that followed. The omens assume this form: "if such and such happens, then such and such will occur." Again, this is a form of ancient science, though we moderns would consider it bunk. The ability to predict the future was of paramount importance to ancient peoples, particularly political leaders, who had to make important decisions about warfare and policy that had serious repercussions. Akkadian scribes composed anthologies of these predictions. Both the literature on exorcism and divination literature represents the bulk of Akkadian compositions.

Related to the divination texts were the manuals of jurisprudence or what scholars erroneously have called law codes (Bottéro 1995, 2299), as in the famous "Code of Hammurabi." These also have the following caustic structure: "if someone does this, then this is the punishment."

As for know-how literature, the word lists were continued in the Akkadian literature (Bottéro 1995, 2299-2300). Technological treatises were also studied like the raising and training of horses, cooking recipes, and medical and pharmacological treatises.

Egyptian Scribalsim

The Egyptian word for scribe is *zakhau*: "one who uses the brush," which includes not only writing but drawing and painting (Wente 1995, 2211). Egyptian scribes, like their Mesopotamian counterparts, could serve as high officials because the ability to read and write was a necessary prerequisite for any career in the administration. The role of scribe, however, did not necessarily mean high rank in Egyptian society. Elite administrators looked down on lower level scribes who were essentially copyists or secretaries.

Egyptian scribes used red and black ink for their compositions (Wente 1995, 2212). The standard scribal kit consisted of a palette with two depressions for the colored ink and brushes. This kit could be linked together by a cord, and scribes are often depicted in this way, with the kit draped over their shoulders. In fact, the scribal kit was the standard hieroglyph for "write" and "scribe."

Illustration 10. Egyptian Scribes

The literacy rate in ancient Egypt was very low, as in the rest of the ancient Near East (Wente 1995, 2214). In the Old Kingdom (2650-2135 B.C.E.), it was 1 percent, reaching 5 percent during the New Kingdom (1550-1080 B.C.E.). Unlike most Mesopotamian kings, pharaohs were usually literate, though they used personal secretaries to handle their correspondence. In the Old Kingdom, only the sons of officials were educated to become scribes. In the Middle Kingdom (2040-1650 B.C.E.), we begin to see democratization of the selection process. In order to ensure loyalty to the Pharaoh and bureaucracy, boys of diverse backgrounds were recruited. In the New Kingdom, boys of modest background were also educated, some becoming high officials. For young boys, the military also offered an alternative route to advancement.

Scribal Education

In the Old Kingdom, scribal training was a sort of apprenticeship, usually a father teaching his own son or an official a "spiritual" son (Wente 1995, 2215). This intimate relationship is indicated by the usual term for the student: "son." During the First Intermediate Period (2135-2040 B.C.E.), when the central bureaucracy collapsed and the land was governed by local rulers, we have the first mention of a school. This provided greater standardization in education and enabled more students to be taught simultaneously. In the Middle Kingdom, a school existed in Memphis, where elite as well as less advantaged boys attended.

In the New Kingdom, a boy usually started scribal training at age 10 (Wente 1995, 2215). The oldest pedagogical text is the "Book of Kemit" or "summation/completion." It contained vertical columns filled with phraseology of letters and tomb biographies in hieratic, a cursive type of hieroglyphs. After this, the student learned to write hieratic in horizontal lines by copying texts like "Satire on the Trades" or "Instruction of Khety." The scribal instructor would provide a sample text, which the students copied on ostraca or pieces of pottery. As they progressed, the teacher would simply recite the passage orally for the students to record. The students then memorized the text and wrote it from memory.

In the New Kingdom, during the elementary education, which lasted 4 years, students focused on learning the classics composed in the Middle Kingdom (Wente 1995, 2215-16). After completion and in his teens, the student had to decide if he would pursue more advanced studies, whether serving in the administration, priesthood, or military as an officer. This more advanced stage could last 12 years, and he had to learn colloquial Late Egyptian and study mathematics, accounting, geometry, surveying and elementary engineering. As an apprentice, the student copied model compositions from his master, which included a diversity of texts called "Miscellanies." The most boring part of his training was memorizing word lists which included the names of occupations, localities, body parts, etc., organized topically like an encyclopedia.

Candidates for the priesthood studied at the House of Life at a temple (Wente 1995, 2216). Here the student copied old religious and magical texts. In New Kingdom times, priests had to manage large temple estates and were trained accordingly as both administrators and ritualists. At the Houses of Life, future physicians, astronomers, magicians, and dream interpreters were also educated.

Roles and Status

Scribes worked for either the state (civil or army) or the temples (Wente 1995, 2217-18). Since the economy of ancient Egypt was dependent on agriculture, most scribes worked for the treasury as tax assessors. Lower echelon scribes went throughout the land surveying fields and estimating yields. Higher level scribes would take these local accounts and create a unified report. Some of these higher level scribes could become quite powerful, even building tombs for themselves. Scribes were also involved in building projects, serving as civil engineers who estimated the number of days of work a group of workers needed to complete a project or the total rations needed to complete a task. Army scribes were responsible for taking a census for recruitment purposes. Scribes enlisted soldiers and informed them of their duties, including sometimes labor projects. These particular skills were more highly esteemed than registering incoming grain at the temples.

Scribes were advantaged in that they were not subject to taxation (Wente 1995, 2218-19). A scribe was a tax collector rather than a taxpayer. However, the scribe was not always of the highest status. The Ramesside scribes who organized the royal tomb artisans at Deir el-Medina had homes that did not differ much in size from the laborers. Also, their salary in grain was only 35 percent more than the artisans and equal to the two foremen, who technically outranked them. Some scribes, though, could become wealthy, owning lands and slaves. Scribes were generally liked by the villagers, but some were oppressive and known for taking bribes.

Egyptian Literature

Old Kingdom (2650-2135 B.C.E.)

Tomb Autobiographies

In Egypt, writing first appeared as brief notes designed to identify a person, place, event or possession (Lichtheim 1975, 3-4). The Egyptians viewed this early writing as both magical and divine. Its first major application was the offering list that was inscribed on tomb walls. It named the tomb-owner and his family, listing his ranks and titles and the offerings he needed for the afterlife, like fabrics, ointments, and foods. The list eventually developed into a prayer for offerings, which requested offerings and a good reception in the West (abode of the dead). From this came the autobiography which emerged during the Early Dynastic Period and became a truly literary phenomenon. The tomb autobiography was a way for the dead to speak to posterity (Redford 1995, 2232). The dead enjoined the living who passed by to provide him offerings or at the least pronounce the offering formula. The autobiographies warned against decimating the tomb.

The autobiographies functioned similarly to the self-portrait in sculpture and relief: to sum up the essence of the person's character positively and in view of eternity (Lichtheim 1975, 4). To moderns, they seem very self-laudatory, but this was because they were simultaneously a kind of epitaph and a bid for immortality. Confession of sins was not appropriate. The bid for immortality was both magical and moral. Statues, food offerings, and rituals would help ensure existence in the West, but living a good moral life was essential. It had to be lived in accordance with Maat, the divine order. Thus emerged a catalog of virtues practiced and vices avoided as a standard feature of the autobiography. This closely resembles the list of vices not practiced in Job's vow of innocence (Job 31), when he places a curse on himself if he has mistreated other people, particularly the poor.

Instructions

The genre of instruction is basically a development from the autobiographies (Lichtheim 1975, 1, 5). This genre reflected the hierarchic society of the Old Kingdom, which in turn was seen as reflecting the divine order. The instructions combined pragmatic advice gleaned from experience with religious piety to form maxims. The instruction is usually framed by a father who instructs his son with worldly wisdom. The instruction was very popular, useful, and entertaining. While the form remained basically the same throughout the ages, the content varied somewhat. It mainly displayed an aristocratic flavor. In the New Kingdom, it became more "middle class" in perspective. The instruction represents the distillation of the nation's wisdom and replicated the morals of the autobiographies. Most Egyptologists believe the instructions are all pseudepigraphical ("false writing") or not really written by whom they purport to be. This lent them more authority.

One of the oldest examples is the "Instruction of Ptahhotep." This work contains 37 maxims and is very socially self-conscious. Much of the instruction treats the appropriate behavior before one's superiors and inferiors:

> If you meet a disputant in action,
> a powerful man, superior to you,
> fold your arms, bend your back,
> to flout him will not make him agree with you.
> Make little of the evil speech
> by not opposing him while he's in action;
> he will be called an ignoramus,
> your self-control will match his pile (of words)
> (Lichtheim 1975, 63-64).

To put it in modern parlance, "Ptahhotep" extolled the virtues of being a gentleman (Lichtheim 1975, 7). Though the book is supposed to be from a vizier to his son, the instructions apparently have little to do with the vizierate (Lichtheim 1975, 7). However, like the "Instruction of Shuruppak," this is not the intent. Even a vizier would need to know how to assess various social situations. Few of the other genres that scribes studied were self-consciously scribal in flavor. The scribes were expected to learn a broad curriculum that went beyond just practical and explicitly professional concerns. They were to become well-rounded officials.

First Intermediate Period (2135-2040 B.C.E.) and Middle Kingdom (2040-1650 B.C.E.)

During the First Intermediate Period society shifted from a centralized monarchy to a decentralized polity where local politics prevailed (Lichtheim 1975, 8). Though some scholars characterize this period as socially anarchic and a sort of Dark Ages, it was not. The artwork of this period does not represent a decay from the previous era but rather the contributions of ordinary people who could finally build tombs and monuments for themselves.

A new type of instruction was created during this time represented by the "Instruction to King Merikare" (Lichtheim 1975, 8-9). It is royal instruction that is in the form of a testament and represents a treatise on kingship. However, most scholars believe it was written by a court scribe at the command of King Merikare.

The Middle Kingdom can be described as Egypt's classical age, which produced a variety of genres and with great sophistication (Lichtheim 1975, 9). Two new genres include hymns to gods and praises of the king. Royal monumental inscriptions that have a historical character became exquisite.

Protest Literature

The instruction changes form in the Middle Kingdom, largely due to the effects of the First Intermediate Period (Lichtheim 1975, 9). It becomes admonitory and "prophetic." For the first time, Egyptians begin to ponder the problem of evil in literature. All was not well in the land. People were evil. Civil war had divided the nation. The order of the Old Kingdom had been disturbed, yet the gods did not intervene! An example is the "Admonitions of Ipuwer," which paints the world as bleak and dark and turned upside down:

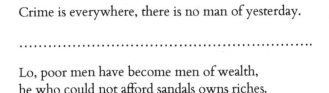

Crime is everywhere, there is no man of yesterday.

. . . .

Lo, poor men have become men of wealth,
he who could not afford sandals owns riches.

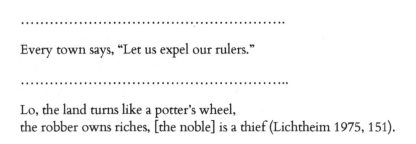

Every town says, "Let us expel our rulers."

....

Lo, the land turns like a potter's wheel,
the robber owns riches, [the noble] is a thief (Lichtheim 1975, 151).

At the end the sage reproaches the king for allowing this state of affairs to happen and encourages him to act like a king and do his religious duties. The king speaks at the end and blames the people. This instruction may have served as propaganda for the reign during which it was written, serving to contrast the former chaotic times with the current situation (Faulkner 1973a, 210).

Similarly, in the "Prophecies of Nefertim" the chaotic society theme is used for rhetorical effect (see Lichtheim 1975, 139). A sage is summoned to court to entertain King Snefru of the fourth Dynasty. During the event, the sage is asked to prophecy concerning the future. He prophecies the devastation of the land by civil war and the rise of great king Amenemhet I. The topsy-turvy world depicted in the instruction would contrast with the time of its composition during Amenemhet's reign. Thus, similarly to "Ipuwer," this poem serves as royal legitimation. Though the text is labeled a prophecy, in fact it is *ex eventu* prophecy or prophecy after the fact. This occurs in the Hebrew Bible as well, as in the apocalyptic oracles in Daniel 7-12, when a book written in the Seleucid period (160's B.C.E.) "divines" contemporary events as though from the earlier Babylonian period (sixth century B.C.E.).

Similar to the dialogues of Mesopotamian wisdom literature is the pessimistic "The Dispute between a Man and his Ba" (see Lichtheim 1975, 163). It is in the form of a dialogue between a man who wants to commit suicide and his Ba, a sort of alter-ego that must remain with him in the afterlife in order to survive. The man complains about the misfortunes of life and wants to die. His Ba threatens to leave him, which horrifies the man, who implores the Ba to remain. The Ba advises him that eternal life is not guaranteed and not everything he imagines. Those with fine tombs and proper mortuary fare are no better off than those without. The Ba advocates a carpe diem ethic, but the man does not agree. In the end, the Ba agrees to remain with him. However, this nod toward orthodoxy at the end cannot conceal the fact that the Ba seems to have the better argument (Redford 1995, 2234). This work resonates well with Ecclesiastes, with its fixation on death, its skepticism and pessimism, and carpe diem ethic. Also, the interaction between the man and his Ba resembles the way the teacher in Ecclesiastes speaks to his own heart (e.g., 9:1) as he observes the dark realities of life (see Holmstedt 2009, 1-27).

In line with this skepticism are the "Songs of the Harpers." These were songs found in the tombs that usually praise death and affirm the joy of the afterlife for the deceased. Harps are mentioned as imaginatively accompanying the recitation of the poems. However, one of the songs in the tomb of King Intef started a tradition of skepticism that continued in the "Harpers' Songs" of later periods. In it doubt is cast on what happens in the afterlife and about the effectiveness of the mortuary cult. In the New Kingdom, evidence shows that this skepticism is actually countered a bit and softened in the tombs. The following song from Intef's tomb describes the sad fate of the long dead, including two famous sages, and then advises a life of ease and joy:

(Yet) those who build tombs,
their places are gone,
what has become of them?
I have heard the words of Imhotep and Hardedef,

whose sayings are recited whole.
What of their places?
Their walls have crumbled,
their places are gone,
as though they had never been!

....

Follow your heart as long as you live!
Put myrrh on your head,
dress in fine linen,
anoint yourself with oils fit for a god.

....

Make holiday,
do not weary of it!
Lo, none is allowed to take his goods with him,
lo, none who departs comes back again!
(Lichtheim 1975, 196-97)

Once again, the wordage of the harper's carpe diem ethic is striking similar to Eccles. 9:7-10.

This literature of protest and despair represents a period of introspection among the Egyptians after the collapse of their majestic Old Kingdom (Redford 1995, 2233). For the first time, space was made for heterodox ideas to be expressed that went against the grain of orthodoxy. A certain kind of individualism permeates the writings of these authors.

Didactic Literature

A more optimistic example of didactic literature is "The Satire of the Trades," which aims to humorously promote the superiority of the scribal profession over against all the other vocations. It is framed by the story of an official walking his son to scribal school and on the way begins to speak of the many advantages of the scribal profession. The satire assumes that even elite scribal students found their homework and studies difficult and so were in need of encouragement from time to time. He begins this way:

> I have seen many beatings—
> Set your heart on books!
> I watched those seized for labor—
> There's nothing better than books!
>
> ....
>
> A scribe at whatever post in town,
> he will not suffer in it;
> As he fills another's need,
> he will [not lack rewards].
> I don't see a calling like it
> (Lichtheim 1975, 185).

Later he states, "See, there's no profession without a boss, except for the scribe; he is the boss" (Lichtheim 1975, 189). The father exaggerates the unpleasantness and drudgery of other vocations. The smith's fingers end up looking like crocodile claws, and he stinks worse than fish roe. The jeweler wearies his arms, only rests when the sun sets, and his knees and back are cramped. The potter is described as working under the soil and digging in the mud more than a pig. Ben Sira is dependent on this work, even if indirectly, when he too lauds the benefits of scribalism (38:24-34). He also makes fun of the other professions but at least acknowledges that the other guilds are necessary for society to operate (38:32)!

Narratives

Several prose tales were popular as well. That the Egyptians valued rhetoric is indicated by "Tale of the Eloquent Peasant," which was mentioned earlier. The highly artistic "Story of Sinuhe" is described by famed Egyptologist Miriam Lichtheim as "the crown-jewel of the Middle Kingdom literature" (Lichtheim 1975, 11). Sinuhe is an official of Pharaoh Amenemhet 1 (1991-1962 B.C.E.) and served his daughter, Neferu, and her husband, Senwosret (see Matthews and Benjamin 2006, 137). When Amenemhet dies, Sinuhe witnesses a developing coup d'état and flees to escape death at the traitors' hands. He travels to Syro-Palestine and is rescued from starvation by some herders. He eventually makes it to Byblos, a significant coastal city on the Mediterranean. Because he was both honest and wise, the leader of this region, Ammunenshi, gives his daughter to him in marriage, and Sinuhe has children. He serves as a gracious host to travelers. Once he is challenged to a duel by a valiant warrior, but Sinuhe shoots him in his neck with an arrow and kills him with his own ax. This story is strikingly similar to the story of David and Goliath (1 Sam. 17). Though happy, Sinuhe becomes homesick and finds out that he can return in good favor to Egypt because Senwosret has become king. Sinuhe leaves his eldest son behind to run his household.

The New Kingdom (1550-1080 B.C.E.)

Continuity as well as change characterizes the literature of the New Kingdom (see Lichtheim 1976, 3-5). After the Hyksos, the Semitic foreigners who had subjugated Egypt, had been expelled from Egypt, the age of empire began for the Egyptians. The pharaohs began to invade and conquer Syro-Palestine. Palestine consisted of a series of city-states, which became vassals to Egypt and had to pay tribute. Egyptian garrisons were installed in important cities.

Foreign princes were brought to Egypt to be trained in Egyptian ways (see Lichtheim 1976, 3-4). Treaties were made with the Hittites,

Mitannians, and Babylonians. Daughters of these kings were sent to live in Pharaoh's harem, thereby establishing strong alliances. This was a period of great internationalism for the Egyptian empire and a golden age of wealth and luxury. Egyptian scribes prided themselves in their knowledge of far way places and peoples, while foreigners could come to Egypt and attain positions of high rank (cf. Joseph in Genesis). Many Egyptian scribes and their foreign counterparts were required to become bilingual. The great Egyptian gods became the gods of all the lands, a kind of universalism.

During the second half of the New Kingdom, the Ramesside kings (1305-1080 B.C.E.) emerged, and control of Syro-Palestine was the main concern (Lichtheim 1976, 4-5). The Hittites rose to become a great and threatening power but eventually became allies of the Egyptians. Ramses II stands out as a great pharaoh and is often believed to be the king of the Exodus. He is known for his numerous and enormous monuments. During the Ramesside period the proliferation of literature was also great. After the death of Ramses III, Egypt fell into a decline and lost most of its territories outside Egypt. It was during this vacuum in power that Israel and its neighbors were able to develop into small, independent nations.

The tomb autobiographies and prayers continued, as did the building inscriptions and annalistic historical accounts (Lichtheim 1976, 5-6). An example of the latter is the "Annals of Thutmose III," who engaged in a series of 16 campaigns in Syro-Palestine to establish Egypt's dominance. It is framed by a report to his divine patron, Amon-Re, the sun god, that the king had secured the land belonging to the deity (Matthews and Benjamin 2006, 142-45). Especially interesting is the account of the conquest of Megiddo, later to become an Israelite city. Narrative poems emerged also during this period that resemble epics, such as the "Annals of Merneptah," which includes the earliest reference to Israel outside the Bible (Matthews and Benjamin 2006, 97-98).

Hymns to the gods progressed beyond those of the Middle Kingdom (Lichtheim 1976, 6). An example is the "Hymn to the Aten," which praises the solar disk, which is technically distinct from Amun-Re, the sun god. This hymn was composed during the revolution of Akhenaten, formerly Amenophis IV and the father of king Tut(ankhamen). He had moved the capital of Egypt to Amarna from Thebes and had made the Aten the supreme deity. Akhenaten wanted to increase his own power as pharaoh at the expense of the priests at Thebes, where Amun-Re was worshipped (Matthews and Benjamin 2006, 275-79). His son, king Tut, overturned this revolution and restored the former status quo.

Instructions and School Texts

One example of the instruction genre most important for illuminating Israelite wisdom literature was composed during this period: "Instruction of Amenemope." This is because most scholars believe that the author of Proverbs 22-23 was dependent on this text due to the striking similarities in content and phraseology. As compared to the former period, the values in this instruction have subtly shifted (Lichtheim 1976, 7). Maat still governs one's life and the cosmos. Success still is dependent on one conforming to its dictates. But emphasis is placed less on material rewards and more on humility toward god and humanity. A more modest individual is presupposed for the addressee here.

Related to the instructions is a new genre known as "school texts" (Lichtheim 1976, 7). These consist of compositions used as models for copying by students. They are strung together to form a "book," like the "Papyrus Lansing." In one of these is a text radically skeptical for

Egypt called "The Immortality of Writers." In it the author argues that the only afterlife that really exists is the memory of scribes who leave behind compositions! Instead of copper tombs or children to continue afterlife existence through mortuary care,

> They made heirs for themselves of books,
> of Instructions they had composed.
> They gave themselves [the scroll as lector]-priest (a mortuary specialist),
> the writing-board as loving-son.
> Instructions are their tombs,
> the reed pen is their child,
> the stone-surface their wife (Lichtheim 1976, 176).

Then the author recommends becoming a scribe:

> Be a scribe, take it to heart,
> that your name become as theirs.
> Better is a book than a graven stela,
>
> ....
>
> Man decays, his corpse is dust,
> all his kin have perished;
> but a book makes him remembered (Lichtheim 1976, 177).

Then the poet mentions famous sages who had gained such immortality: Hardedef, Imhotep, Nerferti, Khakheperree-sonb, and Ptahhotep.

This text also refers to these scribes as very interested in prognostication: "Those learned scribes, since the time of those who existed after the gods, those who predicted what was to come . . . Those sages who predicted what was to come—what issued from their mouths happened" (Williams 1990, 24). Similarly, in the eighteenth dynasty, Thuty, the royal builder and herald of Queen Hatshepsut, recorded on his stele, "I investigated a time and predicted what was to come, (being) one who was skilled in looking at the future, aware of yesterday and thoughtful concerning tomorrow, ingenious regarding what would happen" (Williams 1990, 28).

Another school text is the prayer to a deity (Lichtheim 1976, 110). The following comes from a prayer to Thoth, the Egyptian god of wisdom and scribalism:

Come to me, Thoth, O noble Ibis (bird which symbolizes the god),

....

O letter-writer of the Ennead,

....

Make me skillful in your callings,
it makes (men) great.
He who masters it is found fit to hold office;
I have seen many whom you have helped;

....

They are strong and rich through your help (Lichtheim 1976, 113).

Prayers are also composed for Amun. These prayers reflect the individual piety typical of the New Kingdom.

Mortuary Literature and Love Lyrics

The "Book of the Dead" represents a modification of the "coffin texts" of the Middle Kingdom (Lichtheim 1976, 7). Instead of being written on coffins, these texts were written on papyri and provided guidance to the afterlife. Like the autobiographies, these texts emphasize morality as a key to attaining immortality but magic is blended in as well. The mixing of morality and magic is typical of the Egyptians.

A new genre to emerge is the "love lyric," which is skillfully composed (Lichtheim 1976, 7-8). These were usually narrated in the first person and the lovers call each other "brother" and "sister" (Redford 1995, 2237). Themes include a list of the lover's charms, love sickness, separation, dawn emerging, and the locked door, most of which resonate with the biblical Song of Songs. Here is an example:

> With flashing eyes of beauty,
> her lips sweet of speech—
> yet she lacks a word too much—
> with lofty neck and radiant breasts,
> real lapis lazuli her hair;
> her arms outdo gold,
> her fingers are like locus flowers;
> with declining rump and trim waist,
> whose thighs show forth her beauty,
> of graceful step when she treads the earth,
> she has seized my heart in her embrace!
> She causes the neck of every male
> to turn about at the sight of her;
> happy the one whom she embraces!
> He thinks himself the foremost of lusty males!
> (Redford 1995, 2237).

Narratives

Narratives and tales were composed that add new themes, are longer, and involve more complexity (Lichtheim 1976, 8). Some of the tales are mythological. "The Book of the Cow of Heaven" describes how the sun god Re attempts to wipe out humanity because of a plotted rebellion. He invokes the aid of the goddess "Eye of Re" to do it. After much decimation, Re repents and uses deceit to stop the goddess from completing her task by getting her drunk. This resembles Ea's aiding of Athrahasis with instructions to build the ark so that humanity might survive the flood sent by the gods.

The story of "Wen-Amun" is also interesting because it reflects the declining power and fortune of the late New Kingdom during the twentieth Dynasty (1196-1070 B.C.E.). Wen-Amun is a priest of the temple Amun-Re, who is sent to purchase cedar timber from Lebanon. In earlier days, this would have simply been tribute paid by a vassal Canaanite king. Here Wen-Amun experiences numerous insults and deception at the hands of Semites before he finally obtains the timber.

The tale of "Truth and Falsehood" is actually a satire that involves the personifications of truth and falsehood as they competed for supremacy. The story begins as Falsehood claims that he lent Truth a fantastic dagger but never returned it. Falsehood takes him to court before the gods and has him blinded and made the door-keeper for himself. Falsehood finally sends Truth away to be killed, but he is secretly saved. Truth eventually is admired by a woman who has a son by him and raises him alone. When he reaches maturity, the boy finds out who his father is and seeks vengeance. In the end, he demonstrates to the gods that Falsehood had lied about a dagger that had never existed and is exposed for trying to kill his father. Falsehood is blinded and made door-keeper for Truth.

Late Period (1080-332 B.C.E.)

For the most part, the literature of the Late Period can be characterized as a reuse of the past genres and themes but in creative ways (Lichtheim 1980, 3-10). We will only note one instructional work, the "Instruction of Ankhsheshonq." It is composed in demotic script, which is a type of cursive Late-Hieratic (Lichtheim 1980, 9). The instruction departs from earlier ones, especially in genre, in that, instead of poetic units that treat a particular theme, it consists of a series of miscellaneous independent sentences or short maxims written in prose. This means that this instruction closely resembles Proverbs 10:1–22:16 and chaps. 25–29. "Ankhsheshonq" is characterized by a strong utilitarianism, and its moralizing is very down-to-earth rather than lofty and idealistic (Lichtheim 1980, 160). It is also humorous at times. The text is framed by a story similar to the late Mesopotamian tale of the sage Ahiqar, who was accused of treason by his adopted son. Anshesheshonq had tried to talk a friend out of assassinating the pharaoh, but it backfired on him when he did not report it. Anshesheshonq supposedly wrote his maxims on pottery while he was in prison for his youngest son. Here are a few examples:

> He who sends spittle up to the sky will have it fall back on him (Lichtheim 1980, 168; cf. our "What goes around comes around").

> Speaking without thinking causes suffering. Do not say everything you think (Matthews and Benjamin 2006, 311).

> Enjoy your body when you are young. Death comes to all (Matthews and Benjamin 2006, 311).

> Do not do evil to someone unless you want others to do evil to you (Matthews and Benjamin 2006, 313).

Summary

In both Egypt and Mesopotamia scribes performed numerous roles that benefitted both the private and public sectors. As administrators for kingdoms and empires, they were the nexus from which the business of government was controlled and managed. In many ways they were the glue that held these polities together and made sure they operated smoothly and efficiently (see Carr 2005, 33). It is no exaggeration to say that without the scribes no kingdoms or empires would have existed. Because few people could read and write in the vernacular, let alone understand foreign languages, the scribes were considered extremely valuable. This is why they were held in such high esteem. The education of scribes was arduous and difficult but would pay large dividends if the student completed his studies. Scribes were trained fundamentally to be copyists who could aid others in numerous practical ways. But beyond this level, many scribes chose advanced studies that allowed them to become experts in various areas of knowledge and often serve as high officials. These scribes were trained broadly and drank deeply from the well of cultural knowledge of their respective societies. Part of their training involved reading and studying numerous genres of literature that reflected the various facets and values of their respective societies. This broad training prepared them to serve competently as either scholars or as administrators. This body of literature, and especially the wisdom literature, trained them beyond the practicalities of their future jobs; it made them well-rounded. In fact, it fashioned them into "gentlemen," who could mingle among the elite as well as the commoners and assume significant roles, including as leaders.

4

Western Periphery Scribalism

The scribes of Syro-Palestine were a component of the larger trans-national polity known as the Western Periphery (WP) (of Mesopotamia). "Syria" and "Palestine" are actually artificial terms that do not conform to geographical or political entities (Lemche 1995, 1195). We have already mentioned that "Palestine" comes from the word "Philistine," but this ethnicity only occupied a small section of Southwestern Palestine. "Syria" actually comes from the name "Assyria," and so Syria actually occupied Northern Assyria, though the Assyrians never fully dominated this area. Syro-Palestinian scribalism largely constitutes an extension of Mesopotamian scribalism, including its literature. This is because of frequent Mesopotamian control of these areas and its trade relationships. Israelite scribalism reflects both Mesopotamian and Egyptian influences, the latter due to its proximity to Egypt. Canaanite scribalism includes Ugarit, Israel, Moab, Edom, and Ammon, which form a cohort within Syro-Palestinian scribalism in that they all used the alphabetic script to compose their vernacular languages.

Figure 5: Table of Ages and Periods		
Mesopotamia and Palestine	Egypt	Israel
Early Bronze Age or **EBA** (3500–2100 B.C.E.)	Old Kingdom (2650–2135 B.C.E.)	
Middle Bronze Age or **MBA** (2100–1550 B.C.E.)	First Intermediate Period (2135–2040 B.C.E.)	
	Middle Kingdom (2040–1650 B.C.E.)	
	Second Intermediate Period (1650–1550 B.C.E.)	
Late Bronze Age or **LBA** (1550–1200 B.C.E.)	New Kingdom (1550–1080 B.C.E.)	
		Iron Age I (1200–1000 B.C.E.)
		Iron Age II (1000–587 B.C.E.)
		Neo-Babylonian Period (587–539 B.C.E.)
		Persian Period (539–332 B.C.E.)
		Ptolemaic Period (332–198 B.C.E.)
		Seleucid Period (198–140 B.C.E.)
		Hasmonean Dynasty (140–37 B.C.E.)

We will first generally introduce WP scribalism and then focus on two important cities: Ugarit and Emar. We first discuss the scribes who worked at Ugarit during the Late Bronze Age (LBA: 1550–1200 B.C.E.). Then we will examine the scribes at Emar or Imar, a northern Syrian city on the banks of the Euphrates that has revealed families of scribes who worked during the LBA from the mid-fourteenth century to 1185 B.C.E. We will briefly discuss the Amarna letters, which were unearthed in Amarna Egypt and reflect the Middle Bronze Age (MBA, 2100-1550 B.C.E.) and later periods, revealing the relationship between the Canaanite city-states and Egypt during this time. The scribes, of course, are the medium between the pharaoh and the Canaanite rulers in this correspondence. Finally, we will examine the Canaanite and Phoenician literature and mythology, with which the Israelite scribes would have been familiar. In distinction from the previous chapters, this one aims to provide the more immediate background to Israelite scribalism. The greater influence of this region on Israel, as opposed to Egypt and central Mesopotamia, is indicated by Israel's having been heavily influenced in its blood rite (the ritual slaying of animals and applying their blood to objects) by the Hittites. The way the Hittites used their blood rite is strikingly similar to Israel's practice and distinct from Mesopotamia and it appears that the flow of influence was from Turkey to Israel (see Feder 2011, 124-25).

The Western Periphery

Emar was part of what is known as the schools of the Western Periphery of the MBA and LBA (Cohen 2009, 46-47). During the LBA the lingua franca had long been Akkadian, the language of bureaucracy. Scribes and scholars from Anatolia (Turkey), Syria, Canaan, and Egypt copied, studied, and translated Mesopotamian lexical texts, omens, incantations, and literature such as myths and epics. This curriculum allowed them to communicate in a foreign tongue and at a later and more advanced stage enabled them to develop technical expertise in such practices as divination, magic, and medicine.

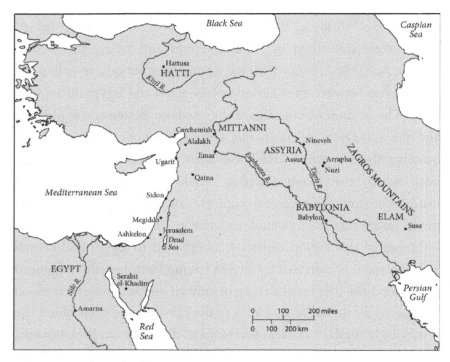

Map 3: Syro-Palestine in the Late Bronze Age

The WP of the MBA and LBA followed the Old Babylonian (OB) curriculum (Cohen 2009, 48). Mathematics was a subject in the OB curriculum, but only one math text (at Hazor) has been found in the WP schools. Instruction in letter and contract writing (models) was also a component of the education, some of these in fact becoming "literary" in that they treated student lore. These have been found at Ugarit but not Emar. Also, metrological texts have been found at Ugarit, which is the science of measurements.

Emar was not alone when it comes to cuneiform scribal education in the WP during the Middle and Late BA (Cohen 2009, 50-51). Cuneiform literacy is also found at sites in Egypt, Canaan, Syria, Lebanon, Anatolia (Turkey), and Elam. However, only two sites reveal enough evidence to reconstruct the nature of scribal schools:

Ugarit on the Mediterranean coast, parallel in latitude with Emar and Cyprus, and Ḫattuša in Turkey (the Hittites).

Important Sites

Ugarit

Ugarit (or Ras Shamra) was a significant city-state of the second millennium (van Soldt 1995, 1255-59). It was on a natural harbor on the Syrian coast, which proved to be very profitable for its economy. To the north of the city was a large mountain ("Sapanu"; cf. Hebrew *zaphon* = "north") that played an important role in the area's religion. The city was inhabited as early as 6500 until around 1200 B.C.E., which means it has one of the longest habitation records of any city. There were temples for Baal and his father Dagan ("grain") in the city. The city's location made it one of the most significant trade centers in all of the ancient Near East. It was on the crossroads of an east-west (Cyprus-Syria) and a north-south (Egypt-Anatolia) route. The city was more significant for its wealth than its military, and, thus, was susceptible to being dominated by other powers like Egypt and the Hittites.

Five archives have been excavated in the royal palace (van Soldt 1995, 1261). Three of these were used for administrative purposes. These archived lists of persons who received rations or paid taxes, lists of land owners, etc. The other archives contained documentation of land sales within the city-state and international records, including treaties with foreign kings. An archive consisted of several rooms, one of which was the secretariat, in which were found bronze styli, the instruments for writing on the clay tablets. This room was normally next to the court, and scribes could work here or in the court since the lighting was better.

The Scribes of Ugarit

From the excavations and records recovered, it is evident that many "guilds" which served the palace were operative in the city, such as smiths, soldiers, priests, builders, boat and cart makers, and weapon makers (van Soldt 1995, 1262-63). The best known of the guilds is the scribes, since they left documents behind. The profession apparently remained within the same family for a long time. A scribe could serve in non-scribal functions, such as a diplomatic mission. For example, the scribe Attenu not only had his own school but was high priest and a diviner.

Ugaritic Schools and Their Curriculum

The training of scribes took place over many years. Instruction did not occur in the palace but was private (van Soldt 1995, 1263). Four such schools were in existence at Ugarit, where the students wrote practice texts that they signed with their own names and those of their teachers. The schools were conducted in private houses, like the House of Rap'ānu (an important official), which held 250 Mesopotamian scholarly texts, and the Lamaštu Archive, which held 76 texts (Cohen 2009, 51). The latter was perhaps home to a Babylonian teacher, and there is evidence for an Assyrian scribe who taught Ugaritic scribes. While some documents were in Ugaritic and alphabetic, most of the documents were in Akkadian (van Soldt 1995, 1263). This meant the learning of over 600 cuneiform signs by the scribe.

According to the standard Mesopotamian curriculum, the students' studies gradually increased in level of difficulty, starting with the writing, translating, and memorizing various kinds of lists like syllabic and vocabulary, such as all the divine names, all wooden objects, all professions, etc. (van Soldt 1995, 1263-64). The next level involved copying of literary texts. The Ugaritic students were not very good at this. Some of these texts are not known from Mesopotamia and some have parallels at Emar and at the Hittite city Ḫattuša. Among these texts are omens and incantations, one against the demon Lamaštu, who would snatch infants from their mothers' laps. One text instructs on how to ward off various diseases. Also found were an astronomical text that reports an eclipse, musical texts, hippiatric texts (treatment of horse diseases), and farmers' almanacs (Mack-Fisher 1995b, 75-79).

Wisdom texts have been found, such as the instructions of a father to a son and the poem of a righteous sufferer who prays to his deity for deliverance (van Soldt 1995, 1264). An instruction to a messenger on how to recognize the sender's mother resembles the Song of Songs. Also, there is the ballad song of ancient heroes, a drinking song advising the carpe diem ethic. A brief account of the great flood has been found (Atraḫasis), and the "Epic of Gilgamesh" (Cohen 2009, 51).

Scribes who completed their studies were employed by the palace or high officials of the city (van Soldt 1995, 1264). Scribes could eventually become high officials themselves. They sometimes were given cities to govern, and this, of course, would mean considerable power (Mack-Fisher 1995a, 113-114). One scribe, Šapšumalku, is given the title "expert scribe," but even higher in status was a "vizier" or "counselor," and several scribes attained this rank. One of these viziers and scribes may have signed the copy of the flood story found at Ugarit.

The other script taught to scribes was the thirty-letter alphabet, which was comparatively easy to learn. The student merely had to compose a few practice texts to master it. Several abecedaries have been found in Ugarit, as well as various practice exercises, such as lists of names, epistolary exercises, and a literary text. Most of the significant Ugaritic (and Canaanite) myths have been unearthed at Ugarit and were composed by the scribe Ilimalku in the home of the high priest. These include "Cycle of Baal," the "Epic of Keret (Kirta)," and the "Epic of Aqhat." These works will be discussed later. Ilimalka may be the scribe who composed contracts in Akkadian for an overseer.

The scribes of Ugarit were trained in the Babylonian tradition and studied all the various genres of literature (Mack-Fisher 1995a, 115). They were very astute politically, which enabled them to often work for more than one king.

Hattuša

The capital of the Hittites was Ḥattuša or Boğazköy, which has revealed a number of Mesopotamian school texts (Cohen 2009, 51-52). There is evidence that the Babylonian genre *naru* or inscriptions on entitlement monuments (or boundary stones) have influenced the Hittite scribes in their composition of annalistic literature. Beginning in the fourteenth century B.C.E., there is Hurrian as well as Old and Post-Babylonian influence on the Hittite school literature. Asyyro-Mittannian medical and magical texts found here probably arrived after Shuppiluliuma I conquered Mittanni and brought them back as booty. Some of the scholarly Hittite literature found at Ugarit and Emar point to this mysterious transmission of Hittite lore throughout the Hittite Empire in the LBA.

Schooling at Ḥattuša probably occurred in the temple or palace (Cohen 2009, 52). One "library" was found that held incantations and lexical lists, and it may have served as a school. Assyrians and Babylonians who served as diplomats at the capital may have also functioned as teachers at the school. Hurrian scribes in the Hittite

Empire had an important role in diffusing Mesopotamian and Hurrian scholarly materials. Their greatest contribution was their omen literature, which has been found not only at Ḫattuša but also at Ugarit and Emar.

Other Western Periphery Sites

Other sites of the Western Periphery have revealed evidence of schooling activities such as Mesopotamian academic texts, but the evidence is too meager for any definitive conclusions (Cohen 2009, 53). The MB city of Alalakh, just northeast of Ugarit, contained a collection of lexical lists, omens and incantations. Qatna, just southwest of Ugarit, also contained omen literature. In the Lebanon Beqaa valley, 9 tablets were unearthed, 8 of which were letters and one is perhaps a school text intended to teach scribes the basics of cuneiform. At Sidon a cuneiform tablet of an inventory of wooden objects from the LBA was found.

In Palestine, evidence for schools is meager for the MBA and LBA (Cohen 2009, 53). Several tablets containing lexical lists, liver model omens, a mathematical text, and a fragment of "Gilgamesh" have been found in the following sites: Ashkelon, Aphek, Hazor, and Megiddo. It is not too speculative to suppose that at these sites the same type of instruction was practiced as that in Northern Syria and Mesopotamia.

Illustration 11. Megiddo King and Courtiers

A small cache of Mesopotamian scholarly texts that included lexical lists and Babylonian myths were also found in Egypt at Amarna (Cohen 2009, 53-54). The building they were found in is called "The Bureau for the Correspondence of Pharaoh," which suggests a diplomatic archive, though scribes could have been trained there as well. Hittite scribes may have served as the instructors here, while the Mesopotamian texts suggest Babylonian scribes. Also, part of a cuneiform letter to Ramses II was found in the Delta. This in conjunction with fragments found in Anatolia of Egyptian correspondence to Ḫattuša demonstrate that cuneiform was often employed during the thirteenth century B.C.E.

Emar

Scribes of Emar in the Late Bronze Age

Yoram Cohen has documented the lives of more than 50 scribes who were employed in Emar during the LBA (Cohen 2009, 1). Cohen finds that there were two types of scribes that existed during this time. First are the Syrian scribes, who can be further divided into scribes who composed ephemeral documents like letters and contracts and those who were real scholars who copied and studied actual literature. Then later come Syro-Hittite scribes, who produced both ephemeral and scholarly documents and reflect a Hurrian (or Mitannian) influence.

Archaeologists uncovered the city of Emar at Balis-Meskene when the Syrian government in the 1960's was planning to dam the Euphrates for agricultural purposes and wanted to preserve the information from sites that might be damaged by flooding (Cohen 2009, 7-9). The Emar textual remains can be divided into three groups: ephemeral documents, cultic texts, and scholarly documents.

Ephemeral documents included mainly sale contracts of property (fields, gardens or houses), either between private individuals or the city (or royal family) and individuals (Cohen 2009, 9). The royal family sometimes presented land grants to people. There were also testaments and adoptions, with witnesses recorded. Documentation of slavery sales, debt-notes, and other disputes are also represented. A few letters regarding administration of the temples were found as well, such as lists of donations or cultic personnel and dockets listing temple equipment.

Cultic texts concern the city's rituals and festivals (Cohen 2009, 9-10). They include details of the celebrations of the city gods in yearly and monthly cycles and the installation of religious personnel. The scholarly materials consist of all the genres of the scribal school curriculum such as syllabaries, lexical lists, literary texts, and exercise tablets, which are extractions from the literary texts. Also found were omen texts and magical/medical incantations for the training of diviners and doctors. Cohen points out that the fact that these various genres were found at the same spot and composed by the same scribes indicates that functional boundaries for these scribes were blurred.

Emar was on a very important trade route on the way to Aleppo and Carchemish, which made it a mercantile city (Cohen 2009, 15-17). It functioned as a significant trading point and caravan route since the Old Babylonian period. It was never autonomous and was under the control of the Kingdom of Yamhad and Mari. Later, the Hurrians controlled it as part of the Mittanian domain. In the fourteenth century B.C.E., it came under the rule of the Hittites via Carchemish. It was finally destroyed around 1185 B.C.E., most likely by the Arameans.

Sidebar 7: Scribal Dictation and Memory

Though scribes are often thought to have recorded dictation accurately, so that their "hand matches the[ir] mouth," most scribes did not take dictation in this sense. They did not transmit verbatim or use shorthand. Rather, they outlined what they heard in very compressed entries such as the following: "—About not meeting each other—About [not?] conferring with Hammurabi and Qarni-Lim—About not sending a messenger—About the topic (with) the following: 'I will write wherever I want to; but you need not write where you do not want to write'—About the topic not to write Hammurabi and Qarni-Lim during troubles." With this kind of outline, the scribe would later reconstruct the commissioned letter. This method also helped the scribe determine what size tablet would be needed for the letter (Sasson 2002, 215-16).

The scribes at Emar were part of the ancient and venerable Mesopotamian tradition, which was quite prestigious (Cohen 2009,

26-27). The scribes at the end of the Mesopotamian tradition in fact traced their lineage back to famous authors who lived long ago, such as the alleged author of the "Epic of Gilgamesh." These scribes saw themselves as an established community of cuneiform users, who studied a common curriculum. Especially in the second millennium b.c.e., scribes interacted with their colleagues in other cities and countries and in other languages because they shared the same linguistic and conceptual world. The Mesopotamian scribes also shared their own distinctive religious perspective, with veneration for the gods Nisaba, Nabû, and Ea as their patrons. This community of scribes across the ages and spaces considered itself elite and privileged. They also were cognizant of their power to control information in the courts and other institutions which employed them, which meant they were not expendable within the larger political systems.

At the provincial center of Emar, 40 scribes composed ephemeral documents, while more than a dozen scribes were scholars/teachers and their students (Cohen 2009, 27-28). The regular city sacrifices to the gods Ea and Nabû indicate the seriousness with which the citizens of Emar viewed the scribal profession. Unfortunately, no women scribes are evident as serving in Emar.

Scribes at Emar are not infrequently identified simultaneously as diviners (Cohen 2009, 40-42). The roles are distinguished in the cultic texts, but still there seems to be a natural correlation. Scribes were also frequently found participating in cultic activities: "The king of this land, the diviner, and the chief scribe consecrate the ḫukku bread(s) and the barley beer" (Cohen 2009, 40). After the consecration, the scribe receives a nice piece of meat. That this particular scribe performed alongside the diviner and king demonstrates his high status.

The scribes at Emar were not completely homogenous ethnically or nationally (Cohen 2009, 42-46). Most of the names of scribes were

West Semitic and similar to other names in this region. However, there were also some "Mesopotamian" names that include the names of deities like Marduk, Ea, and Sin, and one with the name of the scribal god Nabû. These names indicate the tendency to connect the sons of scribes with the prestigious Babylonian tradition. Other names indicate the presence of scribes who had come to the city for trading or teaching purposes.

Scribal Schooling at Emar

Most of the scribes at Emar are known from their ephemeral documents (Cohen 2009, 54-55). However, we are fortunate that archaeologists have uncovered a private home that served as scribal school for the family of Zū-Baʻla, who were Syro-Hittite scribes. The building was once thought to be a temple, but Cohen disagrees and believes it is a private dwelling large enough to accommodate a family and students. The building has relatively thick walls, is 15 by 7 m in size, and has a central hallway and three adjoining rooms. In the building were found many exercise tablets and copies of Mesopotamian scholarly texts, a library, which contained omen, literary, and ritual texts, and an archive that contained a mixed assortment of documents relating to the Zū-Baʻla family and others.

We know a few things about the structure and personnel of the school (Cohen 2009, 56-59). There is direct evidence of the school in a list of sacrifice distributions: "Ea of the scribes, Nabû of the schools." Ea, of course, is the Babylonian god of wisdom, and Nabû is the god of the scribes. Note the plural for "schools," which may indicate more than one school in the city. In an allocation list, the supervisor of the scribes is mentioned: *ugula é-dub-ba-a*. "Ugula" is also the same title used at Ḫattuša and similar to another title used at Ugarit of bureaucrats and senior scribes. Under the supervisor would be the teachers and students, and two of the teachers' names are known from the colophons (information about the document found at the end of the tablet) and ephemeral documents. The colophons at Emar usually give the following information: the scribe's name and lineage, his profession and status, whether he is a student or teacher, and his patron gods. The students can be identified from the colophons with two names: either "novice diviner" or "junior scribe" and "student" or "apprentice." There is indication that the profession often passed from father to son here at Emar, even within the Zū-Ba'la family. The school at Emar was rather small, with two teachers at the most, with one of them the supervisor, and no more than three to four students. The school of the Zū-Ba'la family may have been in existence for four generations.

The Syrian Scribes at Emar

Cohen examines the documents created by four types of scribes at Emar according to role and chronology. The first type is what he calls non-scholarly, Syrian scribes, who only composed ephemeral documents and worked in the city before it was controlled by the Hittites. The second type are what he calls the non-scholarly Syro-Hittite scribes, who reflect a strong Hurrian influence when Emar was dominated by the Hittites before its destruction. Then he discusses their scholarly counterparts chronologically, Syrian then Syro-Hittite scholarly scribes. In the following, I will group both types of scribes (non-scholarly and scholarly) together chronologically for convenience sake

There were 29 Syrian scribes who only composed ephemeral documents (Cohen 2009, 65). For example, Abī-kāpī (Cohen 2009, 74–77) composed 16 documents and, thus, is one of the best attested scribes of this type. Most of his documents are the records of property purchased from the temple of the warrior god of Lagash, Ninurta, in the city. More interesting is a royal land grant given to a certain diviner and scribe who received a field for his service to the king. Also, in another purchase record there is a note about how the property of one individual was sold to another because of some offense he had committed against the king. Abī-kāpī's son may have served as a scribe too because of his name as a witness in a document.

After examining all the data for this type of scribe, Cohen concludes the following (2009, 89-90). During the reign of each king, only about 4 scribes were active. These scribes did not work exclusively for either the palace or temple. Scribes with only one or two documents in evidence usually wrote private deeds. Thus, these scribes may be considered part-time scribes, who were competent in composing legal and business documents but whose main vocational role was not as a scribe. This indicates that scribes were employed often on an ad hoc basis. In contrast to the Syro-Hittite scribes to be presently discussed, it appears the Syrian non-scholarly scribes served in minor roles in the city administration.

There were five scholarly Syrian scribes who copied Mesopotamian scholarly texts (lexical lists, incantation, and a literary text) (Cohen 2009, 121-25). One of these scribes also produced ephemeral documents: Ba'al-bārû. He composed a lexical list and identified himself in the colophon in this way: "The hand of Ba'al-bārû, the diviner, servant of Nabû and Nisaba" (Cohen 2009, 122). Nisaba was the divine patroness of the scribal arts. This diviner appears to have a son, Mašru-ḫe, whom he mentions in an ephemeral document as receiving a royal land grant: "When the Hurrian troops surrounded the walls of Emar, Mašru-ḫe was then the diviner of the king and city. Now, his divination (about the enemies being defeated) came about. Therefore, the king Pilsu-Dagan has given him this very field as a gift" (Cohen 2009, 123). Mašru-ḫe himself composed 5 documents, including a sophisticated lexical list, which probably served as a library copy for students.

Another interesting scribe is Rībi-Dagan, a novice diviner, who composed an incantation and a lexical list (Cohen 2009, 126-31). In one of his colophons, he identifies himself as the servant of Nabû and Nisaba and the servant of Ea. Another colophon reveals the only personal circumstances of a scribe at Emar: "The hand of Rībi-Dagan, servant of Nabû and Nisaba. I wrote this tablet when I was placed in bronze chains during the period of . . ." (Cohen 2009, 129). Apparently, Ribi-Dagan had become indebted and was metaphorically placed "in chains" until he could pay his debt. Also, he copied a *Sammeltafel*, a tablet that includes more than one genre (here an incantation on one side and another genre on the other), used as part of the students' practice exercises.

Another scribe, Tuku-dÉḫursag, copied a literary prayer of blessings to be bestowed by Enlil, god of the wind and a chief deity, and other deities on the king (Cohen 2009, 135-36). It is similar to the Sumerian prayers. In his colophon, Tuku-dÉḫursag identifies himself as a priest of Dagan. This tablet was probably a library copy, shelved to demonstrate the scribe's accomplishment.

There were several omen compendia composed by these scribes (Cohen 2009, 136-44). These were collections of omens related to the examination of the condition of the livers of sacrificial animals (extispicy). In ancient Mesopotamia, these texts were put into practice when a king consulted his scholars to discern the will of the gods. In addition to these, there were clay models of the liver and lungs found, used to educate and aid the diviners in their soothsaying. These texts and clay models were not only found in Babylonia but also in the WP, such as Hazor, Megiddo, Alalakh, and Ugarit. A representative of a celestial omen text was also found, concerning the moon.

To summarize, the Syrian scholarly scribes produced the following genres of texts: lexical lists, omen compendia, incantations, and a literary composition ("Benedictions for a King") (Cohen 2009, 145-46). Since the extispicy omen texts were only of single copies, these probably served as reference works or library copies.

Syro-Hittite Scribes

There were 13 Syro-Hittite non-scholarly scribes (Cohen 2009, 99-116). Nothing is known about their education. For example, Ba'al-mālik was a scribe who wrote two private purchase documents. He identifies his father as Imlik-Dagan. There are 9 persons designated as scribes who appear to have been more bureaucrats than scribes in the traditional sense in that they played extensive roles in the Hittite administration. There were also 3 foreign scribes in the city who were involved in merchant activity. They served in both scribal and mercantile capacities, and one was a scribal teacher.

Most of the Syro-Hittite non-scholarly scribes had Semitic names and never attained high status within the Hittite bureaucracy, but some locals were incorporated within it (Cohen 2009, 118-19). The foreign scribes show that the scribes at Emar were not insular and could be influenced from abroad.

As opposed to the Syrian scholarly scribes, we have much more information because of the Zū-Ba'la family of diviners whose archive was filled with documents (Cohen 2009, 147). The nature of this scribal family can, thus, be more fully fleshed due to both ephemeral documents and scholarly texts in the home, their archive, and scriptorium. We can also follow their family for four generations.

One of the Zū-Ba'la family scribes is Šaggar-abu, who wrote letters to a Hittite overlord, Adda, concerning administrative affairs of the city and cult (Cohen 2009, 165-69). In one of these, Šaggar-abu informs Adda and his wife that the sacrificial animals they had sent had arrived, which were most likely then offered to the gods of Emar on behalf of Adda. Šhaggar-abu was also explicitly involved in the school, evidenced by his colophons. He had copied a syllabary, a vocabulary, a lexical list, an omen, and "Lunar Eclipses." The documents indicate that he had been both a student and teacher there. He also copied two literary texts: the "Ballad of the Heroes" and a wisdom text called "The Fowler." In the colophon of the latter, Šaggar-abu identifies himself as a "diviner, servant of Nabû and N[isaba], servant of Marduk . . ." (Cohen 2009, 169).

Another interesting scribe is Ba'al-malik, who was a scribe and the chief diviner of the gods of the city (Cohen 2009, 170-75). His seals, including those found on two cultic inventories in the temple's archive, indicate his responsibility for the gods' cultic belongings. Documents indicate that Ba'al-malik's uncle, Kāpī-Dagan, attempted to usurp his role as chief diviner. Ba'al-malik wrote a letter to a Hittite official about it and also reported that his uncle had withheld offerings for the gods. From the evidence it is clear that Ba'al-malik was the winner in this struggle. Ba'al-malik also was involved in the acquisition of slave labor for the cult and even ransomed a slave by paying his debt. We also have instances where debtors were required to sell their property, family or even themselves to Ba'al-malik. A man from a nearby city sold himself and his two wives and gave his property to Ba'al-malik so that Ba'al-malik would pay his debts. In another case, parents sold their 4 children to Ba'al-malik in a time of duress. Due to the degree of indebtedness and the small amount Ba'al-malik gave them for the transaction, the family was probably never reunited. We know from documents that the children were ages 2, 1 (two twins), and one not yet weaned, whose feet could not be impressed into the clay. The latter probably was not removed from her mother until she was weaned.

In addition to all his administrative and business affairs, Baʻal-malik was also a scribe and teacher at the scribal school (Cohen 2009, 175-79). This is indicated by the colophons on some school texts like omens and a syllabary. One colophon is by a student who lists Baʻal-malik as his teacher. In addition to scholarly compositions, Baʻal-malik also composed a votive inscription in which he and his two sons present expensive offerings to the god Ninurta. Baʻal-malik's sons were the last generation of the family of diviners before the city was destroyed, and they probably were active at their father's school.

A scholarly scribe outside the Zū-Baʻla family is represented by Madi-Dagan (Cohen 2009, 189-94). He is unique in that he was both a scribe (chief) and doctor. He is connected to ephemeral documents as the first signatory on a private land sale and as a signatory and witness on other documents. More interesting is the medico-magical incantations he was responsible for copying. On one of them he identifies himself as both a scribe and *apkallu* priest. The latter is quite unique for scribes and was a highly prestigious title among Mesopotamian scribal circles and is even the description used for the famous 7 antediluvian sages of Sumerian mythological lore.

The scholarly compositions of the Syro-Hittite tradition included lexical lists like syllabaries, vocabulary, and a god list (Cohen 2009, 194-216). In the omens, auspicious and non-auspicious days are listed according to month. Celestial omens involve predicting the future by observing celestial bodies on the occasion of their eclipses, colors, movements, and conjunctions with other bodies. In the lunar eclipses, it is revealed that the omens are dependent on the celestial bodies which had been stationed in the skies at the beginning of time. The scribes considered the omens to be the work of Ea. Other omens concern the appearance and behavior of sheep as they are led to slaughter and afterwards, animals born malformed, the physical appearance of humans, and even diagnostic omens concerning the description of a physical malady in humans. There were various medico-magical incantations, like one against headache. Among the gods implored were Marduk and Ea, and various manipulative agents were alluded to, like magical stones.

Finally, various literary texts were part of the school's curriculum (Cohen 2009, 219-23). The "Ballads of the Heroes" were found, and scholars today regard these as wisdom texts, though these contain "historical" traditions about long dead kings (see Alster, 2005, 288-326). A wisdom text called the "Fowler" was found. In its colophon, the scribe identifies himself as a diviner. Another wisdom text is named "Hear the Advice," which contains a series of short precepts for instruction, which places it firmly within the Babylonian wisdom tradition, though it is only represented in the WP. Recensions of this work have also been found at Ḫattuša and Ugarit. The "Epic of Gilgamesh" is also represented and has been found among other scribal schools of the WP like Ḫattuša, Ugarit, and Megiddo. Also found was "The Disputation between the Date-Palm and the Tamarisk," a debate about which is most beneficial to humans, which is part of the OB and Assyrian traditions, and is the only representative from the WP. A letter from the king of Larsa to the sun god, Utu, was found as well. It represents a genre of literary letters addressed to the gods and was part of the OB scribal curriculum.

Cohen concludes that the Zū-Ba'la family of diviners was respected enough that they were recognized by the Hittite king (Cohen 2009, 231-35). On several occasions the family members interacted with Hittite officials, usually concerning the cult. As the diviners of the gods of Emar, the major cultic responsibilities were theirs. The only other scribe outside this family securely identified was Madi-Dagan, the chief scribe and *apkallu* priest, who practiced magic and medicine.

After mastering the signs with the aid of lexical lists, the students at the school next studied the omens and incantations and the literary texts (Cohen 2009, 235-38). How the technical literature served their training as scribes is not completely understood. However, one cannot deny that for the Emar diviners it was at the heart of their education. The relative paucity of the literary compositions over against the lexical lists and omens at Emar and the WP demonstrates that they were secondary to the main interest of the school. The main goal of the school was to instruct novice scribes in mastery of the script, achieved through the lexical lists, and then in mastery of the divinatory techniques expressed in the omens and incantations. The literary texts were merely part of the broader standard WP education and may have helped in creating a scribal ethos common to the scribes of LBA.

The Scribes of Emar: Concluding Remarks

Cohen has demonstrated that the scribal tradition at Emar fits the prototype of the rest of the WP (Cohen 2009, 241, 243). There are even some compositions like certain omens that are almost identical with those from Ḫattuša. It is interesting that the Emar scribes never composed in their own native tongue, unlike their counterparts in the WP such as in Lebanon, Canaan, and Anatolia. This is probably because Emarite was not that different from Akkadian, since Emar was part of the Middle Euphrates region. In comparison to Ḫattuša and Ugarit, the richness of the textual finds at the minor city of Emar, the number of scribes, and the presence of a foreign teacher there cause us to discern how significant the WP was to central Mesopotamia.

The Amarna Letters

The Amarna letters are named for the site where they were found: Tell al-Amarna, a.k.a. Akhenaten, the capital city of Pharaoh Akhenaten (Amenhotep IV), who had transferred the capital from Thebes and had started the Aten (deity represented by the sun's disk) heretical reform (see Izre'el 1995, 2411). The bulk of these letters were written during the fourteenth century B.C.E. between the Pharaoh and his officials and the leaders of the various city–states in Canaan. This was a very volatile time in this region. The Egyptians controlled the Levant (literally "the rising" of the sun; the Eastern Mediterranean) up to the border with the Mitanni Kingdom (the Hurrians). This kingdom as well as Assyria and Babylonia had good relations with Egypt. However, the new power in the equation was the Hittites, who had recently conquered and claimed the land of the Amorites, and threatened Egyptian control of the Levant. Another troublesome element in the Levant were the 'apiru, which appears to be a term that designated trouble-makers, who resisted Egyptian domination of the region.

Though Egypt had a writing system almost as old as Mesopotamia, it communicated with foreign nations but also with its vassals in Akkadian (Izre'el 1995, 2412). During the second millennium what can be called peripheral Akkadian was the *lingua franca* of the ancient Near East.

The Amarna letters are very formulaic and sensitive to social status (Izre'el 1995, 2413). A person of lower status would address his superior with the title "my lord." Kinship terms were often used like "father," "son," "brother," and "family." Aziru of Amurru (Amorite) writes to Tutu, an Egyptian official, "To Tutu, my lord, my father: Message of Aziru, your son, your servant: I fall at the feet of my father. May all be well with my father" (Izre'el 1995, 2413).

The leaders of the vassals often found themselves in dire straits due to the troublemakers who rebelled against Egyptian dominance (Izre'el 1995, 2414). One of them, Bibhaddi, the ruler of Byblos, had to flee his city when his own people turn their allegiance to Aziru (an Amorite). He constantly appeals to the pharaoh for help: "Why are you (the pharaoh) silent (and do not speak)?"; "all my cities have been captured"; "all the countries have joined the Apiru"; "there is war against me" (Izre'el 1995, 2414). Similarly, Abdikheba of Jerusalem seeks assistance: "May the king take counsel concerning his land! All the land of the king is lost!" (Izre'el 1995, 2414). The pharaoh in fact tries to persuade this same Aziru, who has switched allegiance to the Hittites, to become loyal again to him: "Have you not written to the king, your lord, thus: 'I am your servant like all the loyal (or former) mayors who were in the city?'" (Izre'el 1995, 2014). But originally Aziur probably had no intention of keeping his word.

In the first millennium, Hebrew letter writing generally reflects influence from both Mesopotamian and Egyptian letter writing (Izre'el 1995, 2414). Even Ps. 21:2 reflects the formulary of diplomacy: "The desire of his heart you have granted, and the *request* of his lips you have not withheld." The word in italics is a *hapax legomenon*, which means it occurs only once in the entire Hebrew Bible. Avi Shveka argues that this word, which is found in Akkadian and Ugaritic, was used in diplomatic communication between a king and his counterpart and expresses a brotherly relationship (2005, 297–320). Here it is used of the relationship between the Israelite king and God. Shveka argues that the word dropped out of contemporary Hebrew and that the royal scribe who composed this psalm decided to employ it here, knowing that his colleagues would catch the diplomatic nuance.

Canaanite Literature and Mythology

Narrative

Because the clay tablets of Ugarit were preserved, we are fortunate to have recovered a few of their narratives, which are mythical. "Myth" is not used primarily to denote stories that are false. Rather, employing the anthropological definition, myths are stories about society and how it understands itself in its various facets (see Smith 1995, 2031). Carl Jung defined myth as the unfolding of human consciousness. This terminology is appropriate for the literature of ancient Canaan.

The Story of Aqhat

Although Ugaritic texts are not Canaanite per se, since Ugarit is technically north of Canaan in Syria, the biblical allusions to Canaanite lore, especially the Baal cycles, demonstrate that these stories were known in both ancient Canaan and Israel. The story of Aqhat resonates with several biblical stories and the "Gilgamesh Epic" (see Coogan and Smith 2012, 27-55). Though the story is named for the son of Danel, one named Aqhat, Danel is really the protagonist of the story. Aqhat does not live long enough to merit this title. Danel, whose name carries the meaning of "judging," is described as a hero and ruler who sat at the gate of the city and "judged the cases of widows, presided over orphans' hearings." (Coogan and Smith 2012, 39). In ancient Near Eastern societies, widows and orphans were considered the most vulnerable category of people, with few rights without an adult male to fend for them. Rulers were expected to be their protectors, and judging them would require wisdom. Danel's wisdom, in fact, is alluded to in the book of Ezekiel: "Behold, you are wiser than Danel; no secret is hidden from you" (28:3). Ezekiel is here speaking to the king of Tyre.

While Danel is a great leader, he has no heir. This meant he would not have a son, who could maintain the mortuary rituals necessary for his afterlife existence. He goes to the temple and laments to El, who decides to grant his wish. After the son is born, the god Kothar, the Skillful Craftsmen and magician, makes a splendid bow for him. Kothar is the Canaanite god of wisdom. Anat, the goddess of war and the hunt and sister of Baal, envied the bow (a symbol of Aqhat's masculinity and adulthood) and tried to persuade Aqhat to give it to her, offering wealth and even immortality. The request may have a latent sexual connotation (Smith 1995, 2031). Anat is notorious for her violence and is depicted as wearing a necklace of human heads and a belt of human hands (Coogan and Smith 2012, 7). Aqhat refused her request, even insulting her with, "Bows are for warriors—do women ever hunt?" (Coogan and Smith 2012, 42). This is similar to "Gilgamesh" rebuffing Ishtar's amorous passes at him. And like Ishtar, who then pouts and goes to her father, Anu, the Mesopotamian sky god and head of the pantheon (similar in status to El), in order to have Gilgamesh punished, Anat goes to El, who grants her permission to do as she wishes. Anat employs her henchman Yatpan, who assumes the form of a bird that sneaks up to Aqhat, who is preparing game he has killed, and slays him.

After Aqhat dies, a drought covers the land. Vultures start flying over Danel's house, and he and his daughter Pugat began to mourn for their dead son/brother. In the end, Pugat avenged her brother's death by dressing seductively, hiding her weapon, getting Yatpan drunk, and slaying him (the text ends before this actually happens). Two common motifs are present here: a warrior killed shamefully by a woman (Judg. 4:9, 21 [Jael]; 5:26-27; 9:53-54; Judith 12-13) and the hidden weapon (Judg. 3:16). Pugat is frequently depicted as a dutiful daughter: "She who carries water, she who collects dew on her hair, she who knows the course of the stars" (Coogan and Smith 2012, 31). Even though she is a leader's daughter, she was expected to go fetch the water from the well before dawn broke.

Within the story several common motifs emerge: a concern for fertility, whether human or the natural world, the righteous leader, the courageous but rash son, and the dutiful daughter (Coogan and Smith 2012, 32-33). All of these would serve as models for potential warriors and leaders. Behind these characters loom the gods and goddesses, who interacted directly with mortals in those days and often capriciously!

The Story of Kirta

The story of Kirta is another significant Canaanite tale (see Coogan and Smith 2012, 65-95). King Kirta had to face three problems: no heir or wife, an illness, and his son's usurpation. The king was responsible for supplying order and security in society. He was also supposed to provide a smooth succession from his reign to a son's. The story starts out with the perishing of Kirta's family and then his eventual sickness, which resonates with the story of Job. El appears to him in a dream, and Kirta is told to make his way to the king of Udm and lay siege to his city, during which he is to demand the king's daughter in marriage, who is described as vary beautiful, like Anat or Astarte. On his march toward the city, Kirta stops at a shrine of Asherah (the consort of El) and promises an offering if she helped him achieve his mission. She did, but he failed to fulfill his vow, and, as a result, was stricken with a disease. Nature also suffered because a famine occurred throughout the land. Finally, because of the prayers of the people for their king, El intervened and restored his health. After this, another of his sons threatened to usurp his throne because he had failed to assume his royal responsibilities during his illness. Kirta cursed his son, and the tablet is broken as this point. The point of the tale appears to promote the power, wisdom, and benevolence of El and Kirta's total dependence on him (Parker 1995, 2403).

The Baal Cycle

The "Baal Cycle" (fourteenth century) describes the emergence of the young warrior and fertility god as head of the Canaanite pantheon, which compares to the role of Marduk in the "Enuma Elish," the "Babylonian Genesis" (see Coogan and Smith 2012, 97-153). El has consigned Baal to submit himself to the domination of Prince Sea or Yam, but Baal refuses. Prince Sea correlates with the dragoness Tiamat (depicted as multi-headed) and represents chaos and evil; he has an array of demonic minions. A battle ensues and Baal is at the point of defeat when Kothar intervenes and supplies Baal with some magical weapons that allow him to be victorious (Smith 1995, 2031). After the battle, Astarte (goddess of love, war, and the hunt, like Anat) proclaims:

> Hail, Baal the Conqueror!
> Hail, Rider on the Clouds!
> Prince Sea is our captive,
> Judge River is our captive
> (Coogan and Smith 2012, 99).

Anat fights for her brother Baal, mainly against humans who were on the side of Prince Sea.

Baal has demonstrated his great power in defeating the Sea, but he cannot be considered a king unless he has his own palace (see Coogan and Smith 2012, 101-106). Anat convinces El to give Baal permission to build one with the aid of Kothar as architect. But he must also get Asherah's (El's consort) permission. Baal bears gifts, and she is persuaded. Kothar builds Baal's house with the finest cedar from Lebanon and with precious metals and gems. This establishes Baal's role as storm god and demonstrates his emergence as head of the pantheon. At first Baal refuses to have a window constructed in his palace for fear that Death (Mot) might enter therein, but he finally agrees to its installation, and sends word of his refusal to pay the required tribute to Death, who, in many respects, is the counterpart of Yam but more powerful.

Death sends messengers to inform Baal that his punishment would be death and captivity in the Underworld (see Coogan and Smith 2012, 106-53). When Anat and El received the news, they mourn, and Anat buries her brother. With the storm god's death, the earth dies, with drought and infertility. Anat then goes into battle against Death and slices him in two, planting him in the ground—symbolic of the death that grain must endure in order for life to spring up from the seed. Death died and Baal revived, reveling in his reemergence and proclaiming his domination. But after 7 years, Death returned to conquer him and bind him in the Underworld again. This symbolizes the recurrence of drought about every 7 years in the Levant; ultimately, death cannot be conquered (Parker 1995, 2406). Although Baal is declared king and keeps the Sea and Death at bay, he is never the single dominant character (Smith 1995, 2032).

Sidebar 8: Scribes, Dictation, and Competition

In the days of King Zimri Lim, ruler of the city-state of Mari in Northern Syria and on the Euphrates, one of his officials, Ibalpi-El, writes a letter to him, via his scribe, explaining why he had made a mistake in a previous letter sent. While he blames the mistake on another official's (Hamman) scribe, he is really pointing the finger at Hamman, who competes with him for the king's favor. The nature of the mistake shows that it was not due to the accuracy of the scribe's recording of the dictation but to a failure in oral communication before the message was relayed. Though Ibalpi-El attempted to slight Hamman in the eyes of the king, both officials had long and prosperous careers. And it is interesting to note that Ibalpi-El actually attempted to protect Hamman's scribe because he refers to him anonymously. Apparently, King Zimir-Lim was tolerant of such frequent mistakes (see Sasson, 211-28).

At the end of the tale, two allies of Baal are mentioned, the Sun god, who rules over the Rephaim or dead ancestors, and Kothar, Baal's diviner and god of wisdom, who will use magic to restrain Prince Sea and his minions (Coogan and Smith 2012, 152-53). The colophon ends: "The scribe: Ilimiku from Shuban, student of Attanu, the diviner, chief of the priests, chief of the herdsmen, the officiant of Niqmaddu, king of Ugarit . . ." The city of Ugarit considered Baal-Haddu (or Hadad) to be its patron deity, and the publication of this cycle at the city legitimated the king there, who is represented as Baal, and also reaffirmed the political values of the dynasty (Smith 1995, 2032).

Similarly, a second millennium letter from King Zimri-Lim of Mari (in north Syria and near Emar) quotes his divine patron, the storm god Adad or Haddu = Baal: "I s[et] you on the thr[one of your father]; the weapons with which I battled against Sea (similar to the name Tiamat) I gave to you" (Smith 1995, 2033). This is the very first West Semitic allusion to the Canaanite conflict story and demonstrates how the mythology correlates with the earthly reality (politics).

Shorter Narratives

There is an interesting series of rituals and stories contained in "The Rituals and Myths of the Lovely Gods" (see Coogan and Smith 2012, 155-66). Coogan and Smith describe "lovely gods" as a euphemism because these gods are actually destructive and malevolent and symbolize the dryness of the desert. The "lovely gods" are allowed to participate in a feast with the benevolent deities and even Death, who eventually dies. This mythology is an attempt at integrating both the life-giving and destructive forces of nature, especially as demonstrated in the autumnal equinox when the dry summer gives way to the winter rains. This mythology also represents the treatment of Death and his demise without Baal as an opponent. One interesting segment of the myth is the story of how El, who has several erections, finally impregnates his two wives, who give birth to Dawn and Dusk and other divine children. Interestingly, in this story El is not depicted as the old, gray-haired man but in his prime.

In "The Rephaim," one finds devotion to the "Healthy Ones" = "Rephaim," who appear to be the gods of the Underworld, originally dead ancestors (Coogan and Smith 2012, 57-63). This is further evidence that ancestor worship was a reality among the Canaanites and the rural Israelites as well. These deities were worshipped so that they might provide aid in human fertility. These deities were also consulted as oracles to predict the future. Micah and his mother (Judges 17-18) may have erected an image (a teraphim or "household gods") of the recently deceased patriarch for oracular purposes (see Cox and Ackerman 2012, 1-37). The teraphim may also have been involved in land rights.

In "El's Drinking Party," an etiological tale, the head of the Canaanite pantheon is displayed in a rather comical and unflattering manner (see Coogan and Smith 2012, 167-72). El makes preparations for a *mrzh* for the gods. A *mrzh* was a party or gathering of elite males, often for funerals, similar to the Greek symposium. In Hebrew it is *marzeah* (Jer. 16:5; Amos 6:7). Several deities, the Moon (depicted as a dog), Anat, and Astarte = Ishtar, go hunting for wild game to supply the party. In the meantime, El gets very drunk and has to be helped by the women to return home. Along the way he sees a precursor to the devil, with horns and tail, and soils himself. Anat and Astarte go hunting to find ingredients to help alleviate El's hangover. The final lines of the text contain a magical prescription for treating hangovers: dog hair is placed on the head, and dung and olive oil are mixed and either applied or ingested, perhaps to induce vomiting. Most of these elements are reflected in the myth. The story was probably recited as the treatment was applied.

The first millennium story of "Baalam the Seer" was found on an inscription in plaster fragments from Deir 'Alla in ancient Moab. Its specific title is "Inscription of [Balaam son of Be]or, seer of gods." This same Baalam is in Numbers 22-24, where this prophet is employed by the king of Moab to curse Israel. This backfires and the prophet is taught a lesson by the donkey he rides, who sees an angel blocking his way on the road. The donkey speaks to him, and he is startled. Instead of cursing Israel, he ends up being forced to bless them because of God's power. In ancient times, a curse was a real phenomenon that had to be dealt with by magical means to stop the effects. The Moabite inscription tells of Baalam being visited by the gods during the night. He arose the next day in great distress and began fasting. The people ask him why he is so upset. He had bad news for them.

The Aramaic tale of Ahiqar, which also includes a collection of proverbs, involves a vizier of the Assyrian king who had no heir (see Parker 1995, 2407). He plans to adopt his nephew, Nadin, to succeed him in his profession and instruct him in wisdom. Once Nadin is installed, he accuses Ahiqar of treachery. The king commands Ahiqar to be executed. Fortunately for Ahiqar, the executioner had himself previously been accused in the same manner and Ahiqar had saved his life by hiding him and telling the king he had killed him. Later, Ahiqar eventually vindicated the officer, who was then reinstalled. The executioner in turn does the same for Ahiqar. Later the king wishes Ahiqar was still around, and the executioner then unexpectedly produces him. Ahiqar is reinstated, and Nadin is punished.

The story of Ahiqar is the typical ancient Near Eastern story of court intrigue. The hero is a remarkably wise and pious person who is victimized but, in the end, prevails over his enemies. It is similar to the story in book of Esther when Mordecai is reinstated because the Persian king remembers that Mordecai had once saved his life. The stories of Joseph and Daniel also reflect these kinds of plots. Also, the story is strikingly similar to the "Instruction of Ankhsheshonq," as mentioned previously.

Cultic and Wisdom Literature

The lament psalms in the biblical Psalter have close parallels in the Ugaritic literature and Levantine inscriptions (Parker 1995, 2407-2408). A ritual text from Ugarit begins this way:

When another power attacks your gates,
a warrior your walls
lift up your eyes to Baal:

"O Baal,
if you drive the power from out gates,
the warrior from our walls . . ." (Parker 1995, 2408).

Next is a vow with promise of sacrifices and a visit to Baal's sanctuary. Then follows this assurance:

Then Baal will hear your prayer:
He will drive the power from your gates,
the warrior from your walls (Parker 1995, 2408).

Similarly, the Aramaic king Zakkur (Zakir) recorded this in an inscription: "They raised a wall higher than the wall of Hadrak, and plowed a ditch deeper than its ditch. And I lifted my hands to Baal shamein and Baal shamein answered me, and Baal shamein spoke to me through seers and prophets" (Parker 1995, 2408). A prophetic oracle of salvation then follows.

The "Proverbs of Ahiqar" is the one representative of wisdom literature of Syro-Palestinian lore. It contains about 100 proverbs. The earliest form of the story was found in Elephantine Egypt and dates to the fifth century B.C.E. (Goodman 1961, 270). The Jews at Elephantine knew of the story and some of its parables. Here are some examples:

Spare the rod,
spoil the child (Benjamin/Matthews 2006, 303).

Two kinds of people are a delight.
A third pleases Shamash, the divine Judge:
Those who share their wine,
those who follow good advice,
those who can keep secrets. . . .
(Benjamin/Matthews 2006, 304).

Choose words carefully to teach another.
The word is mightier than the sword (304).

A thorn bush asked a pomegranate tree:
"Why so many thorns to protect so little fruit?"
The pomegranate tree said:
"Why so many thorns to protect no fruit at all?"
(Benjamin/Matthews 2006, 308).

Do not send the Bedouin to sea, or the sailor into the desert.
Everyone's work is unique (Benjamin/Matthews 2006, 309).

Summary

We have examined the training of scribes and their roles in society within the WP. The training of scribes and the curriculum follows a standard pattern that reflects the Mesopotamian system. Students first become familiar with cuneiform and the tablets. Next they memorized lexical lists that introduce them to different domains of their world (names of gods, objects, professions, etc.) that will help them both culturally and professionally. Next, memorization and copying of phrases and sentences further reinforces their learning of cuneiform but also introduces them to literary texts that would help form their cultural perspective. Next, actual literary texts were studied and parts memorized like liturgical texts (hymns, etc.), mythical narratives, various types of wisdom literature, and "scientific" texts like omen literature. Also, more practical texts were studied and copied such as model letters, inscriptions, and business contracts. Finally, there was specialized training such as in divination, medicine, or perhaps the priestly arts.

There is evidence of scribes who served in both academic and professional capacities and both copied and studied literary and scholarly texts as well as composed ephemeral or practical documents, a combination of the practical and the academic, though some scribes appear to have been employed exclusively within the business and administrative world. But the relationship between the two worlds was close. A scribe who was trained broadly in the academic realm became a better scribe in the professional arena. And because scribes were employed to serve in so many capacities, it made sense to supply a broad education that included both cultural and literary elements as well as practical ones.

The scribal training of the WP strongly reflected the Mesopotamian ethos and culture and included study of its lore and literature, a way to homogenize the spread of cuneiform culture and make communication easier and more efficient throughout the realm. But, as in Ugarit and even at Emar, there were indigenous elements. At Ugarit, in addition to the Babylonian materials, the scribes also studied their own religious mythology involving the Canaanite pantheon. And while these texts resonate with the Mesopotamian mythos, such as Anat resembling Ishtar and Yam echoing Tiamat, they are distinctive. However, in the end it is the universal themes that resonate with both the Mesopotamian mythos that are the most important for understanding the scribal ethos and its worldview: fertility versus bareness, rainfall versus drought, loyalty versus treason, courage versus cowardice, kingship versus anarchy, obedience versus rebellion, order versus chaos, life versus death, etc.

The scribes were in essence the cultural repositories of their respective cultures. Whether serving in the private business world or the administrative world, they represented the ideals and values of the states or cities who trained them. As the tiny few who could read and write in the lingua franca of their world and sometimes in their own mother tongue, they were extremely valuable and could sometimes wield considerable power. How the Israelite version of scribalism reflects this WP and its cultural milieu will be discussed next.

5

Israelite Scribalism and the Place of Wisdom Literature within It

In this chapter, we finally situate the scribes who composed the biblical wisdom literature within their own particular social and historical contexts. We will first discuss literacy in Canaan, then the critical importance of the emergence of the alphabet there during the second millennium. Next we will examine some of the epigraphic and textual evidence for Israelite scribalism in the Iron Age. Then we will examine the various roles Israelite and Jewish scribes assumed during the Iron Age and postexilic period. Drawing on comparative epigraphic and archaeological evidence, we will finally speculate on the place of wisdom literature in a theoretical Israelite scribal curriculum.

Writing in the Second Millennium B.C.E.

Before the alphabet arose in Canaan, hieroglyphic and cuneiform writing is represented there (see Millard 2011, 14). Potsherds bearing the name of Pharaoh Narmer were found at Arad and Tell el-'Areini, while seal impressions with the names of other early pharaohs and officials were discovered at 'En Besor. Thus, writing existed in Canaan during the EBA (3500-2200 B.C.E.), whether or not the local people could read it. The earliest cuneiform tablets found in Canaan come from the Old Babylonian period or MBA (2000-1550 B.C.E.). These include seven incomplete tablets, two liver models, and part of an inscribed stone jar discovered at Hazor, possibly a letter from Shechem, an administrative text from Hebron, a fragment from Gezer, and several inscribed cylinder seals. Numerous scarabs (beetle shaped jewelry)[1] with inscribed names of officials were found, which probably served as magical amulets.

Egyptian and Babylonian writing in Canaan is better represented in the LBA (1550-1200 B.C.E.), when Egypt controlled this area (see Millard 2011, 14-15). Pharaohs had inscriptions made on rocks and stelae, while officials erected monuments for themselves or their pharaohs (Beth-Shan, Gaza, and Jaffa). These officials ensured that taxes were collected. Though hieroglyphs are found throughout Canaan during this period, the official mode of communication between Canaan and Egypt was cuneiform, as demonstrated by the Amarna letters. At Shechem and Tell Ta'annek tablets and fragments were found that show that Babylonian cuneiform was used for local administration and correspondence. Canaanite scribes had to learn cuneiform and Akkadian, and at Aphek and Ashkelon, lists of words were found, and in one case, with Canaanite equivalents.

---

1. The dung beetle represents the sun in that their egg laying habit involved rolling a sphere of dung along the ground like the sun circuiting in the sky.

The Emergence of the Alphabet

The alphabet emerged unexpectedly from common laborers (turquoise miners) and not the elite. Previously all writing was very complicated and either consisted of pictographs like Egyptian hieroglyphs or Mesopotamian cuneiform, which meant the learning of hundreds of signs instead of a simple alphabet. The first alphabetic writing emerged at Serabit el-Khadem in the Sinai (see Goldwasser 2010, 38-50). There was an Egyptian turquoise mining operation here during the Middle Kingdom (1950-1800 B.C.E.). Canaanites were employed to do the mining. This new script (Proto-Canaanite) uses the Egyptian hieroglyphs for its letters, which the Canaanites could not read but saw every day. Ingeniously these miners imitated the hieroglyph signs creating pictographs as signs for consonants and not words or syllables as in hieroglyphs. In a few cases the miners directly copied hieroglyph signs. For example, the Egyptian hieroglyph for foreman is a man with upheld arms as if issuing a command. The miners often heard the foreman calling out to work with "Hoy!" meaning "Get to work." The miners then used the symbol for their letter "h."

The miners inscribed prayers on stelae, stones, and the walls of the mining caves with this new script (Goldwasser 2010, 38, 42, 44). They were for protection in the dangerous caves. A sphinx dedicated to the bovine-shaped goddess Hathor, the protective deity of the site, was found. Inscribed on it, in hieroglyphs, is "the mistress of turquoise." In the new Canaanite script, the word inscribed is "mistress" or *Baalat*, the feminine form of "Baal," which means "lord" or "master."

The invention of this Proto-Canaanite script had far-reaching social consequences because it meant that "writing broke out of the 'golden cage' of the professional scribal world" (Goldwasser 2010,

41). Scribes no longer had a monopoly on writing, though they were still the only ones who could read and write proficiently and at a high level. It meant that the time needed to learn to read and write was reduced.

In the city of Ugarit, during the LBA in the fourteenth and thirteenth centuries B.C.E., Ugaritic scribes adopted the Proto-Canaanite script and created a similar alphabet, with the same order, but, instead of using pictographs, they used the cuneiform wedge-shaped marks that they had been using for years in their communication with Egypt and Mesopotamia (Goldwasser 2010, 50). In Canaan, during the thirteenth and twelfth centuries, two writing systems existed side by side. In the urban centers, the Ugaritic system was used, but in the countryside, the script of the "caravaneers," similar to the Proto-Canaanite script, was prevalent.

With the first Canaanite alphabet, there were no vowels since no word began with a vowel among Semites (see Millard 2011, 15-16). The language could be written clearly enough without them, as was true for hieroglyphs, and remains true for Hebrew and Arabic even today. In the early stages, there were only 26 letters.

With the decline of the great powers at the end of the LBA, new peoples settled the region like the Aramean (Syrian) kingdoms, Israel, and Ammon, Edom, and Moab. At this time the only vestiges of the LBA Caananite kingdoms were the Phoenicians at Tyre, Sidon, and Byblos (see Millard 2011, 17-19). The new West Semitic kingdoms could now adopt the 22 letter Canaanite linear alphabet (written across lines) for their own purposes. One of the earliest forms was graffiti on a bowl (1200 B.C.E.) from Qubu al-Walaydah, near Gaza, that contained the owner's name and was perhaps a votive gift to a deity. In the twelfth century a student at Izbet Sarteh, near Tel Aviv, composed the 22 letter alphabet in order, except *peh* precedes *'ayin*, an order found in some later Hebrew inscriptions like those found at

Kuntillet ʿAjrud and in biblical acrostics (a poem with lines structured alphabetically; e.g., Lamentations 2-3). At Byblos, a spatula (end of the eleventh century) was found with alphabetic writing but it is hard to decipher. Also of the same date is an ostracon (piece of pottery used as a writing medium) found at Khirbet Qeiyafah, near the valley of Elah where David fought Goliath, similarly hard to interpret. It is debated whether it is actually Hebrew or not. There have been 50 or more arrowheads found with the word "arrow" (*chetz*) usually incised along the spine, followed by a name and patronymic (father's name), and, occasionally on the other side, a title. Their function is disputed. Five arrows were found in Bethlehem.

Both Seth Sanders and Ryan Byrne have pointed out that during this period scribes were not controlled by the state but rather served as freelance experts. They could be hired by the elite for prestige purposes, like having one's name inscribed on an arrowhead (Sanders 2004, 45-46; 2008,105-107; Byrne 2007, 1-31).

The oldest continuous, legible, alphabetic texts come from Byblos in the tenth century (see Millard 2011, 19-20). Around 1000 B.C.E., the son of Ahirom, king of Byblos, had an epitaph chiseled into his father's sarcophagus. A graffito on the tomb wall warns robbers of their grave danger entering any further. In the tenth and early ninth centuries, other kings of Byblos had notices engraved on stone, some referring to Canaanite deities like *Baʿal Shamêm* and the "lady of Byblos." From this tenth-century material, the development of the national alphabets can be traced. The script from the Byblian texts is the prototype from which all the others came: Phoenician, Hebrew, Aramaic, Transjordanian, and Greek. Because the Phoenicians were not imperial powers or colonists in the Levant, their alphabetic script spread via their mercantile activities.

The earliest Hebrew texts appear to be the Gezer calendar and the Tel Zayit abecedary, if in fact they are actually Hebrew (Millard

2011, 22). The calendar is not in Classical Hebrew script and is closer to Canaanite (Schniedewind 2004, 58-59). The Greeks adopted the Phoenician alphabet due to trading needs in the eighth century and turned some of the consonant symbols into vowels because the Greeks had words that started with vowels like their negative particle *ou* (Millard 2011, 24-25). The Greeks, thus, produced the first true alphabet. The Hebrews eventually did something similar, in imitation of the Aramaeans, by allowing certain consonants to serve simultaneously as vowel letters.

While the Israelites adopted the Phoenician script for their own national script, they adopted the Egyptian hieratic for their numbers and even for some of their measurements (Millard 2011, 26). This may be because in the LBA Egyptian scribes were in Canaan. Also, David and Solomon seem to have had close Egyptian ties. Egyptian influence was at a peak during the eighth century, when this system becomes most discernible.

Scribalism and Literacy in Ancient Israel

Chris Rollston's recent book, *Writing and Literacy in the World of Ancient Israel*, has created quite a stir among biblical scholars. He has challenged many scholars who have advocated a general literacy among the ancient Israelites and has confirmed the notion of state sponsored scribal education among the Israelites. Rollston earned his doctorate at Johns Hopkins and is one of the most respected epigraphers of paleo-Hebrew (the earliest Hebrew) today. While scribalism in ancient Egypt, Mesopotamia, and the Levant is documented by large amounts of data from archaeological finds, like clay tablets and actual school buildings, Israelite scribalism, in comparison, largely lacks this kind of evidence. Rollston's book is invaluable because it fills in that gap by examining the extra-biblical epigraphic evidence, which can indirectly support the theory of scribal education in ancient Israel and demonstrate state sponsorship of such an institution.

Sidebar 9: Kuntillet 'Ajrud 3.9
[ ] to YHWH of the Teman and to his Asherah. [ ] all that he asks from God, he (God) will favour; and if he entreats, that which he desires (Wearne 2014).

By examining very closely the Hebrew inscriptions that have been found in ancient Israel Rollston has demonstrated that Hebrew became first standardized in the ninth century (2010, 44). He follows the diachronic development of Hebrew as well as its synchronic consistency, even discerning a North Israelite and Judean dialect (2010, 109). He argues that standardization of Hebrew could only occur if there was some kind of state sponsored institution, what he calls "formal, standardized education" instead of using the term "school" (2010, 95). Rollston's ninth-century dating for standardization actually fits with Lipiński's (1988, 157-58) observation that the first actual royal annals were produced only after the days of king Rehoboam (930-913 B.C.E.), when monarchic reigns were given actual years instead of the earlier stereotypical accounts (40 years each for the reigns of David and Solomon).

Schools in Ancient Israel?

Rollston's avoidance of the word "school" is due to the accusation by other scholars that it is anachronistic. However, André Lemaire has avoided that problem by comparing Israelite education with Koranic schools (1984, 278). These did not necessitate any buildings delegated exclusively for education. Rather, a Koranic teacher could gather "in a square or the corner of a court or in a public place" to teach students. Lemaire points to two archaeological sites that might fit this description. At Kuntillet 'Ajrud numerous school exercises were found in the same place, in a room with benches (first half of the eighth century B.C.E.). And the number of school exercises at Kadesh-Barnea suggest the existence of a schools, where a room or corner of a court may have been used (600 B.C.E.).

Kuntillet 'Ajrud is the famous site where inscriptions were found on two large pithoi or jars, one of which reads "Yahweh and his Asherah," with a possible artistic rendition of both. Gareth Wearne has recently argued that one of the "blessings" is actually a non-canonical psalm, whose lacunae should be filled in with a verb of praise and not of blessing. He compares the two lines to several psalms like 29:1-4, which has a similar pattern. He theorizes that this psalm was part of a school exercise for scribes (Wearne 2014).

Also, Rollston has pointed out that Israelite scribal education probably followed the apprenticeship model, which occurred within a domestic context (2010, 115-16). This means that a scribe would pass on his trade to his son(s) in his home. This, of course, is corroborated by the Emar evidence that we have looked at, particularly with the Zūba'la family, where there is documentary evidence of fathers teaching their own sons and maybe another student or two. It is also suggested by biblical evidence such as David's scribe Seraiah (2 Sam. 8:17) or Sheva (2 Sam. 20:25), who had two sons, Elihoreph and Ahijah, who served as scribes under Solomon (1 Kgs. 4:3). Shaphan is the royal scribe who was part of the team that found the book of the Law (2 Kgs. 22:3-14), and his sons and grandsons appear to be scribes closely connected with

Jeremiah (Jer. 26:24; 29:3; 36:10; 39:14; 40:1-41:10). Elishama was a royal scribe during the reign of Jehoiakim (Jer. 36:12, 20-21), and his son, Ishmael, was responsible for the murder of Shaphan's grandson, Gedaliah (Jer. 41:1-10).

Sidebar 10: Lachish Letter No. 3
Your servant, Hoshayahu, sent to inform my lord, Yaush: May YHWH cause my lord to hear a report of peace and a report of good things. And now, please explain to your servant the meaning of the letter which you sent to your servant yesterday evening because the heart of your servant has been sick since your sending to your servant and because my lord said "you do not know (how) to read a letter." As YHWH lives, never has any man had to read a letter to me. And also every letter that comes to me, surely I read it, and, moreover, I can repeat it completely! . . . (Schniedewind 2004, 101-102).

Lemaire has also argued that schools would have been necessary during Solomon's reign (1984, 276-77). With Egypt in view, he defends the use of the comparative method, historically and sociologically, for speculating about Israel's early administration as it developed a monarchy. He points out that Egypt had had a tremendous influence in Canaan in the LBA and during the emergence of the Israelite nation and monarchy. Evidence for these close ties is the administration under Solomon resembling the Egyptian model, the adoption of a section of the "Instruction of Amenemope" by Judean scribes preserved in the book of Proverbs (22:17-23:11), and the employment of hieratic script for writing numbers in paleo-Hebrew, which is substantiated by an ostracon found at Kadesh-Barnea that contained a table of weights and measures with numbers from 1-10,000. Lemaire concludes,

> . . . [T]he existence of an important administration (which cannot be reduced to ministers!) as a result of the creation of a united kingdom of David-Solomon supposes a development of the employment of writing and the creation of schools (in the ancient manner!) for forming, in particular, the future functionaries of the royal administration, the best example of the development of this scribal administration being the practice of census (2 Sam. 24:1-8; 1 Chr. 21) (1984, 277; translation mine).

Corroboration of this is provided by four ostraca found at Tel Arad, a southern fortress used during the time of Solomon, in the tenth century. It reads:

Son of B[. . .]M[. . .]

Son of H[. . .] *hekat* (barley) 10

Son of MN[. . .] 100 *hekat* (barley)

[. . . *hekat* (barley)] 2[0] (Schniedewind 2004, 62).

This is an accounting text, and *hekat* is an Egyptian term for measuring barley. The numbers are in hieratic.

Literacy beyond Scribes?

Rollston has challenged the view of some scholars that the alphabet enabled persons to learn to read and write in only a few days or weeks (2010, 92-97). Rather, based on modern education systems that employ alphabetic writing, Rollston argues that it still took years. Also, he counters scholars who have argued for a high percentage of literacy among the Israelites due to the fact that beginning in the eighth century Hebrew inscriptions become much more prominent.

Importantly, Rollston admits that literacy was not confined solely to scribes (2010, 128-32). He gives the example of the Lachish Letter No. 3, which reflects the literacy of an elite military officer. In this letter Hoshayahu writes to his superior officer, a certain Yaush, and complains to him of having suggested to Hoshayahu that he use a scribe because he had misunderstood a previous missive. Hoshayahu boasts that he had never needed a professional scribe for such purposes. But Rollston notes that this officer is still elite, a high ranking military officer.

Though this officer was proficient at least in reading and composing letters, it is doubtful that Hoshayahu could have read the literature of the Hebrew Bible as well as he claims to have been able to read letters. And likewise it is doubtful that he could compose literature of any type. That would be reserved for the scribal elite or other literati, like priests and perhaps some prophets. Thus, a distinction needs to be made between a low literacy, where one could write his name or read simple compositions, and a high literacy that would have been required of scribes, who could read and write literature.

During the late Judean monarchy several archaeological finds indicate that writing may have been produced by the hands of non-scribes. The Mesad Hashavyahu ostracon is a letter from an agricultural worker who complains about one of his garments taken in pledge without being returned (cf. Exod. 22:26-27). It is dated to the late Judean monarchy and was found in a guardroom of the fortress. It is often assumed that a scribe composed the letter for the worker, but Schniedewind points out that this is conjecture (2004, 103). Graffiti has also been found. One found at Khirbet el-Qôm asks for a blessing from "Yahweh and his Asherah" (Schneidewind 2004,

104). At Ketef Hinnom silver amulets were found that paraphrase the priestly blessing of Num. 6:24–26 ("The Lord bless you and keep you . . .") and Deut. 7:9–10 (see Schniedewind 2004, 105–106). They were worn around the neck and may have had magical connotations. But none of this substantiates the view that a high percentage of Israelites were truly literate.

The Status of Scribes

Rollston has also argued that the Israelite scribes should be considered elite, certainly highly respected in Israelite society, chiefly because of the rarity of persons who could read and write Hebrew fluently and sophisticatedly (2010, 85–90). He also notes that Israelite scribes were sometimes powerful. He discusses Mesopotamian and Egyptian literature that lauds the position of the scribe in the respective societies, such as the Egyptian "Satire of the Trades," which compares the cushy job of the scribe with the lowly and difficult professions of various guilds like potters and smiths. It does this to motivate young scribal apprentices to study harder. Rollston also cites Ben Sira (38:24–39:11), who similarly contrasts the high position of the scribe with the arduous but necessary vocations of other professions. Rollston also attempts to counter the argument that many Israelite scribes occupied more lowly positions. He rightly maintains that even scribes who served as business professionals would have been perceived as having high status because of their ability to do something few could do. Rollston's description of the social status of scribes will be further nuanced in a later chapter.

Scribes and the Matrix of the Hebrew Bible

Recently, there have been three biblical scholars who have theorized that the emergence of the Hebrew Bible is intricately connected to the onset of literacy and scribalism. William Schniedewind maintains that writing played only a limited role in the early period of Israel and Judah's statehood (2004, 48-63), when it was restricted to only royal and temple scribes and no substantial literature was composed. However, he speculates that during the days of Hezekiah, in the eighth century, when the king attempted to centralize the nation and reform it religiously, writing started acquiring religious authority and Israel's culture began transforming from an oral to a literary culture (2004, 64-90). This is basically confirmed by David Jamieson-Drake (1991), who argued, based on archaeology, that the earliest that "schools" could have existed in ancient Israel was the eighth century B.C.E. Schniedewind connects the Hezekiah proverb collection (Prov. 22:17-23:11) with this period and argues that literature during this period, like the earliest stage of the book of Kings, was composed for royal propaganda in order to legitimate the Davidic dynasty when the Assyrians were threatening the Judean kings (2004, 75-81). But during the time of Josiah literacy expanded exponentially with many non-scribes becoming literate, like soldiers and priests (2004, 91-117). One of Schniedewind's main theses is that most of the Hebrew Bible was written during the eighth through sixth centuries B.C.E., a conclusion with which most scholars will not concur.

David Carr compares the scribal curricula of ancient Mesopotamia, Egypt, Greece, and ancient Israel and finds striking similarities in terms of curriculum and sequence of educational stages. He believes this scribal curriculum was primarily intend to enculturate the young scribes and the elite to prepare them for governmental service and leadership roles (2005, 119, 126). He argues that the very first corpus of school texts may have been the wisdom literature, specifically the book of Proverbs, some material maybe even going back to the days of Solomon, with other genres studied as well (2005, 126-34). Later came the Deuteronomistic History[2] (Joshuah-2 Kings), which he describes as an alternative curriculum (2005, 134-42). The prophetic corpus, in turn, became even a counter-curriculum (2005, 143-51). He believes the Hebrew Bible canon was largely set during the days of the Hasmonean dynasty, which had its own library and was influenced by Greek models (2005, 253-72). Differently from Schniedewind, Carr argues that ancient Israel retained its oral culture as writing become more dominant and that scribes recited their written texts and memorized them. The notion that the Hebrew Bible began as a curriculum has not won general acceptance, but I believe his thesis can help illuminate the place of wisdom literature within the scribal curriculum.

Karel van der Toorn also argues that our Hebrew Bible is essentially the product of scribes. He maintains that originally the contents of the Hebrew Bible were composed by scribes and for scribes (2007, 2). He also supports the idea that literacy was very low in ancient Israel as in the rest of the ancient Near East (2007, 10-11). He believes the very first segment of what became the Hebrew Bible was the Torah (2007, 249). Later came the collection of prophetic books, and so forth (2007, 252). Toorn does not believe the Hebrew Bible was formed originally as a scribal school curriculum because so many of the genres in it are not paralleled in the Mesopotamian curriculum, particularly the technical divinatory and exorcism texts, but instead represent general literature (2007, 247). He argues that eventually in the Hellenistic period what was originally scribal

---

2. This corpus is called this because these books have been heavily influenced by the book of Deuteronomy in style and content.

literature became sacred literature, and, thus, the canon began to formulate (2007, 252).

Types of Scribes and Their Social Roles in Ancient Israel

Delineating the types of scribes and their various social roles is very difficult because of the number of types and vastly differing roles. Also, a complication is that a particular scribe often assumed several roles simultaneously.

General Types

Scribes can be divided up and categorized in various ways. One way could be according to status. There were certainly upper level scribes who served in important administrative and governmental positions as leaders. Some in fact could become quite powerful. But most scribes occupied a lower ranked position of administrators, who mainly did the "grunt work" for senior scribes or patrons. Just their ability to read and write in Hebrew made them invaluable for various people, whether great or lowly.

Another basic categorization would be based on the type of employer. One division would be between scribes who were employed at the palace and those employed at the Temple, thus, royal and temple scribes. Of course, after the exile, the Temple was the primary locus for scribal activity. But there were also scribes who served in administrative centers outside the capitals of Samaria or Jerusalem. And then the smaller cities and towns certainly would need scribes. No doubt every village required a scribe to conduct its business and be accountable to either the monarchy or powers during the postexilic period.

Specific Roles

Heralds

The Hebrew word for scribe is *sopher*, which comes from a verb that is used in the *qal* stem, its most basic form to denote counting and reckoning. In the *piel* stem it means to recount or relate, declare (Brown, Driver, and Briggs 1980, 707-708). The latter meaning fits the role of scribes throughout the ancient Near East, who were often simultaneously messengers or heralds because they were the only ones who could read. One of Solomon's officials, Jehoshaphat, is listed as a "herald" (1 Kgs. 4:3), from the word *mazkir*, which comes from a root that means to remind. It could either be translated as "recorder" or "herald," but either way, this position would have necessitated training as a scribe in order to be able to read the Hebrew. Also, Shaphan, a scribe, had to read the scroll of the Law found in the Temple for Josiah and his ministers (2 Kgs. 22:8-10). And Habakkuk is told to record the prophecy given to him on a tablet so that a herald may go and proclaim it (2:2); the intended herald is no doubt a scribe.

Teachers

Along with priests, scribes taught the people the law (Ezra 7:6; Nehemiah 8). These perhaps were Levitical scribes, but scribes, none-the-less. The authors of the Wisdom literature in the Hebrew Bible were probably primarily teachers and scholars, what we would call professors. Ben Sira, a scribal scholar, refers to what may be his own "school" (51:23). The address to the "son" by the "father" in the prologue to Proverbs is certainly a rhetorical device meant to lend legitimacy to the wisdom tradition and the aphorisms that begin in 10:1. But it also was a common address of a teacher to his pupil.

It reflects the reality that many biological fathers who were scribes taught their own sons. The superscription "the words of the wise" that mark two collections of aphorisms in Proverbs (22:17; 24:23) point to scribal scholars as their authors. The degree of literary sophistication and moral discernment in them indicate scholars as authors.

The "Preacher" (from Martin Luther's "*Der Prediger*") or "Teacher" (NIV) in Ecclesiastes is described by the frame-narrator to the book as "teaching the people" (12:9). "Teacher" is a guess for translating the Hebrew penname "Qohelet" used in the book to describe the protagonist. It comes from a Hebrew verb that means "to gather," say, people, as in an assembly. The word "synagogue" was often a translation of the noun form of the verb in the Septuagint. So, the translations "Preacher" or "Teacher" are educated guesses of what the participle form of the word means. A teacher or preacher speaks to a gathered assembly. But the penname could also refer to the gathering or collecting of aphorisms (12:9). Also, in the latter part of this verse, the narrator describes Qohelet's activities as "he weighed and searched and arranged many aphorisms." As mentioned earlier, Michael Fishbane has demonstrated that all of these descriptive phrases are technical terms that scribes used to depict their own activities (1988, 29-32).

Administrators

Scribes often functioned as governmental officials, whether for the monarchy or Temple and later the Temple alone. There was probably a scribe in every village who composed business and marriage contracts and divorce decrees for peasants, as well as serving as notaries and witnesses to oaths, and perhaps functioning as lawyers, treasurers, land surveyors, and tax collectors—basically, anything that involved writing and record-keeping. There would be more scribes, of course, in the administrative cities, like Megiddo, and even more in the capitals. A scribe would have been integral to the operation of both village and city, the hinterland and urban centers. As we saw earlier, scribes served as the glue that enabled the earliest civilizations to operate and function smoothly.

Interestingly, Mark Christian argues that middle level, Levitical scribes served as liaisons between the urban elite in Israel and the rural villagers (2009, 1-81). These scribes helped produce the laws in Deuteronomy, which do not solely reflect the interests of the upper class and, thus, as a whole, represent a compromise, of sorts.

The necessity of the scribal system for the monarchy is indicated archaeologically by possible scribal chambers found in two administrative cities, Megiddo and Hazor, and one capital, Samaria. Following Yeivin, Ze'ev Herzog has argued that scribal chambers have been found in these cities (1992, 229-30). The administrative character of the chambers is indicated by their location, symmetrical plan, and the distinctiveness of their design in contrast to other typical IA dwellings. Also, at Samaria, numerous ostraca were found in the building, which has been called the "Ostraca House." The plan of the chamber is a basic unit that could be either doubled or tripled. Each unit contained a long, narrow corridor or inner court, on whose long sides were doorways to square rooms. These date to the ninth century.

The earliest chambers are at Megiddo and date to the tenth century B.C.E. There were two northern chambers found here and one southern one. Each unit comprised a court and on its long sides were three square rooms. These chambers may have been treasuries. At Hazor, from the eighth century, two scribal chambers were found. Each unit has a broad court, divided by a row of pillars, with a row of rooms on each side. The pillars indicate that part of the court was covered and provided a shaded area.

There is also evidence for Judah. During the eighth century B.C.E. Hezekiah created four administrative cities (Schniedewind 2004, 71). These are indicated by royal storage jars and their seal impressions. The seals were stamped on their jar handles while the clay was wet. They contain the royal insignia, which is a flying sun disk, reflecting Egyptian influence. Above the insignia are the words "belonging to the king," and the name of one of four cities: Hebron, Socoh, Ziph, or *MMŠT*, which is probably Ramat Rahel.

Royal scribes would have also served as letter writers for the king and rulers. Though several Hebrew letters have been found on ostraca, none are royal. However, fragments of letters are found in passages in the Hebrew Bible (see Lipiński 1988, 158). David's letter to Joab concerning Uriah's fate may be a genuine verbatim letter: "And he wrote on a scroll saying, 'Set Uriah in the front in the heat of the battle and retreat from him so that he will be smote and die.'" Another famous example would be Queen Jezebel's letter to the notables of Jezreel in order to eliminate Naboth, who would not sell his vineyard to her husband (1 Kgs. 21:9-10). Also, in 2 Kgs. 5:6 a letter from the king of Syria to the Israelite king begins with "and now," which is the regular formula that introduces the main part of a letter (cf. 2 Kgs. 10:2-3).

The royal scribes who served as governmental officials basically fit Leo Oppeheim's category of Mesopotamian "bureaucrat-scribe," who served in both the palace and temples (1975, 39). They served the needs of the bureaucracies of both the palace and temple as copyists and record keepers. He states, "In that situation the most obvious and best known activity of the scribes is the recording of the flow of goods, staples, animals, and workmen through the circulation channels that keep the organization functioning" (Oppenheim 1975, 39).

Courtiers

A royal scribe who served as courtier is distinguished from administrative scribes by his higher positions and mainly his function as advisor. When priests, prophets, and sages are formulaically combined, the "sages" are most likely courtiers. The standard passage cited is Jer. 18:18: "Then they said, 'Come, let us devise plots against Jeremiah for instruction will not cease from the priest, nor advice from *the wise*, nor an oracle (word) from the prophet. Come, let us smite him by tongue and let us not listen to all his words.'" The courtier who served as advisor for the Assyrian king Esarhaddon, Ahiqar, was both a scribe and courtier. He describes himself as a "wise scribe and counselor of all Assyria," and also as a seal-bearer to the king (Pritchard, 427-28).

As mentioned earlier, not all courtiers were scribes, however. Ahithiphel, who served David as a courtier, is distinguished from Jonathan, David's uncle, who is described as both a counselor and a scribe (1 Chron. 27:32-33). The wisdom writers of Proverbs seemed to assume that some of their audience would serve as courtiers, even if only occasionally, because several of the aphorisms reflect a courtly setting (e.g., 23:1-8; 25:1-7). The reference to Hezekiah's men copying maxims (Prov. 25:1) could refer only to royal scribes. Similarly, the maxims in the "Words of Ahiqar" would purportedly have been composed by a scribal courtier.

The connection, though largely legendary, of Solomon's court and wisdom is indicated by 1 Kgs. 5:12-13: "He uttered three thousands maxims, and his songs were one thousand and five. And he spoke concerning trees, from the cedar, which is in Lebanon, to the hyssop, which goes forth from the wall. And he spoke concerning the beast and bird and creeping thing and the fish." These allusions to classified lists of flora and fauna correspond to the Mesopotamian lexical lists and the analogous Egyptian onomastica. This indicates that it is possible that a "similar series of lexemes were compiled or copied by scribes at Solomon's court" (Lipiński 1988, 159-60). Abecedaries in combination with lexical lists would have been necessary to help scribes learn the Hebrew language (Lipiński 1988, 160).

Royal scribes were no doubt also involved in the composition of what can be called royal propaganda (see Lipiński 1988, 160-61). These texts would most likely have been read to the illiterate masses (2 Kgs. 23:1-2; Jer. 36:9-26; Neh. 8:1-3). For example, in 1 Kgs. 5:11, Solomon is said to be wiser than Ethan the Ezrahite to whom is attributed the authorship of Psalm 89. The purpose of the psalm is to assert the divine election of David and his dynasty and dates to between the tenth and eighth centuries B.C.E. No doubt Ethan was a royal scribe who worked at the Jerusalem court.

Another example is what is called the Succession Narrative (2 Samuel 9-20 and 1 Kings 1-2). Lipiński points out that its prose is quite sophisticated and it displays a type of realism similar to modern standards without the miracles found, say, in the prophetic accounts about Elijah and Elisha (1988, 160-61). He theorizes that its original intent may have been to demonstrate the illegitimate nature of Solomon's claim to the throne, which was reversed by another scribe who turned the work into a pro-Solomonic composition by adding the phrase "and the kingdom was established in the hand of Solomon" (1 Kgs. 2:46b) This renegade scribe may have been an eye-witness to the events or perhaps even the priest Abiathar who belonged to the ousted party of the heir apparent and brother of Solomon, Adonijah. Most scholars, however, view the Succession Narrative as a whole as an apology that legitimates the succession to Solomon and discredits Adonijah as unworthy and not chosen by God. Either way, as the story stands, it is an example of royal propaganda, written by scribes in service of their regal employers.

Royal scribes were especially utilized as diplomats and often had to know more than Hebrew. That they were usually bi- or tri-lingual certainly further qualified them for this kind of position. Baruch's brother Serayah was a royal scribe who was sent on a diplomatic mission to Babylon (Jer. 51:59). In the story of the Rabshakeh's confrontation with Hezekiah's officials, the ambassadors claim to understand Aramaic (2 Kgs. 18:26; Isa. 36:11), and Ahab had to deal with Aramean messengers (1 Kgs. 20:2-5). Aramaic was probably the diplomatic language during the eighth-seventh centuries B.C.E. and maybe earlier since the name of David's scribe, Shay-Shi', is an Aramaic name (Lipiński 1988, 159).

Muster Officers

The earliest Israelite scribe mentioned in the Hebrew Bible is in the Song of Deborah (Judg. 5:14): "from Zebulon, the marchers, with the staff of the scribe." Here his function is that of a muster officer, who is one who takes an account of troops, and of their equipment, i.e., a mustering officer; an inspector. It makes sense that any army would need a number of scribes to keep inventories and continually draw up an up-to-date census of soldiers. Numbers and records are extremely important for any military, and the use of literate messengers is as well.

Judges/Attorneys

At the village level and beyond, scribes would have been necessary for composing various legal documentation and to serve as witnesses to contracts. This would enable them to offer legal advice, especially since they were the few who could read the Torah and interpret it competently. The "officials" installed by the monarchy as judges (Deut. 16:18-20; cf. 2 Chron. 19:4-11), perhaps in place of the traditional elders, may have been trained as scribes. Again, being literate would have greatly enhanced the ability to serve in this role.

Specialists

This category includes scribes who specialized to work in certain professions that required technical training beyond the basic scribal education or specialized in the composition of a particular mode of literature (prophetic or priestly/legal literature) or worked exclusively with certain professional groups like the prophets and priests.

Prophetic Scribes

Prophetic scribes are defined as scribes who followed prophets and recorded their oracles. They appear to have largely specialized in the composition of prophetic literature and perhaps in bioi of the prophets' lives. Baruch is the quintessential prophetic scribe who recorded the oracles of Jeremiah, whom he followed, apparently as both a disciple and as his personal scribe. Baruch and Jeremiah had support from the powerful royal scribal family of Shaphan. Baruch even read from a scroll containing Jeremiah's prophecy in two scribal chambers (Jer. 36:10, 12, 15). There has even been a bullae found or clay seal found that contains the name of this prophetic scribe: "[Belonging] to Berachyahu, son of Neriyahu, the scribe," with a fingerprint, though its authenticity has been disputed (see Cook 2005, 73-75).

Since Jeremiah needed a scribe to record his oracles, it seems to imply that prophets were often not literate and had to rely on scribes to record their lives and words. Jeremiah is said to have sent a letter to the exiles in Babylonia in chapter 29, but it is not indicated whether Jeremiah himself composed the letter or dictated to a scribe. Or it could suggest that Jeremiah could write simple letters but not compose literature, like the complex poetry that is reflected in his oracles. Similarly, Isaiah is told by God to write out the name of his son, "Maher-shalal-hash-baz," i.e., "The spoil speeds, the prey hastens" (Isa. 8:1). This assumes that the prophet had "at least a rudimentary knowledge of how to write" (Schniedewind 2004, 86).

Anson F. Rainey has argued that much of the material in the books of Samuel, Kings, and Chronicles comes from two prophetic schools, one from the north and the other from south (Rainey and Notley 1996, 171-74). He points to references to accounts made by prophets like Samuel, Nathan, and Gad, who are listed as sources for the reign of David by the Chronicler (1 Chron. 29:29-30). Other prophetic materials are said to come from the prophets Jehu (2 Chron. 20:34), Isaiah (2 Chron. 32:32), and Iddo (2 Chron. 12:15). He maintains that these prophets served as both prophets and advisors to the various kings and that they essentially served as biographers for the respective kings. Rainey even suggests that the alleged "E" ("Elohist") and "J" ("Yahwist") documents of the Pentateuch are the products of these prophetic schools, the former from the north and the latter from the south (1996, 174).

This is certainly possible. It is similar to the roles that many of the Emar scribes assumed, who worked closely with the king, with some even being in charge of cultic activities. These prophetic accounts, if not fictive, would mean that these writing prophets would have to have received scribal training in order to compose the biographies. Nathan is an interesting example of how the various professional roles overlapped in ancient Israel. He worked closely with both David and Solomon. He is technically a prophet, but if he composed these accounts then he would have had to receive scribal training. Note also that Nathan served simultaneously as a courtier since he served in the capacity of trusted advisor for David during his reign.

Similarly to Rainey, David Peterson refers to a type of prophet he calls a prophetic historian, who does not actually have any title in Hebrew (1997, 29). They are untitled intermediaries "who wrote the prophetic speeches, stories or comments embedded in the deuteronomistic history" (Peterson 1997, 29). They valued the prophetic word highly and testified to their power (1 Kgs. 12:15; 2 Kgs. 24:2).

Annette Schellenberg has argued that the prophetic compositions are not likely to have been authored by royal scribes because they would have been too loyal to the king to criticize him (2010, 285–309). She believes the prophetic literature was created without any institutional support but rather by followers and disciples of the prophets, and many would follow her. However, the Deuteronomistic History, which is frequently viewed as being authored by royal scribes, often expresses a critical perspective regarding the monarchy and the individual kings (e.g., 1 Samuel 8). And further, the finished form of all the prophetic books would have been produced during the exilic and postexilic period, when there was no Israelite king!

Priestly Scribes

Not all priests were probably literate. A book like Leviticus no doubt required an author(s) who was both a priest and scribe because of the technical knowledge required for writing about all the rituals and tabernacle architecture. The authors of the "Priestly" source, no doubt, were simultaneously priests and scribes, though much of this source does not reflect exclusively priestly concerns. But priests who mainly conducted rituals or served as custodians (at one time, the Levites) would not need to be literate.

Physicians/Diviners/Oneiromancers

Levitical priests probably served as "physicians" who treated the various diseases of the ancient Israelites. The concern for skin diseases, inaccurately translated as "leprosy," indicate such a profession (Leviticus 14). Max Weber, in fact, theorizes that Levitical priests were catalysts in the comparatively greater degree of rationalization in the Israelite religion through their diagnosis and treatment of various diseases/crises and through their discernment of legal infractions (1976, 212-18, 222, 228-29, 235). The Israelite treatment of disease was more rational in that the cure for diseases involved atonement for sins rather than the appeal to magic typical of other ancient Near Eastern medico-exorcist practice. It makes sense that literate Levitical priests would be necessary for this profession since the commandments were so varied and complex.

Daniel was a wise scribe trained in all the Babylonian literature (Dan. 1:17), but he also appears to have specialized in the art of the interpretation of dreams (oneiromancy), a form of divination. Though Joseph's life does not indicate scribal training, his expertise in dream interpretation would have normally required such an education and specialization, though God's inspiration is the biblical source of his skill (Gen. 40:8).

Yoram Cohen and Late Bronze Age Wisdom Literature

In this last part of this chapter, we want to appeal to two Assyriologists for help with theorizing the place of wisdom literature within the Israelite scribal curriculum. The first is Yoram Cohen again, who has written on LBA wisdom literature, particularly focusing on the scribal schools at Emar, Ḥattuša, and Ugarit. Cohen briefly surveys how Assyriologists have reacted to the utilization of a concept from biblical studies to categorization wisdom-like texts, which began with William Lambert, a famous British Assyriologist (2013, 8). While Assyriologists have generally found the classification an empty literary category (Cohen 2013, 12), Cohen and a few others are not so negative and find the category useful (12-13).

His own approach involves looking at three facets: the Mesopotamian view of wisdom literature, key themes, and contextualizing wisdom literature. As for the Mesopotamian view of wisdom, Cohen believes that there is evidence, such as the Old Babylonian library catalogs, that the Mesopotamians did recognize a genre we would call wisdom literature, even though its boundaries are fuzzy (2013, 13-14). As for key themes, Cohen categorizes wisdom literature into positive and negative wisdom, the former being more traditional and conservative, while the latter refers to a more critical or subversive perspective (2013, 14-16). Positive wisdom is represented by the Sumerian "Proverb Collection" and "The Instructions of Shuruppak," where a "father instructs his son on how to achieve a proper life," and for the LBA by the first part (the father's advice) of *Šimâ Milka* or the "Instructions of Šūpê-amēli" (2013, 14). Negative wisdom is more critical and involves two themes: the view that everything is valueless, and, thus, the admonition to enjoy life before the eternal sleep (carpe diem ethic) (2013, 15). It is represented by the Old Babylonian Sumerian compositions "Nothing is of Value," and in the LBA by "The Ballad of the Early Rulers," "Enlil and Namzitarra," and the son's part in *Šimâ Milka.*"

Cohen ends by pondering what the matrix and purpose of critical or negative wisdom was (2013, 15-16). He maintains that it emerged in the Old Babylonian period as the scribes began to come to terms with the mortality of humanity and began to feel the great distance between the gods and mortals. He believes it did not emerge from particular historical crises or social circumstances but represents more a perennial intellectual concern. It is reflected beyond the wisdom literature in the heroic epics where the protagonists experience tragedy and disaster in the end, such as in the "Epic of Gilgamesh."

As for the third facet, that of contextualization, Cohen focuses on the specific function the wisdom literature had among the Mesopotamian and LBA scribal curricula and its connection with the larger respective socio-historical and political milieus. He assumes an intuitive approach that perceives wisdom literature as a common humanistic tradition, and he hints that this literature functions as one component of a larger system of thinking among the scribes. Cohen spends most of the rest of his introduction on this third facet, which we will now summarize.

Cohen focuses on the archaeological contexts of wisdom texts at Ugarit, Ḫattuša, and Emar (2013, 21-35). He emphasizes that wherever cuneiform tablets were found, school materials were present with them. This suggests that learning to write occurred in "schools" and not outside this institution (2013, 23). Since we have already discussed the curriculum in the OB schools and the WP, I will not repeat Cohen's summary here.

Cohen next exams the archaeological context of the three cities and shows how wisdom literature is always found within a "school" context (2013, 37-54). The following will present a few examples of finds at the cities that indicate the nature of the scribal curricula. At Ḫattuša, three wisdom texts were found; one was unprovenanced (the location of its finding was not recorded) (2013, 40). But two others were found in the Lower City in the House on the Slope. A collection of proverbs were found within the vicinity of various rituals, a myth, and an administrative list. A fragment of the *Šimâ Milka* was found also next to ritual, oracle, and historical texts, cult inventories, and some divinatory materials. And immediately outside the house were found schooling materials: lexical lists, *naru* literature (fictitious autobiography), a hymn, and also ritual and historical texts. Also found in the Upper City of Ḫattuša in Building K, which may have been an administrative center, were a selection of rituals, festivals, Hittite historical compositions, some international letters, instructions, oaths, the Hittite Law Code, and a Hittite version of the "Epic of Gilgamesh" (2013, 42-43).

At Ugarit, in the Lamaštu archive, named after an incantation found there against a demoness, lexical texts as well as omens, grammatical texts, and incantations were found (Cohen 2013, 49). It may have served as a school. One manuscript of the "The Ballad of Early Rulers" was also found here. North of this archive is the House of the Hurrian Priest, which contained tablets concerning magic, rituals, and mythology. Also, divination was studied here because a collection of inscribed clay models of sheep livers was found. The wisdom composition "The Righteous Sufferer" was found here. In the archive of the *Maison aux tablettes*, lexical, literary, and omen texts were found. A manuscript of the *Šimâ Milka* was found, copied by a student. Nearby was found a copy of "The Ballad of Early Rulers" (2013, 49-50). Also, a fragment of "Atraḥasis" was just outside. Finally, the House of Urtenu contained royal letters, commercial transactions, administrative texts, and school texts such as lexical lists, fragments of the "Epic of Gilgamesh," and omen literature (50).

At Emar, in the Temple of the Diviner, which Cohen believes was a school and run by the Zāba'la family, were found three broad genres: administrative texts; cultic or religious texts; scholarly materials, including lexical lists, omen compendia, incantations, and Mesopotamian literature, in which category wisdom compositions are to be included. (Cohen 2013, 52) The wisdom texts were the *Šimâ Milka*, "The Ballad of Early Rulers," "Enlil and Namizaitarra," and "The Fowler and His Wife."

Finally, Cohen theorizes about the place of wisdom literature within the scribal curriculum at these three cities (2013, 55-77). To do this, he first discusses the sequence in which wisdom literature was studied within the curriculum of the OB and Kassite periods because they represent the paradigm from which the LBA curricula develop (2013, 55-64). He first treats proverb collections (2013, 57-59) and points out the two standard theories about their function: 1) didactic, in that they taught scribes societal values; 2) pedagogical, in that they enabled scribes to learn Sumerian grammar more easily before moving on to more complex compositions. He shows how the evidence supports both views to some extent. He then discusses the wisdom literature in general (2013, 60) and notes that the short wisdom compositions were studied at the end of the first stage of the curriculum, while the longer compositions, like "The Instruction of Šuruppak," "The Farmer's Instructions," and the debate poems, were studied in the second stage.

Cohen then discusses the relationship between the wisdom compositions and the other genres of the OB curriculum (2013, 60-61). Several works could be placed on a *Sammeltafeln* (collection tablet). For example, The "Ballad of Early Rulers" appears with a "Prayer of Marduk," a "Praise of Abi-ešuḫ," and the wisdom text "Nothing Is of Value." The wisdom text "Enlil and Namzitarra" was found on the same tablet with "Nothing Is of Value," a lament, a literary letter, and a school composition. And a collection of proverbs was included with "Nothing is of Value" on the same tablet. He also points out how wisdom compositions were often grouped together in catalog lists.

Cohen emphasizes that wisdom compositions were studied in tandem with other types of literature (2013, 61-62). He also notes that the proverbs and lexical lists reinforce each other. The epic literature often cites proverbs found in the collections and vice versa. He notes that there are close ties between the proverbs and laments. Based on the *Sammeltafeln* phenomenon and the regular listing of wisdom texts together in catalogs, Cohen concludes that in the OB curriculum there was a self-consciously recognized genre of wisdom literature that was an important part of the scribal curriculum within a larger body of texts and literature.

Cohen then treats the Kassite period that represents a renaissance of literary activity and notes that the important wisdom texts *Ludlel Bēl Nēmeqi* and "The Babylonian Theodicy" were produced during this time (2013, 63-64). The former was studied in the more advanced stage of scribal education during the first millennium, so it probably occupied the same role during the Kassite period. Much of the OB wisdom corpus was apparently studied and copied during this period.

Finally, Cohen attempts to reconstruct the LBA scribal curriculum and the place of wisdom literature within it (2013, 64-72). Using the OB curriculum to fill in the gaps, he theorizes that there were two stages of education. The first stage began with a study of the lexical lists, which acquainted the scribal apprentice with cuneiform. The second stage involved the introduction of more complicated lists, like a list of deities. At Emar one of these lists is accompanied by a popular incantation on the same tablet. Supposedly, the student studied the incantation after the lexical assignment. In the more advanced second stage, scholarly or professional literature was studied: omen literature, incantations, and magic-medical texts. Epic literature was also probably studied at this stage, like "Gilgamesh" and "Atraḥasis." Cohen argues that the longer wisdom compositions were studied during this latter stage, while he implies that proverbs were used in the first stage.

Paul-Alain Beaulieu and Babylonian Wisdom Literature

The second Assyriologist is Paul-Alain Beaulieu, who summarizes the social history of the Babylonian wisdom tradition. He points out that the Babylonian words for wisdom, like *nēmequ*, are associated with the deities, Marduk, and his father, Ea. The Babylonian terms overlap largely with Hebrew wisdom terms like *chokmah* but primarily refer to skills and then more largely to "all the skills and knowledge necessary to civilized life" (2007, 4).

Beaulieu theorizes that in the OB period wisdom was intricately connected with kingship and was divine in origin, ultimately going back to the antediluvian divine sages and passed down through kings (2007, 5-7). He points out that Zisudra or Utnapishtim, the Babylonian Noah, represents a watershed for the transmission of wisdom. He was the son of Shuruppak and the last king before the flood. Through him wisdom is passed on to humans, and specifically through Gilgamesh. Beaulieu in fact argues that in the "Epic of Gilgamesh," the protagonist is involved in a search for wisdom, which Zisudra supplies to him. Again, wisdom means the cultural knowledge that brings civilization that is connected intricately to kingship. In the "Death of Gilgamesh," the notion of wisdom included also the cultic rites in service of the deities, which extends even to the art of exorcism and incantation. Gilgamesh becomes the culture bearer who passes on wisdom and the art of civilization to the postdiluvian kings. In fact, in the "Instructions of Ur-Ninurta," a king of the First Dynasty of Isin, the king is portrayed as a restorer of justice, order, and ritual practices after the flood. Thus, this wisdom composition represents direct royal ideology.

Beaulieu theorizes on how the realm of wisdom eventually passed from the hands of kings and his scribes (*edubba*) to the expertise of the exorcist, the lamentation singer, and the diviner, all united in placating the angry deities and demons who brought disease (2007, 8-18). The wisdom works "*Ludlul bēl nēmei*" ("Let me praise the Lord of Wisdom") and the "Babylonian Theodicy" are critical in discerning this transformation. In the former, the problem of theodicy is essentially resolved through the art of exorcism, though the real cause of the sickness is never discerned. In fact, the author identifies himself as an exorcist! Beaulieu notes that "*Ludlul*" was studied in the Neo-Babylonian schools in the second stage of education, which was devoted to the craft of exorcism and prepared scribes for further specialization in various disciplines.

The Place of Wisdom Literature within the Israelite Scribal Curriculum

The following is speculative because we do not have the kind of archaeological and epigraphic evidence that has emerged at Ugarit, Ḫattuša, and Emar. However, reasonable conjecture can be made about the education of scribes and their curriculum in ancient Israel. First of all, scribalism in EIA Palestine was not institutionalized at first, as early abecedaries such as that found at Tell Zayit, a small village, attests. During the reigns of David and Solomon, Israelite scribalism was co-opted by the monarchy and developed quickly. During the reign of Rehoboam scribes were competent enough to create annals that accurately recorded the years of a king's reign.

Only a few decades later did Hebrew become standardized, eventually with two dialects, northern and southern.

In the first stage of scribal training, we can conjecture that abecedaries were used in conjunction with lexical lists (Solomon's flora and fauna lists) to enable the Israelite scribe to learn the basics of Hebrew and prepare them for eventual specialization. Proverbs were studied early on during this first phase. Something like the proverb collections represented in Proverbs 10-29 were studied. This did four things. First, it taught them literary skills, such as the art of parallelism, the fundamental structure of all Hebrew poetry, to be examined later. Second, it also reinforced standard Israelite values, norms, and sometimes folkways, like how to behave before a ruler (e.g., Prov. 23:1-8) or how to deal with trouble-makers (fools). This would have served them well if they worked later as governmental officials or were employed in the private sector. Third, it also reinforced religious values and emphasized sole loyalty to Yahweh, the chief deity of the nation. And, fourth, many sophisticated kinds of aphorisms (more on these later) would have stimulated the scribes cognitively. This function is significant because a smart scribe makes a better one.

During the later phase of the first stage, Israelite scribes may have had to memorize excerpts from other genres of literature like psalms, erotica (Song of Songs), historiographical, and/or legal material, and then copy it down from memory. Scribes would probably also have studied more complex lexical lists. They were probably also taught basic administrative genres during this stage, such as letters and diplomatic documents, various contracts, inventory lists (learning the Egyptian hieratic symbols for numbers), etc.

During the second stage of education scribes would have been exposed to longer compositions like mythological texts and historiographical or epic literature, perhaps some form of the story of

David or even the patriarchs. Perhaps some version of the creation accounts was studied (Genesis 1-3). And as the legal material in the Pentateuch developed, this may have been studied too. The prophetic texts emerged early, so they may have been studied as well. These, in many ways, parallel the omen texts of the Mesopotamian curricula. The Israelite scribes would have been very interested in discerning the will of God and in divining the future, which was also a primary concern of the kings. As already noted, Egyptian scribes were also very interested in prognostication.

During the postexilic period, the book of Proverbs as a whole, as opposed to the sentence collections, would probably have been studied at this more advanced stage, with the sophisticated introduction (Proverbs 1-9) (see Weeks 2007) that introduces wisdom and folly as personifications. The instruction of king Lemuel's mother and the ode to the virtuous wife, both in Proverbs 31, would be appropriate during this stage. During the postexilic period, the books of Job and Ecclesiastes would also have been studied at this stage, which largely bring the negative or critical perspective into view, a necessity for scribes as they matured.

After this second stage, scribes could specialize and become priestly or prophetic scribes, specializing in these respective modes of literature and working for the priests and prophets. Or they might become physicians, as Levitical priests. Or they might specialize in the military sciences and become military scribes. Specialized scribes would attain high positions within whatever institution they were employed.

Conclusion

All the evidence points to Israelite scribes having been trained similarly to the system employed in the WP, especially the city of Ugarit, with its alphabetic script. Though it would have been easier for Israelite scribes to learn alphabetic Hebrew, it still required a lot of training and practice. One should distinguish between functional literacy, where one could write one's name and do other simple tasks, and a literacy that involves the reading and composition of sophisticated texts, especially literature. Israelite scribes were most likely bi- or trilingual, in view of the necessary diplomatic assignments. Some sort of educational system had to have been in place by the ninth or no later than the eighth century B.C.E., as indicated by the standardization of Hebrew in Judah and North Israel. Because scribes would have been in such great demand, whether by the court, Temple, or village, their status would have been relatively high. Israelite scribes would have served numerous roles, often occupying more than one station simultaneously. This fits the picture found within WP scribalism and would have been necessitated by the tiny size of the nations of Judah and North Israel.

Israelite apprentice scribes would have never just studied the wisdom literature in their training. They would have had to work with a number of genres, both administrative and scholarly. Many of these scribes would not have had to specialize in a specific genre and would have simply worked as a lower level administrator for the palace or Temple or simply at an administrative center or village. At the village level they would simply have helped the masses with the various documentary needs, but their broader training would have helped them serve as intellectual functionaries for the people and to serve as liaison between the villagers and the larger political entities.

Interestingly, a recent archaeological find supports the view that wisdom texts were never studied in isolation by scribal apprentices. Aramaic scribal exercises on bowls were found at Maresha in Idumaea (Edom) dating to the early second century (Eshel, Kloner, and Puech 2007, 39-62). On the bowls were found a wisdom text, a harvest registration, a receipt, a blessing, and a marriage contract.

6

The Wisdom Corpus as a Mode of Literature

Genres

We ended the last chapter by speculating on the place of wisdom literature in the Israelite scribal curriculum. In this chapter we want to focus on the nature of this corpus. This will involve looking at the conventions that distinguish it from the other modes of literature in the Hebrew Bible but also how this mode interacts and relates to the other modes. But first a brief introduction to genre theory is necessary.[1]

Genres are basically templates formed in the minds of people that enable them to recognize types or kinds of literature that share what can be called a family resemblance. This implies that genres involve literary patterning. This patterning is important for understanding

1. For introductions to genre criticism (literary theory), see Frow (2005); Fowler (1982); Hirsch (1967, 68-126); Dowd, Stevenson, and Strong (2006). For its application for biblical studies, see Sneed (2011); Sparks (2005, 6-21); Sandy and Giese (1995); Newsom (2007, 19-30).

genres. That a particular speech or literary form shares features with other forms means that it somehow belongs to this same group and attains an identity of sorts by belonging. The sharing of features also reveals that certain expectations are inherent to this grouping of literary forms. Thus, a degree of predictability is intrinsic to genres, and this reveals an important component of their function. When a reader or hearer is exposed to a genre, immediately certain conventions and assumptions come to mind and prepare the reader/ hearer for what is to follow. For example, the cinematic horror fan knows just from the title or from previews that a certain horror movie can be expected to have things going bump in the night, dark and dreary scenes, and unusual music. And there are always certain rules involved. For example, in one subgenre of horror movies, the vampire films, vampires cannot enter a home without being invited, are repelled by crosses and garlic, and must avoid the sun, etc.

The conventional nature of genres mitigates unnecessary shock to the person and actually enables a smoother flow of communication. Because of this predictability one could say that genres are the "lubrication" of communication. They help grease the tracks of communication and ease the conveyance of information to the recipient. Without genres, communication would in effect come screeching to a stop, and one would constantly have to stop and invent the wheel every time she wanted to express herself.

The patterning involved in genres is what is referred to as its universalism—what is held in common among the examples of a genre. A work of literature or speech does not technically belong to a particular genre. Rather, it participates in it; it shares in the genre's conventional world to one degree or another. However, the universalism or patterning implied in genres also simultaneously implies its opposite: the particularism of any communicatory event. Every example of communication participates in one or more genres, yet it is more than these. All verbal and literary forms, thus, are unique in certain ways. They are more than the patterning.

A special type of particularity involves the actual activation of a genre. An author can choose to depart from the rules, to an extent. Since genres bring to the reader/hearer certain assumptions and conventions, it enables an author who utilizes a particular genre to do something unexpected. In other words, it allows authors and speakers to shock their audiences who have been lulled into simply accepting the conventions of the particular genre.

As an example in the wisdom literature, the author of Ecclesiastes uses the genre of royal autobiography in the book unconventionally. In royal inscriptions in the ancient Near East, this genre is used, and it basically brags about all the king or pharaoh's accomplishments, especially his construction projects and military victories. The inscription is usually inscribed in a stone monument like a stele or on the side of a palace or temple for all the public to view. The function of such inscriptions is obviously royal propaganda, and exaggeration and hyperbole is to be expected. The author of Ecclesiastes assumes the role of a great oriental king who builds immaculate buildings and gardens and attains great wealth, no doubt alluding partially to Solomon's reign (2:1-10). Yet, what is shocking is that instead of bragging about how grand and great the things he accomplished were, the Teacher proclaims the whole endeavor as futile and empty (2:11)! In a sense, the Teacher deconstructs the stereotypical royal autobiographies (see Seow 1995, 275-87). This represents a subversion of the generic conventions, a deliberate sabotaging of it for the author's own purposes. So, one can see the delight in the Teacher's eyes as he knows that he will be leading his readers down a particular, conventional path that will allow him to suddenly ambush them in their complacency and shock them with an unexpected assessment of royal accomplishment. So, here we see the tension between the universal and the particular used for rhetorical and literary effect.

Sidebar 11: Mesha Stone

I am Mesha from Dibon, ruler of Moab . . . Omri, ruler of Israel, invaded Moab year after year because Chemosh, the divine patron of Moab, was angry with his people. When the son of Omri succeeded him during my reign, he bragged; "I too will invade Moab." However, I defeated the son of Omri and drove Israel out of our land forever . . . I built Qarhoh with gates and towers, a palace and reservoirs. I also decreed: "Every household in Qarhoh is to have its own cistern." I had my prisoners of war from Israel dig the cisterns of Qarhoh. I built Aroer and a highway through the Arnon valley. I also rebuilt the cities of Beth-bamoth and Bezer for fifty households from Dibon. I reigned in peace over hundreds of villages which I had conquered . . . (ninth century B.C.E. Moab) (Benjamin and Matthews 2006, 168-69).

Generic Worlds versus Worldviews

Genres create worlds, not worldviews. When an anthropologist or religion expert speaks of worldview, he means the way the people of a particular culture see the world. All members of a particular culture share the same worldview. The worldviews of ancient Near Eastern peoples were largely the same. They differed only in the details. For instance, the Israelites were monotheists, while their neighbors were polytheists. However, both shared a supernatural view of the world. They also believed that medical illnesses were caused by the anger of a deity or demons. The New Testament is more explicit about the connection of demons with illness than the Hebrew Bible. Thus, the ancient Near Eastern people shared a worldview that was largely the same, and the differences among themselves are insignificant in comparison with the distance between our own modern, secular worldview and theirs.

Generic worlds are an entirely different matter. They constitute literary worlds that an author enters into and decides to engage, in order to organize and shape the material and information she wants to communicate. Again, for example, horror flicks usually concentrate on the night time instead of the day to convey a literally dark ambiance to match the dark content of the movie. There is a reason why vampires are active only during the night. The *Alien* movies are almost totally shot during the night. Storms and rain are also a typical convention. Eerie or anticipatory music also helps to create the effect of the horror world.

Another example is noir movies, from the French word for "night." These movies began to be produced after WWII and are basically very dark and cynical gangster movies (see Crowther 1989, 7-12). Usually there is a detective and femme fatale involved, and the protagonist knows that he is doomed to die in the end, yet he presses on. These movies have a number of conventional features like narration of the protagonist, unique camera shots, and shooting at night and in the rain. Many psychologists believe these films arose to deal with disillusionment and trauma many Americans, especially soldiers, experienced during and after the war (see Bould 2005, 49).

More recently the old noir movies have been revitalized, including some of the standard conventions. This time they are not usually gangster related and are called neo-noir. A cult classic, *Blade Runner*, is an example. The original ending of this movie did not have the happy ending of Decker and the female robot flying off into paradise in the bright sunshine. This change was due to the typical audience that wants a happy ending, which a true noir movie resists. The rest of the movie is set in a future Japanese setting and is shot entirely at night and in the rain. The ending of the movie, *No Country for Old Men*, was also disappointing to audiences who wanted justice for the villain Anton Chigurh. The latter film is also a neo-noir but does not utilize literal darkness to convey its dark world, which shows that horror or noir movies have all sorts of conventions but there are no hard and fast rules about which must be used. A classic neo-noir film that involves a femme fatale is *Basic Instinct*. The *Sin City* movies are also classic noir and filled with femmes fatales.

Generic worlds then are fictive, artificial worlds that are fashioned to help create the mood or atmosphere and features most conducive for communicating the message or content the author/director wants to convey. One should never confuse these conventional worlds with the actual worldview of the same author or director. That the Coen brothers love to create noir dramas, often simultaneously comedies, does not mean they are dark people themselves or see the world in terms of the cynicism. It is rather that they have chosen to use a particular genre in which to convey whatever truth or message they want to put forward or even no message at all! This choice has nothing to do with the way they see the world. Their worldview is the typical perspective of middle class suburban America, from which they hail.

Biblical Generic Worlds

Genres can be either simple or complex (Frow 2005, 29-50). Simple genres do not convey much of a world. One of the simplest biblical genres is the aphorism, such as in the aphoristic collections in Proverbs, e.g., the maxims in 10:1-22:16. These have been improperly called proverbs, for proverbs are by definition current sayings known by everyone in a society. But these sayings are identified as coming from the hand of King Solomon (Prov. 10:1). This means that here, whether one believes the historicity of the superscription or not, these sayings are presented as the creations of the king and not true proverbs.

The maxims themselves do not convey a clear and definitive world because each deals with various topics that range widely. One might call the world of the Hebrew aphorism the world of values and social norms because that is generally what they treat. But this is not very helpful and largely abstract. However, one could argue that certain aphorisms convey a particular world, the world of the scribe or courtier. For example, there are two groupings of instructions (Prov. 23:1-8; 25:1-7) that are rather "courtly." The following verses assume that the original addressee would appear regularly before the king and rulers, an expectation that certainly fits the courtier:

When you sit to eat with a ruler,
indeed consider what is before you.
Set a knife to your throat,
if you have an appetite (23:1-2).

Do not boast before the king
and do not stand in the place of the great,
for it is better for one to say to you,
"Come up here," than to be placed lower,
before the nobleman whom your eyes have seen (25:6-7).

However, most of the maxims do not reflect strictly courtly concerns, so one would be amiss to describe the world reflected by the aphorisms in Proverbs as reflecting a professional code or class ethic (see Kovacs 1974, 176). Since the book of Proverbs is mainly about values, societal norms, and ethics, these concerns would be true of any Israelite, not just the scribes. However, this does not mean the audience was not scribes, only that the world it projects is not overtly scribal! The "Instructions of Ptahhotep," however, project a more overtly scribal world.

Complex genres, however, create more complete worlds. For example, apocalyptic literature found in the both the Hebrew Bible and Christian Bible has a sophisticated and fairly comprehensive world. Daniel 7-12 is considered full-blown apocalyptic, while Ezekiel 38-39 and several of the Minor Prophetic books, like Joel and Zechariah (1-8), contain apocalyptic elements, called proto-apocalyptic. This literature is usually viewed as a development from Israelite prophetic literature. Apocalyptic literature conveys a very colorful world marked by epochs, celestial omens, earthquakes, monsters, angels, plagues, pestilence, mysteries, revelations, blood, fire, and death.

Technically speaking, apocalyptic literature is not a genre but rather a mode of literature. This is indicated by the use of the adjective "apocalyptic" modifying "literature." Similarly, one speaks of a *comic* play or *heroic* epic. Mode operates on a higher level of abstraction than a genre. The apocalyptic literature is a mode of literature that includes numerous genres within it: symbolic dream vision, epiphany, angelic discourse, revelatory dialogue, midrash, etc. (see Collins 1984, 6-9). Other modes of literature in the Hebrew Bible would include the prophetic literature, historical literature, and the legal material, etc. And, of course, the wisdom literature is also a mode of literature, not properly a genre, that includes a whole host of genres: aphorisms, dialogue, narrative, monologue, etc.

The world of apocalyptic literature is especially apt for those at the bottom of the social hierarchy, suffering oppression and persecution, such as the original audiences of Dan. 7-12 and book of Revelation.

The sociologist Karl Mannheim called this a utopian worldview, which wants to change the way the world is currently, in contradiction to an ideological worldview, which seeks to maintain the status quo (Mannheim 1936). This implies that the differing social classes may see the world in different ways, at least to a degree.

Modern Genres and Social Settings

Genres are intricately connected to social settings. As Frow put it, "The work of a genre . . . is to mediate between a social situation and the text which realizes certain features of this situation, or which responds strategically to its demands. Genre shapes strategies for occasion; it gets a certain kind of work done" (2005, 14). For example, a proverb is frequently used to clinch an argument with someone you are debating. A well-placed proverb can sometimes be more effective in winning a debate than logical argumentation. This is due chiefly to the high ethos of a proverb. Ethos is a rhetorical term that refers to the credibility of an author or speaker. Proverbs convey a sense of unquestioned and impeachable veracity because everyone is taught them from the time they are small and discern their axiomatic character. Their currency also helps buttress this effect since proverbs are known by all people in a community and, thus, are part of the public domain and represent the people's wisdom.

In the judicial arena there are a number of genres that help the legal process run more smoothly during a trial. For example, a juror has to affirm an oath to weigh the evidence and not let biases color his/her judgment. Similarly, a witness must also affirm an oath to only speak the truth. Often, lawyers will refer to dispositions that have already been given orally but now are written records. The question and answer format of dispositions is part of the genre, and it enables lawyers, whether for the plaintiff or defendant, to better analyze the evidence of the case.

More complex genres, like literary genres, are less tied to specific social contexts (see Frow 2005, 16-17). This is because they are more abstract and are less dependent on a particular concrete context. For example, the detective novel is found in book or electronic format and can be purchased and read almost anywhere, so it has few limitations. It is usually read for entertainment purposes.

Biblical Genres and Their Social Setting

All biblical genres are obviously literary and, thus, are not as bound to a particular social context. In written form they are confined only to the scroll and so limited to how that particular scroll was used. But determining this is somewhat speculative. For example, most scholars believe the songs in the Psalter were originally used in the worship at the Temple or perhaps at other cultic sties. For example, in 1 Sam. 2:1-10, Hannah brings little Samuel back to the shrine at Shiloh to dedicate him to the service of Lord because the Lord had answered her prayer for a son. However, the "song of thanksgiving" she sings is actually a hymn similar to the ones in the Psalter, which celebrate God's character as creator and sustainer in a very general way (e.g., Pss. 29, 33, 68). In fact, it could be ripped out its context here and placed in the Psalter without any ill effect. It contains no allusions to anything specific in Hannah's crisis. So, one see here evidence for the oral performance of a psalm in a cultic context, but, simultaneously, the literary character of the song and its suitability as one of the psalms in the Psalter scroll, where it could be sung by someone else besides Hannah.

One can go another step and ask if all the psalms in the Psalter were used in cultic contexts? Psalm 1 is usually considered a wisdom psalm because it reflects many features of the wisdom literature. It is also not addressed to God but rather to any reader or hearer who will listen: it is didactic. This psalm could have been sung no doubt, even in a cultic setting. But it also could have been simply read and studied for devotional purposes. But the other psalms, even the non-wisdom ones, could have also been studied, and not sung, as well, much as we study the psalms today. This shows the complexity of context and how the original context is only the first of many latter contexts that reactivate a particular genre.

The social setting of the wisdom literature is more complex but in a different way. Unlike the story of Hannah, we do not have stories where regular Israelites employ aphorisms (they do employ proverbs: Judg. 8:21; 1 Sam. 24:13; 1 Kgs. 20:11) or use other sapiential genres. The book of Job contains the dialogue Job has with his three friends. In the dialog, each often cites aphorisms (e.g., Job 32:7; 34:3). However, all of this appears contrived. Their interactions are all in poetry, and there is no evidence that Israelite debates were actually performed in this manner. This again points to the literary character of the wisdom literature. While this is self-evident and seems insignificant, it is extremely important to consider. The pertinent question is then not how were the sapiential genres employed orally in Israelite society, which is all highly speculative. Rather, the important question is how this literary corpus was used and by whom? What was its original *Sitz im Leben* (or "situation in life") as literature? This too is speculative but not to the same degree.

For the book of Proverbs, we have more hints than in the other wisdom books, but even it is quite limited. The collections of aphorisms in Proverbs are introduced by a long introduction (chaps. 1-9) that begins with a prolog, which provides this information:

The aphorisms of Solomon, son of David, king of Israel.

For knowing wisdom and discipline, for comprehending words of insight;

for learning the discipline of insight, justice, judgment, and integrity;

for giving the simple cleverness, and to the youth knowledge and discretion.

Let the wise hear and increase learning, and let the insightful attain wise counsel.

For understanding an aphorism and enigma, the words of the wise and their riddles.

The fear of the Lord is the beginning of knowledge,

but wisdom and discipline the fool despises (1:1-7).

And then the reader is immediately addressed in v. 8: "Hear, my son." The problem with his description is that it is incredibly vague. Who are the "wise" and the "simple"? We know who Solomon is but who is "my son"? Does he intend Rehoboam?

Most scholars do not take the attribution of the aphorisms to Solomon seriously. As in the rest of the wisdom literature in the ancient Near East, wisdom compositions are generally ascribed to a wise, well known sage or king. But these ascriptions are generally regarded as fictitious and intended to lend more credibility to the composition. In the "Instructions of Shuruppak," the oldest wisdom text ever (ca. 2600 B.C.E.), the work is presented as the words of the king of the city of Shuruppak (or is that his name?) to his son by a narrator. There is no purpose given for the instructions, only that the son should listen to his father's words (Alster 2005, 57). The father is described as being wise and good with words (Alster 2005, 56). The impression is that the son will become wise and better at rhetoric by reading these maxims. The problem is that the maxims do not reflect a princely addressee but rather any owner of a household

(Alster 2005, 33). There are even some maxims that are critical of those in power: "The strong one takes away from a man's hand" (Alster 2005, 76). And they also often reflect agricultural concerns: "Don't buy an ass that brays; it will split your yoke!" (Alster 2005, 58). Thus, the information in the prolog of the collection appears to be clearly fictitious and its perspective does not fit with the content of the maxims.

Though one might think from just reading the content of the proverbs that the authors and audience were maybe farmers or the average man with a household, from our previous discussion we know that this collection was written by scribes and for scribes. The underlying assumption is that a scribal composition should reflect solely or mainly the professional or vocational concerns of scribes. But this forgets that scribes were persons like anyone else. And the daily concerns of the average Sumerian or Babylonian would have been the concern of scribes too. Sumerian scribes were certainly raised in a very agrarian milieu and most likely had their own farms that may have been tended by servants. In fact, Robert Gordis has theorized that the authors of the wisdom literature in the Hebrew Bible were absentee landlords, who made most of their earning through stewards who managed their estates in the countryside (Gordis 1971, 162). Thus, attempting to discern the intended audience and author of a composition from the content of the literature alone can be very misleading.

Along with the lexical lists that they studied, the "Instructions of Shuruppak" would have helped scribes learn Sumerian in the early stages. These maxims were also "used as a kind of source book from which the students could learn how to use apt rhetorical phrases" and, thus, are examples of scribal wit; they were not most likely actual proverbs (Alster 2005, 25). Though the "Instructions of Shuruppak" never explicitly designates scribes as the intended audience, we are practically certain that this is the case. The royal fiction in the prolog would have simply lent more authority and gravitas to the collection and helped motivate novice scribes to study the maxims more diligently.

Similarly, the "Instruction of Ptahhotep," the oldest Egyptian wisdom text (ca. 2150 B.C.E.), shares the same characteristics and fictitious nature but is even more closely aligned with the aims of the prolog to Proverbs. The instruction is not a collection of short aphorisms but rather more cohesively structured short sections that include aphorisms, although mainly consisting of short units of thematically arranged exhortations and admonitions. The "instruction" is the same genre as Proverbs 1-9, which is filled with wisdom poems and short units of thematically connected exhortation.

The "Instruction of Ptahhotep" is attributed to a revered sage who purportedly was the vizier of King Isesi and mayor of the capital. In the prolog he asks the pharaoh for permission to pass his wisdom on to his son because he has become quite old and then provides the pharaoh's response:

> May this servant be ordered to make a staff of old age,
> so as to tell him the words of those who heard,
> the ways of the ancestors,
> who have listened to the gods.
> May such be done for you,
> so that strife may be banned from the people,
> and the Two Shores may serve you!
> Said the majesty of this god:
> Instruct him then in the sayings of the past,
> may he become a model for the children of the great,
> may obedience enter him,
> and the devotion of him who speaks to him,
> no one is born wise (Lichtheim 1975, 63).

It is interesting that the sage argues that the future of the kingdom (strife eliminated and the people obedient) is dependent on forming a suitable replacement so that he might advise the pharaoh wisely. It is unlikely the pharaoh would have viewed the office of vizier so highly. But this correlates with the reference to instruction on justice and judgment in the biblical prolog (Prov. 1:2). There is no reference in the biblical prolog to the audience serving as models for the elite children but many of the maxims in the collection assume that the students will someday be governmental officials and some that indicate their character is under scrutiny (e.g., maxim about false weights: Prov. 20:10) (see especially Ansberry, 2011). In a later chapter we will examine the evidence that the intended audience of Proverbs were sons of the elite. The intended purpose of the "Instruction of Ptahhotep" to pass on the traditions of the past is not found in Proverb's prolog, but this is implied in the introduction when the father alludes to his having been educated by his own father (4:4). The emphasis on piety in "Ptahhotep" (listening to the gods) resonates with the motto of Proverbs (1:7). Its instilment of loyalty and obedience is not a part of the biblical prolog, but both the service of the king (e.g., Prov. 22:29) and, of course, God is encouraged in the collections. The pharaoh's last words discern the difficulty in educating the young and that in many ways it is unnatural. This correlates with the emphasis on discipline in the book of Proverb's prolog, and there are a few proverbs that assume this notion of the naturalness of folly (e.g., 13:24).

Concerning the themes and content of "Ptahhotep" itself, Miriam Lichtheim, the famous Egyptologist, says that it is

> . . . noteworthy that of the thirty-seven maxims with which Ptahotep instructs his son, the future vizier, not one has any bearing on the vizierate—a strange situation if the work were the genuine legacy of a vizier who is introducing his son to the highest office of the land. In fact,

the maxims embody the pragmatic wisdom of the upper-class Egyptian, and formulate a code of behavior befitting the gentlemen of the Old Kingdom (Lichtheim 1975, 7).

But again, this does not mean that a young vizier would not profit from studying the instructions. There would be more to the education of a vizier than specific instruction about his specific role as vizier. Certainly, one would have expected a vizier to be a gentleman, a man of good manners and appropriate demeanor. If the author is fictive, so is the purported audience. The work is certainly intended to go beyond the literal son of the Chief Vizier! And we know that Egyptian scribes studied this oldest genre of instruction. The instruction is very conscious of social position and one's relationship to others above and below one's station. All of this material would have been important for a scribe's training. Again, this apparent incongruence between the content of the material and the actual intended audience is exactly as in the case of the "Instructions of Shuruppak," and I would argue is true for the case of Proverbs. Rarely does one find a maxim in Proverbs whose message would be restricted to only a courtier or vizier. But this does not mean that a vizier would not profit from the book as a whole and that the majority of non-courtly aphorisms would not be salient for his education.

The tension between the prolog and the contents of both the "Instruction of Ptahhotep" and the "Instructions of Shuruppak" demonstrate that although we do not know with certainty the *Sitz im Leben* of the book of Proverbs, we can be fairly confident that it originally had a scribal audience and pedagogical purpose. The fact that Proverbs never clearly identifies its true author or audience should not hinder us from concluding that the book was important for the training of scribes, even if it was used for other purposes in latter times.

The Elusive Nature of Genres

It is important to emphasize that genres certainly exist. They are real. However, their existence is only in the minds of those who use them. Genres are simply patterns that particular texts reflect to one degree or not. This means that genres are meta-textual and that texts share in genres but do not belong to them (Frow 2005, 11).

There are innumerable ways to define or categorize a genre. It could be thematic. For instance, romance novels are categorized this way because they treat the subject of love. Detective novels contain stories about detectives who seek out cold-blooded murderers. But content is not the only feature that can identify a genre. Form and style are also an important element. For example, proverbs are not just wise sayings. Their pithy and poetical form is a necessary element. The Haiku is certainly identified by its structure and not its content. In the beginning, it treated the subject of nature, but today this is no longer the case. This shows that a genre does not necessarily demand the combination of both form and content. Haiku is formed by structure alone.

Another identifying feature of genres is mood. For example, the horror genre is primarily formed by the mood it creates in its intended audience: fear or disgust. Horror movies also have thematic aspects as well. Romance novels also share in this emphasis on mood because though the stories are about relationships between people, the mood that is elicited in the reader is the amorous. And when these end up arousing sexual images then the mood of eroticism comes to the fore and the novel begins to take on pornographic features, another genre! Tragedies and comedies obviously have a heavy mood component. But a genre can be created by a combination of these features or even only one.

A particular literary work can share in more than one genre simultaneously or be categorized generically in more than one way. Ecclesiastes provides a biblical example. Scholars have debated the specific genre of Ecclesiastes for centuries. Tremper Longman argues that the book compares favorably with fictional Akkadian autobiographies and concludes that the book's genre is a "framed wisdom autobiography" (1998, 17). Scholars today often speak of the book as framed because a third-person account of the words of "Qohelet" or the Teacher in the body of the book literally frames these words: 1:1-11//12:8-14. In contrast to Longman, Michael Fox designates the book a "fictional royal testament" (1999, 155), though he describes the book as a framed-narrative as well (1977, 83-106).

While the specific ancient Near Eastern generic categorizations are helpful, several scholars, including myself, have found it more helpful to categorize the book more broadly as pessimistic literature. This defines the book's genre in terms of mood and demeanor. Also, a closely related genre, skeptical literature, is often employed to describe Ecclesiastes. There are several ancient Near Eastern works that reflect a pessimistic and, often simultaneously, skeptical mood. For example, we have mentioned "The Ballad of Heroes" that was a standard Mesopotamian work that contains both the declaration that everything is vanity and simultaneously the carpe diem advice. The theme of death is almost always connected to the carpe diem ethic in this genre.

We have already mentioned the Egyptian "Songs of the Harper" found in tombs, which are sometimes skeptical about life after death and contain the carpe diem ethic. Both are also found in Ecclesiastes:

For the living know that they will die, but the dead know nothing. And there is not for them any reward for their memory has been extinguished. Also their love, their hate, their envy have already perished. And there is no longer a portion for them forever in what is done under the sun. Go, eat with joy your food and drink with a happy heart your wine, for God has already approved your activity. . . whatever your hand finds to do, do it while you have the strength for there is no work or planning or knowledge or knowledge or wisdom in Sheol to which you are going (9:5-7, 10).

We have already mentioned another Egyptian example of pessimistic literature is the "Admonitions of Ipuwer," which displays the topsy-turvy world motif. "Admonitions of Ipuwer" is technically an Egyptian instruction but is very bleak. It depicts the world of the former pharaoh, a world where everything seems upside down and quite anarchic. Ecclesiastes also employs this specific motif:

> There exists an evil I have seen under the sun, as an error which goes forth from a ruler. A fool is set in high places, whereas the rich abide in a low estate. I have seen slaves on horses and princes walking around like slaves on foot (10:5-7).

The topsy-turvy motif is part of the author's general depiction of a generally dark and unpleasant world, which he frequently describes as filled with "evils." One of the author's favorite ways to make his case is to provide anecdotes. For example, in Eccles. 6:1-6, the Teacher says that he has seen an individual to whom God has given wealth, possessions, and honor, and yet does not allow him to enjoy them. Instead God gives all these things to a stranger. The Teacher then concludes by saying that even if a person lives a long time and has many children but cannot enjoy his possessions, he would have been better off stillborn! The author employs numerous anecdotes throughout the book, and in none of them is there a happy ending! It is evident that the Teacher is deliberately painting a very negative view of the world. The significant question is why does he do this? What is he attempting to relate to his readers by creating such a dark world?

In the "Admonitions of Ipuwer" the answer to this question may be more evident. As already noted, one Egyptologist speculates that the dark and inverted world painted by the author is meant to legitimize the current regime by contrasting it with the "anarchistic" and "disorderly" former one (Faulkner 1973a, 210). This is common strategy in other types of Egyptian literature and inscriptions. For example, in the "Prophecies of Neferti," composed during the reign of Amenemhet I at the beginning of the Twelfth Dynasty, a priest and sage of the Fourth Dynasty "prophesied" that there would be a chaotic period, the First Intermediate Period, which would be overcome by the rise of a child (Amenemhet), who would someday bring order to it and establish peace. This is known as a *vaticinia ex eventu*, a prophecy written after the fact and then promoted as an old prophecy that has come true. The "Prophecies of Neferti," thus, is really political propaganda used to legitimize a dynasty that had no connection with the earlier dynasties (Van Seters 1983, 173).

Similarly, after the Second Intermediate Period, when the foreign Hyksos dominated Egypt, Queen Hatshepsut assumed the throne after the death of her husband, Thutmose III. She was technically coregent with his son, who was a minor. Because of these circumstances and particularly because of being female, she felt compelled to legitimate her rule. On the façade of a cliff-temple is inscribed her claim that she brought order to the Egyptian world that had gone to pieces during the Hyksos period (see Seters 1997, 174). She also declares that the Hyksos did not rule by divine decree as she does. All of this conveniently overlooks the intervening reigns that actually accomplished the restoration of indigenous rule.

From this discussion of the category of pessimistic and skeptical literature one can perceive its significance for understanding a particular work's rhetoric and especially its *Sitz im Leben*. This particular categorization is defined by mood primarily, though thematic elements are present such as the focus on death and the carpe diem ethic. Now, being aware that Ecclesiastes is formerly related to royal autobiography or testimony and that it is a framed narrative are all important for better understanding the book. But I would argue that its inclusion in the broader category of pessimistic/skeptical literature is more important for understanding its function and rhetoric. Thus, a work can share in numerous differing generic categories, with certain generic identifications more relevant than others. This also demonstrates that genres are in "the mind of the beholder," that they are mental templates that constitute agreed upon conventions by authors and readers. In turn, this means modern interpreters might even classify certain works in ways the ancients might not have. But, again, this is simply acknowledging the ethereal character of genres. And when biblical scholars speak of biblical genres they are largely employing them as heuristic devices, which means there is a subjective element involved here that cannot be eliminated. We will later explore how the author of Ecclesiastes uses pessimism in his composition for a particular purpose.

The Instability of Genres

Genres are inherently unstable and are constantly changing and morphing over time. Some genres even morph into new genres. This realization is actually a very recent discovery. In former times genres were considered stable and ontological entities, and the job of the literary critic was to simply determine by what genre a particular work was to be classified. This taxonomical approach is similar to the method an entomologist utilizes when he finds a specimen of bug and carefully determines the genus and species. This is known as generic realism (Sparks 2005, 6). However, modern genre critics no longer view genres in such an outdated way. The modern approach is called generic nominalism. It assumes that "there is a flexible and partially arbitrary character to all classifications . . . generic categories are essentially taxonomic inventions" (Sparks 2005, 6).

One aspect of this instability is the constant evolution of new genres and the transformation of old ones. The history of music supplies a couple of examples. Folk dances were transformed by aristocrats into the minuet, which is, in turn, appropriated anew in romantic music (Jameson 1981, 141). Blues guitar music is another example (see Roberts 2000, 89). It emerged as a genre during the slavery days of the African-Americans. But today it is one of the most lucrative types of music in the world. Prime examples are the Rolling Stones and Eric Clapton. And though the form and content of the early and most recent blues music may not differ terribly, there has been a significant metamorphosis. One only has to compare the blues of Robert Johnson and the Rolling Stones to discern the difference.

This demonstrates that genres often originate in one setting and among a particular social group but then eventually diffuse into the public domain where they are accessible to the general public. Thus, social groups never completely "own" or control genres; they cannot be contained.

An ancient example would be the evolution of the biography or autobiography genre (see Lichtheim 1975, 3-5; Redford 1995, 2232-33). This is the earliest genre found among the Egyptians. The biography was inscribed in tombs and represented a very positive self-portrait of the deceased in hopes that this might aid the individual in securing eternal life instead of damnation. These contained a catalog of virtues practiced and vices shunned during the lifetime of the deceased. The deceased enjoins future generations to provide him/her with offerings or to at least pronounce an offering formula, and forbidding them to damage the tomb. These were at first prose but then grew to become genuine pieces of literature. Here is part of a catalog of morals from a biography of Sheshi during the Sixth Dynasty:

> I rescued the weak from one stronger than he
> as much as was in my power.
> I gave bread to the hungry, clothes <to the naked>,
> I brought the boatless to land.
> I buried him who had no son ... (Lichtheim 1975, 17).

During the politically decentralized First Intermediate Period, when a rugged individualism first appeared, a summary of military accomplishments was the norm (Redford 1995, 2233). During the Middle Kingdom the form became more polished. During the New Kingdom, in the Ramesside age, instead of lauding one's feats while alive, the emphasis was on piety and the inclusion of hymns of praise to the deity. During the Twenty-fifth and Twenty-sixth Dynasties of the Late Period, there was a return to recording one's good deeds but the focus was on benefactions made for the temples and gods on behalf of the king.

The second main genre of ancient Egypt was the instructions. These also changed over time. The "Admonitions of Ipuwer" and "Prophecies of Neferit" are actually a new form of the traditional instruction that takes on a prophetic or admonitory tone (Lichtheim 1975, 9). We have already seen how their "topsy-turvy" theme was used as royal propaganda.

An example in the Hebrew Bible would be to compare how the Qumran wisdom literature, which is very apocalyptic, and a book like Ben Sira, both considered types of wisdom literature, differ from the earlier wisdom books in the Hebrew Bible. For example, Ben Sira incorporates within his book not only the typical genres found in wisdom literature like aphorisms and instruction but also prayers, hymns, aretology (self-praise), and biblical paraphrase. There is even a long, poetical account of the heroes of the faith in Israel's history

(Sir. 44:1-50:24). Unlike other books in the Hebrew Bible, we know who the author is because of the prologue added by Ben Sira's grandson. The book reflects Greek influence. Unlike the previous wisdom books, Ben Sira closely connects wisdom with the Torah. In chapter 24 wisdom is personified and praised, and she tells of how after her creation by God she went forth around all the world seeking a place to abide. She is eventually told to dwell in Israel. At the end of the poem, Ben Sira comments:

> All this is the book of the covenant of the Most High God,
> the law that Moses commanded us as an inheritance for the congregations of Jacob (14:23; *NRSV*).

Excluding the Torah psalms, viewed as a type of wisdom psalm by some wisdom experts (more on this later), before Ben Sira's time, there is no direct or explicit reference to the Law or the covenant with the patriarchs or even to any historical events in the wisdom literature. There are allusions to the Law, such as in Eccles. 5:4-5 (Deut. 23:21-22), but no explicit reference to the law at large. This, of course, is to be expected in the development of genres. In Ben Sira, this simply points to the great significance and centrality for Jews that the Law had attained by his day. Like the Egyptian instructions, the content and form of Hebrew wisdom literature changed over time.

Economy of Genres

Genres never exist as isolated and independent entities. Rather, genres are systemically related to all the other genres that exist in the generic "universe" of a particular culture. This means that each genre occupies a particular niche within this universe, something it does that the other genres do not. Thus, what makes a genre a genre is not just what it is but also what it is not (Frow 2005, 125). Genres defined themselves and have an identity only in relation to other genres. Martin Buss noted, "*The Hebrew Bible is largely arranged according to what appear to be culturally significant genres, which each represent a dimension of life and which engage metaphorically in a dialogue with each other*" (2007, 13). If Buss is correct, then the Hebrew Bible represents a compendium of various genres that systemically treat at least most of the facets of the Israelite life, whether socially, religiously, ethically, etc. The various genres and the various topics that are discussed in the Hebrew Bible are so varied and diverse that most areas of human existence are touched on. This is not to suggest that the Hebrew Bible is exhaustive in this regard or that the matters it addresses were a concern for every Israelite, whatever the social status.

This is a very important point, though it has been largely unknown among biblical scholars and especially wisdom literature experts. Many wisdom literature experts have seen great significance in the fact that the Israelite wisdom literature does not allude to many of the significant theological tenets or events of the Israelite religion such as the covenants, the Law, and *Heilsgeschichte* (German for "salvation history," the view that God directs history for Israel's benefit). In fact, James Crenshaw, one of the most prominent wisdom literature experts in the U.S. puts it most eloquently:

> Within Proverbs, Job, and Ecclesiastes one looks in vain for the dominant themes of Yahwistic thought: the exodus from Egypt, election of Israel, the Davidic covenant, the Mosaic legislation, the patriarchal narratives, the divine control of history and movement toward a glorious moment when right will triumph. Instead, the reader encounters in these three books *a different thought world*, one that stands apart so impressively that scholars have described that literary corpus as an alien body within the Bible (Crenshaw 2010, 24-25).

He believes that the sapiential tradition originally did not appeal to revelation and was based primarily on experience (2010, 11).

Crenshaw goes so far as to consider the worldview of the wisdom corpus "an alternative to Yahwism" (2010, 229)! He also views this literature as representing a distinctive movement among the Israelite literati (Crenshaw 1969, 130 n. 4).

But Crenshaw is not alone. The majority of wisdom literature scholars view the corpus as representing a distinctive worldview within the Hebrew Bible at large, even if they do not go as far as Crenshaw and see it as non-Yahwistic. But a growing minority view is challenging this position.

The wisdom "tradition" began to make more allusions to the core theological tenets and events of the Israelite faith with Ben Sira. We have already cited a few of these. But Ben Sira goes even further when he discusses the curriculum studied by wise scribes. Like the Egyptian "Satire of the Trades," Ben Sira contrasts the hard and difficult, though necessary, work of common laborers, like the farmer and smith, with the work of the scribe:

How different the one who devotes himself
to the study of the law of the Most Hight!
He seeks out the wisdom of all the ancients,
and is concerned with prophecies;
he preserves the saying of the famous
and penetrates the subtleties of parables;
he seeks out the hidden meanings of proverbs
and is at home with the obscurities of parables (38:34–39:3; *NRSV*).

Because Ben Sira includes the study of literature other than wisdom literature, as well as almost equating wisdom with the Torah, Crenshaw views this as a radical transformation of the wisdom tradition (2010, 216–19, 224–25, 245). These new elements are seen as an anomaly and not indigenous to the origins of wisdom.

Another more sophisticated example of the consensus is Michael Fox. He does not go as far as Crenshaw and others who view the wisdom literature as foreign to the canon or as non-Yahwistic. But he does assume that that absence of allusions to the major theological tenets and events is significant. Fox maintains that the wise men who wrote Proverbs did not feel that these other traditions were necessary for instructing young men on ethical behavior: "The primary axiom of Proverbs' ethics is that the exercise of the human mind is the necessary and sufficient condition of right and successful behavior in all reaches of life: practical, ethical, and religious" (2007b, 6). Related to this, Fox argues that the epistemology (the branch of philosophy that treats how we know what we know) of Proverbs is distinctive in the Hebrew Bible (2007a, 669-84). He avoids the label of empiricism to describe the epistemology of Proverbs, though he does argue that it is appropriate for Qohelet (Fox 1999, 71-86). Instead of empiricism, Fox describes the sapiential epistemology as a coherent system of ethical harmony, based on both empirical and non-experiential principles, where what is fitting ethically is also beautiful and pleasing and just. He defines wisdom in Proverbs as a moral aesthetic, which the wise man learns to develop so he can discern the appropriate action for a particular situation. Discerning the right action is a balancing act, which he describes in this way:

> If Yahwism were iconic, Yahweh could be pictured like the Egyptian Thoth, judging everyone by his balance scales. This is the essence of God's justice and his demands in Proverbs, and it is fully sufficient. No promises to the forefathers, no covenantal ties, demands, or rewards, not even divine laws, come into the picture. They are not rejected: they are simply unnecessary in Proverbs' system (Fox 2007a, 681-82).

Thus, Fox explains the lack of allusions to the core theological tenets of Yahwism in the book of Proverbs and, more generally, in the wisdom literature as signifying a unique epistemology that rests on a different foundation, that of the mind alone and the ability to discern the fitting action in a particular situation without referral to the other traditions.

In response to their arguments, I would suggest Crenshaw and Fox are guilty of employing the *argumentum ex silento* or "argument from silence." The assumption is that if the biblical wisdom literature does not include such core theological tenets of Judaism as focus on the Torah, the covenants, and God's action in history, then the authors must not have viewed them as significant, and, consequently, their worldview is idiosyncratic and distinctive. However, philosophers and rhetoricians point out that the argument from silence is an inherently weak form of argument. In fact, it is usually treated as a fallacy (Duncan 2012, 83). This is because "the assumption that considering apparent lack of evidence as evidence of actual lack of evidence is to go too far, which in turn raises the question of how any lack of evidence can ever be established as meaningful" (Duncan 2012, 84). In other words, the absence of evidence is not evidence of absence! The argument from silence is technically a variation of *argumentum ad ignorantiam* or appeal to ignorance, such as someone arguing that there must be ghosts because no one has ever demonstrated that they do not in fact exist (see Copi 1982, 101).

However, Mike Duncan (2012, 83-97) does not throw the argument completely out. While acknowledging it as a very weak form of argument, he maintains it can be useful as a stepping stone to further research and for counter arguments that eventually arise (2012, 88). Conveniently, Duncan alludes to an example from biblical studies. The argument is made that because Paul does not allude much to Jesus' pre-crucifixion life found in the Gospels, then that means he was largely ignorant of it (Duncan 2012, 89-93). This has produced counter-arguments to explain the absence: Paul viewed his own revelation as more authentic than the experiences of the Twelve apostles, so he avoids alluding to this information; Paul assumed his audience would have already known this information, so he does not mention it; Paul saw it as authentic but not agreeable with his teaching and emphases.

In the vein of Duncan's comments, there have been several counter-arguments to the view that the wisdom literature must represent an idiosyncratic tradition within the canon of the Hebrew Bible because it ignores significant theological tenets and events in the canon. David Carr has argued that the wisdom literature does not reflect what are considered the core Yahwistic elements because these tenets had not yet become dominant among the Israelites (2004, 12). This is possible. However, by the time the introduction (chaps. 1-9) to Proverbs was added during the Persian period, the Law appears to have been firmly established as the dominant core of what would become Judaism and the stories of the patriarchs would have been well known.

But the most devastating counter-argument, however, is the one I have already appealed to: the systemic nature of genres. Raymond Van Leeuwen puts it aptly:

> This silence does not imply that the various authors of the book had no interest in matters of redemptive history or in other biblical books . . . Like most books, Proverbs does not reveal the full range of its authors' concerns. . . . Such silences in wisdom writings are a function of their genre and purpose, and too much should not be concluded concerning the isolation of the sages from Israel's historical traditions (1997, 21).

Van Leeuwen is correct on both counts. First, the wisdom corpus does not reflect all of the concerns of its authors. This is another way of saying that as a mode of literature, it does not represent a complete worldview. As we said earlier, genres only convey a conventional world, nothing more. A genre is not comprehensive enough to reflect a worldview. And the same holds true for modes of literature, to an even greater degree. And as we have seen, the scribes who composed and studied the wisdom literature, composed and read various other genres, all of which occupied important niches in their training.

Second, Van Leeuwen is correct that the wisdom corpus as a mode of literature is focused on its own purposes and not those of the other modes like the historical, prophetic, and apocalyptic literature and the legal material. In other words, what makes the wisdom literature wisdom literature is its differences from the prophetic literature, the Torah, and the apocalyptic and historical literature. As Derek Kidner points out, the book of Proverbs as wisdom literature addresses the domain of values and ethics: "There are details of character small enough to escape the mesh of the law and the broadsides of the prophets, and yet decisive in personal dealings. Proverbs moves in this realm, asking what a person is like to live with, or to employ; how he manages his affairs, his time and himself" (1964, 13). Similarly, Richard Clifford, referring to the wisdom literature, notes, "Missing from them are politics, economics, and history as well as national and international affairs, for these are not (for the most part) subject to *personal* decision and reflection. Wisdom literature is personal and familial" (1998:19).

If one considers the other ancient Near Eastern wisdom literature as whole, there is a similar pattern. There are few allusions to core theological tenets or historical events of the respective cultures. For example, the "Instruction of Ptahhotep" makes few allusions to the main tenets of Egyptian theology. It occasionally refers to the gods but only generally. It alludes occasionally to the concept of Maat, but this notion is highly relevant for a discussion of ethical behavior, which is the focus of the work. Also, the maxims in the "Instructions of Shuruppak" make even less references to respective core beliefs or historical figures/events. Again, all of this suggests that this feature is in the nature of wisdom literature, which focuses on the mundane and ethics, and not on historical or international events or core mythological stories.

This leads to another counterargument that helps explain the lack of distinctively Israelite tenets within the wisdom corpus: its rhetoric. Since wisdom literature seeks to counsel moral guidelines for daily life, these instructions must assume the ideology of universalism (see Eagleton 1991, 56-58). In other words, the truths and knowledge about living wisely promoted in the wisdom literature cannot be parochial, for sectarian "truth" is no truth at all. The instructions that wisdom literature promulgates must be true for any individual, not just a particular ethnicity or nationality. For example, the wisdom writers prohibit the well-to-do from taking advantage of the poor:

Oppressing the poor to increase himself,
giving to the rich,
only results in loss! (Prov. 22:16).

The author of this maxim would not have thought that it would only apply to Israelites. Like Immanuel Kant and his categorical imperative, he would have viewed his aphorism as being valid only if it applied to everyone, no matter what ethnicity or nationality. Concern for the poor is also a frequent motif in the other non-Israelite corpora of wisdom literature. For example, in the "Instruction of Ptahhotep," there is counsel against attacking a poor man when in a dispute with him and the statement: "Wretched is he who injures a poor man" (Lichtheim 1975, 64). The-non Israelite sapiential authors have also adopted the same universalistic ideology as the Israelites.

The Israelite author of the book of Job employs this universalistic rhetorical strategy to strengthen the book's teaching. The characters in Job are all non-Israelite (Job and his friends are apparently Edomites). This scheme is also employed in Proverbs when the "oracle" of a foreign queen mother, the mother of king Lemuel, is included (31:1-9). And even in Ben Sira, as Woman Wisdom seeks a place to dwell before lighting upon Judah (Sirach 24), she assumes the nature of a universal being, without nationality.

A final counterargument is that much of the terminology in the wisdom literature makes little sense without the rest of the canon. Words like "wisdom" and "righteousness" remain largely abstract concepts without the narratives in the Hebrew Bible that provide concrete examples of what these characteristics mean. We have already mentioned the example of Abigail who demonstrates what Israelite "wisdom" means when she uses her wits to save her family from slaughter by David, whom her husband Nabal, nickname meaning "fool," had insulted (1 Samuel 25). She is described as *tovah sekel*—literally "good of insight" (v. 3). And David pronounces her wise because of her deeds: "Blessed be your good sense (*ta'am*)" (v. 33). "Wisdom" becomes defined as "intelligence" but also as "respect" and "self-sacrifice" for the good of the family. Nabal, to the contrary, demonstrates what folly looks like: greed and disrespect. It is highly doubtful that the sages of ancient Israel would have considered such stories as *unnecessary* for developing the skill of moral discernment!

Sidebar 12: Modal Repertoire of the Wisdom Literature
THEMES: Wisdom, knowledge, success, discipline, discernment, theodicy problem, paradox, etc.
FORMS: Framed poetry; numerous genres: aphorism, instruction, dialogue, soliloquy, poem, hymn, ode, anecdote, reflection, etc.

Conclusion

The wisdom literature is a mode of literature that was studied primarily by younger but also older scribes to help them develop their skill at moral discernment. This is in addition to the pedagogical role played by aphorisms in the learning of Hebrew during scribal training. Keen moral discernment would have been invaluable for the scribes' vocation as governmental officials or in other capacities. This mode of literature creates a conventional world—not a worldview—that focuses on the niche of morality, social norms, and values. The numerous genres used in this corpus in turn created their own worlds, which each have their particular focus and purpose. As such, the wisdom corpus is by definition not as concerned about the other domains of life treated by the other modes in the Hebrew Bible. This literature has a particular focus and purpose. Scribes did not only study this mode of literature. It was only one of several that were necessary for the training of scribes. But without it, it would not have been complete. All the modes of literature that the scribes studied served to provide them with the maturity and breadth that would have well served them in the numerous, often difficult, tasks that they were called on to serve.

7

The Poetics, Axiology, and Rhetoric of Wisdom Literature

In the prolog to the book of Proverbs (1:6), we see a dimension to wisdom that goes beyond the moral and ethical (axiology):

> To comprehend an aphorism and an enigma,
> the words of the wise and their riddles.

This verse points to a more exclusive definition of wisdom for the sages. It is not just a particular lifestyle that any Israelite could adopt. To be wise one must learn the aesthetics of their literature: "the words of the wise." This means wisdom, as understood by the sages, is not just the content of their teaching but simultaneously the medium or form in which it is cast. In other words, wisdom is not just sound advice but also involves the pretty package in which it is placed. Further, the genres "enigmas" and "riddles" transcend literary niceties and include cognitive stimulation. Also, closely related to wisdom's literary and cognitive facets is its rhetoric. Wisdom needs credibility and appeal. This chapter will thus discuss the basic properties of its literary, cognitive, and rhetorical dimensions, as well as nuancing its ethical focus, which is also ensconced in its aesthetics.

Wisdom Literature as Poetry

The wisdom literature as a mode of literature is composed almost completely in poetry. There are narrative elements certainly. The book of Job is framed by a prose narrative that sets up the dialogue between Job and his three friends, the latter of which is entirely in poetry. The wisdom book that contains the most narrativity is Ecclesiastes. In fact, Eric Christianson has recently interpreted it from a narrative perspective (Christianson 1998). However, the hybrid character of Ecclesiastes is best characterized by Robert Alter as "cadenced prose" (Alter 1985, 167).

Thus, the appropriate question to ask is: why is all the wisdom literature in poetry? One answer might be poetry is the language of the gods! It is significant that the divine speeches (chs. 38-41) in Job are in poetry. And, as Alter suggests, even the poetry in the speeches is more majestic than in the poetic dialog of Job and his friends (1985, 96). That God's speaking in ornate poetry only serves to magnify his status is somehow fitting. The divine oracles in the prophetic books are all also in poetry.

But another reason is that poetry can do things that prose and narrative cannot. Basically poetry is usually a better medium for conveying emotion. Poetry pulls at the heart strings better than prose. It also uses more vivid imagery than does prose, and this further enables it to elicit a variety of emotions. It also is generally more symbolic than prose, utilizing metaphors and similes to convey its truths. This means that poetry can take the reader to a higher level of consciousness, so to speak, i.e., a deeper transcendent state.

Simultaneously, because the language of poetry is so symbolic, this means it is much more ambiguous than prose. This ambiguity provides poetry much more flexibility than prose in order to create all sorts of effects. It also means that reading poetry requires much more work than does prose. The ambiguity stimulates the brain to attempt to "pin down" the symbolism and provide closure to a form of literature that seeks to escape any such containment. The ambiguity of poetry then can serve as a cognitive stimulant. Thus, there are both important cognitive and emotive facets to poetry that provide this medium with unique potential.

These two features of poetry are ideal for the pedagogical purposes of the wisdom literature. As we have shown, this corpus was most likely intended originally to train scribes. First, it would have helped them learn Hebrew when used in conjunction with lexical lists. Second, it would have "trained" them in the sphere of values and morality. Poetry would be ideal for the latter. Though this will come as a surprise to most, the area of values and morality is technically not the realm of rationality, at least not primarily. Rather morality is within the domain of the irrational or non-rational, which is the sphere of the emotional. Values and morality are not about the way the world is but the way it should be or the way we want it to be. Values come from desires and needs, whether volitional or instinctive. A particular societal value represents what a specific society has agreed to desire, and these are not always logical. For example, the value of caring for the vulnerable is frequently found in all societies. This is not exactly rational because a particular society might be better off generally ignoring their vulnerable and focusing their energies on the healthy majority. And it certainly is not the rational choice for the healthy individual who strives to benefit himself or herself.

Thus, when the wisdom literature intends to promote and reinforce certain values in the young scribes who originally studied this material, the use of poetry was ideal because the rhetoric it uses often involves the emotional and the ethical, the domain of the prescriptive and not the descriptive. As we shall see, the wisdom literature certainly uses logos in its rhetoric, where it tries to rationally appeal to its readers. Logos is related to the word "logic," and involves a speaker or author attempting to use human reasoning to persuade an audience. But this is often reinforced emotively, and so pathos is a more common rhetorical strategy in the wisdom literature. Poetry is the ideal medium for pathos! The rhetorical strategy of pathos is utilized when a speaker/author appeals to the audiences' emotions and their passions in order to persuade them to either do something or embrace a particular lifestyle.

What is Hebrew Poetry?

Hebrew poetry is characterized by the same features as English poetry: terseness (concision and gaps in information usually provided in prose, called "ellipses"), striking images, meter or rhythm, and rhyme. Hebrew prose can share to a degree in all these features. The difference between the two is in degree. One should think of it in terms of a continuum, with Hebrew poetry having more frequent incidences of these features (after Longman 1996,169).

Terseness

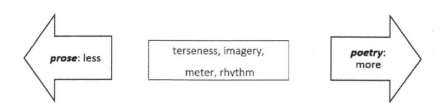

Figure 6: Terseness

Terseness is found where words are left out to create a more compact effect. An example is found in Prov. 1:8-9:

Hear, my son, the instruction of your father,
and do not forsake the teaching of your mother,   ] Bicolon

For they *shall be* a graceful wreath upon your head,
and a necklace upon your neck.

In the last bicolon (or couplet) there are no verbs, so the italicized words are actually not in the Hebrew and must be added. And then in the last bicolon the "added" verb must do double duty for both cola. Like in English, Hebrew poetry has a tendency to leave out a number of lines in the second colon that were used in the first. In a sense, they are carried over into the second colon.

Rhyme or Parallelism

Semantic Parallelism

In English rhyme is achieved *phonologically* by having the last words of a couplet *sound* the same in the last syllable:

Hickory, dickory, *dock*,

the mouse ran up the *clock*.

Hebrew, too, has a rhyming feature of sorts like this in that it employs alliteration (words with the same or similar consonants) and assonance (words with the same or similar vowels). But Hebrew poetry also forms rhymes with thought (semantic), grammar, and form (morphology). This type of rhyming is called parallelism, where two couplets or cola "parallel" or mirror each other. In the above quote from Prov. 1:8-9, the two bicola involve semantic parallelism. The instruction of the father is parallel or generally equivalent to the mother's teaching. And the wreath and necklace are both adornments worn on the body. This is called semantic parallelism because it sets two thoughts or ideas alongside each other, thus, it is a cognitive type of rhyming.

Types of Semantic Parallelism

Synonymous Parallelism

The type of parallelism just examined in Prov. 1:8-9 is called synonymous parallelism or equivalence or elaboration (Alter 1985, 169) because the two cola are basically saying the same thing and, thus, echo each other. Here is another example:

As one with lying lips conceals hatred,
and one who spreads a rumor, he is a fool (Prov. 10:18).

While the two cola do not say exactly the same thing, they unite two negative traits about the fool: slander and deception. Putting the two together, the foolish slanderer's modus operandi is deception; he hurts others behind their backs. Often parallelism is not 100 percent aligned (see Heim 2013, 53, 638). This means that the reader has to figure out how to connect the two cola, which entails a cognitive stimulation.

Antithetical Parallelism

Another main type of semantic parallelism is exemplified by the following "sentence" or short maxim in Prov. 10:1:

A wise son will bring joy to a father,
but a foolish son is the grief of his mother.

Here the two cola are saying the same thing cognitively: being wise makes your parents proud. However, they do it by using opposite language and concepts. "Wise" is the opposite of "foolish"; "joy" is the opposite of "grief"; "father" is the opposite of "mother." But the two cola combined are meant to say: be a wise son! This is called antithetical parallelism.

Synthetic or Progressive Parallelism

A third category of semantic parallelism often employed was called years ago synthetic or progressive parallelism. Here is an example:

A club and a sword and a sharp arrow,
is a man who bears false witness against his neighbor (Prov. 25:18)

THE SOCIAL WORLD OF THE SAGES

The second colon completes the thought of the first. Some, like Robert Alter, would call this proverb a riddle (1985, 169). This is shown by the awkward lumping together of weapons in the first colon without explanation. Only after we read the second colon do we understand the author's intention. One could rephrase the first colon as "What is like a club and a sword and a sharp arrow?" The answer is found in the second colon. In the first colon something is said that is jarring or incongruent, and so the reader is forced to ponder what the colon means. The anxiety created is only reduced by reading the next colon, and, so, one gets the punch line.

Another example of this third category of semantic parallelism is what has been called the "better than" proverb:

Better a meal of herbs with love there,
than a fatted cow and hatred there (Prov. 15:17).

Here the second colon completes the first by providing the less valued item in contrast to the preferred item.

Some scholars, however, see the term synthetic parallelism as problematic because it has become a catchall term for any type of semantic parallelism that is not synonymous or antithetical (Petersen and Richards 1992, 26). However, it is still useful as a heuristic or teaching device.

The basic function of parallelism should be that the two cola modify each other, complete each other, or interact with each other in some way. The possibilities for the cola interacting with each other is almost without limit! This allows for a great deal of creativity on the part of the authors. Alter describes parallelism in Proverbs as different than in other parts of the Hebrew Bible due to the compressed length of the cola. He also emphasizes that the final word in the second colon often functions as a punch-word that delivers something unexpected or drives home the point in a satisfactory way (1985, 168)! Below is depicted graphically the basic relationship between the cola:

A ⟵————————————————————————— B

Figure 7: Relationship between Cola

Effects of Semantic Parallelism

Focusing

One of these effects is what Alter calls "focusing" (1985, 173-74). This is where a concept represented by a word in the first colon that is rather broad is narrowed or focused in a concept represented by a word in the second colon:

> A foolish son is an *engulfing ruin* to his father,
> and a contentious wife is a *leaky roof* (Prov. 19:13).
> *Acts of judgment* are reserved for scoffers,
> and *blows to the backs* of fools (Prov. 19:29).

A leaky roof is more specific and less abstract than a great ruin, and physical blows to the back is a more specific concept than general acts of punishment.

Intensification

Intensification is where the concept represented by a word in the first colon gains more emotional weight and a stronger connotation in a concept represented by a word in the second colon (Alter 1985, 173):

> A noble women is a *crown of honor* for her husband,
> like *rottenness in the bones* is a wife who brings shame (Prov. 12:4).

> One who disturbs his own home *will inherit the wind*,
> but a fool is *a slave to the wise of heart* (Prov. 11:29).

In Prov. 12:4, cancer in the bones is more graphic than a crown. In Prov. 11:29, while it is bad to create chaos in one's own house, it is worse to be a fool and a "slave," who cannot inherit like an heir (Alter 1985, 174).

Narrativity

Alter speaks of the narrativity of a number of aphorisms (1985, 171-72). This is the notion that the maxim tells a little story. Note the following examples:

> A man who wanders from the path of intelligence,
> he will be led to the assembly of the ghosts (Prov. 21:16).
> The lazy buries his hand in his bowl,
> he will not even return it to his mouth! (Prov. 19:24).

In Prov. 21:16, one sees sequential action or cause and effect, with the action of the first colon leading to the consequences in the second. Proverbs 19:24 is quite humorous, and it actually shows the reversal of what would be expected. One would expect the lazy person to at least retrieve food already in a bowl, but this individual is portrayed as so lazy he is not even able to do this.

Grammatical Parallelism

Parallelism does not always occur through the rhyming or juxtaposition of thought. It can also occur through grammatical form. Note the following example from Deut. 32:1 (after Longman 1996, 173):

Listen, O heavens, and I will speak,

Verb   Subject   Modifier

hear, O land, the words of my mouth!

V   S   Object

Thus, the parallelism here is produced by the pairing of different parts of speech. Note that the second colon departs from the pattern by switching the modifier with an object at the end. Here is another example from the next verse in Deut. 32:2 (after Longman 1996, 174):

Let my teaching drip like rain,

         S   V   Prepositional Phrase

let my speech trickle like dew,

         S   V   PP

like showers upon the grass,

    PP   PP

like rain upon the herbage.

    PP   PP

Note that in both passages a combination of semantic (synonymous) and grammatical parallelism occurs.

Morphological Parallelism

Another type of non-semantic parallelism is called morphological parallelism. This can be created by contrasts or equivalences through the forms of words in Hebrew (suffixes added to nouns and conjugations of verbs). Examples include gender (masculine or feminine), number (singular or plural), definiteness (the Hebrew word with or without the article "the"), and conjugation, tense, and number (see Petersen and Richards 1992, 32). Some of these, like gender (e.g., a masculine noun) and number (distinguishing between second person singular and plural), may be missed by students who do not know Hebrew.

Examples of Morphological Parallelism

Gender

> Even in *laughter* the *heart* may have pain,
> and after its *joy* there may be *grief* (Prov. 14:13).

The two nouns in the first colon are both masculine; the two in the second are feminine.

Number

> Ask *your father* and he will tell you,
> *the elders* and they will speak to you (Deut. 32:7b).

The singular father is contrasted with the plural elders.

Tense

> The Lord *sat enthroned* at the flood,
> and the Lord *sits enthroned* as king forever (Ps. 29:10).

God built his heavenly temple after defeating chaos represented by the flood, and now he sits enthroned as Israel's king.

Proper Noun and Pronoun

Praise *the Lord* with a lyre,
with a harp of ten strings sing to *him* (Ps. 33:2).

Chiasm

Another frequent type of parallelism is called chiasmus, from the Greek letter *chi*, which has the "ex" shape. This is where the sequence of the concepts in a colon are inverted by their corollaries in the second colon. Here is an example:

One who withholds his rod hates his son,
one who loves him chastises him often (Prov. 13:24).

I will break this down into its parts:

A: One who withholds his rod	B: hates his son
B': one who loves him	A': chastises him often

As one can see, "one who withholds the rod" correlates with "chastises him often" in that both concern discipline. Correspondingly, "hates his son" correlates with "one who loves him" in that both concern emotional reaction to the son. Thus, one can see half of the chiastic arrangement in the following:

Figure 8: Chiastic Arrangement of Prov. 13:24

The following illustration will show the full chiastic shape:

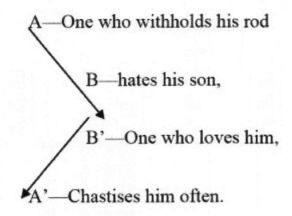

A—One who withholds his rod

B—hates his son,

B'—One who loves him,

A'—Chastises him often.

Figure 9: Full Chiastic Shape of Prov. 13:24

Imagery

Much of the intensity that poetry provides, in English and Hebrew, is its employment of colorful imagery. A great example of this is provided by Hosea 13:3:

Therefore, they will be like a morning *cloud*,
and early *dew* that departs,
like *chaff* that is blown away on the threshing floor,
like *smoke* from the window.

What is interesting is how the wicked are described in such graphic ways, which only poetry can do. Note that the visual, tactile, auditory, and olfactory senses are appealed to for dramatic effect. This verse is also a rare example of a quatracolon or 4 cola.

The imagery of nature is also beautifully presented in the book of Job in the divine speeches. God challenges Job and questions him about his ability to create something as wondrous and frightening as the battle horse:

Did you give to the horse might?
Did you cloth his mane with quivering?
Did you cause him to spring like a locust?
The majesty of his snorting is dreadful!
He paws in the valley and rejoices in his strength,
he goes forth toward weaponry.
He laughs at fear and is not dismayed,
he does not retreat before the sword.
Upon him the quiver rattles,
the flashing point of the spear and javelin.
In quaking and excitement he swallows up the land,
and he does not stand still at the blast of the trumpet.
As often as the trumpet sounds, he says, "Aha!"
and from afar he smells battle,
the thunderous shouting and loud noise (Job 39:19-25).

Prose just would not do justice to this material. The size, power, and grandeur of the battle horse and the human emotive response to it cannot be adequately conveyed through prose alone.

An important facet of the use of imagery in Hebrew poetry and especially in the wisdom literature is the use of metaphor. Metaphor is similar to simile, which uses "like" or "as" to compare one thing with another, but metaphor does not use these words. Many of our examples of various features of poetry have included similes, such as Hosea 13:3, which describes the wicked as being *like* clouds, dew, chaff, and smoke. Though similar in function, a metaphor is more jarring and shocking because it does not make the comparison explicit. But this also means that metaphor can be a powerful way to create more meaning and in fresh ways. In fact, the conjoining of two different entities through metaphor creates a new meaning that is impossible to achieve with comparison alone (Potts 1995, 505). Here is an example that is actually what Robert Alter (1985, 176) calls a "riddle," and it is rather startling:

A gold ring in a pig's snout,
is a beautiful woman who turns aside from discernment (Prov. 11:22).

Many translations blunt the force of the metaphor by adding "like" or "as" at the beginning of the verse (e.g., ESV, KJV). A gold ring in a pig's snout creates a bizarre image in the reader's mind. It is contradictory and baffling. Who would waste such a valuable commodity on a pig? But the incongruity is exactly the point. From the Israelite and ancient Near Eastern perspective, beauty and wisdom belonged together, and to have one without the other was unthinkable—like expensive jewelry on a pig! Now no one would say that a beautiful dunce is literally a gold ring in a pig's snout, but the comparison gets the mind to ponder how such an image is true to the nature of beauty and folly combined.

Interestingly, Babylonian popular sayings suggest that the Mesopotamians viewed the pig as foolish or dumb (contrary to modern science that considers pigs highly intelligent):

The pig is unholy [. . .] bespattering his backside,
making the streets smell, polluting the houses.
The pig is not fit for a temple, lacks sense,
is not allowed to tread on pavements,
an abomination to all the gods, an abhorrence [to (his) god,] accursed by
Šamaš (Lambert 1996, 215; cf. Hurowitz 2013, 98-99).

As another example, the book of Proverbs emphasizes the importance of the ability to speak effectively in various situations. One of the most popular metaphors used to reinforce this is the eating of fruit. Here is an example:

By the fruit of a man's mouth his belly is satisfied,
by the yield of his lips he is satiated (Prov. 18:20).

As William Brown aptly puts it, "As delectable fruit is happily consumed, so a well-turned phrase renders pleasure and sustenance to the speaker" (2004, 141). This aphorism also reflects the importance of persuasive speech for the role of scribes and officials.

Meter or Rhythm

All scholars believe that ancient Hebrew had some kind of meter but attempts to delineate it have not been successful (Petersen and Richards 1992, 39). Meter is the relationship between syllables and accents. For example, earlier we cited the following nursery rhyme:

Hickory, **dick**ory, **dock**, (trimeter)

The **mouse** ran **up** the **clock**, (trimeter)

The **clock** struck **one**, (dimeter)

The **mouse** ran **down**, (dimeter)

Hickory, **dick**ory, **dock** (trimeter).

The meter is the accented syllables in conjunction with the unaccented ones. The bold syllables indicate the accented ones. The first two lines are trimeters, followed by two dimeter lines, then finishing with a trimeter line. Thus, one sees that both rhyming and meter combine to create a nice effect for this nursery rhyme, and this helps in memorizing it, which is especially good for children. However, for Hebrew, since scholars cannot determine the specifics of the ancient system, it is preferable to refer to the rhythm of the poetry. Obviously, only students of Hebrew will be able to detect this feature.

The Aphorism as the Primary Genre
of the Wisdom Literature

While there are many genres used within the wisdom literature of
the Hebrew Bible, the most frequent, and, one could argue, the most
basic, is the aphorism, i.e., the sentence. Even when a larger genre is
involved, as in instructions (e.g., Prov. 1-9), individual aphorisms are
often cited to buttress the instruction (e.g., Prov. 1:17). Instruction
represents an elaboration on the basic aphoristic form. In the
following we will examine the poetics of the aphorism or maxim,
both cognitively and emotively. The larger wisdom genres will be
discussed when the individual wisdom books are treated in the latter
part of this book. By treating the most basic genre of this corpus, this
will enable the reader to enter into the literary world of the sages and
better comprehend the nature of their generic and modal repertoire
and the skill necessary for utilizing them.

As mentioned earlier, the "proverbs" in the book of Proverbs are
not actually proverbs. While they are related, the difference between
an aphorism and a proverb is significant. All the standard dictionaries
include a characteristic of proverbs that is not true of the sentences or
short pithy sayings in the book of Proverbs: that is, being current in a
society. A proverb is a pithy, often witty, wise saying that is found in
the mouths of the common people, not just the elite, sometimes called
a folk proverb. In many ways, folk proverbs represent the public
domain. All people of a particular culture are taught these proverbs
when young, and so folk proverbs represent the popular wisdom of
the people.

This is not true of the sentences or aphorisms in the book of
Proverbs. The book of Proverbs is not a collection of folk proverbs
that have been gathered and recorded to preserve for the posterity
of the Israelite people. This is indicated simply by the superscriptions

in the book, which ascribe the authorship of these maxims to either a king or famous sage: "the sayings of Solomon, son of David, king of Israel" (1:1); "the sayings of Solomon" (10:1); "Extend your ears; hear the words of the wise. Let your heart heed my knowledge." (22:17); "also, these are by the wise" (24:23); "these are also the sayings of Solomon which the men of Hezekiah copied, king of Judah" (25:1); "the words of Agur, son of Jakeh, an oracle" (30:1); "the words of Lemuel the king, an oracle, which his mother taught him" (31:1). The point is that the sentences in the book of Proverbs are not presented as if they are folk proverbs but rather as aphorisms or epigrams composed by famous people. They may have been in circulation among a segment of the elite or among the scribes who studied them, but that does not make them folk proverbs in the true sense. Unless they had wide circulation, they cannot be considered proverbs (or folk proverbs). Thus, the title of the book of Proverbs has been mistakenly translated and their nature as proverbs a misnomer. The book of Proverbs should be titled the "Book of Aphorisms"! That the "proverbs" in the book of Proverbs are really aphorisms also comports with their usual high literary sophistication. Though these aphorisms could have been quoted orally—and their alliteration and assonance points to this—their primary function appears to be as something that is aesthetically pleasing to the eyes!

The Weighing of Values: A Structural Approach

As T. A. Perry cogently states, "[P]roverbs are *assertions of value*" (1993, 23). This fits with what we have already claimed about the wisdom literature, that it primarily focuses on values and ethics. Perry argues from a structural perspective that aphorisms have a quadripartite "deep" structure, which means that below the surface every maxim implies four possible propositions, whether explicit or implied. He also divides these values into positive and negative. For example, consider Prov. 12:9 (see Perry 1993, 42):

> Better to be dishonorable and own a slave,
> than to play the great man and lack bread.

He divides the maxim up into four values:

1. To lack respect (-)

2. But able to eat ( )

3. To pretend greatness ( )

4. But not able to eat (-)

The maxim reflects a hierarchy of values that would be true for ancient Israel and the rest of the ancient Near East. Sustenance is valued more than even honor, and honor ranks near the very top for ancient Near Eastern societies (more on this in the next chapter). But being honorable while starving is not deemed by the Israelites as a viable option. This seems to reflect Maslow's hierarchy of needs (see Burton 2012), which is illustrated below:

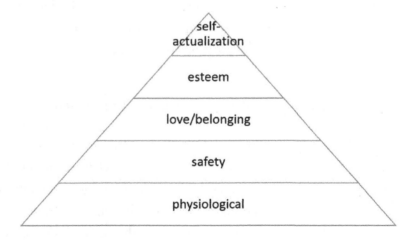

Figure 10: Hierarchy of Needs

According to this pyramid, the maxim is simply noting the significance of physiological needs over those of esteem.

However, it is interesting that honor is esteemed more than wealth in ancient Israelite society, and many proverbs reflect this. Here is an example:

> Better a little with righteousness,
> than much income without justice (Prov. 16:8).

Here to act honorably or righteously though poor is better than to be dishonorable or wicked and be rich. Poverty is considered a bad thing (-) yet not as bad as being wicked (-). But poverty is not the same thing as starving.

Another connection with the hierarchy of needs is expressed by this similar maxim:

> Better a meal of vegetables and love there,
> than a fatted cow and hatred there (Prov. 15:17).

Instead of righteousness, here we have the value of love emphasized. Eating vegetables represents the diet of the poor. But this is better when accompanied by love than being wealthy within a dysfunctional family. Again, poverty does not mean the lack of physiological necessity but bad circumstances where opportunities and goods are limited.

Perry provides a summary of the primary values found in the book of Proverbs: "work, fear of God, love, righteousness, lowliness of spirit, slowness to anger, quiet (peace), integrity, openness, nearness, and wisdom" (1993, 42). I would add wealth and honor or prestige as top values. More on these latter two in the next chapter. One could call several of these values virtues, and several scholars, most notably William Brown, have compared the Hebrew value system with Greek virtue ethics (see Brown 1996). Virtues are simply cultural values put into practice. Virtue ethics has become a popular topic among scholars of late. More on this as well in the next chapter. One should compare Perry's list with the one Miriam Lichtheim formulates for the "Instruction of Ptahhotep": "The cardinal virtues are self-control, moderation, kindness, generosity, justice, and truthfulness tempered by discretion" (1973, 62).

The book of Ecclesiastes reflects the same assessment and calculating of values. As Scott Jones states, "Ecclesiastes is a book about values, and one of Qohelet's primary tasks is to give an account of the pluses and minuses of life under the sun" (2014, 21). J. A. Loader has also shown how the book places the traditional values of Israelite society, like wisdom or wealth or honor, in juxtaposition to life's eventualities (bad happenings), whereby the particular value is exposed as illusory or less than desirable (1979). These juxtapositions form polarities that exist as tensions that cannot be resolved.

Again, values are technically non-rational. They express desires, interests, and needs, and, thus, they have a strong emotive component. As humans, then, we are a wonderful combination of the rational and irrational, and both facets of our selves seem to compete and struggle with each other. We often talk of how hormones seem to control our lives more than our cognitive powers, but such is not the case.

One might think that by removing human emotions or emotional intelligence, this would make us more rational and better able to make decisions and live our lives with fewer frustrations and obstacles. However, the opposite is the case. The social psychologist Jonathan Haidt studies patients who have suffered from damage to the ventromedial prefrontal cortex, the region of the brain that controls emotions (2012, 39-41). As a result, their emotional capacity is eliminated, though they retain 100 percent of their rational thinking capacity. Instead of simplifying their lives, this damage seriously disrupts them. They can no longer make the simplest decisions, like what to order at a restaurant or any decisions that involve values. Basically, they shut down when faced with such dilemmas. Thus, instead of enabling them to be superpowers cognitively, it cripples them and makes them dysfunctional.

The focus on values in Proverbs and the rest of the wisdom literature, then, is an important component of the human life, and especially for young scribes who someday would become important leaders in ancient Israel. As the intellectuals of their society and its administrators, their ability to make important ethical decisions would have been crucial. And, so, the ranking and discernment of which values rank the highest would have been a significant exercise for the training of the young scribe's mind. Scribes needed to be trained emotively and ethically as well as cognitively and rationally.

Disjointed Proverbs

To shift more to the cognitive aspects of the scribes' training, there is a special subgenre of aphorisms that Michael Fox has dubbed "disjointed proverbs" (2004, 165-77), what Richard Clifford has called "elliptical sayings" (2004, 158-59) and Knut Heim calls "imprecise parallelism" (2013, 683). Basically, a disjointed proverb is a maxim whose second colon does not directly and logically follow from the first one. Here is an example (after Fox 2004, 171):

In the house of the righteous is much wealth,
but the income of the wicked is cut off (Prov. 15:6).

The conclusion in the second colon does not technically follow from the first; it is a non sequitur. But if we add the following line, it becomes complete:

In the house of the righteous is much wealth,
The wealth of the righteous is not cut off.
But the income of the wicked is cut off.

Here is another example (after Fox 2004, 168):

A fulfilled desire is pleasing to the soul,
but the abomination of fools is to turn from evil (Prov. 13:19).

Again, the second colon is a non sequitur. The following line connects the two thoughts:

A fulfilled desire is pleasing to the soul,
Fools desire evil.
But the abomination of fools is to turn from evil.

The purpose of these disjointed proverbs is to get scribes to think hard and to try to fill in the logical gaps. This is similar to the function of riddles, which were discussed earlier (cf. Prov. 11:22). A jarring incongruity in the first colon ("A gold ring in a pig's snout") leads to the scribe attempting to come up with the answer before reading the second colon ("a beautiful woman without discretion"). Both riddles and disjointed proverbs serve to cognitively stimulate the scribes and literally help make them become wise. They help expand the thinking capacity of the scribes, which would certainly come in handy in the various administrative positions scribes would eventually occupy.

Paradoxes

One further point that deserves discussion is the fascination of the sages with paradoxes. While the sages believed that God had created an orderly and just world, the wise were intrigued by what seemed like contradictions in it. Here is an example:

> There exists some who relinquish their goods and yet become richer,
> and others who withhold their wealth and yet become poorer (Prov.
> 11:24).

Here the sages are fascinated by the incongruity of a generous person, who, though he freely showers gifts on others, seems to increase his wealth all the same, while the hoarder or greedy person seems to impoverish himself! This maxim also indirectly recommends generosity, one of the significant values of Israelite society.

Here is another example that we have already cited earlier:

> He who withholds his rod hates his son,
> while one who loves him chastises him often (Prov. 13:24).

The sages were perplexed about the seeming incongruity that those who actually love their children will discipline them and do things to them that the children will not like, while those who spoil their children and give them everything they want end up producing persons whom others avoid, and, as a result, are not successful in life! It is interesting that this maxim has been abbreviated in America and turned into a proverb: "Spare the rod and spoil the child!" The "rod" is a metonym for discipline and should not necessarily be taken literally.

From these paradoxes and others one can see that the sages were keen observers of the world. In many ways, they were the first psychologists and sociologists as well as ethicists and philosophers. They delighted in incongruities because these provided an unexpected surprise in what could seem like a monotonously orderly and harmonious world.

The Rhetoric of Wisdom

We have already touched on the rhetoric of the wisdom tradition with the concept of universalism. The wisdom literature in general is not too ethnically Israelite or parochial. Rather, it presents its "goods" as universally applicable, which is a necessary condition for what can legitimately be called truth. The reader addressed by this literature is, thus, "Every person," who, if he or she will only enact the advice given, will be successful in life in general. But this corpus uses more than one rhetorical trick. In the rest of this section we will focus on these.

Brief Introduction to Rhetoric

The field of rhetoric is closely aligned with the literary studies in that it refers not only to oral communication but also written. Rhetorical criticism, when directed at literature, asks the fundamental question, "How does the author persuade his/her audience?" Rhetoric, then, is the art of persuasion. This field of study actually began with Aristotle's book on rhetoric. Much of the terminology and concepts go back to him. There are three main types of rhetorical appeal that come from the Greek nomenclature: logos, pathos, and ethos. Logos is the logical reasoning used to persuade an audience. It involves the use of reason and rationality. Pathos refers to emotional appeal. This is where the writer attempts to tug at the heart strings in order to elicit a response from the audience. Ethos refers to the authority and credibility of the author. This facet involves the author trying to earn the respect of the audience and demonstrate that he/she is trustworthy and has earned the right to speak on the topic at issue. As James Crenshaw has pointed out, ethos, pathos, and logos correspond to the following goals respectively: to charm, to move, and to persuade (1980: 12).

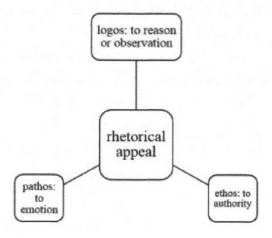

Figure 11: Rhetorical Appeal

Ethos

One particular wisdom work will serve nicely as illustration of rhetoric: Ecclesiastes. The ethos of the book is established in a number of ways. First of all, note the superscription to the book:

The words of the Assembler, son of David, king in Jerusalem (1:1).

Though scholars disagree on how to translate and understand the designation of the persona "Qohelet" or the "Assembler," it is obvious that the superscription is appealing to the authority of Solomon. Persona comes from a Greek word that originally designated a mask that an actor wore during a play. The frame-narrator uses this persona to present his message to the readers. The persona in fact puts a little difference between himself, the narrator, and Qohelet's words, which are technically distinct. More on this later.

In the first two chapters, the authority of an oriental, Solomon-like king is deployed to make the case that all is vanity. In these chapters, and some have argued that this royal conceit exists throughout the book (see Christianson 1998, 128-72), Qohelet assumes the role of such a king in order to more effectively argue that all human labor is futile. What better person to test the various pleasures and means of human happiness and well-being than a great king who has the means and intelligence to engage in such a exercise? The argument of the first two chapters would not be nearly as effective if the royal experiment in these chapters was engaged by a common person.

Logos

Argument by logos is also a significant facet which Qohelet uses to make his case. Qohelet uses his own powers of observation and reasoning to make his case that all human labor is futile. One of his favorite forms of evidence is the anecdote. While in academics today an anecdote is not as credible as hard evidence, in the ancient world it was seen as quite authoritative. Here is an example:

> There exists an evil I have seen under the sun, and it is severe upon humans. There is a man to whom is given riches and wealth and honor and there is nothing lacking to his soul of all he desires. And yet God does not allow him to consume it, for a stranger will consume it. This is a vanity and a sore disease (Eccles. 6:1-2).

Qohelet's argument that all is vanity is buttressed by a situation he apparently has observed recurrently. A person is given the two things that mattered to ancient peoples: material luxuries and a great reputation to accompany it. Yet, this person loses it all to a stranger. This may reflect a foreign despot who arbitrarily removes the property of a native nobleman and gives it to one of his cronies, who will now assume the position of the former (Lauha 1981, 400-401). At any rate, to have many valuable assets but not be able to utilize them is one of the pieces of evidence Qohelet uses to argue that all human toil is ultimately futile. The person here has no doubt worked hard for all his possessions and built up a good reputation, yet both of these things are destroyed through no fault of his own. He is powerless to prevent it. The anecdote helps clinch Qohelet's argument that human labor and effort are largely ineffective. In other words, it never "delivers the goods."

Pathos

Though Douglas Miller (2000, 224) argues that ethos is the most important rhetorical strategy for the book of Ecclesiastes, I would argue that it is pathos. On the surface Ecclesiastes appears to be a very cerebral book with its skepticism and arguments from observation. However, a closer look reveals that its primary form of argumentation is an appeal to the emotions. The theme of the book is found in the refrain that envelopes the words of Qohelet:

"Vanity of vanities," says Qohelet, "All is vanity" (1:2; 12:8).

The word for vanity is *hebel* in Hebrew, and it literally means "vapor" or "wind" and metaphorically "emptiness," "futility," and "worthlessness." It is often used to describe the futility of idols, which are gods made of metal or wood that can do nothing (e.g., Jer. 10:14–15). The word is used 38 times in the book and represents its leitmotif.

Hebel in Ecclesiastes can have the neutral meaning of "fleeting," referring to the transitory character of youthfulness (Eccles. 11:10), but its predominant usage is strongly negative. Thus, it is evaluative and negative (Seybold 1978, 319). It places a negative evaluation on traditional wisdom and other forms of human striving. Since it is evaluative, it represents the realm of values, and is, thus, emotive and technically non-rational. Qohelet and the frame-narrator use the word to lower expectations about God, the world, and humanity, especially human striving. For example, consider Eccles. 7:15:-18:

> I have seen everything in my *vain* days. There exists the righteous person perishing in his righteousness and there exists the wicked person living long in his wickedness. Do not be too righteous and do not be too wise. Why ruin yourself? Do not be too wicked and do not be foolish. Why die before your time? It is better that you grasp onto the one and not let your hand rest in regard to the other. For he who fears God will go forth from them both.

Here Qohelet first observes what he sees during his *vain* days as a human being. It is not pretty. What should be the reward for the righteous in fact becomes the reward for the wicked and vice versa. In this crazy, disordered world Qohelet advises taking a middle road. Do everything in moderation. Caution is the word of the day. Piety and wisdom cannot deliver on their promises. It is thus best to live life cautiously and carefully. Avoid all extremes. The God-fearer, which in Qohelet is not to be equated with the pious person, will have the best chance of survival because he/she is cautious. Qohelet's use of *hebel* in this passage serves to lower expectations in the reader about the world and human effort. It serves to help him/her resign him/ herself to the lack of control in such an inhospitable world.

Declaring everything vanity is certainly a very bleak and pessimistic perspective. All the anecdotes in the book are negative, and so, the narrator produces a very dark and weary world where everything goes wrong. The mood of the book, pessimism, thus, serves to persuade the reader that the best policy in life is caution and not putting all your eggs in the basket of piety or wisdom. This is an emotive appeal. In fact it is psychological. More on this when we discuss the book of Ecclesiastes.

Types of Public Argumentation

In classical rhetoric, there are three types of argumentation: judicial or forensic, deliberative or hortatory, and epideictic or demonstrative. All of these were originally germane to ancient Greek society, so employing them for studying ancient Semitic texts like the Hebrew Bible is technically anachronistic. However, most scholars view this move as heuristically beneficial, and employing this framework often brings a different perspective to the biblical texts.

Figure 12: Rhetoric in Threes			
Rhetoric in Threes			
Types:	judicial (forensic)	deliberative (hortatory)	epideictic (demonstrative)
setting	*court*	*assembly* (legislative)	*ceremony (civic)*
purpose	*persuade*	*persuade*	*please/inspire*
time orientation	*past*	*future*	*present*
focus	*justice*	*expediency*	*praise/blame*
emphasis	*speech*	*audience*	*speaker*

(adapted from Trible 1994, 9)

Judicial Rhetoric

The judicial type was originally situated in the courts of ancient Greece. The speaker or lawyer would try to persuade the judge to decide in favor of his client in a particular case. Judicial rhetoric is meant to defend or condemn a person or event (Miller 2000, 224). The focus is on the speech itself, and the time orientation is the past.

Judicial rhetoric is found in the book of Job when he debates his three friends, who try to convince him that he is guilty of some sin. It also found in the divine speeches when God defends his own integrity because Job has accused him of injustice (e.g., Job 27:2-6). He asks Job a series of rhetorical questions to get him to see that he is in no position to judge Him:

> Who is this who darkens counsel
> by words without knowledge?
> Gird up your loins like a man,
> and I will ask you and you will answer me!
> Where were you when I established the earth?
> Tell if you have understanding!
> Who set their measurements, if you know?
> Or who extended upon it a line?
> On what were its foundations sunk?
> Or who has lain its cornerstone,
> when the ringing in unison of the morning stars
> and all the sons of God shouted? (Job 38:4-7)

In the end, Job agrees that he was wrong to accuse God of injustice (Job 40:4-5). There is a strong appeal to authority (ethos) here with God's incomparable status contrasted with Job's.

Deliberative Rhetoric

Deliberative rhetoric focuses on expediency and attempts to persuade an audience to engage in a particular action; the time orientation is the future. It occurred in ancient Greece in the public assemblies. The emphasis is on the audience. There is no deliberative rhetoric in the wisdom literature because it does not attempt to call people to take action for a particular cause. However, the Psalter is filled with deliberative rhetoric because in the laments the psalmists attempt to persuade God to act on their behalf. Psalm 13 is good example:

How long, O Lord, will you continually forget me?
How long will you hide your face from me?
How long will I worry in my soul and be grievous in my heart daily!
How long will my enemies be exalted over me?
Pay attention and answer me, O Lord my God.
Cause my eyes to shine, lest I sleep the sleep of death,
lest my enemy say, "I prevailed over him,"
my enemy rejoice that I am shaken.
But I will trust in your kindness.
My heart will rejoice in your salvation.
I will sing to the Lord for he has dealt with me.

Here the psalmist raises the issue (see Charney, 2010) of God's failure to come to his cause. He hints at the problem that involves his enemies and perhaps an illness. He proposes a solution: rescuing him and avoiding unwanted consequences like being shamed or "dying." The last verse supplies further motivation for God: when rescued/healed, the psalmist vows to repay God with singing. One sees that the audience (God) is the focus and that there is a specific action being proposed: rescuing the psalmist. The future is the time orientation: God will hopefully deliver the psalmist soon! One sees here a strong appeal to pathos. The psalmist tries to get God to see that letting one of his own be humiliated, mistreated, or left to die would only bring shame or dishonor to Him as well as the psalmist. God's reputation is at stake, and, thus, he must act quickly. The psalmist also appeals to pathos in accusing God indirectly of not being a faithful covenant partner in that he has ignored his plight. This is an accusation of disloyalty and reflects the honor/shame culture that existed at the time. More on this in the next chapter.

Epideictic Rhetoric

The last kind of rhetoric is epideictic. This kind is not intended to call the audience to action for a particular cause. Rather, its aim is to praise and blame a person, event, or idea. Epideictic rhetoric is ultimately about reinforcing or challenging the values and ideas held dear to a particular culture (see Sheard 1996, 765-94; cf. Perelman and Olbrechts-Tyteca 1971, 51). Again, this is connected to the honor culture of the ancient Mediterranean world. With the wisdom literature, the goal is to praise wisdom and to laud its advantages and benefits, while simultaneously blaming folly for all kinds of disastrous consequences. Rather it extols and promotes a particular way of life: the way of wisdom and life. And it simultaneously denigrates the path of folly and death. Its favorite form of argument is comparison, typical of epideictic rhetoric.

For example, much of Proverbs 1-9 functions as a praise of wisdom and the simultaneous denigration of folly. This is achieved by the words of the parental voice (e.g., 1:8) and likewise with the personification of wisdom and folly. The latter two compete for young male disciples and attempt to "seduce" them to come follow them. They appeal to them both cognitively with arguments but also emotionally with suggestions of food and drink (symbols for sex). Woman Wisdom praises wisdom, of course, throughout her speeches. And then she invites the young men to her large manor:

> Wisdom built her house; she hewed out her seven pillars.
> She slaughtered her animals; she mixed her wine;
> she has even arranged her table.
> She has sent out her maidens;
> upon the heights of the city she has called out.
> "Whoever is young, turn here!"
> Whoever is uneducated, she speaks to him.
> "Come, eat my bread and drink my mixed wine!

Forsake simplicity and live. Advance in the way of understanding"
(Prov. 9:1-6).

Woman Folly never praises folly per se but instead distracts the young
suitors from its undesirable effects and emphasizes the immediate
pleasures of doing evil:

> Woman Folly is loud;
> she lacks understanding and does not know anything.
> She sits at the doorway of her house,
> upon a seat at the heights of the city.
> To call to those who pass along the way,
> those going straightway on their paths.
> "Whoever is young, turn here."
> Whoever is uneducated, she speaks to him.
> "Stolen water is sweet and hidden bread is pleasant!"
> And he does not know that the departed spirits are there;
> in the depths of Sheol are her guests (Prov. 9:13-18).

The last sentence is the narrator pointing out what Woman Folly is
careful to leave out. This also resonates with the father's warning to
the young man about the adulterous woman in Proverbs 7. She too
leads to Sheol:

> For many she has caused to fall slain; the mighty are all slain by her.
> The way to Sheol is her house; they descend to the chambers of death
> (7:26-27).

Thus, in the interaction between Woman Wisdom and Woman
Folly, wisdom is praised and has many positive consequences, while
folly gets blamed for all sorts of evils and disasters.

Even the book most critical of wisdom, Ecclesiastes, is epideictic
for just that reason. Qohelet points out the many liabilities of one
particular kind of human toil: wisdom. While he sees benefits to
being wise, he also recognizes its many disadvantages;

I saw that there exists a benefit to wisdom over folly,
as the benefit of light over darkness.
The wise person has his eyes in his head,
but the fool walks about in darkness.
Yet I know that one fate will befall them both!
I said in my heart, "As the fate of the fool, so will it befall me!
And why then have I been so wise?"
And I said in my heart, "This also is a vanity!"
For there is no remembrance
of the wise person along with the fool throughout eternity
because in the days to come everything will have been forgotten.
How the wise person dies along with the fool! (Eccles. 2:13-16).

Though Qohelet cannot totally praise wisdom and certainly does not think folly is the answer, there is one category that he can extoll without qualification: God fearing, which Qohelet means as being very cautious before what he perceives is a capricious God. He notes that God-fearers will come through the difficulties of a world that operates in unexpected ways. This is because the God-fearer is cautious and respects God's mystery. This notion occurs five times in the book (Eccles. 2:26; 3:14; 5:6; 7:18; 8:12-13). We have already considered Eccles. 7:15-18, where Qohelet recommends taking the path of moderation and concludes with the concept of God-fearing. Nowhere does Qohelet qualify this concept. It represents his alternative to both piety (righteousness) and wisdom. God-fearing in Qohelet does not have the usual pietistic connotation found throughout the rest of the Hebrew Bible, including the wisdom literature. With Qohelet, it connotes the literal fear and trembling before God, whom Qohelet conceives as arbitrary and capricious. Thus, Qohelet praises God-fearing but blames non-God-fearing, which might include the traditional notions of righteousness and piety.

The Distinctiveness of the Sapiential Ethos

We want to end this section of rhetoric by focusing on the distinctiveness of the authority of the wisdom writers. Wisdom experts generally assume that the wisdom literature is distinctive here, that as a corpus it does not have the same level of authority as say the Torah with its divine laws or the "Thus, says the Lord" of the prophets with their verbatim quotes from God. As James Crenshaw states:

> So long as wisdom represented human achievement, the authority conveyed to counsel and sapiential reflection lacked divine backing. This does not imply that the sages' observations had no authority, for they carried the weight of parental standing and compelled assent through logical cogency. . . . That is why the wise refused to reinforce their teaching by appealing to belief in creation. They could easily have said, "Do this because God created you and certain actions naturally follow." Instead, they appealed to a sense of self-interest and relied upon a capacity to reason things out (2010, 13-14).

This understanding of wisdom's authority is gravely mistaken. First of all, it fails to understand that the appeal to divine inspiration on the part of prophets and priests is a form of rhetoric itself. And in spite of both intellectual groups drawing on this type of authority for their words and writings, they resort to other types of ethotic rhetoric as well. For example, almost all the prophetic books give biographical information about the prophet in the superscription to their books. If the verbatim quotes from God that appear throughout their books are authoritative enough for these books, why do they include information about the prophet himself? If the prophets are merely conduits of God's word, why include information about the prophets? The answer is that the prestige and credibility of the prophet is also an important component in the overall ethotic strategy of the prophetic book as a whole.

Second and more fundamental, this perspective is wrong about the sages' understanding of the divine inspiration of their writings. The sages, evidently, believed their words to be divinely inspired as well or at least wanted them to be perceived as such. Brian Kovacs puts it best (I provide translations of his transliterations):

> What is the wise man's warrant? The prophet has *koh 'amar yhvh* ("thus says the Lord"); the priest has torah, tradition, and rite. . . . *'etsah* ("counsel") does not mean simply giving advice which can then be accepted or rejected according to the whims of the hearer. When given as counsel, it is the divine word no less than torah or oracle. Not surprisingly, then, 'mashal' ("proverb") can mean 'oracle' as well as 'proverb." The word of Ahithophel amounted to a divine oracle (2 Sam. 16:23). In the admonitions of the wise, the motivating clause is no more essential to the saying's authority than are such clauses for torah and oracle. In this sense, wisdom is authoritative *dabhar* ("word"), the word of Yahweh (1974, 184-85).

If Kovacs is correct, and I think he is, then the words of the wise would have been considered just as divinely inspired as those of the prophets or the priests or even Moses! Just because they do not often include verbatim quotes from God—though this occurs in Job 38-41—does not mean their words are any less inspired. In fact, though the prophets often include direct citations from God, most of the other material is in their own words—they either paraphrase God or they interpret his oracles; it is not all verbatim!

The Solomonic Ascriptions

The fact that the wisdom writers ascribe their words to Solomon in their superscriptions (Proverbs, Ecclesiastes, Wisdom of Solomon) further supports wisdom's inspired status. No doubt Solomon's name in the superscription to the book inter-textually brought to mind for the reader/hearer the famous dream at Gibeon in 1 Kings 3. Here the person who would become the father of the wisdom tradition in Israel is approached in the manner of the calling of a prophet in a dream and asked by God to request whatever he so desires for himself. Because he chooses wisdom to rule his people justly, God grants him long life, honor, and great riches. What is most important for our purposes is that wisdom here is portrayed as a gift given by God. Thus, Solomon's wisdom is a divine charisma, and the attribution of the sentences in Proverbs to Solomon serves to connect them with divine inspiration, even if indirectly. Though the sentences may not be coined by God himself, he provides the source for their production. Thus, in practical terms, what is the difference between divine revelation as in a citation from God in a prophetic oracle and divine charisma that is given to the father of wisdom, who purportedly composed thousands of *meshalim* ("maxims") (1 Kgs. 4:32)? Thus can the wisdom tradition claim inspiration and ultimately divine origin.

Woman Wisdom and Divinity

Most interesting for the divine inspiration of wisdom is Proverbs 8, where wisdom and divinity merge very closely. God creates wisdom as a frolicking maiden before he creates anything else. She was created before the rest of creation, a place of great honor. The whole scene ascribes divinity to her. For Christians, this of course brings to mind Christ's exalted status as the "firstborn of creation" (Col. 1:15).

Richard Clifford (1999, 99-101) makes an interesting and compelling argument about the translation of a key word in this passage in Prov. 8:30: *amon*. Woman Wisdom states, "I was by his side an *amon*, and I was a delight daily, playing before him continually." While one lexicon (Brown, Driver, Briggs 1980, 54) translates this word as "artisan, artificer, architect, master-workman, as firm and sure in his workmanship . . . craftsman," others have opted for "trustworthy friend" or "ward" or "nursling." But Clifford vocalizes the word as *oman*, an Akkadian loanword from *ummanu*, meaning "scribe, sage; heavenly sage," which had fallen out of usage by the time of the Septuagint and other versions. Clifford notes that an *ummanu* was "a divine or semi-divine bringer of culture and skill to the human race" (Clifford, 1999, 101). This, of course, alludes to the Mesopotamian antediluvian semi-divine sages who passed on their wisdom to humans through Zisudra or Utnaphistim, the Babylonian Noah, after the flood, in the form of the buried tablets that contained the "Instruction of Shurupak." In other words, Woman Wisdom here is the Hebrew Prometheus! Though she might not be involved in any acts of creation, she stands alongside God ready to transmit wisdom to the crown of his creation: humanity.

Summary

According to the wisdom literature in the Hebrew Bible, becoming wise meant more than just living a conformist and pious life or even being clever in making important decisions. Being wise, according to Proverbs, meant being able to read and comprehend the beauty and wit of the aphorisms composed by the sages. It meant being literate and catching the subtle nuances of these compact sophisticated sayings. It also meant being able to fill in the logical gaps of say a disjointed proverb and to guess the solution to a difficult riddle. But the wisdom literature did not confine itself to aesthetic and cognitive niceties. The aphorism involves the sophisticated assessment of values and how these are actuated in the real world. All of the aesthetic, cognitive, and moral dimensions of the wisdom literature would have served well the training of young Israelite scribes, who would someday serve in various governmental positions, as well as among the general populace.

But in order for the wisdom tradition to be effective in the training of scribes, it needs authority and appeal. The rhetoric of the sage is not much different from that of the priest or prophet. The sages too claim divine inspiration, though rarely via direct citation of the deity. All wisdom ultimately goes back to God. And the sages' reverence for Solomon, who received his wisdom in a dream, points in the same direction. Wisdom rhetoric is epideictic; it praises wisdom and blames folly. And it appeals not just to the rational side of humans but especially their emotions and values, which is what morality is all about.

8

Social World of the Sages

Honor and Shame in Israelite Society

Introduction

The social world of the ancient Israelites was quite a bit different from our own in the Western industrialized countries. In the last two decades, New Testament scholars have begun to use a grid to better understand that social world (for a recent review, see Esler 2012, 35-76). It is known as the Pan-Mediterranean honor culture. Anthropologists have studied certain subcultures of the modern Mediterranean world which display features of a very old culture that has persisted for millennia and have mapped out its elements. New Testament scholars and classicists have then used this grid to interpret archaeological artifacts and ancient texts. It is felt that these Mediterranean subcultures are basically a continuation of the old Greco-Roman culture. This anthropological perspective can help fill in cultural gaps that texts create for modern readers. Hebrew Bible scholars have also utilized this grid but not as extensively. Two exceptions would be Victor Matthews and Don Benjamin, who apply it to the notion of wisdom (Matthews 2000, 91–112; Matthews and Benjamin 1993, 142–58). Wisdom experts have rarely utilized it, but there are exceptions (in the case of Ben Sira, see Claudia Camp 1997, 171–87).

A good example of a clear vestige of this culture in our own world is the notion of honor killing. In many Arab countries today, if a young girl is raped, one sometimes hears of one of her brothers killing her. This is shocking and repulsive to modern Western sensibilities. The governments of these Muslim countries often ignore such killings because this phenomenon is so deeply ingrained in their cultures. Our inability to make sense of what is for us a misdirected and brutal act of violence demonstrates the great divide between our own culture and the world of the Hebrew Bible, which basically shares the same perspective as the modern Arab countries.

While the Hebrew Bible does not provide examples of honor killings of the victim per se, it does indicate that brothers were responsible for protecting the virginity of their sisters (cf. Song 1:6). If for some reason they failed to do this, they were required to avenge the disgrace and kill the perpetrators. In Genesis 34, Dinah, the only daughter of Jacob, is raped by Shechem. He later wants to marry her and tries to negotiate with Jacob and his sons for her hand in marriage. The brothers request that in order for this to happen, all the males of the city of Shechem must be circumcised. When they were recovering from the surgery, Simeon and Levi, Dinah's full brothers, killed all the males of the city. Also, in 2 Samuel 14, Tamar, the beautiful sister of Absalom, who lived at his home, is raped by her half-brother Amnon. Absalom conspires to slay his brother, which happens two years later.

All of these stories reflect the high value placed on virginity. In an honor culture, honor and shame are channeled sexually, i.e., they are gendered (see Delaney 1987, 35-48; Campbell 1974b, 270-71, 276). Virgins were a valuable commodity in the Mediterranean culture because they were a guarantee that a child was the future husband's progeny, on which his honor depended (see Delaney 1987, 40). The males of the household, especially brothers, were expected to do whatever necessary to prevent their virginal sisters from being penetrated by other males. This meant that they often veiled their women, which is reflected in the burkas of Muslim women today. Basically, the woman's sexuality was not to be exposed in any way (see Bourdieu 1974, 221). Even after marriage, the wife was treated in a sense as a virgin and kept from the eyes of non-family onlookers by coverings and veils.

If a girl or woman was penetrated and not married, then she became stigmatized and marked. A "tainted" woman had few prospects for marriage. She might marry a widower or divorced person and maybe a disabled man (see Campbell 1974b, 303-304). She was "damaged goods" essentially and the stigma could not be removed. Even if her perpetrator is killed, she is still marked for life. This is clearly seen in Tamar's case. Tamar pleads with Amnon not to do the terrible deed:

> No my brother, do not humiliated me, for *such a thing is not done in Israel*! Do not do this *disgraceful thing*! Where will I go with *my reproach*? And you will be one of the *good for nothing persons* in Israel! Speak to the king for he will not withhold me from you! (2 Sam. 13:12-13).

Tamar is rhetorically appealing to Amnon's sense of honor. She suggests that their father would allow an incestuous marriage. Anything would be better than raping one's sister! She indicates that basically her life will end if he does this deed. She will find it difficult to marry and have children, which is the means that women in ancient Israel achieved honor and elevated their status. At least in an incestuous marriage, married to a man she did not want to marry, she would have the opportunity to have children and live a fulfilled life of sorts. But once she has been penetrated by him illicitly, she becomes tainted for life.

Honor also necessitates that when one's own honor has been challenged or been impugned, some sort of retaliatory measure must be performed or the one challenged becomes shamed or dishonored. In the case of this story, Absalom's honor is challenged when Amnon violates his sister (see Esler 2012, 322-56). Absalom will remain in a state of dishonor or shame until he can reciprocate and attain his honor again. A male shamed must respond to a greater degree and force than the one who impugned his honor or else become shameful forever. From a modern Western perspective, Absalom's two year premeditated plan is brutal and extreme. But from the perspective of an honor culture, it is perfectly predictable.

Feasibility of Applying the Honor Culture Grid to the Hebrew Bible

A word of caution is advisable here. Though many biblical scholars believe that the honor culture paradigm is applicable to the biblical texts and world, anthropologists are less enthusiastic. In a book on applying this model to the Bible, two anthropologists responded to articles by biblical scholars. One was more positive about the venture though cautioned that it should be applied with more sophistication (Chance 1994, 139-49). The other did not believe that Israelite culture was really related to the Arab honor culture (Kressel 1994, 153-61). For example, Dianne Bergant (1994, 23-40) argues in her book that Song of Songs does not seem to reflect the typical features of an honor culture. She points out that the Shulamite is rather liberated and unconstrained in the book. The anthropologist thought she was too indecisive and speculated that the book represents a counter-text that resists the typical constraints of an honor culture (Chance 1994, 143-44). Similarly, W. R. Domeris (1995, 86-102) argues that the honor culture grid does not exactly fit the role of women in Proverbs. I think, however, she goes too far in her conclusions. The way women are depicted in the Proverbs is much closer to the Arab culture than she claims, as we shall see later. In general, however, the grid has been found to be very helpful for the biblical world by many scholars.

There is always the danger of applying this grid naively to the texts of the Hebrew Bible. It should always be emphasized that every culture, even today, displays aspects of honor and shame. Yet each differs in the way honor and shame is defined and applied. One must not force the text to conform to the paradigm and be sensitive to nuances that do not appear to fit.

Honor Culture: The Basics

Honor societies are those where one's relationships with family, friends, and allies are as important as one's social position (see Peristiany 1974, 11). This is different from our own Western societies that are bureaucratic and where one interacts often with anonymous individuals and engages indifferent institutions and laws. In honor societies, honor and shame are basically forms of social control that operate externally (Bourdieu 1974, 211-12; Brandes 1987, 130-31). This is also distinct from our modern Western societies where behavior is largely controlled internally by the individual's inward conscious. The allotment or distribution of honor and shame serves to reinforce a particular culture's cherished values and norms (Peristiany 1974, 10; Campbell 1974a, 150-51). Thus, an honorable person is one who exemplifies the virtues and desirable behavior that a specific culture values (see Campbell 1974b, 268). Conversely, a shameful person is one who does not abide by a particular culture's values and norms, is not "a team player," so to speak, and practices what that society would define as vices. Honor societies exert a lot of pressure on their members to conform to the values they hold dear. A person who acts honorably is rewarded with praise and other advantages. His/her ranking in society is also elevated.

Conversely, a person who acts shamefully is laughed at, ridiculed or mocked. His status is low. If his behavior is bad enough, he will even by shunned, sometimes by his own family! Gossip is one of the most important external forms of social control or sanctioning that works to ensure that people conform to the standards of society (see Asano-Tamanoi 1987, 115-16; Brandes 1987, 130; Giovannini 1987, 68-69; Campbell 1974b, 312-15). Instead of relying solely on an internal moral compass, in honor/shame cultures the populace puts social pressure on its members so that it will make it easier to conform. In modern Western societies, we generally disdain this kind of pressure and instead relish non-conformity. But in honor/shame cultures, to be a non-conformist is the greatest of sins!

Wisdom and Honor

In many ways, the wisdom literature reflects such a perspective. We have already cited a number of passages from the wisdom literature in the last chapter that reflect the importance placed on honor: Proverbs 8; 12:4; 12:9; 16:8; Eccles. 6:1-2, not to mention the non-wisdom passages that also allude to honor: Psalms 13; 1 Kings 3. In the wisdom literature, honor is social capital worth attaining! Here are a couple of examples:

A gracious woman attains honor,
but the powerful attain wealth (Prov. 11:16).

By prudent speech a man is praised,
by a twisted heart he will be contemptible (Prov. 12:4).

In Prov. 11:16, one sees a distinction between honor and wealth. Having wealth will not automatically bring one honor. It must be accompanied by generosity and benevolence, not violence. In Prov. 12:4, one sees a direct link between honor and wisdom. The Hebrew word for "prudent" (*sekel*) is within the semantic field of typical wisdom terms. The "twisted heart" is a perverted heart and connotes wickedness, as well as folly. This person will only suffer shame before others. In the wisdom literature in general one often sees the following correlation:

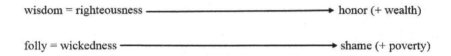

Figure 13: Correlation in Wisdom Literature

Thus, the wise person is largely a conformist, while the fool flaunts the rules of society and is subversive. Both are rewarded or punished with honor from society and wealth from God or shaming from society and poverty from God, respectively. In the wisdom literature, however, the wise person follows not only the basic norms of Israelite society, what we have called lifestyle wisdom, but is also held to a higher standard. He must be educated, a "gentleman," and discern the literary sophistication of riddles and aphorisms!

Prestige and Social Stratification

Honor or prestige is also intricately connected with social stratification, the pecking order of a society. The more honor or prestige a person accrues, the higher his ranking in society. Thus, honor is a social variable that is closely connected with wealth and power, the other variables of the trinity of social stratification (see Weber 1978, 302-307, 926-40). One's social class is her economic position within society. It designates a stratum of people who share similar economic interests and life chances (Weber 1978, 302-305; 926-32; Swedberg 2005, 37-38). Classes in ancient Israelite include the aristocracy (the upper class) or the peasantry. There are different ways to divide this pie. Groupings of prestige, like a status group (e.g., Levites, scribes, Nazarites), are also distinct from class in that they involve clusters of people who share a similar lifestyle (Weber 1978, 302-307, 926-40; Swedberg 2005, 38).

Power refers to the ability to force other people to do what you want done (Weber 1978, 53, 926; Swedberg 2005, 205-6). Groupings of power are called parties (e.g., patrons, Pharisees, Hassidim, Essenes) (Weber 1978, 284-88, 938-39; Swedberg 2005, 194). Wealthy people usually have more power in society than do the poor. And governmental officials can have more power than wealthy people, depending on the situation. Thus, being a member of the upper class does not automatically mean an extensive amount of power, though power gravitates toward wealth. Even the poor have a degree of power and can exert a certain amount of influence in society, especially if they band together, though nothing like the wealthy (cf. Foucault 1980, 72, 142).

Prestige or honor also tends to gravitate toward wealth and power, but not always. For example, a mafia don has incredible amount of power within the mafia community. He also usually has much wealth and high status among his peers. However, outside this community a don is viewed with disdain or shame. He may be powerful and wealthy but outsiders do not usually view him with respect. Also, university professors usually have high status but are not usually of the upper class and do not hold a lot of power. Thus, while power and wealth can increase your prestige within society, this is not always the case, especially if you are corrupt and abuse your power.

Corporate versus Individualistic Identity

Honor cultures are very family-centered, and one's identity and status is essentially determined by the family one is born into (see Peristiancy 1974, 11; Bourdieu 1974, 229). One's primary role in the family is to bring honor to it and avoid bringing any shame. Members of a family then share in the status of the family as a whole, and they all will defend the honor of their family, even to the point of death, if necessary (see Campbell 1974b, 272). Honor and shame always then involve a corporate dimension. Archaeologically, for rural settings in Iron Age II (eighth -seventh centuries B.C.E.), during the monarchy, the family to be honored was an extended one. But for city dwellers, the nuclear family was the norm (Faust 2012, 111). The wisdom writers seem to focus more on the nuclear family than the extended (e.g., Prov. 31:10-31), though there are aphorisms that speak of grandparents: "A crown for the elderly is grandchildren, and the glory of sons is their parents" (Prov. 17:6).

This does not mean that there is no concept of individuality in honor cultures (see Esler 2012, 57). There will be competition among the siblings for preeminence within the family. The story of Jacob and Esau is the classic example of this struggle. The older brother automatically is ranked higher because of his age, but younger brothers can certainly attempt to challenge that, as Jacob indeed did (Genesis 25, 27). Jacob himself also had favorite sons, who were the youngest: Joseph and Benjamin, born from his favorite wife Rebekah. When David appears before his brothers to provide them with food, they are offended that their younger and lower status brother is asking questions about the military challenge of Goliath. Eliab, the eldest brother, attempts to rebuff him but to no avail (1 Sam. 17:28-30). When David ends up killing the giant, his rank escalates far above his brothers, and he then becomes predominant within his own family. Thus, there certainly was "sibling rivalry" among Israelite families even as today.

Degrees of Relationship and Ethical Behavior

In honor cultures, there are basically three levels of relationships, each involving a different code of ethics (see Campbell 1974a, 142; 1974b, 38-42). First are the kinsmen by blood. While there is competition among siblings in the family, all are expected to be honest and candid with close family members. One can feel free to be completely open and reveal emotions within this context. Next is the broader kin relations that extend to the affines, people related by marriage. Here one is expected to be honest but complete openness is discouraged. One keeps family matters within the confines of the home. One reciprocates gifts with comparable gifts (see chapter one). The concealment of information is allowed. The third level would be strangers. Ethically there are "no holds barred" in this relationship. Dishonesty and cheating, in fact, are valued as honorable endeavors (see Bourdieu 1974, 228; Campbell 1974b, 282-83). One attempts to take advantage of strangers, and no guilt is felt in doing this. That the Israelite laws were intended to be an inner-Israelite code, not valid for enemies, is indicated by Jesus' universalistic reinterpretation of them in the Sermon on the Mount (Matt. 5:38-48).

The Perspective of Limited Good

In honor cultures one finds the notion that goods are always limited and in short supply, whether wealth, honor, or power (see Campbell 1974b, 204; Neyrey 1998, 122-27). Anthropologists refer to this as the perspective of limited good. This is the idea that someone's wealth, power, or prestige, is always at the expense of someone else. In other words, the ancients believed in what we call today a zero sum game. They saw all of the world as connected, as systemic, one part directly affecting the other parts. No one is an island to herself. For example, in the New Testament, the parable of the "Rich Man and Lazarus" (Luke 16) insinuates that the rich man's great abundance is at the expense of Lazarus. That the two are paired together indicates this. Being wealthy was certainly not condemned in the ancient world, but the rich were expected to be very generous with wealth, with abundant acts of charity, to compensate somewhat for the inequality. Because the rich man in the parable is not generous with his wealth, not even extending charity to Lazarus, the rich man is condemned.

Another example is in Genesis 27, where Isaac is deceived into pronouncing upon Jacob Esau's firstborn blessing (see Esler 2012, 66-67). When Jacob is blessed, he is told God will bless him "from (partitive *mem*; see Westermann 1985, 443) the dew of the heavens and from the fatness of the land, and much grain and new wine" (27:28). Here fertility is the focus and great wealth will be the result. Also, Jacob is told that he will be "lord over his brothers and your mother's sons will bow down to you" (27:29). When Esau discovers the scheme he begs his father for a blessing, "'Do you only have one blessing, my father? Bless me also, my father!' And Esau lifted up his voice and wept." Isaac pronounces what one could call an un-blessing:

Away from (privative *mem*: Westermann 1985, 443) the fat of the land
will be your dwelling,
And away from the dew of the heaven above.
You will live by the sword and will serve your brother.
But when you become restless, you will break his yoke from upon your
neck (27: 39).

Jacob's increase must simultaneously mean Esau's decrease. There is
only one firstborn blessing. Once it is pronounced, it can neither be
retrieved, nor duplicated, because even blessings are limited and not
infinite, even from a patriarch.

Also, in terms of prestige, God in Judges 7 commands Gideon to
whittle down the men who will fight against the Midianites to 300,
who drink water in a particular way (see Esler 2012, 67). God does
this because he did not want the Israelites to claim the victory as their
own:

And the Lord said to Gideon, "The people who are with you are too
many to give Midian into their hand, lest Israel will *glorify* itself over me
saying, 'My hand has delivered me!'" (Judg. 7:2).

The Hebrew verb for "glorify" (*pa'ar*) is semantically related to
"honor" (*kaved*), both terms of social stratification. Thus, even honor
is limited in connection with God. Israel's increase in honor
simultaneously means God's decrease in honor. And, conversely,
Israel's diminishment in honor simultaneously means the
enhancement of God's honor.

We have already mentioned the evil eye as a type of magic that is
found in Proverbs. It relates to the notion of limited goods because
the wealthy were expected to avoid being ostentatious and were to
be very generous simultaneously. A stingy wealthy person risked
being envied by the poor, who could cast an evil glance at them that
essentially becomes a curse. Among the Sarakatsani shepherds of the
Greek mountains, old women are feared for displaying the evil eye

(Campbell 1974b, 290-91). The wealthy are also warned by God that he is the guardian of the poor and oppressed and that he will take vengeance on the wealthy who abuse them (e.g., Exod. 22:20-26; Deut. 10:18; see Sneed 1999b, 501-503).

Challenge and Riposte

In an honor culture, one's honor can always be challenged (see Esler 2012, 61-64). The challenger can, if fact, increase his own honor by challenging someone else's honor, if that person does not respond appropriately and he does not delay too long. A challenge to one's honor can be countered either with violence or verbally. When Amnon violated Tamar, he insulted Absalom's honor (see Esler 2012, 322-56). If Absalom had done nothing, he would have remained shameful and considered weak. Thus, his slaying of Amnon two years later would have been considered an appropriate response, though the delay is unusually long. We have mentioned the story of David and Abigail, when David's men request permission to enjoy some of the food Nabal has recently prepared during the sheep shearing (1 Samuel 25). Nabal insults them by questioning David's family status: "Who is David and who is the son of Jesse?" (v. 10). David's planned response is to meet insult with violence. Fortunately, Abigail, Nabal's wife, intervenes and prevents the slaughter of the males of her household.

Even the giving of gifts, a type of reciprocity, can serve as a challenge to someone, who in turn must answer with an ever more elaborate gift or suffer disgrace (see Bourdieu 1974, 204). The story of the reunion of Jacob and Esau (Genesis 32-33) provides an example of this. When Jacob learns that Esau has 400 men with him, he sends gifts ahead of his family that go before him to Esau. In Genesis 33, Esau tries to politely refuse the gifts because he knows accepting the gifts would beholden him to his brother and that he would have to reciprocate in some way or suffer shame (cf. Matthews 1999, 96-99; Stansell 1999, 76-78):

> "What is all this caravan of yours I encountered?" And (Jacob) said, "To find favor in the eyes of my Lord." And Esau said, "I have enough, my brother, let yours be yours!" And Jacob said, "No, please, if I have found favor in your eyes, take my gift from my hand, for inasmuch as I have seen your face, it is as an image of the face of God, and you found favor in me! Please take my *blessing* which has been brought to you, for God has favored me and I have everything." And he urged him and he took it. (Gen. 33:8-11).

It is significant that Esau will not take the gift until Jacob refers to it as his "blessing." This alludes to the blessing that Jacob had stolen from Esau by deceiving their father Isaac and pretending to be Esau (Genesis 27). When Esau realizes that Jacob's "gift" is really an attempt to return part of the blessing he deceptively received from their father, he finally accepts the gift. The "gift" then is no gift at all but an attempt by Jacob to repay his brother for the theft of his blessing many years ago. Since no further reciprocity would be involved–because this is "repayment"—Esau accepts the "gift."

A final example of challenge and response will come from the wisdom literature in the book of Proverbs:

> Do not answer a fool according to his folly,
> lest you be like him.
> Answer a fool according to his folly,
> lest he become wise in his own eyes (Prov. 26:4-5).

Many wisdom experts have pondered these verses trying to explain why they seemingly contradict each other. There have been numerous explanations, most leaving the conundrum unresolved (see Fox 2009, 793-94). Fox sees the second admonition qualifying the first.

This is reasonable, but what is the reason for the qualification? As far as I can tell, no wisdom expert has resorted to the honor culture paradigm to explain these verses. From an honor culture perspective, these verses certainly involve the situation of challenge and riposte. In this type of situation, the main concern is in how the one challenged gauges whether he can ignore the challenge and still maintain his honor. And the question of ignoring a challenge always relates to the relative social status of the combatants (see Bourdieu 1974, 197-215). Thus, if the challenger is of a lower status than the one challenged, then he can probably ignore the challenge with impunity. Also, if the challenger is of a higher status than the one challenged, then not reciprocating would be the safest route and would probably incur no loss of face, since the one challenged is essentially under the authority of the challenger and can do nothing about it. However, if the combatants are of the same social status, then the challenged person must respond in some way to preserve his honor intact. Also, if the challenger is belligerent and keeps challenging the person, then the intensity of the attack demands some kind of response in order to preserve the honor of the one challenged.

And so I would argue that the fool is technically of a lower status than a sage, and, so the normal approach would be for a sage to ignore him or respond to him in a less belligerent way. As Roland Murphy points out for Prov. 26:4, "[D]eigning to an answer is to give honor to one who does not deserve it, 26:1" (Murphy 1998, 199). In 26:1, one finds, "Like snow during the summer or rain the harvest, thus honor is not befitting the fool." However, Prov. 26:5 would apply in situations where the honor of the sage is challenged to such a degree that some kind of response is necessary. Thus, the fool must be put in his place! It could also be that wisdom is at stake and to ignore the fool would be to admit that folly prevails—something that could not be countenanced—and this is still an honor concern.

Different policies prevailed in different cultures. In dealing with quarrelers in Egypt, apparently one size fits all! Scribes are advised to be silent before quarrelsome persons. This is confirmed by the "Instruction of Ptahhotep," which provides an example of the effectiveness of silence before an aggressive quarreler in maxims 2-4. Lichtheim's summary captures the gist:

> If the quarreler is a powerful man, keep silent; for opposing him will harm you, and his evil speech . . . will reveal his ignorance.
>
> If the quarreler is a poor man, keep silent, do not oppose him, for "vile is he who injures a poor man."
>
> If the quarreler is on your level, keep silent while he speaks evilly,
>
> and the listeners will recognize your worth (1997, 24).

Lichtheim concludes, "Silence, then, is an active virtue which stops quarrel and combat." She also concludes, "[T]he overall thrust of the teachings is that none of the virtues and vices are specific to a class" (Lichtheim 1997, 24).

There are a couple of consecutive maxims about scoffers that reinforce this notion:

> One who admonishes a scoffer receives shame,
> and the one who reproves the wicked, he is repulsive.
> Do not reprove a scoffer lest he hate you,
> reprove a wise man and he will love you (Prov. 9:7-8).

These show that how one responds to a scoffer or fool depends on gauging the effects of shame. As a general policy it is better to ignore the fool (or respond benignly) because to engage him further would be to elicit insult and challenge. However, as Prov. 26:5 indicates, there are times when the appropriate response is to defend one's honor and turn the table or else experience loss of face before the audience.

Patron and Client

Another special type of relationship that is significant among honor cultures is the patron-client relationship (see Pitt-Rivers 1974, 58; Campbell 1974b, 211-62). This type of relationship occurs outside kin relations. It is important because it is a way that poorer families within poorer clans can gain political leverage that their own extended families cannot provide. It can also help families gain access to the larger power structures. The classic example often given to explain this phenomenon is from the movie *The Godfather* (cf. Lemche 1994, 119-20). In the movie, the godfather meets with a relatively well-to-do father whose daughter had been brutally beaten by her boyfriend and his friend. They practically receive a slap on the wrist in the judicial system. The godfather acts as if he is surprised the father has come to him for redress because the father had never submitted himself to the Godfather's protection. Only now when he finds himself in trouble does he come to the Godfather. The father finally kisses the Godfather's ring and becomes his client. Soon justice occurs. The father is now expected to honor the Godfather and become subservient to him. In return, he can expect the Godfather's protection.

Among the Sarakatsani, the godfather system is very popular (Campbell 1974b, 217-24). Poorer families seek an older wealthier man to serve as godfather for their children. The godfather usually attends the baptism of the child, and he is expected to aid her spiritually and sometimes financially. Hospitality is also a type of patron/client relationship with the host serving as patron and guest client (see Herzfeld 1987, 86).

In the wisdom literature, warnings against going surety for a neighbor (Prov. 6:1-5; 17:18; 22:26; 11:15; 20:16; 27:13), particularly for a foreigner, are found. Going surety is comparable to cosigning a loan today. Here is an example from Proverbs and Ben Sira (second century B.C.E.):

> My son, if you serve as surety for a neighbor,
> if you shake hands for a stranger,
> if you are ensnared by the word of your mouth,
> if captured by the words of your mouth,
> do this then, my son, deliver yourself
> for you have brought yourself into the hand of your neighbor.
> Go, humble yourself, implore your neighbor!
> Do not give sleep to your eyes or slumber for your eyelids!
> Deliver yourself, like a gazelle from the hand,
> like a bird from the hand of a fowler (Prov. 6:1-5).

> A good person will be surety for his neighbor,
> but the one who has lost all sense of shame will fail him.
> Do not forget the kindness of your guarantor,
> for he has given his life for you.
> A sinner wastes the property of his guarantor,
> and the ungrateful person abandons his rescuer.
> Being surety has ruined many who were prosperous,
> and has tossed them about like waves of the sea;
> It has driven the influential into exile,
> and they have wandered among foreign nations.
> The sinner comes to grief through surety;
> his pursuits of gain involves him in lawsuits.
> Assist your neighbor to the best of your ability,
> and be careful not to fall yourself (Sir. 29:14-20).

The Dead Scroll 4Q Instruction (4Q416 2 ii, 4-6) includes a similar caution about going surety for a neighbor, although the intended audience would be much poorer than in Proverbs and Sirach (see Goff 2013, 23-26). However, few scholars have speculated about why one would risk such a precarious action, if it could mean the ruin of the guarantor financially. Michael Fox speculates that this act represents charity or in the case of foreigners a service fee (Fox 2000, 215). However, if it is charity, it goes beyond the typical measures of charity. It makes better sense to see the willingness to serve as surety as a desire to form a patron–client relationship. The payoff for this kind of act is considerable. The guarantor receives honor for being benevolent not only from his client but from onlookers who will admire the good deed. A patron with many clients has more honor than one with only a few. And, so, a competition ensues to gain the most clients as possible. There is also the benefit that if the patron falls from grace for whatever reason, he can count on his clients to aid him in turn (see Campbell 1974b, 223). Among the Sarakatsani, lawyers, who resemble the scribes in role, they often assume the role of godfathers for their clients' children (Campbell, 1974b, 244).

In the "Instruction of Amenemope," one finds evidence that being generous entailed receiving honor:

> If you find a large debt against a poor man,
> make it into three parts;
> release two of them and let one remain;
> you will find it a path of life;
> you will pass the night in sound sleep; in the morning
> you will find it like good news.
> Better it is to be *praised* as one loved by men
> than wealth in the storehouse[.] (Simpson 1973, 255; italics mine).

Also, Any, the scribe, notes the ultimately self-serving character of generosity to others:

> One man is rich, another is poor.
> But food remains for him [who shares it].
> As to him who was rich last year,
> he is a vagabond this year;
> don't be greedy to fill your belly,
> you don't know your end at all.
> Should you come to be in want,
> another may do good to you (Lichtheim 1976, 142).

The wisdom writers would have viewed the king they served under as their patron. This is reflected in their seeking his favor or grace:

> The favor of the king is for a wise servant,
> and his anger will be upon one who brings shame (Prov. 14:35).

Grace is what the patron extends to his clients; honor is what the client extends to his patron (Campbell 1974b, 234). The Israelites would have viewed God as their super-patron (cf. Campbell 1974b, 345). He blessed and favored them, while they in return honored him through praise and the offering of sacrifice.

Patron/client relationships are especially exemplified by the LBA Amarna letters. The scribes who composed letters that were sent to the pharaoh assume a client relationship with the pharaoh. The scribes address the pharaohs with patron–client terms like "my lord" or "my father" and "your son" or "your servant" (Izre'el 1995, 2413). What is interesting is that the Egyptians did not accept this relationship. Instead, they saw the Canaanite city states and their administrators more as subjugated peoples or colonies and often ignored the pleas for help that the Canaanites expected as clients (Liverani 2001)! This misunderstanding continually frustrated the Canaanite scribes.

The patron–client relationship is really about reciprocity. There is give and take on both sides. The patron extends his favor in the form of power and financial gifts. But the client extends honor to the patron and supplies him with a loyal group whom he someday may need in the case of his own unexpected political demise or crisis. The larger his following, the greater his prestige within the larger community as a whole.

But the doctrine of retribution is also about reciprocity and the patron-client relationship. God, as super-patron, rewards the loyalty and obedience of his clients, the pious and wise Israelites, with long life and prosperity. Those who demonstrate lack of loyalty or bring shame to his name, the foolish and wicked Israelites, will receive sickness, poverty, and death. Being wise then, within the wisdom literature, is about attempting to live in such a way that God, the super-patron, will be pleased and bestow his favor. Thus, nothing ever escapes the notion of reciprocity!

Wisdom Literature as Eudemonistic

Like other Israelites in an honor culture, the sages would have shared a cooperate identity that was largely tied to their families and their reputations, especially the nuclear family for the urban scribes. However, what will seem odd is that the wisdom literature and especially the book of Proverbs seems to focus heavily on the individual and his interests to the exclusion of community interests. In fact, some have seen the book of Proverbs as appearing to advise selfishness (see Schwáb, 88-90). And even when their advice in Proverbs benefits the larger public, it is usually motivated by appeals to the self-interest of the addressee.

For example, there are many maxims warning against being lazy: "A slack hand creates poverty, but a diligent hand makes one rich" (Prov. 10:4). Laziness would be a vice for not only the scribal novices but for any young Israelite, whether elite or not. A lazy person represents the quintessential narcissist, who does not think of the community but only her own desires. Slothfulness is a vice primarily because of the damage it does to society because every hand was needed in an agricultural society, where laborers were in demand. Instead of promoting the community benefits of industry, this aphorism focuses on the negative results that will accrue to the lazy person, not its effect on society. This can partially be explained as pedagogical rhetoric. By appealing to the addressee's self-interest, the aphorism is more effective in motivation.

Most of the maxims are aimed at benefitting the scribal apprentice hearing or reading it, not the scribal apprentices as a whole. For example, the addressee is told to seek the king's favor through appropriate behavior:

> The favor of kings is upon righteous lips,
> and one who speaks uprightly, he will love (Prov. 16:13).

Remembering our discussion about limited good, when a scribe attains the king's favor or goodwill, another scribe does not. In another case, the addressee is told to control his temper and thereby increase his status:

> An angry man will stir up strife,
> but a patient man will pacify strife (Prov. 15:18).

This would be to the benefit of the individual scribe, not the whole "school" of them. This is advice that will help the individual scribe "climb the latter of success" and attain advantages over his peers. A strong element of competition is implied here.

Some rather strikingly, almost Machiavellian (morally questionable but politically expedient) maxims advise the necessity of gifts or bribes in order to enable a person to have access to someone important:

> A gift is a precious stone in the eyes of its owner,
> to wherever he turns, he will succeed (Prov. 17:8).

However, as already pointed out, a gift used to distort justice is condemned (Prov. 17:23). And a bribe received can corrupt one's heart:

For oppression makes the wise into a fool,
and a gift cause the heart stray (Eccles. 7:7).

The difference is that a gift can be used by an underling to gain greater access, while a judge who receives gifts becomes corrupt.

The most "egocentric" book of the wisdom literature is the book of Ecclesiastes, which seems less concerned about communal needs than any other book. Whatever advice Qohelet gives, it is from the perspective of how it benefits the addressee:

Better two than one, to whom there is a reward for their toil.
For if one falls, his companion will lift him up.
But woe to the one who falls
and there is not a second person to lift him up.
Also, it two sleep together, they become warm,
but if there is only one, how can he become warm?
And if one overpower the one, the two will stand up against him.
A three-ply cord will not be easily torn in two (Eccles. 4:9-12).

Here there is no discussion of the needs of the community, even of a dyad, but only how having a companion benefits someone. In his book, Qohelet never even speaks of bringing honor to one's family but instead counsels enjoying one's family as much as possible (9:9). More on this later. Eberhard Wölfel argues that the inherent egocentrism of the wisdom tradition is what led Qohelet to his pessimistic perspective (1958, 84-88).

Another explanation is to recognize the nature of this mode of literature. It is focused on the individual, and so to expect it to address the needs of the community is unrealistic. And finally, perhaps, the best explanation is to understand the type of ethical system that Proverbs and the other wisdom texts promote. The Greeks help us here. The ethic of the wisdom literature can be described as eudemonism and it goes back to Aristotle (see Schwáb, 91-93).[1] The goal of a eudemonic ethical system is the happiness of the person: what brings her/him the most satisfaction in life. Aristotle's *Nichomachean Ethics* is the standard text for this system. Most of Proverbs exudes this type of ethic. Even as Aristotle intended, though a eudemonistic ethic is focused on the individual, all of this serves the greater good—the political body as a whole. The happy man in Greek society, but also in Israelite society, would make the best citizen. So, the eudemonism in Proverbs and the rest of the wisdom literature does not conflict with the honor culture in which they were ensconced.

Wisdom as a Means Value

We have already mentioned that honor ranks near the top of what Israelites desired most. It ranks second only to the basic essentials for life and to love and companionship. So what is wisdom's relation to honor? What kind of value does wisdom represent? We have already referred to the story of Solomon's dream in 1 Kings 3, where God asks Solomon to ask for whatever he wants. Because Solomon asks for wisdom to lead the people, God gives him everything that a king would usually ask for: great wealth, honor, and long life. So, how would these three values stack up? Which would be core values and which would be means values (values that are in not in themselves core values but enable one to access core values). Of course, from the standpoint of the Maslow hierarchy of needs, wealth would help with the physiological needs in that the basic necessities would certainly be provided for. But beyond sustenance, wealth becomes a means value. Wealth itself does not provide happiness for a person, but it is what wealth does that is important. In an honor culture wealth can bring

---

1. Others who have employed Greek philosophy to understand the ethics of Proverbs are Fox (2007, 75-88) and Ansberry (2010, 157-73); for the wisdom literature as a whole, cf. Brown 1996, 9-11.

power and honor, so it is definitely a means value. Long life, again, is connected to the physiological and safety needs because it implies the ability to live securely and with enough sustenance to reach old age. But living beyond the immediate present was not the major concern for most people of the ancient world, and so long life is largely a dream and not an immediate need, and certainly not really within one's power.

Figure 14: Wisdom and Eudemonism

What about wisdom? Wisdom is a means value in Proverbs (cf. Campbell 1974a, 151–52; contra Domeris 1995, 95–96). Wisdom is valuable because it can lead to all three of the other values: wealth, longevity, and honor, which all contribute toward happiness. But of these three, honor is the only one that is a core value (Plevnik 1998, 106; Pilch and Malina 1998, xix). One becomes wealthy and wise so that one can be honored. Esteem or honor is the only value of the three that one finds on the Maslow hierarchy of needs. One does not find wealth or power there, because these are means values. Even power is a means value because one seeks power not only to perhaps gain greater wealth but ultimately to increase one's prestige! A wealthy and powerful person who does not have the respect of his family and peers or the broader community (i.e., honor) does not have much (cf. Campbell, 1974b, 306)!

Brain Kovacs seems to view wisdom in Proverbs as a core value:

Thus, even if the wise man is oriented toward the acknowledged

Hebrew goods-of-life (long life, success, progeny, and recognition), he may not seek them directly nor by the path of his own planning. Only by pursuing wisdom for its own sake, so that it is good and valuable in its own right rather than instrumentally, by means of the discipline of restraint, can he succeed. It is only a slight exaggeration to say that the wise could seek success only by giving it up (1974, 183).

This is certainly the way the sages saw it, but that does not make it true. The virtuous life could be considered an end in itself, as even Aristotle surmised (1962, 15). However, even Aristotle admits that virtue can also can be viewed as a means value: it leads to happiness. From this perspective, wisdom serves a higher purpose. It is not an end in itself. The reality is that the wise lifestyle that Kovacs argues the sages seek non-instrumentally would not be attractive to the sages if they were not admired by others for being wise. Wisdom for its own sake would not mean much without a community that honored the sages for their wisdom. There is a social element here that cannot be eliminated. The sages at least wanted the respect of their peers and God, even if they could not get it from the broader community. But that is all that prestige demands: the respect of some group, if only a small circle of elites.

Honor as the core value also makes sense in terms of the social location of the sages who composed the biblical wisdom literature. They did not possess great power or wealth. So, status or prestige was an especially valuable commodity to them. It was for them social capital par excellence!

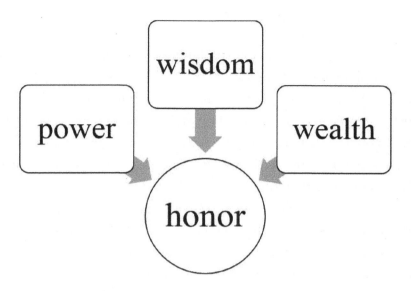

Figure 15: The Israelite Core Value of Honor

Wisdom as Intellectual Pleasure

There were, however, aspects of wisdom that were pleasurable in themselves, with no utility beyond themselves. The sages' relish for cognitive pleasures that included pondering the paradoxes of life and seeking more and more knowledge and insight about the cosmos was equally important for their satisfaction as human beings. And, related, their love of literary aesthetics was also a pleasure in itself that needed no utilitarian function. Beauty is one of those pleasures that is an end in itself (see Bautch and Racine 2013), and as intellectuals, the sages appreciated the literary subtleties that their colleagues were able to create in their compositions. This implies the satisfaction of the life of a scholar—his particular form of happiness.

The Social Class of the Sages

The sages who composed the wisdom literature, except for the Dead Sea Scroll representatives (see Goff 2013, 23-27), can be located within the retainer social class. This is not a middle class (see Sneed 1999b, 53-65). As the word suggests, retainers were retained by the governing or upper class to serve their own personal needs. A classic example of the retainer class is reflected in the popular British TV show "Downton Abbey." The butler, cooks, maids, and other laborers who serve the needs of the aristocrats are examples of the retainer class. Many of the members of the English retainer class, which existed for centuries, were relatively poor, but they were not at the bottom of the rung. Their position was superior to truly impoverished peasants and serfs. And a segment of the retainers could be rather comfortable economically like the chief butler or other high functionaries.

Basically, the retainer class is parasitic on the governing or ruling class, much like the sucker fish that attaches itself to large sharks (on this class, see Lenski 1984, 243-48). Their advantages and benefits come from their close relationship with the governing class. In fact, sometimes retainers, because of the economic advantages they accrue, end up eventually becoming members of the governing class themselves (see Lenski 1984, 244).

Going beyond the British system, retainers also include soldiers and governmental officials. Obviously, they serve the needs of the governing class. High governmental and military officials are usually well remunerated well because of the danger of a coups d'état (see Lenski 1984, 247-48). Revolts often come from this social stratum because of all their connections and the loyalty of those under them. Governmental retainers also served as a buffer zone between the governing class and the masses (Lenski 1984, 246). Aristocrats and the governing elite rarely had direct contact with the lower classes. The retainers essentially served as mediators between these strata. Thus, the governing class never had to feel the direct umbrage of the common people.

Scribes were technically members of the retainer class. As administrators, whether for the public or privately, they served the needs of the truly elite and powerful. As state officials, their power is always derived; they were representatives of the ruling class and only wielded the power they were allotted by it. Some of these scribes became quite powerful and wealthy, as we have seen. But most probably led generally comfortable lives, except for perhaps village scribes, who would have held high status, if not well-to-do. The constant motivation found in Proverbs for attaining wisdom is wealth and high status. This makes perfect sense for the scribal elite. Though not the most wealthy and powerful of their society, Israelite scribes were in a position to take advantage of many economic opportunities beyond their employment by the government, like absentee landlordism (see Gordis 1971, 162) and serving as free-lance administrators for private persons, as we saw earlier. However, the scribes who composed wisdom literature most likely led comfortable lives and were more focused on their teaching and producing their literature than on attaining great wealth.

The sages' location as retainers also explains their conflicted class culture, what Gottwald refers to as class contradiction (Gottwald 1985, 574), a Marxist notion that a person who objectively occupies a particular social class reflects the values of another class. Marxists often describe this phenomenon in connection with intellectuals, a social category we will treat next (e.g., Wright 1978, 5-18; Poulantzas 1973, 38).

Basically, the authors of the book of Proverbs reflect both an aristocratic and proletarian perspective simultaneously. The latter is reflected in their empathetic concern for the poor and in their critical perspective of those above them, viewing wisdom as superior to power and wealth:

> The anger of the king is a messenger of death,
> but a wise man will appease it (16:14).

> A wise man goes up against a city of warriors,
> and he topples the strength of their confidence (21:22).

> A slave who succeeds will rule over a son who brings shame,
> in the midst of brothers he will share the inheritance (17:2).

The latter aphorism ironically questions the status quo (Kovacs 1974, 182).

The sages' aristocratic perspective is reflected in their adherence to the doctrine of retribution, where piety and wisdom issue in wealth and prosperity. This doctrine is akin to the concept of karma, which amazingly justifies the caste system by teaching that everyone's social location is in consequence to the way one lived in a previous life. The result is that no one could complain about the social conditions she experiences!

As Gottwald points out, the wise also vilify the poor on occasion in connecting slothfulness with poverty (1985, 573). Again, here is an example: "A slack hand creates poverty, but a diligent hand makes one rich" (Prov. 10:4). The Sarakatsani also view the very poor as morally culpable (Campbell 1974b, 273). But one could argue that this vilification of poverty is used to motivate the young sages to study hard and become successful so that they do not end up in the same situation. Yet, even this explanation does not completely justify the sages' elitism. The bottom line is that the sages, as represented in Proverbs, reflect a complex class culture because of their complex social location as retainers. They largely share the aristocratic worldview of their employers, yet they distance themselves from this stratum because of their comparatively less advantaged lifestyle and, thus, their perceived connection with the rest of society, who suffered under the hand of the governing class.

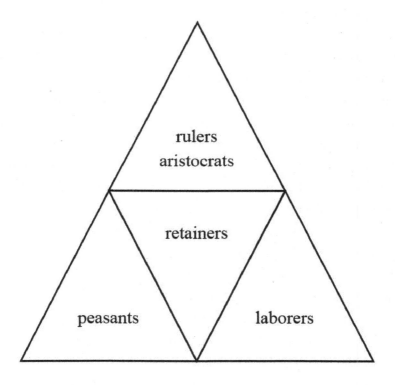

Figure 16: Social Classes of Ancient Israel

The Sages as Intellectuals

Another way to describe this conflicted perspective is to acknowledge another often neglected social category the sages assumed: the intellectual. Intellectuals can be defined as persons who put ideas and their systematization above economic concerns, even if it means those ideas could threaten their social position. They are the masters of culture and systematization; they are culture specialists, who contribute toward the worldview of their respective societies (see Weber 1978, 506, 926; Weber 1958, 324; Swedberg 2005, 127-28; cf. Sadri 1994, 14-15, 29, 58-68, 115).

Because of this, intellectuals actually seem to transcend their own social locations (see Sadri 1995, 58-68). Intellectuals are problematic for Marxists because of this phenomenon, and they often refer to them occupying contradictory class positions. Intellectuals in ancient times usually come from the upper classes because of the necessity of a good education, though many regimes recruited gifted young men from the lower classes to be trained as intellectuals. This is also reflected in the problem that the communists had in Russia in recruiting intellectuals from the proletariat. They often had to recruit them from the bourgeoisie so that they would then serve as the spokespersons for the proletariat.

The intellectual side of the wisdom writers is found in their delight in literary aesthetics, proverbs, and riddles. It is also reflected in their astute assessment of their own culture and their perception of the keys to success for a scribe that are contained in their aphorisms and maxims. But they are also systematizers. The doctrine of retribution is an example. Though this doctrine is almost as old as the planet, they have systemized it and made it more flexible (see Van Leeuwen 1992, 25-36).

Women and Wisdom

Were the Sages Chauvinistic?

Though Carol Meyers (2014, 8-27) argues that early Israelite society was not patriarchal because of the value women held due to their necessary roles in the village and farmstead economy, the wisdom writers were certainly chauvinistic. Two texts are often cited as reflecting misogynistic attitudes. The first is Eccles. 7:23-29:

All this I tested with wisdom.
I said, "I will be wise." But it was far from me.
What has happened is far and very deep. Who can find it?
I and my heart turned to know and to explore
and to seek wisdom and the sum,
and to know wickedness as folly and the foolishness of folly.
I found more bitter than death, the woman, who is a trap,
her heart is a net, her hands fetters.
Those who are pleasing to God will escape from her,
but the "sinner" will be taken by her.
"Look, this is what I have found," says the Teacher,
"One plus one to find the sum."
What my soul still sought I did not find.
One man among a thousand I found,
but no woman among these did I find.
Only this did I find: God made humanity upright,
but they have sought out many schemes.

While some have tried to argue that the woman referred to is not women in general (e.g., Seow 1997, 262-63), this seems to be a case of special pleading. In the ancient Near East, women were often viewed as the weaker sex, not able to control their passions and emotions, especially their sexual desires (cf. the "weaker vessel" [1 Pet. 3:7])—the opposite perspective of our society! Women were often referred to as traps or snares who were constantly seeking a man to seduce and to destroy his career and the reputation of his household. Comparably, the Sarakatsani view promiscuous women as Satan's emissaries sent out to seduce men (Campbell 1974b, 277). In Proverbs 7, the adulterous woman is portrayed as a trap for the gullible youth:

She causes him to turn aside with much persuasion,
with the smoothness of her lips she forces him.
He goes to her suddenly like an ox,

to the slaughter he goes,
and like an anklet for the discipline of a fool.
Until an arrow pierces his liver,
like a bird who hastens to a trap,
he does not know that he risks his life (Prov. 7:21-23).

And compare Prov. 23:27-28:

For a whore is a pit,
and a narrow well is a strange woman.
Indeed, she is like a robber who lies in wait,
she increases the unfaithful among men.

Compare the advice from king Lemuel's mother:

Do not give to women your strength,
and your ways to what destroys kings (Prov. 31:3).

Qohelet's misogyny is no different than Ben Sira's, who is notorious
for his chauvinistic perspective. For example, he states,

Better is the wickedness of a man than a woman who does good;
it is woman who brings shame and disgrace (Sir. 42:14).

And concerning a headstrong daughter he says this:

As a thirsty traveler opens his mouth
and drinks from any water near him,
so she will sit in front of every tent peg
and open her quiver to the arrow (Sir. 26:12).

Also, consider the satirical work "Dialogue between a Master and his
Obliging Servant":

Woman is a pitfall—a pitfall, a hole, a ditch,
Woman is a sharp iron dagger that cuts a man's throat
(Lambert 1996, 147).

Why scholars cannot see Qohelet assuming the same common male perspective is baffling. Qohelet and Ben Sira might represent extremes in their culture, but they still reflect the predominant chauvinistic stereotype of woman of the time.

The Intended Male Audience of the Wisdom Literature

It may seem trite to point out that the intended audience of the wisdom literature is males, especially youths (except for the Qumran wisdom literature: 4Q415 2 ii, 1; see Goff 2013, 31-32), but the full significance of this phenomenon is often overlooked by wisdom experts. The evidence is clear. In Proverbs, the addressee is always "my son" or "son": in chapters 1-9, and then occasionally in the body of the book (e.g., 23:15). The frame-narrator of Ecclesiastes addresses the intended reader as "my son" in the epilog (12:12), as well as referring to the audience as a "young male" (*bachur*) in (11:9). Ben Sira also uses this address (e.g., 2:1). Many scholars agree that "my son" is a metaphorical title that the scribal teachers gave their students, though actual biological fathers would often have been the teachers of their sons at their homes.

Also, there are five aphorisms in Proverbs that mention a "nagging wife," but there is no male corollary (Prov. 26:21 refers to a nagging person in general, not a gendered contrast):

Destruction to a father is a foolish son,
and a leaky roof is a contentious wife (Prov. 19:13).

Better to live on the corner of the roof,
than to be housed with a contentious wife. (Prov. 21:9).

Better to live on desert land,
than with a contentious wife and vexation. (Prov. 21:19).

A leaky roof on a rainy day,

is like a contentious wife.
Hiding her is like hiding wind,
like encountering oil in the right hand. (Prov. 27:15-16).

One can appropriately call this chauvinistic humor that is strikingly modern, though most women would not find it funny today. A comparable viewpoint is found among the Sarakatsani who refer to the type of wife feared as a "quarrelsome grumbler" (γκρινιάρα) (see Campbell 1974b, 153).

Also, one does not find a "Mr. Wisdom," a counterpart to Woman Wisdom, who might woo women to come partake of wisdom as well. Many scholars, including feminist scholars, have found the portrayal of wisdom personified as a female as something positive theologically. Some have even argued that she was a goddess to the Israelites (e.g., Penchansky 2001, 81-92). However, there is a dark side to this portrayal. Wisdom is often personified in ancient lore and literature, but this is primarily because the intended recipient of wisdom is exclusively male. As literary critic Jonathan Culler remarks:

> . . . [D]iscussions of woman that appear to promote the feminine over the masculine—there are, of course, traditions of elaborate praise—celebrate the woman as goddess (the *Ewig-Weibliche*, Venus, Muse, Earth Mother) and invoke a metaphorical woman in comparison with which actual women will be found wanting. Celebrations of woman or the identification of woman as some powerful force or idea—truth as a woman, liberty as a woman, the muses as women—identify actual women as marginal. Woman can be a symbol of truth only if she is denied an effective relation to truth, only if one presumes that those seeking truth are men. The identification of woman with poetry through the figure of the muse also assumes that the poet will be a man. While appearing to celebrate the feminine, this model denies women an active role in the system of literary production and bars them from the literary traditions (1982, 166-67).

Similarly, wisdom expert Carol Fontaine argues that the figures of Woman Wisdom and Woman of Worth (Prov. 31:10–31) "may be inversely proportional to the truth of real women's lives. That is, such fine figure may just as easily be an index of women's lack of power and status as a reflection of a gentler, kinder social reality for women" (1995, 25).

There is also no comparable "Ode to the Virtuous Man," who might serve as the ideal companion for the wise woman. Rather, Prov. 31:10–31 represents the ideal wife for an ambitious scribe. This woman is well-to-do: she owns slaves (v. 15) and is charitable toward the poor (v. 20). As Meyers points out (2014, 22), her managerial skills are exemplary and she wields much power within the household, as she is involved in agriculture and trade (vv. 15–19) (cf. Lang 2004, 140–57). Yet her primary function is to bring honor to her husband, who occupies public space as an elder at the city gate in contrast to her domain in the household (v. 23).

Though there were a few female scribes in Mesopotamia (see Harris 1990, 3–17), the reality is that biblical wisdom literature was written by males and for males. While a woman could certainly attain a wise lifestyle (e.g., Prov. 31:26), women were excluded from participating in the elite wisdom of the Israelite scribe, who learned to ponder the aphorisms and riddles of his male colleagues and delighted in literary subtlety and sophistication.

Summary

The Israelite wisdom literature reflects the honor culture of its environment. The sages lived the honorable life as a conformist or wise person, which connects with their desire to contribute to the good of society and be cooperative. But as intellectual scribes, they also attained honor via their literary and interpretive skills. They also believed in "limited good," and competed for honor at court or at the Temple and beyond and at the expense of others. The sages would also defend their honor when challenged, whether through ignoring or countering. The sages saw their king or leader as patron and were often tempted to become patrons themselves for the less fortunate—though risky—for the attainment of greater honor. The seemingly self-serving advice in the wisdom literature reflects this competitive spirit and is best described as eudemonistic. The sages worked to bring honor to their own nuclear families. Their identity was chiefly formed through their family, and, secondly, through their vocation as scribes.

The sages occupied the retainer class that adhered to the ruling class. Occupying a stratum "betwixt and between" meant that they reflected an aristocratic perspective but were also sensitive to the plight of the masses, since they interacted with them often. Their complex social location becomes reflected in their complex ideological perspective.

The sages were intellectuals who specialized in the world of ideas and their systematization. They were also typically chauvinistic, with wisdom literature being composed by males and for males. The ideal sages' wife was one who submitted to his authority and brought him honor.

9

The Book of Proverbs

Structure

We have already indirectly referred to the structure of the book of Proverbs when we discussed the superscriptions to the book (1:1; 10:1; 22:17; 24:23; 25:1; 30:1; 31:1). These superscriptions represent "seams" that demonstrate that the book is essentially an anthology of collections that once had independent existences. They divide the book into six parts, which can, in turn, be divided into two broad types of Egyptian genres that we have already referred to: sentences (10:1-22:16; chs. 25-29) and instruction (chs. 1-9; 22:17-24:22; chs. 30-31); exceptions include the speeches of Woman Wisdom (1:20-33; ch. 8); numerical poems (6:6-15; 30:11-31), and the encomium on the good wife (31:10-31).

Basically, the sentences are much shorter, being bicolon, and are only loosely related to their surrounding literary contexts (the adjoining sentences), if at all. The instructions are called this because of their similarity to the Egyptian instructions. For example, the

"Instructions of Ptahhotep" begins with an introduction that precedes 45 maxims which are more than one sentence, mainly containing admonitions, with verbs in the imperative mood, which revolve around a single topic. Compare the following maxim from Ptahhotep with an instruction from Proverbs:

Do not copulate with a woman-boy, for you know that/what is (generally) opposed will be a necessity to his heart, and that which is in his body will not be calmed. Let him not spend the night doing what is opposed in order that he may be calm after he has quenched his desire (Faulkner 1973b, 171).	Hear, oh my son, and be wise and lead your heart in the way. Do not be among those who imbibe wine, among those who squander themselves on meat. For the imbiber and squanderer will become impoverished, and slumber will cloth them with rags (Prov. 23:19-21).

Most scholars believe that the lectures in Proverbs 1-9 were the last section of the book to be added. Many see these chapters providing a necessary theological introduction to the rest of the book, particularly the pithy sentences (contra Weeks 2010, 47). This is because the sentences by themselves as independent units can seem rather haphazard and generally irreligious, though this is a misnomer. Most of the sentences do not mention God, but certainly he is assumed to be always in the background. Their pithiness prevents them from mentioning God every time. The lectures, then, serve to hermeneutically orient the reader to interpret the sentences more effectively and appropriately.

Interestingly, the lectures in chapters 1-9 and the encomium on the virtuous woman (31:10-31) serve as a frame for the body of the book. Both are focused on women. Proverbs 1-9 includes the competition between Woman Wisdom and Folly to seduce young men to come follow each respectively. The encomium of ch. 31 provides a portrait of the ideal scribe's wife. The lectures also include the motto of the book in 1:7a: "The fear of the Lord is the beginning of knowledge"; while Prov. 31:30b alludes to it: "by the fear of the

THE BOOK OF PROVERBS

Lord a woman will be praised." Relatedly, there is also an inclusion involving God-fearing in the lectures that is formed by 1:7a and 9:10: "The beginning of wisdom is the fear of the Lord, and knowledge of the Holy One is understanding" (9:10). But as we have seen, this focus on women is not necessarily a redeeming feature of the book, with its implicit chauvinism.

Figure 17: Diagram of the Relation between Instruction and Sentences				
Instruction (chs. 1-9)	Sentences (10:1-22:16)	Instruction (22:17-24:22)	Sentences (chs. 25-29)	Instruction (chs. 30-31)

The lectures have their own unique structure. Many scholars now believe that there are 10 lectures with 5 interludes in-between (e.g., see Fox 2000, 45–47; Pemberton 2005, 63–64). In each lecture a father speaks to his son(s) and tries to persuade him to accept the father's teaching and to pursue wisdom. The interludes reinforce the father's appeal to pursue wisdom. Three of these include speeches by Woman Wisdom. Here is what the lectures look like graphically (interludes in bold):

Figure 18: Proverbs 1-9 Lectures														
1:8 -19	**1:20 -33**	2:1 -22	3:1 -12	**3:13 -20**	3:21 -35	4:1 -9	4:10 -19	4:20 -27	5:1 -23	**6:1 -19**	6:20 -35	7:1 -27	**8:1 -36**	**9:1 -18**

These lectures can be further divided into three subsets based on their rhetoric, according to Pemberton (2005, 63): calls to attention (1:8-19; 2:1-22; 4:1-9; 4:10-19), calls to remember and obey (3:1-12; 3:21-35; 4:20-27), and warning against the alien woman (5:1-23; 6:20-35; 7:1-27).

Clusters and Twice-Told Proverbs

Recently, scholars have discerned a literary "context" that organizes the sentences (10:1-22:16; chs. 25-29). The two dominant proponents of this view are Bruce Waltke (2004, 21) and Knut Heim (2013). Scholars refer to "clusters" of proverbs, which are sentences that are loosely connected by catchwords, theme, genre, and repetition of phrases and also to what have been called "twice told proverbs," usually involving only a colon, that at least linguistically connect the proverbs. The pertinent question is does this clustering mean the sentences no longer stand on their own but must be interpreted within the cluster? If so, this means essentially one interprets one proverb by another. The great weakness with this perspective is that it violates the nature of the genre in that proverbs stand on their own. And it becomes quite circular.

For example, consider the two twice-told proverbs that Heim pairs:

A wise son [listens to] the father's instruction,
but the mocker does not listen to reproof (Prov. 13:1).

A man's wealth can ransom his life,
but the poor has not listened to reproof. (Prov. 13:8) (trans. Heim 2013, 329).

By comparing 13:1b and 13:8b, along with 10:15b ("the ruin of the poor is their poverty") (2013, 235), Heim suggests that "the poor" in 13:8b must be a foolish person who has continually ignored parental advice and, thus, has become poor (2013, 331-32). Also, Heim believes the wealth of 13:8a is honest wealth earned through hard work, with an eye on 13:7b (2013, 333). Thus, in a crisis, hardworking wealthy persons can bail themselves out with their surplus, while the foolish poor have no such options.

This is certainly an ingenious interpretation. However, it unnecessarily moralizes Prov. 13:8 and tends to vilify the poor. There is no moral to this aphorism. It is simply describing the advantages of those at the extreme ends of the economic scale. The aristocrat can save his own neck with his material possessions, while the poor can afford to ignore rebuke because their economic circumstances will likely not change, whether they heed it or not. Thus, though their poverty is oppressive, they do enjoy a few advantages in this state of affairs. The aphorism then is a paradoxical proverb, where the sages display their relish in the many incongruities of life.

Authorship

We have already mentioned that the ascription of the book of Proverbs to Solomon (1:1) is probably pseudonymous to lend authority to the book. And we have already discussed the other superscriptions. They too may be pseudonymous. Even the superscription that alludes to king Hezekiah's officials is suspect (see Carasik 1994, 289-300). It is certainly possible that an ancient Near Eastern king might compose literature himself. Earlier we mentioned the Assyrian king Ashurbanipal (seventh century B.C.E.) who claims to have studied to become a scribe, learning the secret lore of the diviners. But we have also seen that it was rare for a king to have been literate, let alone highly literate with the ability to compose literature. Gerhard von Rad, in fact, had argued that there was a renaissance of literary activity during Solomon's reign that included some of the wisdom literature (1972, 59). But most scholars today question this and point to the eighth century as the period when literary activity began to flourish in ancient Israel (Schniedewind 2004, 64-90; Jamieson-Drake 1991). So, while it is certainly possible that Solomon himself may have composed the many aphorisms attributed to him or even authorized their composition, it is unlikely.

Not all agree, however. Bruce Waltke follows Kenneth Kitchen's lead and both maintain that at least the collections ascribed to Solomon indeed go back to him (Waltke 2004, 31-36; Kitchen, 1976, 99; 1998, 350). Both argue that we should assume ascribed authorship unless otherwise indicated by the evidence. Both also maintain that we should trust the superscriptions ascribing Egyptian instructions to famous Egyptian sages, courtiers, and pharaohs (Waltke 2004, 33; Kitchen 1977, 93-95; 1998, 347-49), though Egyptologists would not concur (e.g., Lichtheim 1975, 6-7). The danger of this kind of thinking is that it would lead us back to the dark ages of pre-critical scholarship!

Date

The consensus for the date of Proverbs in its final form is the Persian period. Even Waltke admits that the final form of Proverbs may go back to the Persian or even Hellenistic period, while Kitchen refers to the possibility of the postexilic period (Waltke 2004, 37; Kitchen 1977, 102). There is no type of definitive evidence to date the book either during the late monarchy or the Persian period. So, there will always be a certain amount of speculation involved in this issue. One of the popular arguments is that Proverbs 1-9's polemic against the "strange women" fits the context of Ezra-Nehemiah, when the Jews were told to have nothing to do with foreign women (e.g., Washington 1994, 165; 1995,157-84). However, the "strange woman" in Proverbs 1-9 is most likely referring to the woman's married state and not her ethnicity: she is off limits to other men (see Fox 2000, 134-41).

A significant factor is that Prov. 1-9 reflects the language of the book of Deuteronomy, whose core is dated to the reign of Josiah in the seventh century B.C.E. (see Washington 1994, 128-33; Schipper 2013, 57-63). For example, Prov. 6:20-23 has long been recognized as an adaptation of Deut. 6:7-8:

Proverbs 6:20-23	
Keep, my son, the commandment (*mitzvah*) of your father, and do not forsake the teaching (*torah*) of your mother.	Deuteronomy 6:6-9
	These are the commandments which I am commanding (*tzavah*) you this day to be on your heart.
Bind them upon your heart continually. Tie them around your neck.	Repeat them to your sons. Speak of them while you dwell in your house and when you walk about in the way and in your lying down and your rising up.
When you walk about, it will guide you. When you lie down, it will watch over you. And when you get up, it will talk to you.	Bind them for a sign upon your hands, and they will for phylacteries between your eyes.
For the commandment (*mitzvah*) is a lamp, and instruction (*torah*) is a light, and the reproof of instruction is the way of life.	Write them upon your doorposts of your house and in your gates.

And note the following three verses:

Bind them for a sign upon your hands, and they will be for phylacteries between your eyes (Deut. 6:8).

Bind them (kindness and truth) on your neck and write them on the table of your heart (Prov. 3:3).

Bind them (father's teaching) upon your fingers, write them upon the tablet of your heart (Prov. 7:3).

Thus, Proverbs 1-9 surely reflects the book of Deuteronomy by applying the language and phraseology of the Mosaic Law to instruction about wisdom. Of course, for the authors of Proverbs 1-9, *torah* does not mean the same thing as in Deuteronomy (where it means Mosaic ordinances). The wisdom writer's theology certainly differs somewhat from Deuteronomic theology (see Fox 2009, 953). But that the sages are deliberately alluding to Deuteronomy cannot be denied! At any rate, this would mean that the earliest date for Proverbs 1-9 would be the seventh century B.C.E.

Dating the final form of the book to the Persian period does not mean that material in the book did not emerge from an earlier period like the monarchy. There are several Proverbs that refer to the king (*melek*) and the reader as one who served in his presence. Here is an example:

> Do you see a person skillful in is his work *before the king*?
> He will not station himself before the lowly (Prov. 22:29).

However, during the postexilic period, the word for king could have certainly carried a broader meaning for the scribes, like "ruler," meaning the foreign emperor or even a high official. So, reference to a king does not force one to push the date back earlier. Even Ecclesiastes, which almost all current scholars (except for Leithart 2013, 445, n. 12) date to the postexilic period, refers to a "king":

> I say, "Keep the edict of the king,
> and because of the word of oath to God.
> Do not be hasty to go from before him,
> do not remain in an evil matter
> because whatever he desires he does" (Eccles. 8:2-3).

For the period, it either refers to the Ptolemaic king or, more likely, Qohelet is using it generally to refer to a high Ptolemaic official whom the elite Jews and scribes would have frequently encountered.

Archaeologically we can say that by the eighth century literacy begins to become more prevalent in ancient Israel (see Jamieson-

Drake 1991). As we saw earlier, according to Rollston Hebrew becomes standardized in the ninth century B.C.E., which implies an institutional state sponsorship (2010, 44, 95). So, most likely, during the eighth century and the time of Hezekiah, the aphoristic collections of the book began to be composed and collected. One should view the development of the book as stretching several centuries, ending sometime in the Persian or Hellenistic period, with Proverbs 1-9 being added near the end of the process.

Relationship between Proverbs 22:17-24:22 and the Instruction of Amenemope

There is a general consensus among wisdom experts that Prov. 22:17-24:22 has been influenced by the "Instruction of Amenemope," a late New Kingdom wisdom work, dated to somewhere around 1186-1069 B.C.E. (Washington 1994, 14). Washington has in fact argued that the influence of "Amenemope" on the composers of Proverbs has softened its negative view of the poor (1994). The appropriate question is whether the scribe(s) who composed Prov. 22:17-24:22 had a copy before him and simply Hebraized the text or whether there is no direct dependence but only a striking coincidence that can best be explained by a common stock of wisdom tradition disseminated throughout the ancient Near East. Here are some examples from both Proverbs and "Amenemope" that are quite similar:

Proverbs	Amenemope
Better a little with the fear of the Lord than much treasure and turmoil with it.	Better, then, is poverty in the hand of God than riches in the storehouse;
Better provisions of herbs and love there than a fatted cow and hatred there (15:16-17).	Better is bread when the mind is at ease than riches with anxiety (Simpson 1973, 249).
An abomination unto the Lord are lying lips, but those who act faithfully are his pleasure (12:22).	God hates one who falsifies words, His great abomination is duplicity (253).
An abomination unto the Lord is one stone and a different stone, fraudulent scales are not good (20:23).	Do not unbalance the scale nor make the weights false, nor diminish the fractions of the grain measure (256).

I concur with John Ruffle who has examined the supposed resemblances:

> I confess to some doubt about the existence of a direct connection between Proverbs and Amememope. The connection so casually assumed is often very superficial, rarely more than similarity of subject matter, often quite differently treated and does not survive detailed examination. I believe it can merit no more definite verdict than 'not proven' and that it certainly does not exist to the extent that is often assumed . . . (1975, 62-23).

A major reason why early scholars assume such a dependence is because it supports the seeming international perspective of the wisdom tradition. However, we have seen that this "universalism" typical of the wisdom literature can better be explained in terms of its rhetoric, that the truths it proposes must by universal or else they are no truths at all!

Intended Audience

Both Michael Fox and Christopher Ansberry have argued that the original audience for the book of Proverbs is courtiers: Fox suggests chapters 10-29 (2009, 504-505; 1996, 234-39) and Ansberry the entire book (2011, 49, 69-70, 184-90). They base it mainly on proverbs that are rather "courtly" like 25:1 (cf. the reference to Hezekiah's officials in 23:1-8 and 25:1-7). Fox argues that they could not be scribes because the Hebrew word for scribe, *sopher*, does not mean scribe but clerk or scholar (1996, 236). Yet Fox views Ben Sira as a *sopher*, assuming the same role for him as the authors of the Egyptian instructions (236), who were all scribes!

We have seen that scribes throughout the ancient Near East could occupy the lowest rung of administration as copyists or serve in the highest positions as viziers. Scribes assumed many roles within their respective societies, which means they usually had other titles than that of scribe. But this does not mean they ceased being scribes! Certainly the "courtly" character of Proverbs 10-29 would suggest that one type of scribe targeted would be the royal ones, but this does not mean these chapters were restricted to royal scribal apprentices. It would have served nicely as material for the full range of scribes (priestly, prophetic, village, etc.), no matter what their latter specialization.

Sub-Genres

Experiential Saying

The sentence or saying can be classified into two types: didactic or experiential saying. The experiential saying merely presents an observation about reality. It does not provide a moral. It leaves it up to the reader to draw any practical or moral lessons form it (see Murphy 1981, 4). Earlier in this chapter we provided an example of one: "The wealth of a man ransoms his life, but the poor need not heed a rebuke" (13:8). The saying is merely stating the paradox that even poverty can have "advantages." The saying merely depicts an unusual reality about life. Technically, it is morally neutral, and I leave it at that. Here are another example of the experiential saying: "Also the fool who remains silent will be reckoned as wise, one who stops his lips as intelligent" (17:28). The saying simply makes a paradoxical observation that a fool is perceived as wise as long as he does not open his mouth. Technically, the saying is morally neutral. However, one can extract a moral from it, such as silence is an important virtue. This is a hermeneutic move though, and not exegetical.

Didactic Saying

Didactic sayings do not simply make an observation about life that may or may not suggest a moral. These sayings are more explicit about morality than the experiential sayings. A value is always being inculcated and a general attitude is being promoted (Murphy 1981, 5). The vast majority of sayings are didactic. Here are some examples:

One who oppresses the poor mocks his maker,
one who honors him is gracious to the poor (14:31).
The fear of the Lord is the discipline of wisdom,
and before honor comes humility (15:33).

Admonitions

As opposed to sayings which simply state a proposition, with the verbs in the third person, admonitions and their negative counterpart, prohibitions, are in the second person or the imperative mood (and jussive). This makes them related to the broader genre of instruction, which is usually filled with admonition. These sayings are essentially commands, which means they resonate with the legal material in the Pentateuch. The difference is that these "commands" do not have the authority of God or Moses but of Solomon. There is a wonderful example of a didactic saying and related admonition that express the same moral (adapted from Murphy 1981, 6):

One who considers a matter will find good,
and one who trusts in the Lord will be blessed (16:20; *didactic saying*).

Submit to the Lord your works,
and your intentions will be established (16:3; *admonition*).

Here one sees that whether as a proposition or command, one should entrust his plans to the Lord so as to find success. Note that the admonition includes a reason given in the second colon: *your plans will be fulfilled*. This also is similar to the legal commands: "Do not take the name of the Lord your God in vain, *for he will not hold innocent whoever takes his name in vain*" (Deut. 5:11).

Prohibitions

Prohibitions are negative commands and share all the features of admonitions: "Do not say, 'I will repay evil,' *wait for the Lord and he will deliver you*" (20:22). Here the first colon contains the prohibition proper and the second provides the reason. The second colon itself interestingly contains a command (wait!) and a reason (God will deliver).

Demotic Egyptian Sentences

We have already cited several Mesopotamian and Aramaic sentences, which parallel the ones in Proverbs. However, during the Late Period of Egypt (tenth century B.C.E.–first century C.E.) there were instructions that have a prologue which is then followed by a loose collection of sentences. These were written in demotic script, which is a late form of hieratic, the cursive script of hieroglyphs. We will examine two of these. The "Instruction of Ankhsheshonq" (late Ptolemaic period—second and first centuries B.C.E.) is about a priest by that name who goes to visit a childhood friend, who has become the chief royal physician (see Lichtheim 1980, 159-63). Ankhsheshonq goes to his friend for advice. During their visit the friend tells Ankhsheshonq of a plot to kill the pharaoh by the friend and some courtiers. Ankhsheshonq tries to dissuade his friend of doing this, but their conversation is overheard by a royal servant. The friend and courtiers are executed and Ankhsheshonq is imprisoned. In prison he writes his son. This is strikingly similar to the story of Ahiqar. The "Instruction of Ankhsheshonq" is known for being both practical and humorous:

> Even a small concern has a man in its grip (Lichtheim 1980, 169).

> Sweeter is the water of him who has given it than the wine of him [who has received] it (174; cf. Acts 20:35: "It is more blessed to give than receive").

> There is no Nubian who leaves his skin (Lichtheim 1980, 175; cf. Jer. 13:23: "Can the Nubian change his skin or the leopard his spots?").

In the "Instruction of Papyrus Insinger" (late Ptolemaic Period) one finds piety and morality fused (see Lichtheim 1980, 185). It is different from Ankhsheshonq in that it is more organized and arranged topically, with individual chapters. "Insinger" contrasts the "wise man," who endures reversals of fortune and eventually is rewarded, and the "fool," who disregards the common decency but eventually is punished. Here are some examples:

> It is the god who gives wealth;
> it is a wise man who guards (it) (Lichtheim 1980, 189).
> [The] evil that befalls the fool, his belly and his phallus bring it (189).
> Thoth has placed the stick on earth in order to teach the fool by it (192).

Thoth was the god of scribes. The stick brings to mind the leather switch used by scribal teachers to keep students awake during instruction (cf. Prov. 26:3: "A whip for a horse, a bridle for a donkey, and a rod for the back of fools!").

Other Special Genres

Prayers

One does not often find prayers in the wisdom literature. But in the oracle of Agur we find one:

> Two things I ask from you.
> Do not withhold them from me before I die.
> Falsehood and deceptive speech keep far from me.
> Poverty and oppression do not give me.
> Let me devour my appointed food,
> lest I be sated and say, "Who is the Lord?" and lest I become impoverish
> and steal and do violence to the name of my God (Prov. 30:7-9).

Agur prays that God give him enough lest he be tempted to steal but also not too much lest he become arrogant and think he does not need God.

Numerical Proverbs

What might be part of Agur's oracle are the numerical proverbs in Prov. 30:15-33. These usually involve animals but are ultimately about humanity. Here is an example:

> Under three things the land trembles, under four is not able to bear:
> under a slave when he rules and a fool when he is full of food.
> Under a hated woman when she gets married and a handmaiden
> when she disposes her mistress (30:21-23).

The ascending numbers 3 + (3 + 1 = 4) is a literary device that "creates a cumulative effect, a feeling of growing intensity" (Waltke 2005, 483-84). These numerical proverbs may have once been riddles. For example, the first line of this maxim could be phrased as a question, "Under what four things does the land tremble and is not able to bear up?" Then the answers follow. This maxim is not about animals but the significance of social stratification. It ponders the paradoxes that sometimes happen within human society. It implies that slaves should never become rulers, and fools should always be hungry, that a nagging woman should never marry and that a handmaiden should never come to dominate her mistress. These reflect the status quo of the ancient world in which there was no real social mobility. The social class into which one was born was the class one remained as member until death.

Oracle

In Prov. 30:1 and 31:1, one finds two superscriptions that include a generic identification, *massa'*:

> The words of Agur, son of Jakeh, an *oracle*, an inspired utterance of a man, to Ithiel (30:1).

The words of Lemuel, king, an *oracle* which his mother taught him (31:1).

The italicized word is the best translation one can give the term. Interestingly, this term is also found in superscriptions in Isa. 13:1; 14:28; 30:6; Hab. 1:1; Zech. 9:1; 12:1; and Mal. 1:1. Prophetic scholars usually view the word *massa'*, when used as a superscription in the prophetic books, as a technical term that designates a particular prophetic genre or book (e.g., Floyd 2002, 401-22; Sweeney 2005, 38). It apparently has a specific meaning that eludes us but in general means a pronouncement or oracle, implying oracular inquiry (literally "to lift up"). Yet, it is also found in Proverbs, and many wisdom experts find them (and the content of Agur's oracle) problematic (Fox 2009, 861; Schipper 2013, 56-57, 69-75), often resorting to taking the term as a place name for an Arabian territory (Massa) (for Lemuel, see Fox 2009, 884; Clifford, 1999, 260; 268-69, n. a). Prophetic scholars also seem to find them problematic, resorting also to taking the term as a place name or assuming that its meaning is different in Proverbs (e.g., Floyd 2002, 402, n. 3; Weis 1992, 28). The most logical explanation is that the word is a scribal technical term for a specific genre that connotes divine inspiration, which was obviously not perceived as incompatible with the wisdom "tradition." The ancient scribes apparently did not make the distinctions we modern scholars assume and felt comfortable with including a "prophetic" genre in a wisdom book. Both oracles are didactic in content.

Encomium

An encomium is Greek genre that is a "declamation of lofty praise for a person or a type of person" (Fox 2009, 903). The "Ode to the Virtuous Woman" in Prov. 31:10-31 is best described with this generic category. The poem is also an acrostic, with each letter of the Hebrew alphabet beginning each verse. Its basic structure is an introduction (vv. 10-12), an enumeration of virtues/deeds (vv. 13-27), and a concluding praise (vv. 28-31) (see Yoder 2003, 427-28):

א (alef) A noble (or capable) wife, who can find one?

Far more precious than corals is her value.

ב (bet) The heart of her husband trusts her.

And gain he does not lack.

ג (gimel) She does him good and not evil,

all the days of her life.

ד (dalet) She seeks out wool and linen,

and she creates in the business of her hands.

ה (he) She is like a ship that travels,

from afar she brings her food.

ו (vav) And she arises while it is yet night,

and provides food for her house, and portion to her maidens.

ז (zayin) She considers a field and buys it,

from the fruit of her hands she plants a vineyard.

ח (chet) She girds her loins with strength,

and makes firm her arms.

ט (tet) She experiences that her profit is good,

her lamp will not be extinguished at night.

י **(yod)** Her hands she extends upon the distaff,

and her hands grasp the spindle whorl.

כ **(kaf)** Her hand distributes to the poor,

and her hands send out to the needy.

ל **(lamed)** She does not fear for her house from snow,

for all her house are clothed with scarlet.

מ **(men)** Covers she makes for herself,

linen and red-purple wool for her house.

נ **(nun)** Her husband is known at the gates,

as he sits among the elders of the land.

ס **(samek)** She makes a linen cloak and sells it,

she gives girdles to the trader.

ע **(ayin)** Strength and honor are her clothing,

and she laughs at tomorrow!

פ **(pe)** Her mouth opens with wisdom,

and her instruction is gracious upon her lips.

צ **(tsade)** She keeps watch on the doings of her household,

and the bread of idleness she does not eat.

ק **(qof)** Her children rise and they call her blessed,

her husband also, and he praises her.

ר **(resh)** Many daughters have done well,

but you arise above all of them!

ש **(shin)** Elegance is deceptive and beauty is fleeting,

 but a woman who fears the Lord, she is to be praised!

ת **(tav)** Give to her from the fruit of her hands,

 and let her works praise her in the gates.

This shows its primarily didactic intent, aiding the scribe to memorize the poem and recite it. The poem is best understood as legitimation of the feminine traits Israelites (especially elites) found most valuable for wives.[1]

In this passage, it is important to keep in mind that there is an anthropological distinction between a woman's work and her status (see Lang 2004, 142). There are two female activities that are given pride of place: the production of food and clothing (Lang 2004, 142), which are clearly indicated here. In Prov. 31:15, the woman brings food from the store-room and then assigns tasks to her servants. According to Van Leeuwen, the food "brought from afar" may refer to grain brought from the Jezreel valley in the north, Israel's bread-basket (1997, 261). Lang thinks it is probably fish imported from elsewhere.

In Prov. 31:13, 19, and 21-22, one sees a focus on clothing production. Here the making of winter clothing is emphasized. Lang describes the elite character of this production: "Clearly, the Hebrew household considered here belongs to the elite that would produce and use only the best quality. The poet's reference to both the practical winter clothing, and the beautiful, the use of scarlet and purple for dying cloth, is remarkable; aesthetic attractiveness matches functional perfection" (Lang 2004, 143). Lang believes the slaves

---

1. Christine Yoder (2003, 432) translates v. 10a as "her purchase price is more than corals," taking *meker* as literally referring to the woman's "purchase price" and connecting this with her dowry. But this phrase is more easily understood metaphorically as her "great value."

received warm clothing as well, but the expensive clothing was reserved only for the family (Lang 2004, 143).

In Prov. 31:26, one might think that the woman is sagacious in her speech with the use of the word "wisdom" or *chokmah*. However, it most likely refers to her "instructing her maidens in the technical arts" as in craft-making (Lang 2004, 144). As in Ottoman societies, Lang points out that servants or slaves of urban elite women would often relieve the upper-class wife from the dull and tedious household chores (Lang 2004, 145-46). Farmer's wives had no such luxury. The elite women were exempted from such harsh toil but were expected to supervise the servants, as we see in this text. And in ancient Israel, "[t]o have one servant, much less several, was a mark of privilege" (Yoder 2003, 443).

This text demonstrates the separate spheres of husband and wife (see Lang 2004, 146-47). Note that the woman's husband occupies the public sphere at the city gate, while the woman is praised for management of the domestic arena, within the private sphere (31:23, 28). What is interesting is that the Hebrew wife here is also occupied with agricultural activities like buying and tending to a vineyard (31:16). But even in rural areas, there was a distinction between gender roles: men ploughed, sowed, and harvested, while women did the lesser jobs like weeding. Rural women's work never ended, which included child care, laundering, milking, weeding, and baking with manure (Lang 2004, 147). The rural men probably had more leisure time. This is implied when the husband sits at the gate (v. 23), and the wife is always busy (v. 27). Lang, concludes rightly about this passage, "The basic pattern, the woman active in the house, as the man is outside, is clearly visible" (Lang 2004, 147).

Some have suggested that the wife here takes care of all the management of the household and estate so that her husband could be free to engage in political activities (see Lang 2004, 148).[2] However, such a situation would have been dishonorable for the husband (Sir. 25:22). The husband was responsible for supplying food and clothing for his wife (Exod. 21:10). Lang states, "The Hebrew husband is in full control of his estate and responsible for farming, i.e., for the main economic activity done outside the home" (2004, 148). Lang emphasizes that the Hebrew household is still a male-dominated one based on agriculture and not a female-dominated one based on the domestic production of market goods (2004, 148-49). As Lang says, "[t]he male authority encompasses the female" (2004, 149). Yet there were distinct spousal domains.

The reference to the wife buying property (Prov. 31:16) has created a discussion among scholars about whether Israelite women could indeed own property (see Lang 2004, 150-54). The biblical legal codes do not speak of this issue. Lang concludes that customary law in ancient Israel may have allowed some women to own their own property (Lang 2004, 153).

2. This portrayal comes close to Carol Meyers' view of Israelite women. She cites this passage (2013, 191) as evidence of the managerial power of Israelite wives. She does not believe Israelite society was patriarchal (see 2014, 8-27) but rather heterarchical. Men and women's roles were complementary, not hierarchical.

10

The Book of Job

Structure

The book of Job is unique among the canonical wisdom books because it contains a narrative frame (1:1-2:13; 42:7-17) that is in the form of a story with fairy tale-like features. In fact, many scholars find the story in conflict with the body of the book, which consists essentially of poetic dialog between Job and his three friends (and Elihu) and finally God (3:1-42:6) (e.g., Clines 1995, 135-36). They would rather divide the two sections and treat them separately. Some emphasize that the frame assumes the doctrine of retribution and that Job is restored what he lost in the end (ch. 42). They also emphasize that the frame narrative depicts a very pious Job who refuses "to curse God and die" (2:9) and yet the dialog presents a skeptical Job who in fact accuses God of injustice and comes precariously close to committing blasphemy, if not in fact (see 27:2-6; 31:1-40).

However, the dialog would not make sense without the narrative frame because it sets up the contest between God and the satan.

In fact, this explains why the friends of Job are condemned in the end (42:7): they were unaware of the contest and, thus, condemned Job prematurely. Without the epilog, the story and debates would have no resolution. Though the differences in genre and perspective between the frame and body are striking, this is exactly the calculated beauty of this ancient text. It is a complicated book theologically, which befits a text that treats a very complicated issue: the problem of evil.

The book, structurally, then consists of a frame narrative, dialog between Job and his friends, which can in turn be divided into three cycles (chs. 3-14; 15-21; 22-25), Job's soliloquy (chs. 26-31); Elihu's speech (chs. 32-37); and the divine speeches (chs. 38-42:6). The following table shows the structure of the book graphically:

Figure 19: Structure of Job							
Frame narrative (1:1-2:13)	Dialog 1 (chs. 3-14)	Dialog 2 (chs. 15-21)	Dialog 3 (chs. 22-25)	Job's Soliloquy (chs. 26-31)	Elihu's speeches (chs. 32-37)	Divine speeches (chs. 38-42:6)	Frame narrative (42:7-17)

Integrity

The book of Job has a number of integrity issues. First of all, in the third cycle of speeches in the dialog, there seems to be dislocation of passages. In 24:18-24, Job is technically speaking but the sentiments are those of the friends. Job 26:1-4, which belongs to Job's soliloquy, is placed in Bildad's mouth. The section 27:13-24 is Job's speech but again sounds like the friends' positions. Scholars usually just reassign the passages according to the character that fits best. Or else they view Job as parodying his friends (see Newsom 2003, 161-68). Also, chapter 28, which contains a wonderful poem on the

THE BOOK OF JOB

inaccessibility of wisdom to humans, though it is placed in the mouth of Job, actually is more compatible with God's position in the divine speeches. And finally, the Elihu speeches (chs. 32-37) have been viewed as a later interpolation because Elihu is not mentioned among the three friends of Job in the epilog (ch. 42). He is a fourth friend who seems to come and go without any effect on the plot. However, since he is in the final form of the text, one must deal with him. Scholars are divided about what to make of Elihu's particular position theologically. He is viewed either as a young whippersnapper who is basically full of hot wind and contributes little to the dialog (e.g., Clifford 1998, 87) or else he is judged more sympathetically and his statements are seen as precursors to the divine speeches (e.g., Gordis 1965, 115).

Genre

Scholars cannot agree on the genre of the book of Job as a whole. Claus Westermann (1981, 1-15) argues that the book is essentially one large lament, like the ones in the Psalter. While the book of Job contains laments (e.g. ch. 3) and lament-like features, this categorization does not fit the book as whole. Others have suggested that the book is a dialog, which is a common genre in the ancient Near East, like the Egyptian "The Man and his Ba," the "Babylonian Theodicy," and the "The Pessimistic Dialog." But these dialogues are primarily only debates and do not have the fairy tale, narrative frame that sets up the complexity the book of Job represents. Katharine Dell designates the book parody and does not recognize Job as wisdom literature because it constantly subverts the generic conventions of this mode of literature (1991, 147). Others have identified the book's genre as sui generis, which means the book's genre cannot be identified because it is so unique. However, this move is not very helpful heuristically; it simply acknowledges the complexity of the book.

Job as Theodicy?

Others have suggested that philosophical categories best identify the book's genre. They have suggested that the book is a theodicy that treats the problem of evil. The word theodicy comes from two Greek words (*theos* or "God" *dike* or "to justify" meaning "justifying God") and identifies any attempt to justify God's actions in a world filled with evil. The problem of theodicy is usually presented as emerging because of three components of a trilemma: God is benevolent; God is omnipotent; yet evil exists. The following graph indicates this trilemma:

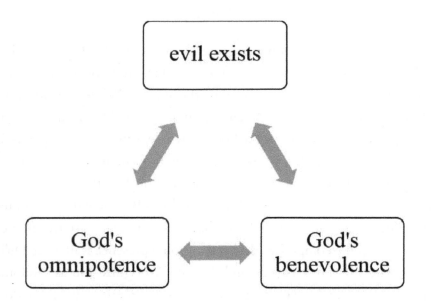

Figure 20: Theodicy Trilemma

A theodicy proper, then, is any attempt to explain how all three points can co-exist. Thus, theodicy is the attempt to defend God's justice in view of evil in the world. Evil can be divided into two kinds: 1) natural evil that wreaks havoc upon humanity (tornados, earthquakes, etc.); 2) moral evil that comes from human acts against other humans (crime, war, oppression, etc.).

Philosophers usually define theodicy narrowly so that it only relates to the three great monotheistic religions: Judaism, Christianity, and Islam (see Green 1987, 430-32). This means that an authentic theodicy only attempts to explain how the three components of the trilemma can co-exist. It cannot explain away any of the points, which would amount to dissolving the problem, not solving it. For example, the Hindus often deal with the problem of evil by redefining evil so that its existence is questioned. Evil, then, becomes only an illusion, and if one gains the proper prospective, evil seems to even have a purpose in the cosmos. Augustine made a similar move when he defined evil as simply the absence of good. Also, Church of Christ Scientists, certainly not a representative of orthodox Christianity, do the same when they define medical illness as an illusion. These "theodicies" in actuality only dissolve the theodicy problem by mitigating one of the points of the trilemma. While polytheistic religions like Hinduism obviously feel the pressure of the problem of evil like any other religion, the need is mitigated somewhat by the fact that the positing of numerous demons and evil deities that can then be blamed for evil. Monotheistic religions do not have this option.

There are two theodicy strategies that seem to be operative in the book of Job. One is the soul-making or educative theodicy (see Green 1987, 433). This form of theodicy was developed by Irenaeus and then was coined from a modern perspective by John Hick (1978). This theodicy states that seeming experiences of evil are actually a form of a test that if endured serves to promote spiritual growth and maturity. This fits Job's character to a degree. Job repents of his challenges to God concerning his justice and assumes a deferential demeanor in the end (40:3-5; 42:1-6). Job endured his suffering and came out with a different perspective about God and the world after the divine speeches. He has matured in his thinking and demonstrated his faithfulness.

The other type of theodicy that appears operative in the book is a postponement of judgment about God's seemingly unjust ways, called deferred theodicy (Green 1987, 434-35). This is most explicit, again, in the divine speeches where God tries to get Job to see the world from his perspective. When God challenges Job about all the wild and cosmic animals (Behemoth and Leviathan) and human disinterest in them, he pushes Job to broaden his horizon and see that humanity is not necessarily the center of God's cosmos, similar to the scientific revolution that de-centered humans and the planet earth within the solar system and cosmos. The point is that God's ways are not human ways, and so Job must learn to trust God and his reasons for creating a world with evil in it.

This theodicy strategy comes close to denying God's justice in that it implies that his standards of justice and rationality are distinct from humans (see Green 1987, 434-35). In other words, God plays by a different set of rules. But if God's standards are different from humans, how can humans know these standards are not wicked or unjust? For all practical purposes, this implies a divine double standard that raises questions about God's justice. Another book of the Bible, Ecclesiastes, in fact crosses the line and essentially denies God's justice. Thus, with God's benevolence denied, the trilemma loses its tension, and the problem is resolved or "dissolved." However, denying God's justice creates its own problems, as we shall see.

In the New Testament this theodicy strategy can be pushed into the next life. The believer is to simply trust God in the meanwhile. The Christian will eventually understand God's ways when she crosses over into the other realm and will then clearly see why God allowed evil to exist in the world (see Green 1987, 434).

Others have viewed the book of Job as functioning as an anti-theodicy, because it seems to counter the traditional types of theodicy strategies like the doctrine of retribution (e.g., Tilley 2000). They emphasize that God's ways are not human and that theodicies are not only useless but end up being detrimental to the cause of defending God. This option is simply another way of denying God's justice and constitutes a redefinition of it, where the divine double standard comes into play.

Another option is to define theodicy more broadly so that even an anti-theodicy is a type of theodicy (see Green 1987, 431). This would incorporate the polytheistic religions as well. This broader definition helps show the positive features of even the denial of God's justice. Max Weber defined theodicy this way, and comparative religionists usually do as well (see Swedberg 2005, 273-74). It will be how we define it in this book. Thus, the book of Job does represent an attempt to deal with the theodicy problem and can be rightly classified as a theodicy.

Job as Skeptical Literature

Another way to generically classify the book of Job is to group it with other ancient Near Eastern skeptical (and its twin sister, pessimistic) literature. The book is not skeptical about God but rather about the doctrine of retribution. It does not completely deny the doctrine, as one sees in the epilog when Job is restored his wealth, honor, and, in a sense, his family. However, the book problematizes the doctrine. It shows that while the rule of retribution is generally true, there are exceptions to it. The book of Ecclesiastes is also often categorized as skeptical literature, though I would prefer the term "pessimistic literature," as we shall see. Ecclesiastes also questions the doctrine of retribution but does not completely negate it. Thus, Job and Ecclesiastes can be viewed as correctives to the doctrine, and, thus, more broadly to what scholars refer to as traditional wisdom, as represented in Proverbs. Many scholars then refer to Proverbs as representing optimistic wisdom, while Job and Ecclesiastes represent pessimistic (or skeptical) wisdom.

This way of generically categorizing the biblical wisdom literature is also true of the ancient Near Eastern parallels. For example, a typical Egyptian instruction like the "Instruction of Ptahhotep" or "Amenemope" are similar to Proverbs in being generally optimistic about the predictability of human behavior. Similarly, the Sumerian "Instructions of Shurupak" reflect the same general optimistic worldview. However, there is a large corpus of ancient Near Eastern works that are either skeptical or pessimistic or, often, both. We have mentioned several of these. The "Adominitons of Ipuwer" represents a shift among the instructions genre, where they started becoming more pessimistic. Some of the "Songs of the Harper" became skeptical about the afterlife, and the "Ballad of the Heroes," found in ancient Mesopotamia and the Western Periphery, look back pessimistically on the age of great heroes and kings, whose greatness had long passed.

Martin Rose implies that these two types of ancient Near Eastern wisdom literature seem to be two sides of the same coin: a wisdom of stability and a wisdom of crisis (1999, 115-34). The first type seems to operate well when social conditions are predictable and reliable and a culture is relatively stable. The second type comes into play when social conditions are more unpredictable and a culture seems to be changing rapidly. Another way to put this is that skeptical wisdom serves as a sort of safety valve that helps its readers cope when times are difficult. Thus, skeptical wisdom helps to maintain a certain degree of flexibility within the sapiential system.

However, the notion of respective types of wisdom for alternating periods of stability and chaos is problematic. Skeptical wisdom is not necessarily operative only when social conditions are less stable. Most of these works were produced during relative stable periods of time. One can discern problems with predictability and difficulties with the doctrine of retribution even during socially calm periods. The Persian and Ptolemaic periods of Judah—when Proverbs, Job, and Ecclesiastes were composed—were relatively stable, except for some occasional battles. The problem of evil is perennial, and it does not apparently take much to induce anxiety about it.

Others have used the related label of orthodoxy to categorize Proverbs and the books of Job and Ecclesiastes. Proverbs, then, represents orthodoxy, and Job and Ecclesiastes represent heterodoxy because they question traditional tenets. However, while this distinction may be heuristically helpful, it fails to explain why both Job and Ecclesiastes were retained within the canon of Scripture. From a canonical perspective, one must designate them both as orthodox, since they passed the litmus test of canonicity. However, one could speak of a continuum where Job and Ecclesiastes are oriented toward the pole of heterodoxy and Proverbs is safely aligned with the pole of orthodoxy.

Per the above discussion, the following diagram will illustrate the corrective relationship between Job and Ecclesiastes and Proverbs and their respective foci.

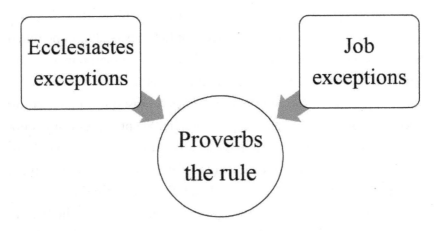

Figure 21: Corrective Relationship between Job, Ecclesiastes, and Proverbs

The corrective function of Job and Ecclesiastes in juxtaposition to Proverbs serves to canonically maintain a sense of equilibrium regarding the doctrine of retribution. But more than a corrective function, they serve to remind the reader of God's mysterious nature and the limits of human rationality.

Authorship and Date

The book of Job never attempts to attribute authorship to anyone. Like all biblical books, this one is authored by a scribe, and certainly one competent to compose in the mode of wisdom literature. The book was probably used in the training of scribes and for advanced students, who had already studied the book of Proverbs.

It is very difficult to date the book of Job, so any discussion of this topic is quite speculative. Its setting appears to be patriarchal, with the wealthy and pious Job resembling the great patriarchs of ancient Israel. But this cannot serve as the basis for dating. Most scholars date the book to the Persian period. The article with the title "satan" (1:7) in the book indicates it was written prior to Chronicles (cf. 1 Chron. 21:1; see Crenshaw 1992, 863), a book usually dated to sometime during the Persian period. While a literary treatment of the problem of evil can occur in relatively stable or even prosperous periods, the subjugation of the Jews by the Persians would be an ideal time to compose such a book. Job's rapid loss of fortune may reflect the Persians' disenfranchisement of the indigenous elite (see Hamilton 2007, 80-89). The book does not appear to be as late as the book of Ecclesiastes because its style of Hebrew does not appear to reflect any proto-Mishnaic characteristics, features Ecclesiastes has. More on this later.

Job and Popular Culture

Job is one of the few biblical books that literary critics in the past and present consider a literary masterpiece. In fact, the American Archibald McCleash, who became the Librarian of Congress, composed a play that is a modernized version of the book called "J.B."—from the name of "J(o)b" himself. The famous English nineteenth-century poet and artist William Blake was fascinated with book and saw himself as modern day Job, who had lived a life of poverty and been largely unrecognized until the latter part of his life. He is famous for painting watercolor scenes from the book of Job and eventually engraving them and selling the prints. Carl Jung, the famous student of Freud, who introduced the notion of archetypes in psychology, wrote a book, *Answer to Job*, where he radically argues that, because of Job's innocence and sustained piety, God is forced to reevaluate himself and become introspective, which led to the necessity of the incarnation of Jesus.

Ancient Near Eastern Parallels

We have already alluded to several parallels to the book of Job from Mesopotamia and Egypt. More discussion of these is needed at this point. "I will Praise the Lord of Wisdom," also known as the "Babylonian Job," involves a righteous sufferer who complains that his deity has abandoned him. Dating to the Kassite period (1531-1155 B.C.E.; see Lambert 1996, 21-27), the poem depicts a man of affluence and authority (a feudal lord) and of model piety, who becomes the object of the king's anger, loses his position, his friends, and even his family, and is finally stricken with a disease. He consults magicians to exorcise demons he thinks have stricken him, but to no avail. He then complains that as a righteous person he has received the fate of the wicked. He concludes that the gods have a different standard of justice than humans and that their will is inscrutable:

> Who knows the will of the gods in heaven?
> Who understands the plans of the underworld gods?
> Where have mortals learnt the way of a god?
> (Lambert 1996, 41)

Then he is visited by priests in three dreams and told that Marduk's wrath has been appeased. The priests perform the proper rituals, and his demons are removed. He goes to the temple of Marduk and proclaims his sin and praises Marduk's mercy.

Another significant parallel is the "Babylonian Theodicy" (1000 B.C.E.), which is structured by 27 stanzas which form an acrostic, with each line in the stanzas starting with the same letter (see Lambert 1996, 63-67). The acrostic turns out to be a title: "I, Saggil-kīnam-ubibb, the incantation priest, am adorant of the god and the king." The poem is a dialog between a sufferer, who bemoans the evils of society, and a friend, who defends the just order of the gods and represents orthodoxy. The sufferer begins the dialog politely.

He bemoans the injustice of being made an orphan because his parents had him late in life. The friend deflects this and says such happenings are the lot of mortals and states: "He who waits on his god has a protecting angel. The humble man who fears his goddess accumulates wealth "(Lambert 1996, 71). The sufferer complains that he is not being listened to. Throughout the dialog, the sufferer questions traditional tenets with evidence that crime does pay and piety does not. The friend counters that piety eventually leads to prosperity and that crime does in fact not pay. For example: "He that bears his god's yoke never lacks food, though it be sparse" (Lambert 1996, 85). He also emphasizes the inscrutability of the divine will: "The divine mind, like the centre of the heavens, is remote: Knowledge of it is difficult; the masses do not know it . . ." (Lambert 1996, 87). The sufferer finally "wins" the argument when he points out that it appears that the gods made humans prone to deception, which the friend cannot deny. In the end, the sufferer pleads with the friend to be more empathetic and asks that the gods resume their protection of him:

> May the god who has thrown me off give help,
> may the goddess who has [abandoned me] show mercy,
> for the shepherd Šamaš guides the peoples like a god (Lambert 1996, 89).

The reality is that this final point does not really solve the theodicy problem. To say the gods made humans evil is to blame the gods, which is not what a theodicy strategy aims to do. But perhaps it is not the particular strategy that is important but rather the debate or discussion itself (see van der Toorn 1991, 59-75). The dialog serves to create room for flexibility in the ideological system as a whole, which is beneficial in itself.

We have already mentioned "The Righteous Sufferer" from Ugarit, a text from the Western Periphery, which is similar to the

"Babylonian Job." In it a righteous sufferer is tormented by physical and social evils and tries to elicit the help of diviners to determine its cause. None could help: "Until Marduk the lord lifted my head, Reviving me from the dead . . ." (Cohen 2013, 167). After Marduk rescues him, the sufferer is led to praise: "[the deeds of] Marduk I praise, [the deeds of] (even) an angry god I praise . . ." (Cohen 2013, 169).

Important Themes

Indifferent Righteousness

The book of Job as a whole focuses on two primary questions: why is there unjust suffering (the dialog), and should we serve God with no thought of reward/retribution (the frame)? The second raises the question of indifferent righteousness. In other words, do we serve God without reward in mind? This is the satan's challenge to God: "Does Job fear God for naught? (1:9; KJV). The satan accuses God of sheltering Job by insulating him with a "hedge" of wealth and manifold blessing. The satan argues that if God were to remove these benefits, then Job would eventually curse him to his face!

The answer to the latter question (indifferent righteousness) actually becomes the solution to the former (righteous suffering). In other words, the problem of theodicy is never really answered in the book. Instead, the focus shifts to the question of the appropriate form of human piety. Thus, the book of Job ingeniously deflects the problem of theodicy by redirecting the issue to anthropodicy and the issue of human integrity, not God's integrity. The focus then switches from the tester to the tested!

Theocentricism versus Anthropocentrism

We have touched on this earlier when discussing how God in the divine speeches attempts to get Job to adopt a broader perspective about his problem. In these speeches God harangued Job with a series of rhetorical questions that he could not possibly answer. This creates a lambasting effect, and scholars have referred to God "bullying" Job, by which he is humiliated and forced to repent in the end. God's questions concern the creation of the world and then shift to the generally unfamiliar or amazing aspects of the natural world, especially wild animals.

Of course Job could not answer any of the questions concerning the creation of the world because he was not there. It is interesting that God's depiction of the cosmogony and its resultant cosmology reflects the typical Semitic view of the cosmos that was discussed earlier, with a giant inverted bowl-shaped firmament. References in Job 38 to the "foundation of the earth" (v. 4) and its sunk "bases" and "cornerstone" (v. 6), the many boundaries placed upon the cosmos (e.g., water: vv. 8-11), "the gates of death" = Hades (v. 17), and "storehouses of the snow" and "hail" (v. 22) all point to the common pre-scientific view of the cosmos, which was geocentric. However, even in its geocentricism, what is significantly left out of discussion is humanity. Rather it is the wonder and grandeur of the natural and cosmological world that demonstrates God's greatness and power in contrast to the insignificance of humanity. Thus begins God's attempt to demonstrate to Job that humanity with all its problems is only a small portion of the vastness of the created cosmos. God is trying to get Job to think beyond humanity to the larger plan of God's designs for the universe as a whole.

At the end of Job 38 (vv. 39-41), God begins the questions about animals by interrogating Job about his power to care for the animal world with all its needs, in order to contrast the mighty power of God with the puniness of humanity. However, it also simultaneously relativizes the significance of humans and their concerns because it addresses the needs of animals, here food for the lion and raven, both wild animals that would not be of much interest for humans. Chapter 39 begins then with God questioning Job about the habits of all sorts of undomesticated animals (except the war horse whose power and majesty are explored (vv. 19-25), which, of course, Job could have had no knowledge about. God interrogates Job about the mountain goat, the wild donkey, and the wild ox, which, it is stressed, are all free of human dominion and constraints, and live their lives in complete liberty and natural splendor. An intriguing piece in the passage focuses on the ostrich:

> The wing of the ostrich flaps joyously,
> it is not the wing of the stork or falcon.
> For she leaves her eggs in the earth,
> and she warms them in the dust.
> But she forgets that a foot might crush it,
> and an animal of the field might trample it.
> She treats cruelly her young as though they were not hers,
> in vain is her toil, yet she is fearless.
> For God causes her to forget wisdom,
> and he does not apportion to her understanding.
> In a high place she flaps away,
> she laughs at the horse and its rider (Job 39:13-18).

In a wisdom book, it is fascinating that this unit actually attributes to God the creation of an animal that is "foolish"! And yet this creature fulfills the function of her creator, though her "folly" makes no sense to humans. But that is the point. The ostrich appears to have been created "dumb," yet she fulfills her purpose in the grand design of God's plan for the cosmos. No doubt this depiction of the ostrich is inaccurate from a naturalistic standpoint—it only appears this way from the perspective of humans. But the point is that God deliberately creates a "foolish" creature that is incomprehensible to humans! Nothing could be more powerful for expanding Job's perspective about the theocentric nature of the cosmos.

This leads to the two other animals that form the climax to the divine speeches: Behemoth and Leviathan. "Behemoth" is merely the transliteration of the Hebrew word that means "beast," while "Leviathan" means "twisted one." The word Leviathan is used frequently in the Hebrew Bible and seems to refer to a sea monster and symbolizes evil and chaos. God is sometimes described as defeating or slaying a dragon, either called Leviathan or Rahab (cf. Isa. 51:9). Leviathan seems to echo the dragoness Tiamat (depicted as multi-headed) that Marduk slays and whose body is then used to create the sky and earth. Tiamat is a watery sea dragoness who represents the danger of the sea and its lethal storms. She is similar to Yam, the Canaanite sea monster that Baal defeats. Both symbolize evil and chaos.

Leviathan and Behemoth may be based on actual animals like the crocodile or hippopotamus. However, they are much more than these. They have been mythologized to become cosmic beasts who represent chaos and malevolent power. Though one can detect in their description features of natural animals, these cosmic creatures cannot be contained by humans. Humans cannot trap or capture them, as they can crocodiles and hippopotami. These are powerful, majestic creatures that God has created, and they serve his purposes. But why would God create such creatures who represent evil and chaos? What purpose could they possibly serve? The book never provides specific answers to these questions. But God has created these creatures nonetheless and keeps them on a leash like pets (implied by 41:5; cf. 7:12). Whenever they get out of line, he jerks the leash and restrains them! The theological point is that God has created evil and suffering for his own purposes. Human beings in their limited and narrow perspectives cannot fathom how these phenomenon serve any purpose. But God apparently has a purpose for them that includes restraining them when necessary. All of this points to the mysterious nature of God whose ways cannot be comprehended by mortals.

Honor and Job

Apparently Job did not suffer from just the loss of wealth and family and the infestation of a skin disease. He also suffered from the loss of status due to the climactic events that happened to him. This was probably just as painful as the disastrous events, if not more so. Lynn Bechtel has focused on how shaming functions in Job (1997, 255-56). She points out that the main aspect of Job's social anxiety stems from the loss of his once esteemed and honorable position as the most pious person on earth, whose wealth was a sign of God's blessing him for his righteous lifestyle.

Job's pious friends perceive him as being guilty of something because of the terrible events that happened to him (e.g., 15:6; 32:3). When their attempt to impose guilt on him fails, they turn to shaming him, a form of social control that involves the attempt to maintain the purity of the community:

> I am a laughingstock to his friends, one who called to God and he answered him, a just and blameless man, am a mockery! (12:4)

> How long will you torment my soul and crush me by words?

> This has been 10 times that you have put me to shame, are you not ashamed to wrong me? (19:2-3)

As Bechtel states concerning Job, "He was bewildered by the fact that his friends were not the least bit shamed of treating him in this way . . ." (1997, 255). Job is even abandoned by his own family, who should have been supportive of him (19:13-19).

The community also abandoned him. In chapter 29, Job described his fall from grace in a dramatic way:

> In my going out to the gate of city, in the open plaza I prepared my seat,
> the youth saw me and hid themselves, and the aged arose and stood.
> The princes restrained their words,
> and they sat a hand upon their mouth.
> The voice of the nobles was hidden, their tongue clung to their palate.
> For an ear heard and called me blessed,
> and the eye saw and testified in my favor.
> For I deliver the poor who cry for help,
> and the orphan when there was no one to help him.
>
> . . . .
>
> But now I am their mocking song,
> and I am to them a by-word.
> They abhor me, distance themselves from me,
> from my face, they withhold not spittle.
> For he loosed my cord and humiliated me,
> and he threw off restraint.
> On my right hand the wretched crowd arises, they push away my feet,
> and they pile up against me their distressful behavior (29:7-12; 30:9-12).

God versus Job

As we have already mentioned, God essentially shames Job in the divine speeches. With the advent of the whirlwind, God and Job engage in a veritable challenge and riposte. Job has accused God of injustice and wants an encounter with him so that he might vindicate himself. Though it takes God a long time to answer, he eventually does, in order to save face. As already mentioned, many scholars have noted that God appears to "bully" Job with his superior knowledge and power. Normally one would not have expected a superior to challenge a person of inferior status. But since Job assumes the role of client to God's patronage, this changes everything. Basically, God dresses Job down and puts him in his place. Like a skilled debater, God delivers a series of rhetorical questions to Job that he embarrassingly cannot answer.

In the end Job repents of his many accusations of divine injustice (42:1-6), though God acknowledges that what the friends said was wrong (42:7). God, then, retains his honor, while Job loses status vis-a-vis God, while retaining his honor before his friends, who had leveled their accusations against Job. The friends lose prestige because of their lack of compassion and support. Though the friends thought they were doing what social custom demanded by shaming Job, they were wrong because they were unaware of the contest between God and the satan and could not think beyond their own preconceptions.

God's honor is at stake also in the frame narrative. As a pious believer in God, Job assumes the role of client to God. As we noted, a client's job is show honor to his patron and be loyal to him, and the patron's job to bestow gifts to the client.[1] When God says to the satan, "Have you considered my servant Job that there is none like him in the land, a man who is innocent, and upright, who fears God and turns from evil?" (1:8), he is boasting about his most loyal client. So, God's honor is at stake in the contest between the satan and himself. Will his servant demonstrate his loyalty and faithfulness to God or not? If God were to lose the contest, he, of course, would suffer a loss of status.

---

1. Since the patron-client relationship is a type of fictive kinship, then the technical type of reciprocity involved here is generalized and not balanced. Ki (2006, 723-49) describes it as a universal gift ethic, but this fails to consider the patron-client relationship between God and Job.

This points to another factor why God engaged in this seemingly dangerous contest. Michael Fox puts it best:

> [O]ne cause of unwarranted suffering, perhaps the only one, is nothing less than God's need for human fidelity. Here is great paradox. Humans are frail and foolish, but they have it in their power to give God something that God places at the top of his scale of values. Inexplicable suffering has a role in the divine moral economy, for it makes true piety possible (Fox 2005, 363).

Just as a patron needs clients to accrue more honor and prestige, God needs loyal adherents, who bring him more honor.

11

Ecclesiastes

Structure

We have already touched on this issue and will repeat it briefly. The book of Ecclesiastes, like the book of Job, has a frame-narrative that encapsulates it: 1:1-11 or 1:1-2, if the poem in vv. 3-11 is viewed as coming from Qohelet, and 12:8-14, which is often divided into vv. 8-11 (or vv. 8-12), from the hand of the frame-narrator, and vv. 12-14 (or vv. 13-14) from the hand of a pious glossator. The hand of the narrator appears in the body of the book in 7:27, with Qohelet referred to in the third person—at the very center of the book! Scholars disagree on how the frame-narrator evaluates Qohelet and his words (12:9-11[12]), whether generally positive (e.g., Fox 1977, 101; Bartholomew 2009, 78-79, 366) or generally negative (e.g., Shields 2006, 5-6). Interpreting the framework overly negatively does not make much sense because it fails to explain why the narrator chose to preserve the Teacher's words in the first place! And how one understands the assessment of the frame-narrator can help with hermeneutical application of Ecclesiastes since he represents the first interpreter of the Teacher's words.

Recently, some scholars have attempted to interpret the gloss at the end, which counsels commandment-keeping, as compatible with Qohelet's words (e.g., Krüger 2004, 213; Batholomew 2009, 372-73): "It is the end of the matter; all has been heard. Fear God and keep his commandments for this is the summation of humanity" (12:13). But few have followed these scholars. It is inconceivable that Qohelet would summarize his words with commandment-keeping, when he often questions the doctrine of retribution:

> And yet I have seen under the sun that in the place of judgment there was wickedness and in the place of justice there was evil (3:16).

> I have seen everything in my futile days: there exist the righteous who perish in their righteousness and the wicked who lengthen their days in their evil (7:15).

> There exists an evil that is done upon the land in that there are the righteous to whom it happens is according to the lifestyle of the wicked, and there are the wicked to whom it happens according to the lifestyle of the righteous. I said that this is a futility (8:14).

Now this is not to say that Qohelet would have recommended wickedness or violating the Torah. In fact, in Eccles. 5:1-7 he counsels to be cautious around God, and especially his Temple:

> Guard your feet when you go to the house of God, and approach to listen rather than to offer the sacrifice of fools. For they do not realize they do evil. Do not hasten with your mouth, and let not your heart act hastily to bring a word before God. For God is in heaven and you are on earth; therefore let your words be few. For a dream comes with much effort, and the voice of the fool with many words. When you make a vow to God, do not delay paying it, for there is no pleasure among fools. What you vowed, pay! It is better that you not vow than to vow and not pay it! Do not allow your mouth to sin against your flesh, and do not say before the messenger that it is was an unintentional mistake. Why let

God become angry at your voice and destroy the work of your hands? For in many dreams are vanities and many words. But fear God!

Concerning the necessity of paying a vow one makes, Qohelet alludes to Deut. 23:22-24. While Qohelet assumes the reader will keep the command here, he negatively qualifies the manner of keeping it and does not positively endorse commandment-keeping in general. Instead, in the rest of the book, Qohelet positively exhorts a carpe-diem ethic—enjoy life now before you die (2:24; 3:12-13, 22; 5:18-20; 8:15; 9:7-10; 11:7-10)—which corresponds with another admonition, one that seems to conflict directly with Torah teaching:

> Walk in the desires of your heart and in the delight of your eyes (Eccles. 11:9).

> Do not follow after your own heart and after your own eyes, which you are inclined to whore after (Num. 15:39).

So, while Eccles. 12:13 is not necessarily incongruent with Qohelet's teaching, it cannot serve as an accurate précis of this teaching. If asked, Qohelet no doubt would caution keeping the Torah, but it never becomes a specific exhortation in his counsel. And he would also probably add that one should not put all of one's behavioral eggs in the basket of Torah-piety.

The following table illustrates the basic structure of Ecclesiastes:

Figure 22: Structure of Ecclesiastes					
Frame Narrative 1:1-2	Body 1:3-7:26	Frame Narrator 7:26	Body 7:27-12:7	Frame Narrative 12:8-12	Glossator 12:13-14

As far as the microstructure of the book as a whole, there are two possibilities. The first views the book as logically and sequentially arranged with progression in thought as the book advances. For example, Craig Bartholomew sees real development in thought in the book, with Qohelet concluding at the end that his flirtation with Greek philosophy was unprofitable (Eccles. 11:7-12:7; 2009, 94).

The second possibility is that the book is more loosely arranged, with no real advancement in thinking. The argumentation of the book, then, is more like the prophetic books and is less linear. The book merely finds different ways of reaffirming its motto statement that all is vanity, which forms an inclusion to the words of Qohelet:

"Vanity of vanities," says Qohelet, "Vanity of vanities, all is vanity! (1:2).

"Vanity of vanities," says Qohelet, "Everything is vanity!" (12:8).

A form of the word "vanity" or *hebel* is used 38 times in the book, so arguably it is the most important concept for understanding the teaching of the book (more on this later).

The most sophisticated treatment of the structure of Ecclesiastes was advocated by Addison Wright (Wright 1968, 325-26). He uses a literary critical approach, and after examining repetition of words, phrases, literary devices, and grammatical features, came up with this outline of Ecclesiastes, largely the basis for all latter reconstructions of the book's structure by Qohelet experts:

"Title (1:1)

Poem on Toil (1:2-11)

    I. Qohelet's Investigation of Life (1:12-6:9)

    Double Introduction (1:12-15, 16-18)

    Study of Pleasure-seeking (2:1-11)

    Study of Wisdom and Folly (2:12-17)

    Study of the Fruits of Toil:

        one has to leave them to another (2:18-26)

one cannot hit on the right time to act (3:1-4:6)

the problem of a "second one" (4:7-16)

one can lose all that one accumulates (4:17-6:9)

II. Qohelet's Conclusions (6:10-11:6)

Introduction: man does not know what God has done, for man cannot find out what is good to do and they cannot find out what comes after (6:10-12).

A. Man cannot find out what is good for him to do

Critique of traditional wisdom:

on the day of prosperity (7:1-14)

on justice and wickedness (7:15-24)

on women and folly (7:25-29)

on the wise man and the king (8:1-17)

B. Man do not know what will come after them

They know they will die; the dead know nothing (9:1-6)

There is no knowledge in Sheol (9:7-10)

Man does not know their time (9:11-12)

Man does not know what will be (9:13-10:15)

Man does not know what evil will come (10:16-11:2)

Man does not know what good will come (11:3-6)

Poem on Youth and Old Age (11:7-12:8)

Epilogue (12:9-14)" (Wright 1968, 325-26)

Authorship and Audience

We have already discussed that Solomon most likely did not author Ecclesiastes. The nickname given is "Qohelet," which means a gatherer of either people (an assembly) or perhaps aphorisms, i.e., a collector of maxims. The name "Ecclesiastes" is the Greek translation of the Hebrew title; Greek students will notice its relation to *ecclesia* or church, which literally means a gathering. "Synagogue" is another translation of the Hebrew noun *qahal*, from which "Qohelet" derives. From the notion of a gatherer comes the translation "teacher" (NIV) or "Preacher," which goes back to Martin Luther: "Der *Prediger.*" But these are guesses, and scholars are not 100 percent sure what "Qohelet" means. For convenience, scholars often use the word Qohelet to refer to the author of the book of Ecclesiastes, while Ecclesiastes is used to refer to the book.

We have referred to Fox's interpretation of "Qohelet" as a persona for the frame-narrative (1977, 83-106). This means that Qohelet is not really a person, but a conceit the implied author uses to distance himself somewhat from the unorthodox thoughts of Qohelet. The other voice is that of the frame-narrator, who cautiously approves of Qohelet's sentiments. Fox ingeniously argues, and I think rightly, that the implied author allows the reader to choose which voice she might gravitate toward: the unorthodox voice of Qohelet or the more conservative voice of the frame-narrator. Fox carefully points out that the voice of the frame-narrator does not dominate or eclipse the voice of Qohelet. Unfortunately, recent interpreters have done just that. Both Martin Shields (2004) and Craig Bartholomew (2009) view the frame-narrative as the dominant voice of the book, which essentially makes the bulk of the words of Qohelet at best tangential theologically and at worse rejected entirely.

The other possibility is to not view "Qohelet" as a persona but as an actual person, whose words have been preserved by the frame-narrator. This makes the narrator simply an editor. This has been the dominant view among Qohelet experts until the time of Fox. With this approach, the description of Qohelet in the epilog becomes paramount for determining authorship. Qohelet is described as "wise," *chakam,* in v. 9 "Besides being wise, Qohelet taught the people, weighing and searching and arranging many aphorisms." This most likely refers to a scribal teacher. In fact, "my son" in Eccles. 12:12 points to this, though this is the frame-narrator's direct address of the intended reader. There is no reason why Qohelet and the frame-narrator would occupy distinct social or professional locations. That Qohelet is being referred to as a scribe is further substantiated by the fact that the description of his professional role in 12:9 ("weighing and searching and arranging aphorisms") constitutes technical language for scribal activities, as already mentioned (Fishbane 1988, 29-32).

"My son" is a typical address for scribal apprentices, as we have seen. That they were young males is indicated in chapter 11, when Qohelet addresses an imagined audience as "young man" (*bachur*):

> Rejoice, o young man, in your youth and let your heart flourish in the days of your youth . . . and turn vexation away from your heart and cause evil to pass from your flesh because youth and blackness (of hair) are fleeting (11:9-10).

The audience, then, appears to be young scribes, as was the case with Proverbs. Like Job, Ecclesiastes was mostly likely a book studied by advanced scribal students and not read in the early stages of their training. No doubt Proverbs was read first, then Job and Ecclesiastes, which both serve to canonically qualify the positive teaching in Proverbs.

Date

The consensus for the date of Qohelet is still the Ptolemaic period. The argument for this date is open to criticism and only represents a consensus. The factors for dating are based on language (evidence of Aramaisms and Greekisms), Greek influence, and the author's psychological disposition. The Ptolemaic dating was essentially the iron clad consensus until C. L. Seow challenged it and argued for a Persian period date (1996, 643–66). But Dominic Rudman essentially deconstructed Seow's main linguistic argument (1999, 47–52). While linguistic arguments for dating a biblical book are notoriously speculative, the book shares features with rabbinical Hebrew, like the use of *she* for *asher* ("which").

There may be evidence of Greek linguistic influence in Ecclesiastes such as the phrase "under the sun" (see Hengel 1974, 117) or maybe the concept of "fate" (9:2) (Machinist 1995, 159–75). Some have argued that the skepticism in the book should be attributed to Greek influence. However, an expert on Greek skepticism discounts that notion (Barnes 1999, 103–14). Qohelet's skepticism and pessimism reflect a long and revered Semitic tradition that goes back to the early second millennium (e.g., "The Ballad of Early Rulers"), as we have seen. Thus, there is no need to attribute these perspectives to the Greeks. Rather, the specific social and historical context best explains why Qohelet chose to adopt these literary strategies to fashion his work.[1]

The references to a bustling economy with some persons becoming suddenly wealthy and then losing everything (e.g., 6:1–2) certainly would fit the Ptolemaic period. In chapter 5, Qohelet warns against materialism as a lifestyle that brings satisfaction. The

1. On the relationship between Qohelet's use of pessimism (and skepticism) and the harsh conditions of the Ptolemaic period, see Sneed 2012.

references to the king and rulers in Qohelet (e.g., 8:2; 10:5) reflect a powerful regime that maintained an iron-fisted grip on its territories. This fits the Ptolemies better than the Persians, who were known for being more benevolent to their vassals, though always to their own advantage. So, the cumulative evidence points to sometime in the Ptolemaic period in the third century B.C.E. Until further evidence emerges, one would be safe to assume this consensus position.

Qohelet's Idiosyncratic Use of Language

Robert Gordis was one of the first to notice that Qohelet often did not employ terms in their typical sense. He explains this as due to Qohelet's attempt to express philosophical concepts in a language not developed for this task:

> At the very outset it must be borne in mind that Koheleth was a linguistic pioneer. He was struggling to use Hebrew for quasi-philosophical purposes, a use to which the language had not previously been applied. . . .Kohelet uses the language in which he was reared, and incidentally, the only one he knew, to express his own individual viewpoint (Gordis 1968, 88-89).

Gordis notes that Qohelet uses certain traditionally moral terms in an ethically neutral sense, like *chote'* in 2:26, which is translated as "sinner" (Gordis 1968, 93-94). Qohelet is using it in the sense of "missing the mark" or a mistake, an un-careful person rather than one who stubbornly resists God and societal norms. This "sinner" God gives the task of collecting for the one "pleasing to God." This person is not the traditional Jewish sinner but rather a dogmatic and narrow-minded individual, who thinks she can predict God's behavior. Also, Gordis notes that "God-fearing" or *yare' elohim* in Qohelet (3:14; 5:6; 7:18; 8:12-13) is usually used in an idiosyncratic way (Gordis 1968, 94). It does not mean a traditionally pious person (except for 8:12-13, according to Gordis), but rather someone who literally "fears" or "trembles" before God and avoids foolish behavior.

The Meaning of *Hebel*

As stated earlier, the word *hebel* occurs 38 times in the book and is considered the leitmotif of the book by most scholars. Scholars disagree on how to translate it. Literally, it means a "breath" or "wind," but it is usually used metaphorically. Sometimes it means "insubstantial" or "fleeting" as when Qohelet bemoans the fleetingness of youth (Eccles. 11:10). However, it usually has the meaning of "futility" in that it is always directed at human activity, never God's. This is seen in the first question the book asks in 1:3: "What profit is there for humanity in all its toil, which it toils under the sun?" The answer in the following poem about cycles of nature and human generations is: none! And in Qohelet's experiment as a royal despot, in the rest of chapters 1-2, the answer is the same: none! This is all directed at human activity and striving. Thus, in this context human aspirations and strivings are evaluated as ultimately futile and meaningless. They do not produce any profit beyond the costs exerted to accomplish them! This does not mean, however, that Qohelet rejects human labor. In fact, he finds it necessary and a means to enjoyment in life. But he seriously qualifies the value of human labor. The striving to accomplish great deeds and build grand monuments is more effort than it is worth. Thus, Qohelet's criticism of human labor is a significant deconstruction of its value for society. Here Qohelet is being the unorthodox sage who challenges traditionally norms.

The translation of *hebel* as "futility," which the New Jewish Publication Society does, fits the context of the book of Ecclesiastes much better than other translations. It suits the popular usage of *hebel* as an polemic against idols, which are portrayed as worthless (*hebel*) pieces of wood or stone that were powerless to help their worshippers (e.g., Jer. 10:15). Also, as Seybold argues, *hebel* in Ecclesiastes is being used as a polemical term directed at the wisdom tradition, which befits Qohelet's aims (1974, 319). It is an evaluative term directed negatively at the sapiential enterprise. Again, this does not mean Qohelet was rejecting the wisdom tradition completely. He certainly found wisdom and righteousness superior to folly and sin. But he seriously qualifies the value of wisdom for guiding life. Qohelet does not believe the wisdom tradition has all the answers. In fact, it can actually lead one astray and down dangerous paths.

One of the most popular translations of *hebel* among scholars is Fox's "absurdity" (Fox 1986, 409-427). This might be okay if one understands it to be directed as human toil. But Fox broadens the scope to refer to the circumstances of the world, which, of course, indirectly implicates God's activities. But as Norbet Lohfink has pointed out, *hebel* is used anthropologically, not theologically (Lohfink 1998, 59). In other words, *hebel* is always directed at humanity, never God. Though Qohelet is not shy to express bitterness about the way God runs the world (e.g., 1:12), it would be unthinkable for him to accuse God's activities as *hebel*. Qohelet might insinuate God's ways appear unjust, from the human standpoint, but never absurd! "Aburdity" would mean *hebel* is being used polemically against God himself! It is more reasonable to see Qohelet's target as traditional wisdom. Even passages that seem to suggest that Qohelet is describing a situation as absurd are rather referring to the futility of human aspiration and striving:

> There is a *hebel* that happens on the earth: there are righteous people who receive what is appropriate to the deeds of wicked and there are wicked people who receive what is appropriate to the deeds of the righteous. I said that this too is *hebel* (translation from Fox 1999, 30).

351

Fox admits that the ambiguous "this" could refer to the futility of the deeds of the righteous whose good deeds do not pan out (1999, 30). But he argues that this cannot be the meaning because the wicked person's deeds indeed profit here because their wickedness proves successful. However, the main problem with Fox's reasoning is that the wicked are not among those addressed by this admonition. The point of this passage is to not put all one's eggs in the one basket of piety. It will not likely result in success. Rather, one should be cautious in behavior; moderation is always Qohelet's favorite advice.

Finally, if Qohelet delights in describing God's ways as "absurd," Fox needs to explain how Qohelet can simultaneously describe the order of God's determination of the activities of humanity and nature in 3:1-8 as "beautiful" or "appropriate" (*yafeh*). Qohelet might have a few bones to pick with God about many matters, but he would never refer to the divine scheme of the world as "absurd"!

Qohelet's Ethical System: Hedging One's Bets

Qohelet's primary ethical system appears to be the carpe diem ethic that we mentioned earlier. Here is the first instance of this ethic, which forms the conclusion to Qohelet's royal experiment in chapters 1-2, where he tests the various attempts humans have made to find meaning in their lives (work, materialism, accomplishment, honor, pleasure):

> There is nothing better for a person than that he eat and drink and that his soul experience goodness in his toil. Also this I have seen is from the hand of God. For who is able to eat and who can enjoy apart from him? For to the person who is pleasing before him, he gives wisdom and knowledge and enjoyment. But to the "sinner" he gives the occupation to gather and collect in order to give to the one pleasing before God. This also is a futility and a chasing after the wind (2:24-26).

Because this ethic begins with "there is nothing better," it indicates that it is secondary to his leitmotif of everything being *hebel* and that it is an ethic of resignation, not one of hope or optimism (see Crenshaw 2010, 144). But it appears to be the one "positive" ethic that Qohelet can advise that is not *hebel*. R. N. Whybray has argued that the pessimism of the book serves as a foil for the carpe diem ethic, which means that joy is Qohelet's actual message, and, thus, Qohelet is not a consistent pessimist (1982, 87-98). Whybray is correct to a point. Qohelet's pessimism is being used rhetorically, but this does not convert his carpe diem ethic into a joyous message. Rather, the pessimism serves it, frames it, and substantiates it. You cannot have the one without the other.

As indicated earlier, Qohelet's carpe diem ethic is another way of expressing the sentiment of 11:9b: "Walk in the desires of your heart and in the delight of your eyes." However, earlier we did not provide the conclusion of this verse: "But know that for all these God will bring you into judgment" (11:9c). Most scholars believe that this ending of the verse is a gloss because it indicates that Qohelet believed in divine judgment, when elsewhere in the book the lack of divine justice is the very problem (3:16; 7:15; 8:14)! However, these same scholars do not usually view the fear of God's judgment regarding improper cultic actions in 5:1-7 as inauthentic. Certainly, this passage assumes the possibility of divine judgment!

These same scholars usually also view Eccles. 3:17 as a gloss, a text which also speaks of divine judgment: "I said in my heart that the righteous and the wicked, God will judge. For there is a time for every matter and for every work." However, here we have a case where Qohelet appears to be using Hebrew terminology in his own distinctive sense. The New Jewish Publication Society has the best translation of this verse:

> I mused: "God will *doom* both righteous and wicked, for there is a time for every experience for every happening" (italics mine).

The point is that God certainly *judges* but he does so arbitrarily from a human standpoint. In other words, God's standards are not human standards. God will certainly judge human behavior but not according to the dictates of traditional Judaism or wisdom!

Another significant passage for this discussion is Eccles. 8:11-14:

> Because punishment is not applied to the deed of a sinner, the heart of the sons of man hastens, therefore, to do evil. *Though a sinner does evil a hundredfold and extends his days, I know that it will be well for those who fear God, because he will fear before him. And it will not be well for the wicked and he will not extend his days like a shadow, because he will not fear before God.*

> There exists a futility which exists upon the land in that there are the righteous to whom it happens according the action of the wicked, and there are the wicked to whom it happens according to the action of the righteous. I said that this is also a futility!

I italicize vv. 12-13 because most scholars believe that either they are a pious gloss or else Qohelet is considering a possibility—that bad things will indeed happen to the sinner—and then goes on to dismiss it in v. 14.

This passage is complex and needs to be carefully considered (see Sneed 2003, 412-16). There are actually two topics being treated here and not one. The first is the problem of delayed punishment (Eccles. 8:11-13). Qohelet reflects on how the wicked often seem to get away with their sinful behavior and even seem to prosper from it. But Qohelet then notes that the sinner will eventually pay the piper, but not for the traditional reasons. Ecclesiastes 8:12-13 point out that the sinner will eventually succumb to punishment not because of his sinful behavior per se but *because he is not a God-fearer.* Here Gordis's notion of God-fearing is relevant. The God-fearer is not necessarily a righteous or pious person. He is merely cautious before the deity. So, Eccles. 8:12-13 are certainly compatible with the rest of Qohelet's theology. A sinner will eventually suffer for his folly but not because of his lack of piety, but rather his lack of caution. The second topic is found in Ecclesiastes 8:14, which is actually the beginning of a new paragraph and is not about delay of punishment but about the lack of a clear connection between piety and one's fortune.

If this interpretation of Eccles. 8: 12-13 is correct, then it means that Qohelet does not completely deny the doctrine of retribution. Rather, he still believes that there is a connection between how one lives and how one fares, except that the rules of the game are different than the perspective of traditional wisdom. Caution rather than piety is the new modus operandi for the wise person. And Qohelet would emphasize that determining the rules of the game is not completely possible. Qohelet admits to a great degree of capriciousness on the part of God and his divine scheme of judgment and retribution.

The relationship between Qohelet's primary and only positive ethic, the carpe diem advice, and his caution about divine judgment mean that Qohelet essentially hedges his bets. Because one cannot count on a clear discernment of the connection between behavior and fortune, Qohelet counsels enjoyment of the present as much as possible and following the "desires of your heart and in the delight of your eyes" (Eccles. 11:9b)! However, this does not mean a total abandonment to hedonistic pleasures, because this might have its consequences as well. Qohelet curtails the carpe diem ethic with the qualification of being cautious in light of God's mysterious divine judgment, which fits with his advice to fear God. Thus, Qohelet's ethical system is strikingly modern. It resembles utilitarianism, where right and wrong depends on the ends. Specifically, utilitarianism teaches that one should act to promote happiness, especially intellectual pleasures, and avoid pain (see Mill 1957, 10-11). Qohelet promotes pleasure (carpe diem ethic) in view of a disconnect between lifestyle and fortune, and he recommends caution in view of possible pain (divine judgment).

Honor and Qohelet

Because the connection between piety and wisdom and the expected results appears to be no longer guaranteed, Qohelet seems to abandon the quest for honor:

> There was a man to whom God gave wealth, and riches, and honor, and there was nothing lacking in his soul of all which he desired. And yet God did not allow him to partake of it, for a foreigner devoured it. This is a futility and a grievous evil! (6:2).

> Dead flies will cause mixed perfume to stink and bubble,
> weightier than wisdom and honor is a little folly (10:1).

Because the traditional values of Jewish society like wealth, honor, and power appear to no longer depend on pious and wise behavior, Qohelet offers another strategy that focuses on other values: pleasure (his carpe diem ethic) and relationships (e.g., 4:9; 9:9; see Sneed 2012, 203-29). This means that on the scale of Maslow's hierarchy of values, Qohelet has rejected the top layers of self-actualization and esteem and focused more on the bottom, more basic and primary layers, like the social and physiological.

But this does not mean that Qohelet completely rejects wisdom. In Eccles. 9:13-16 a poor wise man delivered a city that was being besieged by his wisdom. But everyone forgot about the poor man after the city was saved! Qohelet bemoans this fact: "But I say that wisdom is better than might, though wisdom of the poor is despised and their words are not listened to" (9:16). And this also does not mean that Qohelet completely rejected honor as a means to happiness. Qohelet is described by the frame-narrator as "seeking to find delightful words and upright writing and words of truth" (12:10). This aesthetic and honest endeavor on the part of Qohelet in the composition of his words means that Qohelet hoped to please his intended audience. No doubt Qohelet intended to impress his fellow colleagues as well. This would have brought him a measure of esteem among their number that he might not have enjoyed in the larger public. So, honor was still something sought by the Teacher, but it is no longer the primary value for his circle of confreres: immediate pleasure in view of the uncertainties of life in Ptolemaic Judah.

Comparative Literature

We have already mentioned and cited a segment from the skeptical Egyptian "Songs of the Harpers." The pessimism and skepticism of some of these songs is directly connected with the inevitability of death and the resultant counsel of the carpe diem ethic. The other comparative Egyptian work is "The Dispute between a Man and His Ba," which was also briefly discussed. In it, a man contemplates suicide but his Ba or alter-ego convinces him to remain alive in view of the uncertainties of the afterlife. Again, the interaction between the Ba and the man resembles the way Qohelet often appears to talk to himself as he makes his observations (e.g., "I said in my heart" [2:1]) (see Holmstedt 2009, 1-27).

We have already mentioned the pessimistic "Ballade of the Early Rulers," but another parallel to Qohelet is the Babylonian "The Dialog of Pessimism," where a master and slave debate various options that the master might take. The composition appears to be quite cynical but its function is perhaps to relativize human cognition and emphasize humility (van der Toorn 1991, 59-75). Here are a segment of the debate and the very last one:

> "Slave, listen to me." "Here I am, sir, here I am."
> "I am going to love a woman." "So love, sir, love.
> The man who loves a woman forgets sorrow and fear."
> "No, slave, I will by no means love a woman."
> ["Do not] love, sir, do not love.
> Woman is a pitfall—a pitfall, a hole, a ditch,
> Woman is a sharp iron dagger that cuts a man's throat."
>
> ....
>
> "Slave, listen to me." "Here I am, sir, here I am."
> "What, then, is good?"
> "To have my neck and your neck broken
> and to be thrown into the river is good.
> 'Who is so tall as to ascend to the heavens?
> Who is so broad as to compass the underworld?'"
> "No, slave, I will kill you and send you first."
> "And my master would certainly not outlive me by even three days"
> (Lambert 1996, 147, 149).

But another significant parallel is the "Epic of Gilgamesh." We have already noted the incident of the divine barmaid who counsels Gilgamesh to give up his quest for immortality and adopt a carpe diem ethic, which compares strikingly with Eccles. 9:7-10. However, Qohelet would differ from the "Epic" in rejecting its notion of attaining immortality through legacy or reputation: Gilgamesh resigns himself to mortality by reminding himself of the great city (Uruk) he has built and the many heroic deeds he has accomplished. Instead, Qohelet counsels honest acceptance of death and its uncertainties, which help reprioritize life's values: the present moment is most precious.

12

Sirach and Sapientia

The two books discussed in this chapter are not found in the Protestant Old Testament or Hebrew (Masoretic) canon. They come from the Septuagint and are part of the Catholic canon and are usually designated as apocryphal ("hidden away" from public view) books by Protestants. But all scholars agree that these books are a continuation of the wisdom tradition. Both are focused on the topic of wisdom and both contain stereotypical wisdom genres. Both books are also very late, with Ben Sira (Sirach) dating to the second century B.C.E. and Sapientia (Wisdom of Solomon) usually dated to the first century C.E. And both have the commonality of reacting to the new world of Hellenism, with both resistance and assimilation (Hellenization). And both represent a response to the Greek notion of the immortality of the soul, which will eventually help reconfigure the Jewish doctrine of retribution.

Judaism and Hellenism

Before discussing these books, a few words are in order about the Jewish exposure to the Greek world and culture. In 323 B.C.E., when Alexander the Great conquered the world, the Greeks controlled Palestine and Judah for almost 200 years. This would have had a major impact on the Jews culturally, what is known as Hellenization (from the word for "Greeks," which comes from *Hellēn*, the son of Deucalion, the Greek Noah). While there is evidence that the Greeks left the Jewish nation alone as long as it paid its tribute, there would have been Greek soldiers installed at garrisons throughout the country, various Greek officials living in Judah, especially Jerusalem, and various Greek merchants who traveled through the area (see Sneed 2012, 85-124). Also, there is evidence that the Jews were exposed to Greeks and their culture long before Alexander entered the picture. This would have meant the diffusion of Greek ways and ideas that surely impacted the Jews.

The important questions concerning Jewish Hellenization are to what degree and how quickly? The simple answers are: not much in the beginning and very slowly. We have already discussed how there are few clear indications that Ecclesiastes reflects the influence of Hellenism. But Ben Sira and Wisdom of Solomon were written later, when Hellenization was profoundly affecting the Jews.

The reaction to Hellenization is complex. For example, it usually affects the upper class more than the lower class (Levine 1999, 23-24). And rarely is there a wholesale adoption of the Greek culture without some kind of adaptation and modification. Often there is the adoption of a Greek custom or idea but it is tweaked to make it more compatible with Judaism (see Gardner 2007, 327-43). Both Sirach and Wisdom represent reactions to Judaism. Both are, in a sense, polemical toward Hellenism to an extent but also represent assimilation to its ways and norms.

For example, Wisdom adopts the Greek notion of the immortality of the soul, a very non-Jewish idea at the time, but utilizes it entirely within the theological system of Judaism, where the faithful Jews will be the only ones who will become immortal and their enemies destroyed. And as we have seen, rhetorically, the book of Sirach depicts personified wisdom as first searching the globe for a place to rest but finally lighting upon Judah.

Hellenization in the book is further corroborated by Richard Clifford, who sees Stoicism and Middle Platonism (80 B.C.E.-250 C.E.) in Wisdom, especially chapters. 13-15 (2013, 9). Stoic influence is seen in the use of the concept of a world soul (Wis. 7:24), materialist physics (8:1; 19:18), the proof from design (13:1), and the rhetorical use of *sorites* (chain argument) in 8:17-21. Influence from Middle Platonism includes the pre-existence of souls (8:19), the rigid distinction between soul and body (8:20; 9:15), and the diminished reality of the material world in contrast to the spiritual one in heaven (9:15-16).

Also, Sharon Mattila has shown how Wis 7:22-8:1 reflects a middle to late Stoic imagery, a kind later than that which influenced Ben Sira, where personified wisdom is associated with the divine Logos or rationality that is diffused throughout the cosmos, "while maintaining a very non-Stoic transcendence of God and an eschatological worldview" (2000, 485-87). While Ben Sira has Woman Wisdom be the first of God's creation, like Proverbs 8, the book of Wisdom has her coming directly from God and, thus, partaking of his substance and being more compatible with the divine Logos: "pure effluence," "effulgence," "unblemished mirror," and "image" (Wis. 7:25-26), reinforced by her divine epithets: "all-powerful," "all-surveying" (7:23b; Mattila 2000, 485-86). Instead of her creation by God,

Wisdom portrays her as "the artificer of all things" (7:22a). Yet Wisdom 7:22-8:1 "maintains God's transcendence, because as the *source* of wisdom he remains ontologically prior to her." (2000, 486). Also, while Ben Sira depicts Woman Wisdom at the creation as having "veiled the earth like a dark mist," Wis. 7:22-8:1 identifies her with "an intelligent spirit or breath" which "pervades and penetrates all things" (Wis. 7:22b-24; Matilla 2000, 486-87). The statement after Wis. 8:1b that wisdom "effectively administers" all creation, which refers to her providential role in the maintenance of the cosmos, is very close to the concept of the Logos (Mattila 2000, 487).

Ben Sira (or Sirach) rejects the notion of an immortal soul and preserves the alternative of "immortality" in the sense of legacy and remembrance (see Cave 2012, 201-52). He also encourages the study of the Torah and discourages reading certain writings:

> Neither seek what is too difficult for you,
> nor investigate what is beyond your power.
> Reflect upon what you have been commanded,
> for what is hidden is not your concern (3:21-22; NRSV).[1]

Are these Greek philosophical works or certain apocalyptic writings, like 1 Enoch (Adams 2008, 157) or both (Crenshaw 1997, 626, 663)? At any rate, as David Skelton notes, "Scholars generally agree that Ben Sira is responding to the influence of Hellenistic philosophy by attempting to show that true wisdom lies in Jerusalem, not in Athens" (2009, 1). But Ben Sira also possibly reflects the adoption of Greek ideas. For example, Clifford argues that Ben Sira may have been influenced by both Stoicism and Epicureanism (1998, 117). And this has been fully substantiated by Sharon Lea Matilla (2000, 473-501). Clifford is careful to note that one of the main tenets of

---

1. Unless otherwise indicated, all citations from Sirach and Wisdom of Solomon will be from the NRSV.

Stoicism, that the universe is governed by a divine Logos that humans must conform themselves to by following the dictates of nature and rationality, is incompatible with Ben Sira's thinking. Clifford also points out that the universal perspective of Stoicism would have conflicted with Ben Sira's Jewish perspective, which was covenantal and viewed God as utterly transcendent. However, he sees traces of Stoicism in Ben Sira's ideal of human dignity (41:14–42:8) and of the unity of the world and humanity (36:1–4, 22; 43:27).

Ben Sira

Ben Sira and Egyptian Wisdom

We have already mentioned the connection between the Egyptian "Satire of the Trades" and Ben Sira's similar comparison between scribes and the professions involving manual labor. Here is a comparison of the two by trade:

Satire of the Trades	Sirach
The potter is under the soil, though as yet among the living; He grubs in the mud more than a pig, in order to fire his pots. His clothes are stiff with clay, his girdle is in shreds; If air hits his nose, it comes straight from the fire. He makes a pounding with his feet, and is himself crushed; He grubs the yard of every house and roams the public places (Lichtheim 1975, 186–87).	So it is with the potter sitting at his work and turning the wheel with his feet; he is always deeply concerned over his products, and he produces them in quantity. He molds the clay with his arm and makes it pliable with his feet; he sets his heart to finish the glazing, and he takes care in firing the kiln (Sir. 38:29–30).

The difference between the two is that the Egyptian text is more elitist and condescending toward the menial professions. The "Satire" ends its description of various trades with:

> See, there's no profession without a boss,
> except for the scribe; he is the boss.
> Hence if you know writing,
> it will do better for you
> than those professions I've set before you,
> each more wretched than the other.
> A peasant is not called a man,
> beware of it! (Lichtheim 1975, 189–90).

Of course, one could argue that rhetorically the scribal teacher is merely trying to motivate the student to study harder in order to become a scribe by exaggerating how despicable and demeaning the various professions that involve manual labor. Ben Sira differs in being more appreciative of the non-scribal professions:

> All these rely on their hands
> and all are skillful in their own work.
> Without them no city can be inhabited,
> and wherever they live, they will not go hungry.
>
> ....
>
> But they maintain the fabric of the world,
> and their concern is for the exercise of their trade
> (Sir. 38:31–32a, 34).

Yet Ben Sira points out that members of these professions are not found among the truly powerful and influential (vv. 32b–33). And neither can they properly study the Torah and the secrets of the prophecies and proverbs, nor compare with the scribes' status and reputation (Sir. 38:34–39:1–11).

Text, Authorship, Date, and Audience

Ben Sira comes to us fully only in the Greek language, through its author's son, who introduces his father in the prologue. We can date the book within the year! His grandson, in the prolog, translated his father's work into Greek in 132 B.C.E., the 38th year of Euergetes, king of Egypt (see Clifford 1998, 116). The Dead Sea Scrolls include a few Hebrew fragments, and some were found in Cairo. About two-thirds of the Hebrew text has been recovered, but it is in poor condition textually and has additions to it.

Sir. 50:27 provides biographical material: "Jesus (Hebrew: 'Yeshua') Son of Eleazar, son of Sira, of Jerusalem, whose mind poured forth wisdom" (Clifford 1998, 116). This represents a break with the biblical tradition of anonymous authorship. Ben Sira was a scribe and possibly ran a scribal school (51:23), if "house of instruction" is not being used metaphorically for discipleship. Thus, whether or not Sirach ran a school, the book is intended for young scribes. These scribes would most likely have worked for either the priesthood as administrators, or directly for the Seleucids, the Greeks who controlled Palestine and subjugated Judah as a vassal nation, because indigenous scribes would have been necessary for the Greek administration of the land and its resources (see Sneed 2012, 85-124). They also might have worked for private businesses.

Genre and Structure

The book is certainly modeled as an instructional book similar to the book of Proverbs (see Adams 2008, 158-60). Sirach offers both lengthy discourse and smaller units of sayings. Like Proverbs, Sirach treats such topics as etiquette, wealth, poverty, and death. Also included are numerical and "better-than" proverbs. The book also contains a number of hymns of praise (1:1-10; 18:1-14; 39:12-35; 42:15-43:33; 50:22-24; 51:1-12), like the hymn to Wisdom in chapter 24, which is modeled on Proverbs 8. Sirach also includes a prayer (22:27-23:6)—not entirely new for the wisdom tradition, as Agur's oracle includes a prayer, except this one is not didactic but petitionary. We have already mentioned Ben Sira's version of the "Satire on the Trades" (38:24-39:11), but the most distinctively new formal element for the wisdom tradition is the didactic narrative (see Di Lella 1992, 939) known as the "Praise of the Ancestors" at the end of the book (chs. 44-50), which resembles the Greek encomium. There is also autobiographical narrative in 33:16-18 and 51:13-30, which concludes the book and is primarily didactic. Finally, there are lists or onomastica in the book, used in his creation hymns (39:16-35; 42:15-43:33).

Many wisdom experts believe the "Praise of the Ancestors" is an anomaly for the wisdom tradition since this tradition does not usually make historical or national allusions. However, as we have indicated, this is the argument from silence, which, without other evidence, is very weak. But, even if new, modes of literature are constantly changing, and this should be expected. Certainly, Ben Sira is much more nationalistic and provincial in his casting of wisdom. But his wisdom per se still largely maintains its universalistic appeal because it is focused on the individual. The praise of the ancestors is ultimately used to buttress the didactic intention of the proverbial and exhortatory material in the book as it elevates heroes of the past that could serve as models for righteous and wise behavior.

The structure of the book involves the loose collection of instructions (see Adams 2008, 163). Scholars do not agree on exactly how to divide it. There are some clues however. The midpoint of the book is the hymn to Wisdom in chapter 24, and the praise of the ancestors forms the conclusion. Within the first half there are five passages on Wisdom: 1:1-10; 4:11-19; 6:18-37; 14:20-15:10; and 24:1-34, which seem to indicate chapters. Both Crenshaw and Clifford see 8 main sections, while Adams has 15. The following is a table that illustrates the structure Clifford suggests:

Figure 23: Structure of Sirach									
Prol ogue	1:1– 4:10	4:11– 6:17	6:18– 14:19	14:20– 23:27	24:1– 33:18	33:19– 38:23	38:24 –43:33 Praise of Scribes (38:24 –39:11)	Praise of Ancestors 44:1– 50:24	Conclusion 50:25– 51:30

Key Themes

Wisdom/Torah/Fear of the Lord

One of the most intriguing aspects of Ben Sira's theology and the book's main theme is his connecting of wisdom with the Torah. We have already seen that God-fearing is closely connected to wisdom (e.g., Prov. 1:7), but the equating of Torah and wisdom is distinct for the wisdom tradition, except for Proverbs 1-9 containing allusions to the Deuteronomic Torah and the existence of Torah psalms, which are sapiential as well. The connecting of all three entities is found in two places:

The whole of wisdom is fear of the Lord,
and in all wisdom there is the fulfillment of the law (Sir. 19:20).

Whoever fears the Lord will do this,
and whoever holds to the law will obtain wisdom (Sir. 15:1).

Also, in chapter 24, the connection is made when Wisdom lights upon Judah:

Then the Creator of all things gave me a command,
and my Creator chose the place for my tent.
He said, 'Make your dwelling in Jacob,
and in Israel receive your inheritance.

....

All this is the book of the covenant of the Most High God,
the law that Moses commanded us . . . (Sir. 24:8, 23).

Alexander A. Di Lella's summary of this theological combination
is helpful, ". . . I would contend that Ben Sira's primary theme
is wisdom *as* fear of the Lord, and that his fundamental thesis is
this: wisdom, which is identified with the Law, can be acquired
only by one who fears God and keeps the commandments" (1992,
940). Di Lella also points out correctly that Ben Sira's theology is
mainly Deuteronomistic: "In general, Ben Sira subscribes to the great
Deuteronomic equation: to fear God = to love him = to keep his
commandments = to walk in his ways (cf. Deut. 10:12-13)" (1992,
941). The following is a diagram depicting the relationship between
the three entities:

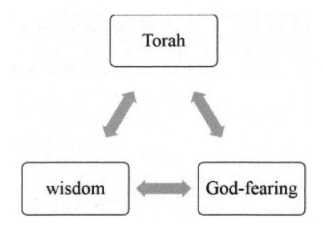

Figure 24: Wisdom, Torah, and Fear of the Lord

Some have argued that Ben Sira subordinates Torah to wisdom. Jack Sanders emphasizes, "Yet what is odd is that ben Sira nowhere cites a commandment from the Torah in support of his moral advice, which regularly follows the traditional conservative ethics of the sages" (2001, 123). Sanders views Ben Sira as essentially assimilating the Torah into the category of wisdom (2001, 125). Similarly, Joseph Blenkinsopp puts it this way, "As much as he insists on the observance of the commandments, it is clear that the category which dominates his thinking is not the law but wisdom" (1995, 163). And finally Gerhard von Rad states it most clearly, "It is not that wisdom is overshadowed by the superior power of the Torah, but, vice versa, that we see Sirach endeavoring to legitimize and interpret Torah from the realm of understanding characteristic of wisdom" (1972, 245).

But the view that Sirach subordinates wisdom to Torah is mainly due to these scholars' inability to conceive of a sage placing the Torah on par with wisdom. Sirach sees wisdom as essentially in harmony with the Torah and certainly compatible with it. There is no such prioritization of one over the other. And Sirach does not need to cite the commandments in his book because his focus is on sapiential advice, not legal. Again, it is absurd to think that a scribe like Ben Sira would somehow see one mode of literature (wisdom literature) as superior to the others, and that he would only see the world through this particular mode!

"Immortality" and National Eschatological Theodicy

Though Qohelet, whose words are dated earlier than Ben Sira, rejects the notion of continued memory or legacy as a means of "immortality" for humans (1:11; 2:16; 9:4-6), Samuel Adams rightly argues that Ben Sira shores up this notion and reestablishes it (2008,

204-208). He assumes the traditional Jewish notion of some kind of afterlife existence, but it is neither clear, nor desirable. At the most it is a shadowy existence, without much substance, and certainly is not the heaven and hell of the New Testament. In 38:21-22, Ben Sira resigns himself to the fact that death is the end of human existence as we know it:

> Do not forget, there is no coming back;
> you do the dead no good, and you injure yourself.
> Remember his fate, for yours is like it;
> yesterday it was his, and today it is yours.

Compare these verses from Ecclesiastes and Ben Sira:

> All go to one place. All came from the dust,
> and all will return to the dust (Eccles. 3:20).
> The Lord created human beings out of earth,
> and makes them return to it again (Sir. 17:1).

Ben Sira also employs the carpe diem ethic but not in a Qohelethian way (see Adams 2008, 204-205):

> Do not deprive yourself of a day's enjoyment;
> do not let your share of desired good pass by you.
> Will you not leave the fruit of your labors to another,
> and what you acquire by toil to be divided by lot?
> Give and take and indulge yourself,
> because in Hades once cannot look for luxury.
> All living beings become like a garment,
> for the decree from of old is, "You must die!" (Sir. 14:14-17)

Ben Sira does not focus solely on present pleasure and completely abandon the notion of immortality as does Qohelet. He embraces the idea of legacy: immortality through being remembered by others: "One who is wise among his people will inherit honor, and his name will live forever" (Sir. 27:26). In chapter 15, Ben Sira speaks of personified Wisdom coming to encounter the God-fearer and one who has attained wisdom (15: 1-2). And then he states:

and he will rely on her and not be put to shame.
She will exalt him above his neighbors,
and will open his mouth in the midst of the assembly.
He will find gladness and a crown of rejoicing,
and will inherit an everlasting name (Sir. 15:4b-6).

In contrast, the fool will "die" before his actual death (see Adams 2008, 207). In 22:11-12, Ben Sira states:

Weep for the dead, for he has left the light behind;
and weep for the fool, for he has left intelligence behind.
Weep less bitterly for the dead, for he is at rest;
but the life of the fool is worse than death.
Mourning for the dead lasts seven days,
but for the foolish or the ungodly it lasts
all the days of their lives.

Adams points out that this qualitative view of "life" and "death" in Ben Sira that affirms the traditional Jewish view of the afterlife is more important for the book of Proverbs than for Ben Sira, where it only receives passing notice.

Though Ben Sira does not extend the doctrine of retribution to an afterlife of reward and punishment, what is known as an eschatological theodicy (see Green 1987, 433-35), he does envision an eschatological theodicy on the national level. In an intriguing article, David Skelton argues that one of Ben Sira's main motives for writing his work was to encourage his readers to not give up on God's providential care of the Jews during their subjugation by the Greeks (2009, 1-2). Skelton argues that Ben Sira foresees God eventually restoring Israel and punishing the Greeks for their oppression of the Jews. Ben Sira exhorts his readers to remain true to traditional Judaism, Torah, the Temple, and the priesthood. Skelton argues that Ben Sira sees Simeon, the high priest, as the new messianic figure, whom he depicts in regal terms. Though Ben Sira never directly mentions the Greeks, he does emphasize God's sovereignty and his punishment of his people's oppressors. In 50:15, Ben Sira emphasizes God's sovereignty by describing him as "the Most High, the king of all." In 17:17, Sirach implies that the Greek's rule over the Jews is illegitimate (see Skelton 2009, 3-4): "He appointed a ruler for every nation, but Israel is the Lord's own portion." In chapter 36, Ben Sira even prays for justice and retribution for his people (vv. 1-22), which Adams considers a later interpretation because he cannot envision Ben Sira adopting an eschatological perspective (2008, 164-69). Compare Sir. 36:1-2, 10a, 12:

> Have mercy upon us, O God of all,
> and put all the nations in fear of you.
>
> ....
>
> Hasten the day, and remember the appointed time[.]
>
> ....
>
> Crush the heads of hostile rulers
> who say, "There is no one but ourselves"

Thus, Ben Sira becomes rather prophetic in adopting an eschatological perspective similar to several of the prophetic books like Ezekiel 38-39, Zechariah 1-8, and Joel 2:1-11; 3-4. We know that Ben Sira is not technically apocalyptic because he does not envision a resurrection from the dead, and there is evidence that Ben Sira is polemical against 1 Enoch, which is apocalyptic (see Adams 2008, 157, 191-98).

Wisdom of Solomon or Sapientia

Sapientia (Latin for "wisdom") or Wisdom of Solomon is certainly a representative of the wisdom tradition, though one that has drunk deeply from the well of Hellenism. Its main significance is its eschatological solution to the newly problematic nature of the Jewish doctrine of retribution, which involves the blending of the both Greek and Semitic notions.

Text, Authorship, Date, Place of Composition, and Audience

The book was originally written in Greek by a Jew, who remains anonymous. The book is similar to Ecclesiastes 1-2 in that it assumes the persona of Solomon. In the Septuagint it is known as the "Wisdom of Solomon." The linking of the book to Solomon alerts the reader to the fact that the book views itself as part of the wisdom tradition, and it also lends legitimacy to the book because Solomon was probably considered by the Jews to be the wisest man who ever lived. The consensus for the date of the book is somewhere between the first century B.C.E. and first century C.E.. This is because the book was composed in Greek and the thinking in the book reflects such Hellenistic Jewish authors like Philo and Josephus, who lived during this period. The place of composition is usually viewed as Alexandria, the grand sea port city named after Alexander the Great (356-323 B.C.E.), and completed shortly after his death. A sizable Jewish population lived there, which may go back to Jews who fled Jerusalem during Jeremiah's days to live in Egypt. These Jews are referred to in the "Letter of Aristeas," which recounts the legend of how the Septuagint was supernaturally translated into Greek from the original Hebrew by 72 scribes (representing the 6 elders from the 12 tribes), in 72 days! The Jews in Egypt could no longer understand the Hebrew text, so a translation was needed.

The intended audience was probably these Jewish Alexandrians, no doubt read to them in synagogues or read in private by those who were literate. These Jews would have been largely Hellenized. The tension in the book between the Egyptians (Exodus section) and the righteous mirrors that between the Alexandrian Jews and Gentiles (see Kolarcik 1997, 439). A poll tax introduced in 24 B.C.E. discriminated against the Jews because they were not Greek citizens, who were exempt. The Jews tried to attain Greek citizenry, but the Greeks opposed it. In 38 C.E. the Jews were attacked and synagogues were destroyed. The Greeks were reprimanded by the Romans, but the Jews were told to be satisfied with their situation, which eventually led to the Jewish revolt in 115-17 C.E.

Overall Genre and Structure of the Book

Scholars disagree on how to designate the overall genre of the book (see Clifford 2013, 9-11). Several possibilities have been suggested: an encomium, where wisdom is praised; an exhortatory discourse, popular among the philosophical schools; a Hellenistic diatribe, a type of moral discourse in the form of a speech intended to convince an audience of a particular course of action (Grabbe 2010, 1427). Michael Kolarcik sees the book structured by two main forces: concentric structure (chiasm) and literary diptych, where two images are set side by side for the purpose of contrast (1997, 444).

However, the tripartite structure of the book is largely now agreed upon. Clifford suggests the book has three parts: Part 1: Wisdom 1:1-6:21, the two worlds in which the hidden one is the authentic world that is governed by justice; Part 2: Wisdom 6:22-10:21, the gift of wisdom that enables a person to comprehend the world and live happily in it; Part 3: Wisdom 11:1–19:22, the Exodus as the grand illustration of how the world operates and how God provides for Israel. Lester Grabbe proposes a similar structure. The following is a table illustrating these two structures:

Figure 25: Structure of Sapientia		
Structure from Clifford		
1:1–6:21 The Two Worlds	6:22–10:21 Wisdom and Finding It	11:1–19:22 The Exodus
Structure from Grabbe		
Chs. 1–6 Book of Eschatology	Chs. 7–10 Book of Wisdom	Chs. 11–19 Book of History

Function of the Book

The book serves as an apology for the Hellenized Jews in Alexandria to help them see that God is still sovereign over the world, though the pagan nations seem to be in control. Special emphasis is given to the notion of the Kingdom of God, which is the expression of God's sovereignty over the world. The book looks forward to the restoration of the Jews as a nation (see Clifford 2013, 11–14).

Important Themes

Immortality of the Soul and Israel's Restoration

As we have indicated, Wisdom is unique in being the first wisdom text to finally embrace the notion of an immortal soul and, and, thus, life after death, and in effect solve the great problem with the doctrine of retribution, which was always confined to life on earth for the

Jews: "For though in the sight of others they were punished, their hope is full of immortality" (Wis. 3:4). This immortality is reserved only for faithful Jews, while the wicked are destroyed. Here the wicked refer to their own demise:

So we also, as soon as we were born, ceased to be,
and we had no sign of virtue to show,
but were consumed in our wickedness.
Because the hope of the ungodly is like thistledown carried by the wind,

. . . .

But the righteous will live forever,
and their reward is with the Lord (Wis. 5:13-15).

But Clifford points out,

Though the book borrows the Platonic language of the immortality of the soul, the context is completely different. For one thing, the author is primarily concerned with the Lord's governing rather than with an individual soul's reward. For another, the governing has a historical context—the restoration of Israel who, the author believes, is still in exile (2013, 12).

And though the author incorporates a very eschatological prophetic view of this restoration, which in Daniel involves the resurrection of a physical body (Dan. 12:2), there is no evidence that the author interprets immortality in terms of a resurrection, though this would not be incompatible with the author's purposes (see Kolarcik 1997, 447).

Torah and Wisdom

While the book of Wisdom never identifies Torah with wisdom, Woman Wisdom seems to direct the narrative about the Exodus story. She opens the mouths of mutes (Wis. 10:21) after the Israelites' deliverance from pharaoh's army, which may allude to the Song of Moses (Exod. 15; Kolarcik 1997, 526). After this, only God acts. This shows the "guiding preeminence of Wisdom" (Sanders 2001, 128). The book also refers directly to the Torah in Wis. 18:4, which was given to the Israelites: "Through whom the imperishable light of the law was to be given to the world." But the book itself never cites any of the Torah legislation, just as is true for Ben Sira. Because of this, like with Ben Sira, Sanders believes the author of Wisdom subordinates wisdom to Torah:

> He blends the rescue narrative of the Torah together with the traditional notion of Wisdom's supreme ability to guide and direct human life; he subscribes to the covenant theology; and he brings in the legal corpus of the Torah only to the degree that he makes the laws Wisdom's laws, from which tactic we may likely conclude that he agrees with ben Sira's position that what the Mosaic Torah teaches is identical with traditional sapiential torah. While the details differ, in principle the author of Wisdom, like ben Sira, incorporates aspects of the Torah into the wisdom tradition while at the same time maintaining the preeminence of Wisdom (2001, 129).

However, as was said concerning Ben Sira, there is no evidence of this. Wisdom and Torah in the book of Wisdom seem quite compatible with each other and on the same level. Though Wisdom in the book of Wisdom is of a higher status than anywhere else in the wisdom tradition and shares in the nature of God, she is still subservient to him, just as the Torah is. Both Torah and Wisdom are his instruments, and, thus, on the same level. So, in the end, the views of Ben Sira and the book of Wisdom concerning the relationship between Torah and wisdom are essentially the same.

13

Wisdom Psalms and the Dead Sea Scroll Wisdom Literature

The Outer Limits of the Wisdom Tradition

We are not entering disputed territory when considering certain psalms that have been classified as "wisdom psalms." James Crenshaw, for example, is quite skeptical about the category:

> My own research in the Psalter leads me to question the very category of wisdom psalms. True, a few psalms treat the same topics that invigorate the author of the book of Job (Psalms 37, 49, 73) and reflect on life's brevity like Ecclesiastes (39), but these subjects probably exercised the minds of all thoughtful people. I do not see any profit in attributing such psalms to the sages when we know so little about the authors and their social contexts. Perhaps we should limit ourselves to what can definitely be affirmed: some psalms resemble wisdom literature in stressing the importance of learning, struggling to ascertain life's meaning, and employing proverbial lore. Their authorship and provenance matter less than the accuracy and profundity of what they say (2001, 94).

Crenshaw is correct that one does not have to identify the authors as sages in order to appreciate these psalms' profundity and realism. However, he is wrong in at least two respects. First, genre is an important component in the production of meaning, and, so, to dismiss its significance so lightly is unwarranted. And second, Crenshaw here reveals his generic realism, which is the old way to approach genre analysis that uses rigid and static criteria for identifying genres. If comparing these particular psalms with the rest of the wisdom literature is illuminating and helpful in better understanding their "world" and function, then what is wrong with doing this? Categorizing them as a type of "wisdom literature," even if we do not know everything about their original *Sitz im Leben*, is helpful. One reasonable hypothesis is that these psalms, as well as the other types, were used by scribal teachers to train their students. This is evidenced throughout the ancient Near East by the many hymns and prayers of various types that were apparently used in scribal training.

Also pushing the limits of a wisdom literature corpus is the category of Dead Sea Scroll "wisdom literature." It is relatively new, with the translation of and commentary on this material only recently undertaken. The new and well-received translation and commentary of the 4QInstruction material (Cave 4; Q = "Qumran"), the largest segment of this mode of literature, was only published in 2013. Dead Sea Scroll wisdom literature contains features of wisdom in terms of form and content, though the vocabulary is different. It represents a blending of sapiential and apocalyptic worlds, which makes it quite unique and in many ways closer to the New Testament literature than the Hebrew Bible.

Wisdom Psalms

The first to identify the category of "wisdom psalms" appears to have been Hermann Gunkel, the father of form criticism (see Gunkel 1967, 38-39). Form criticism developed as a new direction in German biblical scholarship that was distinct from its earlier focus on the presence of literary sources or documents that had been used in the composition of a book or corpus like the Pentateuch. Form critics, instead of focusing on literary sources, focus on the individual stories and units and their earlier theoretical oral usage in particular social contexts. It was Gunkel who applied this type of criticism to the book of Psalms. In many ways the Psalter was ripe for this kind of analysis because the "forms" of the various kinds of songs are more easily discernible than in other types of literature. Gunkel did not rest at identifying a form or genre but also theorized how that particular genre of song was used in Israelite life, among individuals as well as the public.

Gunkel was one of the first to connect the Psalter with the Israelite cult and worship. For example, he identified the genre of lament as the most common type in the psalter, and he demonstrated how these may have been used at the Temple or a shrine or a public assembly. As for wisdom psalms, Gunkel identified them as not prayers, like a lament, but meditations or "pious reflections" and wisdom poetry (1967, 38). He included in their number Psalms 1, 128, 37, 73, and 32. Psalms 73 and 32, he noted, resonate with the struggles of Job about the doctrine of retribution. Gunkel does not really address their specific *Sitz im Leben*, except the implication that they were meditated on, which suggests a literary usage. The following is a chart that provides a sample list of wisdom psalms identified by more recent scholars to show that there is general agreement about a core of "wisdom psalms," but still disagreement about how wide to cast the net:

Figure 26: Wisdom Psalms			
Crenshaw (1981) (hesitantly) 37, 39, 49, 73	Murphy (1990) 1, 32, 34, 37, 49, 112, 128	Whybray (1996) 1, 8, 14, 25, 34, 39, 49, 53, 73, 90, 112, 119, 127, 131, 139	Ceresko (1999) 1, 32, 34, 37, 49, 112, 128 (19, 73, 111, 119, 127, 133—more broadly)
Kuntz (2003) 1, 32, 34, 37, 49, 73, 112, 127, 128, 133	Dell (2004) 1, 34, 37, 39, 49, 73 (14, 19, 25, 32, 33, 36, 38, 51, 53, 62, 78, 90, 92, 94, 104, 105, 106, 111, 112, 119, 127, 128—more broadly)	Perdue (2008) 1, 19B, 32, 34, 37, 49, 73, 111, 112, 119, 127	Weeks (2010) 1, 10, 14, 19B, 25, 32, 34, 37, 49, 52, 73, 90, 94, 112, 125, 128

I regard Perdue's generic categorization as the most helpful, and we will select his list and sub-categorization. He identifies five types of wisdom psalms:

1. Torah psalms (Pss. 1, 19B, 119), which praise the Torah as the means of living a righteous life;

2. Instruction psalms (Pss. 32, 34, 37), which utilize admonitions to instruct in ethics;

3. Proverb (saying) psalms (Pss. 112, 127), which include proverb lists in their structure;

4. Reflective (Joban) psalms (Pss. 49, 73), which deal with the issue of theodicy;

5. A psalm of creation (Ps. 111), which is a creation hymn that emphasizes "fear of Yahweh" as the "beginning of wisdom" (Perdue 2008, 165).

We will briefly examine below two representative examples of these wisdom psalms to show how they resonate with the rest of the wisdom tradition. But before we do this, we must address the socio-historical context of the final form of the Psalter.

Socio-Historical Context of the Psalter in Its Final Form

Perdue's speculation about this issue represents essentially the traditional approach. He proposes that the book of Psalms was not finalized until the Hellenistic period (third century B.C.E. or later). He sees sages working under the direction of the Zadokite priesthood, as the authors of the wisdom psalms, which he believes were added near the end of the book's completion (see Perdue 2008, 158-60, 180-91). He views these sages as redactors who essentially put the book in its final form. He imagines these sages in the vein of Ezra, who was both a priest and scribe. These Temple scribes had begun to equate the Torah with wisdom, like Ben Sira did later, and were employed by the priests to compose the wisdom psalms, which reflect the amalgamation of both the old wisdom tradition and the newer emphasis on Torah piety. The evidence Perdue gives for this "sapiential" redaction of the Psalter is the following:

1. The Psalter is divided into 5 parts, reflecting the Pentateuch.

2. The correlation of the Torah and the wisdom tradition is present in the Torah psalms: 1, 19B, and 119.

3. Psalm 1, which contrasts the way of the righteous and wicked, speaks of meditation on the Torah and provides the hermeneutical lens for interpreting the book as a whole.

4. These scribes composed and inserted 11 wisdom psalms,

which can be identified on the basis of lexicography, semantics, and typical themes (Perdue 2008, 161).

As for social setting, Perdue believes some of these psalms were studied and meditated on in wisdom schools (2008, 195). This would have fostered growth in piety among the students. Others may have been sung at a public worship, where sages would have had an opportunity to speak of their own experiences and offer instruction. Their use in prayer is also implied (2008, 196).

Perdue clearly reveals his generic realism, though he is more sophisticated than most. His lists of sapiential vocabulary for the different wisdom psalms is certainly questionable since all of the terms are found in other modes of literature. One can certainly argue that their increased frequency in the wisdom psalms means they represent a literary tradition, but there are no hard and fast boundaries. But Perdue's understanding of the wisdom psalms as the merging of two separate traditions is the most troubling, as well as his view that this represents the merging of two distinct professional groups: sages and priests.

If, as our evidence has shown, all scribes were given a common core education and studied various genres that certainly included wisdom texts as well as hymns and devotional poetry, why could not any advanced scribe, whether simultaneously a priest, and, thus, Levitical, or a courtier or of some other status, compose wisdom psalms? Why could only "wisdom" scribes (Perdue 2008, 179)—whatever that means—compose wisdom psalms? Scholarly scribes could compose in any genre! Did not scribes compose all the other types of psalms in the Psalter? So, what is the problem with the same scribe who composed laments and hymns simultaneously composing "wisdom" psalms? There is no need for a "wisdom" scribe; it is a redundant role. And where is the evidence for separate scribal schools for priests and sages? The notion of a conjoining of separate traditions implied by the wisdom psalms is simply an illusion that Perdue and the majority of other wisdom experts have assumed without evidence.

And why date all of the wisdom psalms so late? We have already noted the tendency of Proverbs 1-9, dated to the Persian period, to connect wisdom with Torah language in the book of Deuteronomy. So, the connection that the wisdom psalms, especially the Torah psalms, make with wisdom and the Torah is not radically new. Also, Katharine Dell (2004, 445-58) has questioned the dominant view that all the wisdom psalms are late and are essentially non-cultic, meant to be meditated on but not sung in worship. She argues that wisdom psalms were used in worship early on, in pre-exilic or even pre-monarchic period, especially the ones that focus on creation like Psalm 54. She speculates that they were sung during the harvest festivals that celebrated the enthronement of Yahweh, which "was a creative drama to ensure fertility and world renewal" (2004, 458). At any rate, whether one accepts Dell's thesis in part or whole, she has demonstrated that there is no necessary reason to date all the wisdom psalms so late, even if most are.

Psalm 1

We have space to only briefly look at a couple of examples of wisdom psalms. Perdue designates Psalm 1 as a Torah psalm (2008, 165), and I concur. Many scholars have noted that Psalm 1, being the very first psalm and, thus, occupying a very significant position, hermeneutically sets the tone for the rest of the Psalter by introducing it (see Miller 1986, 81-86). In a sense, Psalm 1 turns the many prayers directed toward God into pieces of literature ready for study and mediation. In other words, Psalm 1 turns the Psalter into a book to be read rather than sung. But it also hermeneutically shifts the emphasis in the Psalter to ethics: "The psalm and—by inference from its place at the beginning—the whole Psalter are set to make a primarily positive statement about a mode of life that is ordered to the Lord's way" (Miller 1986, 82).

The song contrasts the two ways of life, a motif found throughout the wisdom tradition. It consists of three parts: the way of the righteous (Ps.1:1-3); the way of the wicked (1:4-5); a final contrast and conclusion (1:6). The psalm begins with "blessed" ('ashre), which indicates that the wicked should be envious of a life that celebrates living according to God's Torah/Law (Miller 1986, 82).[1] Perdue describes this as a wisdom term (2008, 166), though it is used in other modes of literature. Again, one should be flexible with designations like this.

The word "way" here contains two connotations: the manner of one's life and one's ultimate destiny (Miller 1986, 83). The poem uses vivid imagery of a tree in the desert transplanted beside a river, which symbolizes the righteous who delight in God's law and whose lives are fruitful and bountiful, while the wicked are described as worthless chaff, unstable, and blown by the wind (Miller 1986, 83). The expression that "the Lord knows the way of the righteous, but the way of the wicked will perish" implies that the righteous are under God's guidance and care (1986, 85).

Miller points out that divine agency is not explicit in the psalm, and so "it is almost in the nature of things that the wicked way goes under . . . wickedness often does itself in and leads to its own destruction in a world that is shaped by God's moral order" (1986, 85). This is essentially the German notion of Tun-Ergehen-Zusammenhaft, an

---

1. K. C. Hanson argues that this term, a makarism, should be translated "how honorable" and its counterpart, the reproach ("woe"), "how shameful"; he interprets beatitudes and woes in terms of an honor culture (1994, 81-111).

almost deistic notion that God has wound the cosmos up like a clock, and the effects of one's moral behavior are delivered automatically, without God's intervention.

Perdue speculates that the psalm was used to teach young students during the Persian period in Judah, and as a Torah psalm it inculcated Torah piety in them (2008, 167). This is certainly possible, but it could have been used in public worship as well, and in other venues, no doubt.

Again, though the psalm does not explicitly use many "sapiential" terms, this does not negate its categorization as a wisdom psalm. It certainly is a member of the sapiential family, and functions in a very wisdom-like way. It is helpful to interpret it from such a wisdom perspective.

Psalm 73

This psalm is more like Job or Ecclesiastes than Psalms 1 in that it expresses skepticism about the doctrine of retribution. Perdue thus classifies it as a reflective or Joban psalm (2008, 165). It is formally an individual psalm of trust or confidence like Psalm 23, a subset of the individual psalms of lament. The difference is that psalms of trust accentuate the confidence element, a typical component of the lament. But Psalm 73 is unlike other psalms of trust in that it focuses more on the intellectual crisis of the psalmist (theodicy problem) than on his own personal social and physical crisis (73:14).

The psalmist at first expresses confidence that God is good and rewards the upright (73:1), but then he begins to doubt this because it appears the wicked flourish and never suffer punishment (vv. 3-12). The psalmist contrasts this with his pious ways that seem to go unrewarded (vv. 13-14). The resolution to his intellectual crisis occurs when he goes to the "sanctuary of God" (v. 17). Then he realizes that the wicked will eventually be punished (delayed retribution) (v. 19). The psalmist confesses that he at first could not comprehend the problem of theodicy intellectually (v. 16) and, similar to Agur (Prov. 30:1-3), describes himself in this way: "And I was brutish and did not understand; I was a beast toward you" (v. 22). But now he trusts in God and finds satisfaction in a personal relationship with God.

This is clearly deferred theodicy, the notion that God is just but one must wait for his justice to eventually materialize (Green 1987, 434). This makes this solution to the problem of evil similar to Job, but not Ecclesiastes, where the solution is actually a dissolution of the problem by essentially denying God's justice.

Comparative Literature

Perdue astutely points out that wisdom psalms exist outside the Psalter (2008, 156-57). These include Prov. 3:19-20, the aretologies or hymns of self-praise of Woman Wisdom in Proverbs 8, and the many hymns of praise in Ben Sira (the wisdom poems that are interspersed throughout the first half of the book). He categorizes the Egyptian "Satire of the Trades" as a wisdom psalm, as well as seeing wisdom psalms in other Egyptian works, and this seems reasonable. In Mesopotamia literature, Perdue categorizes several hymns to Mesopotamian gods as wisdom psalms, like hymns to Shamash, the god of justice, to Nisaba, the goddess of wisdom, and to Ninurta, the god of fertility and agriculture, all of which are reasonable suggestions.

Dead Sea Scroll Wisdom Literature

One will notice that the more recent introductions to the wisdom literature usually include a section on Dead Sea Scroll wisdom literature (Perdue 2008; Weeks 2010; Crenshaw 2010), as opposed to the earlier ones (Crenshaw 1981; Clifford 1998; Murphy 1990; Ceresko 1999). This is because of the time it has taken for scholars to translate these relatively recently discovered manuscripts (1946-47) and the realization that a large segment of this material is strikingly similar to the wisdom literature of the Hebrew Bible and Apocrypha. Work on the wisdom literature of the Dead Sea Scrolls is all relatively new, and scholarship is still in flux on how to date this material and its relationship to the Essenes, a group that split off from mainstream Judaism and lived in the desert region around the Jordan and Dead Sea. They moved into the desert to escape what they considered the corruption of the priesthood that had begun during the Seleucid period (second century B.C.E.), when the high priesthood began to be sold for profit and was not always occupied by a legitimate Zadokite priest. Most scholars assume some kind of connection between this sectarian group and the Dead Sea Scrolls, but there is no complete agreement on what that was.

We are fortunate that two new translations of this wisdom literature and commentary have been recently published. In 2011, John Kampen published the translation of the broader corpus of Dead Sea Scroll wisdom literature and commentary, which includes more than just 4Q Instruction, the longest and most significant body of this literature. Much of the material in Kampen's commentary is so fragmentary that it is often difficult to read. However, in 2013, Matthew Goff published a translation and commentary on 4Q Instruction, and whose translation is more complete and much less fragmentary because of his more generous use of parallel texts.

4QInstruction was only fully published in 1999 (see Dimant 2012). This text is distinctive in appearing to represent a less sectarian group than the later community, perhaps what can be described as a pre-Qumranian perspective. It is also distinctive in that the social background of the addressees appears to be much poorer (mainly farmers) than for other segments of the Dead Sea Scroll wisdom literature and the other apocryphal, apocalyptic-wisdom literature like 1 Enoch, Baruch, etc.

We will look at a couple of examples of Dead Sea Scroll wisdom literature outside of 4QInstruction before looking more closely at that text. The following is from the Evil Seductress, which is strikingly like the adulterous woman in Proverbs 5-7:

S[h]e lies in wait in secret places, all [. . . .] In the open squares of the city she adorns herself and in the gates of the towns she stations herself. Nothing can make her de[sist] from incessant f[ornicat]ion. Her eyes gaze intently here and there and she raises her eyelids in reckless abandon to seek [out a] righteous ma[n] and overtake him, a [po]werful man and make him fall, to turn the upright aside from the way, the chosen righteous from keeping the commandment; those of firm re[so]lve to bring down with reckless abandon, to make those who walk upright pervert the pre[cept], to make the meek rebel against God, to turn aside their footsteps from the ways of righteousness, to place inso[le]nce in their [hear]ts, so that they do not walk in the tracks of uprightness, to make men attain the ways of the pit and to seduce with flattery [all] mankind (4Q184, frag. 1, 11-17; Kampen 2011, 238).

Kampen argues that she is not a literal prostitute but a symbol for all that the group rejects (235, 236); some see it as an allegory (see Davies et al 2011, 143). This would make it similar to Woman Folly in Proverbs 9.

The following is a section from a document known as the Beatitudes, similar to the beatitudes in Matthew 5. The "her" refers to Woman Wisdom. Note that here, like in Ben Sira, the Torah and wisdom are connected:

> [Blessed is he who seeks her] with a pure heart, he does not slander his tongue. Blessed are those who hold fast to her statutes, they do not hold fast to the ways of injustice. Bles[sed] are those who rejoice in her, they do not spout forth the ways of folly. Blessed are those who seek her with pure hands, they do not search for her with a deceitful heart. Blessed is the man who has obtained wisdom. He walks in the law of the Most High and prepares his heart for her ways (4Q525, frags. 2 3, 1-4; Kampen 2011, 317).

4QInstruction

4QInstruction is considered a sapiential text primarily because of its pedagogical function (Goff 2013, 12). Instead of the typical sapiential address "my son," the addressee of 4QInstruction is *mebin* or the "understanding one." While the addressee is usually in the singular, a group is probably implied because the plural is sometimes used. Though a group is addressed, the focus of the literature is on the life of the individual within the community, such as topics like marriage and faithfulness and paying one's debts and avoiding going surety for others (e.g., 4Q416 2 ii, 4-6).

While much of the composition resembles the rest of the wisdom tradition in content and function, one difference is the frequent allusion to revelation (see Goff 2013, 14). The focus on the work is in fact on the expression *raz nihyeh*, which can be translated "the mystery to be" or "mystery of existence" as Kampen does (2011, 27). Interestingly, in 4Q417 1 i, 8-9, it is claimed that God created the world with *raz nihyeh* instead of wisdom or *chokmah* as in Prov. 3:19 (see Goff 2013, 15)! In fact, one could say that "the mystery to be" replaces "wisdom" in 4QInstruction; or better, it is the "new wisdom." This mystery appears to be God's predetermined plan for the world, from beginning to end. Understanding and studying this mystery has practical implications for daily life and ultimately will ensure the salvation of the *mebin*. The addressee sees himself as the member of the elect, along with the angels (Goff 2013, 17). These elect see themselves as in mourning and strive to attain humility (Goff 2013, 18). Their revelatory knowledge is viewed as actually originating in the garden of Eden when Adam becomes wiser after eating the fruit (Goff 2013, 19). The world depicted is quite apocalyptic (see Goff 2013, 19-23). Interestingly, 4QInstruction never refers to the Torah or equates wisdom with Torah as does Ben Sira and other Dead Sea Scroll wisdom literature.

Goff has identified the social location of the addresses as relatively poor (farmers, artisans, and debt slaves), with some being able to go surety for their neighbors, but most being in debt (2013, 23-27, 207). As opposed to Ben Sira, who encourages his students to lend money to those in need (Sir. 29:1-13), 4QInstruction instructs its audience to be ethical borrowers (4Q417 2 i, 22-23), indicating the stark difference in the audiences (see Goff 2013, 26). "Poor" often takes on the metaphorical sense of "humble" in the composition. The authors would, of course, have been scribes, but no longer retainers for the government, as in previous times.

Goff concludes that the community addressed by 4QInstruction is not the Dead Sea Scroll sect. It neither uses common terminology like the office *maskil* ("sage"), nor are there any references to the Teacher of Righteousness or Wicked Priest. But, again, this is the argument from silence. The composition enabled the poor to live lives of dignity and self-worth amid humbling circumstances (Goff 2013, 27). Like Ben Sira, 4QInstruction was probably written in the second century B.C.E. (Goff 2013, 28).

Sample Topics in 4QInstruction

Women

4Q415 2 ii is the text we mentioned earlier that is addressed to a woman, specifically a wife of the *mebin*, which indicates the addressees were not celibate (see Goff 2013, 31-41). The wife is told to honor both her father-in-law and husband:

Like a father honor your fa[*ther-in*]aw. . . .

Do not depart from his heart and . . .

all the day long and in his bosom (is) [*your*] cove[*nant* . . .]

lest you neglect a ho[*ly*] *covenant* . . .

And one who is hostile to you . . . and . . .

a w[*i*]fe fore[*ver* . . . *You will no longer live*]

in the house of [*your*] ori[*gins*]. Rather in your covenant you [*will*

be faithful . . . *You will become*]

an object of praise in the mouth of all men . . .

. . . from the house of (your) birth . . . (Goff 2013, 31).

Basically this instruction aligns with the encomium of the capable woman in Proverbs 31. The wife's role is to be faithful and submissive to her husband and bring him honor.

In 4Q416 2 ii, 21, one finds: "And also, do not dishonor the vessel of your [*bo*]som." 4QInstruction stresses not only the husband's control over the woman but also his responsibility to treat her with dignity (Goff 2013, 89). Note also that the wife's body is possessed by the husband, similar to 1 Thess. 4:4 (see Goff 2013, 89-90). Note the following verses: "The woman you have taken in your poverty, size [*her*] birth times . . . from the mystery that is to be. When you marry, walk together with the help of your flesh. [*As it is written, 'there a man leaves'*]" (4Q416 2 iii, 20-21; Goff 2013, 93). The reference to her "birth times" indicates her elect status. Again, "your flesh" denotes that the wife is the husband's possession; her body is an extension of his (Goff 2013, 116). The wife as a "help" denotes that she is subservient to him (Goff 2013, 117). Here are two more lines:

> He has given you dominion over her and she will ob[*ey your voice . . . To her father*] (4Q416 2 iv, 2).

> He has given you dominion so that it (her spirit) may walk in accordance with your will (4Q416 2 iv, 7; Goff 2013, 120).

Verse 2 appears to allude to Gen. 3:16 that the husband will rule over his wife. "Her spirit" may denote her elect status (Goff 2013, 131).

Pledges and Debt Slavery

In 4Q416 2 ii, one finds advice relating to pledges: "Do not disho[*nor the pledge of your neighbor lest you st*]umble because of it and] with [his] shame you will cover your face. And with his folly (you will be covered)" (Goff 2013, 59). Here instead of a warning not to go surety for a neighbor, the *mebin* is told not to take lightly the pledge that he has already made for his neighbor (see Goff 2013, 69). The consequences of doing this become clear in lines 7-17:

> Do not oppose] him and do not abandon your obligations. Observe your mysteries

> [*for the sake of*] your [*life*]. If he assigns his work to you [let there be no rest in *your soul and let there be n*]o slumber for your eyes until you carry out

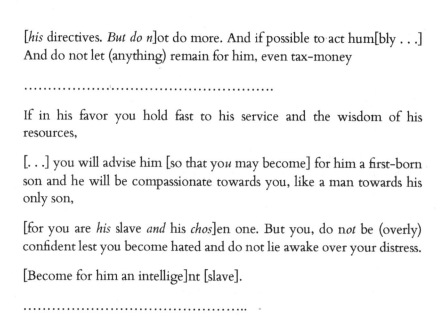

[*his* directives. *But do n*]ot do more. And if possible to act hum[bly . . .]
And do not let (anything) remain for him, even tax-money

. . . .

If in his favor you hold fast to his service and the wisdom of his
resources,

[. . .] you will advise him [so that yo*u* may become] for him a first-born
son and he will be compassionate towards you, like a man towards his
only son,

[for you are *his* slave *and* his *chos*]en one. But you, do n*o*t be (overly)
confident lest you become hated and do not lie awake over your distress.

[Become for him an intellige]nt [slave].

. . . .

[*Do not se*]ll yourself for wealth. It is good you are a slave in spirit and
without wages you serve your oppressors (Goff 2013, 60).

As a result of going surety for his neighbor, the *mebin* has become
a debt-slave here and must pay it off. The *mebin* is being taught
to develop a good relationship with his creditor so that he will not
be too harsh with him. Note that the *mebin* is told to observe his
mysteries, which refers to the teachings of the group that he has
received (Goff 2013, 78). It is interesting that the book of Proverbs
warns against going surety (e.g., Prov. 6:1–5), as we have seen, which
has an audience of elite scribes in view, while Ben Sira counsels going
surety, though with caution (e.g., Sir. 29:14–20), as we have seen, and
has a similar audience to Proverbs.

Eternal Life and the Doctrine of Retribution

Note the following lines, which begin by referring to the fate of the
wicked:

You [*for She*]ol were fashioned, and to the eternal pit is your return. For it will awake and re[*veal*] your sin, [*and the inhabitants of*]

its dark regions will shout out regarding your case. And all who exist forever, the seekers of truth, will awaken for yo[*ur*] judgment. [*And then*]

all the foolish of heart will be destroyed, the sons of iniquity will be found no more, [*and a*]ll those who cling to wickedness will wither aw[*ay. And then*] (4Q418 69 ii, 6-8) (Goff 2013, 224).

4QInstruction assumes two different fates for the dead: Sheol for the wicked but a blessed afterlife for the elect. Goff views Sheol here as neutral (2013, 232), while Adams views it as a place of eternal punishment (2008, 227). There is no clear indication of a resurrection of the body in 4QInstruction, however (Goff 2013, 233). Thus, Wisdom of Solomon and 4QInstruction represent similar attempts to push the doctrine of retribution into the next life (see Adams 2008, 270-71). It is unclear if 4QInstruction maintains the platonic concept of an immortal soul like the Wisdom of Solomon, but some kind of blessed afterlife is clearly depicted. This is known as eschatological theodicy (see Green 1987, 433-34).

Works Consulted

Adams, Samuel. 2008. *Wisdom in Transition: Act and Consequence in Second Temple Instructions.* JSOT Supplement Series 125. Leiden: Brill.

Aḥituv, Shmuel. 2008. *Echoes from the Past: Hebrew and Cognate Inscriptions from the Biblical Period.* Jerusalem: Carta.

Aharoni, Yahonan, Michael Avi-Yonah, Anson F. Rainey, and Ze'ev Safrai. 1993. *The Macmillan Bible Atlas.* Jerusalem: Carta.

Alster, Bendt. 2005. *Wisdom of Ancient Sumer.* Bethesda, MD: CDL.

Alter, Robert. 1985. *The Art of Biblical Poetry.* New York: Basic Books.

Ansberry, Christopher B. 2010. "What Does Jerusalem Have to Do with Athens?: The Moral Vision of the Book of Proverbs and Aristotle's Nicomachean Ethic." *Hebrew Studies* 51:157-73.

————. 2011. *Be Wise, My Son, and Make My Heart Glad: An Exploration of the Courtly Nature of the Book of Proverbs.* Beifhefte zur Zeitschrift für die alttestamentliche Wissenschaft 422. Berlin: de Gruyter.

Aristotle. 1962. *Nicomachean Ethics.* Translated by Martin Oswald. Library of Liberal Arts. Indianapolis: Bobs-Merrill.

Asano-Tamanoi, Mariko. 1987. "Shame, Family, and State in Catalonia and Japan." Pages 104-20 in *Honor and Shame and the Unity of the Mediterranean* (see Gilmore).

Barnes, Jonathan. 1999. "L'Ecclésiaste et le scepticisme grec." *Revue de Théologie et de philosophie* 131:103-14.

Bartholomew, Craig G. 2009. *Ecclesiastes.* Baker Commentary on the Old Testament. Grand Rapids, MI: Eerdmans.

Bautch, Richard J., and Jean-François Racine, eds. 2013. *Beauty and the Bible: Toward a Hermeneutics of Biblical Aesthetics.* Semeia Studies 73. Atlanta: SBL.

Beaulieu, Paul-Alain. 2007. "The Social and Intellectual Setting of Babylonian Wisdom Literature." Pages 3-19 in *Wisdom Literature in Mesopotamia and Israel.* Symposium Series 36. Edited by Richard Clifford. Atlanta: SBL.

Bechtel, Lynn M. 1997. "Shame as a Sanction of Social Control in Biblical Israel: Judicial, Political, and Social Shaming." Pages 232-258 in *Social-Scientific Old Testament Criticism* (see Chalcraft). Repr. from *JSOT* 49 (1991):47-76.

Becking, Bob. 1996. "'Touch for Health . . .' Magic in II Reg 4,31-37 with a Remark on the History of Yahwism," *Zeitschrift für alttestamentliche Wissenschaft* 108:34-53.

Bellafontaine, Elizabeth. 1997. "Customary Law and Chieftainship: Judicial Aspects of 2 Samuel 14.4-21." Pages 206-31 in *Social-Scientific Old Testament Criticism* (see Chalcraft). Repr. from *JSOT* 38 (1987):47-72.

Bergant, Dianne. 1994. "'My Beloved is Mine and I Am His' (Song 2:16): The Song of Songs and Honor and Shame." *Semeia* 68:23-40.

Blenkinsopp, Joseph. 1995. *Sage, Priest, Prophet: Religious and Intellectual Leadership in Ancient Israel.* Library of Ancient Israel. Louisville, KY: Westminster John Knox.

_____. 1997. "The Family in the First Temple Israel." Pages 48-103 in *Families in Ancient Israel.* The Family, Religion, and Culture. Edited by Leo Perdue et al. Louisville, KY: Westminster John Knox.

Bodner, Keith. 2012. *Jeroboam's Royal Drama.* Biblical Refigurations. Oxford: Oxford University Press.

Bottéro, Jean. 1995. "Akkadian Literature: An Overview." Pages 2293-2303 in vol. 4 of *Civilizations of the Ancient Near East* (see Sasson, 1995).

————. 2001. *Everyday Life in Ancient Mesopotamia.* Translated by Antonia Nevill. Baltimore, MD: The Johns Hopkins University Press.

Bould, Mark. 2005. *Film Noir: From Berlin to Sin City.* Short Cuts. London: Wallflower.

Bourdieu, Pierre. 1974. "The Sentiment of Honour in Kabyle Society." Pages 191-241 in *Honour and Shame: The Values of Mediterranean Society* (see Campbell 1974a).

Brandes, Stanley. 1987. "Reflections on Honor and Shame in the Mediterranean." Pages 121-34 in *Honor and Shame and the Unity of the Mediterranean* (see Gilmore).

Brown, F., S. R. Driver and C. A. Briggs. 1907. *A Hebrew and English Lexicon of the Old Testament.* Oxford: Clarendon.

Brown, William P. 1996. *Character in Crisis: A Fresh Approach to the Wisdom Literature of the Old.* Grand Rapids, MI: Eerdmans.

Burton, Neal. 2012. "Our Hierarchy of Needs: Why True Freedom is a Luxury of the Mind." *Psychology Today.* No pages. Cited 11 March, 2015. Online: https://www.psychologytoday.com/blog/hide-and-seek/201205/our-hierarchy-needs.

Buss, Martin J. 2007. "Dialogue in and among Genres." Pages 9-18 in *Bakhtin and Genre Theory in Biblical Studies.* Edited by Roland Boer. Semeia Studies 63. Atlanta: SBL.

Byrne, Ryan. 2007. "The Refuge of Scribalism in Iron I Palestine." *Bulletin of the American Schools of Oriental Research* 345:1-31.

Camp, Claudia. 1997. "Honor and Shame in Ben Sira: Anthropological and Theological Reflections." Pages 171-87 in *The Book of Ben Sira in Modern Research: Proceedings of the First International Ben Sira Conference.* Edited by P. C. Beentjes. Berlin: de Gruyter.

Campbell, J. K. 1974a. "Honour and the Devil." Pages 139-70 in *Honour and Shame* (see Peristiany).

_____. 1974b. *Honour, Family, and Patronage: A Study of Institutions and Moral Values in a Greek Mountain Community.* American ed. Repr. from Oxford: Oxford University Press, 1964.

Carasik, Michael. 1994. "Who Were the 'Men of Hezekiah' (Proverbs XXV 1)?" *Vetus Testamentum* 64:289-300.

Carr, David M. 2004. "Wisdom and Apocalypticism: Different Types of Educational/Enculturational Literature." Paper presented at the Annual Meeting of the SBL. San Antonio, Texas, 21 November.

_____. 2005. *Writing on the Tablet of the Heart.* Oxford: Oxford University Press.

Cave, Stephen. 2012. *Immortality: The Quest to Live Forever and How it Drives Civilization.* New York: Crown.

Ceresko, Anthony R. 1999. *Introduction to Old Testament Wisdom: A Spirituality for Liberation.* Maryknoll, NY: Orbis.

Chalcraft, David, ed. 1997. *Social-Scientific Old Testament Criticism: A Sheffield Reader.* The Biblical Seminar 47. Sheffield: Sheffield Academic Press.

Chance, John K. 1994. "The Anthropology of Honor and Shame: Culture, Values, and Practice." *Semeia* 68:139-49.

Charney, Davida. 2010. "Rhetorical Exigencies in the Individual Psalms." Paper presented at the Southwest Regional Meeting of the SBL. Irving, TX, 14 March.

Christian, Mark A. 2009. "Priestly Power that Empowers: Michel Foucault, Middle-Tier Levites, and the Sociology of 'Popular Religious Groups' in Israel." *Journal of Hebrew Scriptures* 9, Article 1:1-81. Online at http://www.arts.ualberta.ca/JHS/Articles/article_103.pdf (accessed March 18, 2009).

Christianson, Eric S. 1998. *A Time to Tell: Narrative Strategies in Ecclesiastes.* JSOT Supplement Series 280. Sheffield: Sheffield Academic Press.

Clifford, Richard J. 1998. *The Wisdom Literature.* Interpreting Biblical Texts. Nashville, TN: Abingdon.

————. 1999. *Proverbs: A Commentary.* Old Testament Library. Louisville, KY: Westminster John Knox.

————. 2004. "Your Attention Please! Heeding the Proverbs." *JSOT* 29:155-63.

————. 2013. *Wisdom.* New Collegeville Bible Commentary 20. Collegeville, MN: Liturgical Press.

Clines, David J. 1995. "Why Is There a Book of Job, and What Does It Do to You If You Read It?" Pages 122-44 in *Interested Parties: The Ideology of Writers and Readers of the Hebrew Bible.* JSOT Supplement Series 205; Gender, Culture, Theory 1. Sheffield: Sheffield Academic Press. Repr. from pages 1-20 in *The Book of Job.* Bibliotheca Ephemeridum Tehologicarum Lovaniensium 104. Edited by W. A. M. Beuken. Leuven: Leuven University Press/Peeters, 1994.

Cohen, Yoram. 2009. *The Scribes and Scholars of the City of Emar in the Late Bronze Age.* Harvard Semitic Studies 59. Winona Lake, IN: Eisenbrauns.

————. 2013. *Wisdom from the Late Bronze Age.* Writing from the Ancient World 29. Atlanta: SBL.

Cook, Edward M. 2005. "The Forgery Indictments and *BAR*: Learning from Hindsight." *Near Eastern Archaeology* 68:1/2: 73-75.

Coogan, Michael D. and Mark S. Smith. 2012. *Stories from Ancient Canaan.* Second ed. Louisville, KY: Westminster John Knox.

Collins, John J. 1984. *Daniel with an Introduction to Apocalyptic Literature.* The Forms of the Old Testament Literature 20. Grand Rapids, MI: Eerdmans.

Copi, Irving M. 1982. *Introduction to Logic.* Sixth ed. New York: Macmillan.

Cox, Benjamin D. and Susan Ackerman. 2012. "Micah's Teraphim." *Journal of Hebrew Scriptures* 12, Article 1:1-37. Online at http://www.jhsonline.org/Articles/article_173.pdf (accessed August 8, 2014).

Crenshaw, James L. 1969. "Method in Determining Wisdom Influence upon 'Historical' Literature." *JBL* 88:129-42.

———. 1980. "Wisdom and Authority: Sapiential Rhetoric and Its Warrants." Pages 10-29 in *Congress Volume: Vienna 1980*. Vetus Testamentum Supplements 32. Leiden: Brill.

———. 1981. *Old Testament Wisdom: An Introduction*. Atlanta: John Knox.

———. 1992. "Job." Pages 858-68 in vol. 3 of *Anchor Bible Dictionary*. Edited by David Noel Freedman. 6 vols. New York: Doubleday.

———. 1997. "The Book of Sirach: Introduction, Commentary, and Reflections." Pages 601-867 in *Introduction to Wisdom Literature; Proverbs; Ecclesiastes; Song of Songs; Book of Wisdom; Sirach* Vol. 5 of *New Interpreter's Bible*. Edited by Leander E. Keck. Nashville, TN: Abingdon.

———. 2001. *The Psalms: An Introduction*. Grand Rapids, MI: Eerdmans.

———. 2010. *Old Testament Wisdom: An Introduction*. Third ed. Atlanta: Westminster John Knox.

Cross, Frank Moore. 1997. *Canaanite Myth and Hebrew Epic: Essays in the History of the Religion of Israel*. Paperback ed. Cambridge, MA: Harvard University Press.

Crowther, Bruce. 1989. *Film Noir: Reflections in a Dark Mirror*. New York: Continuum.

Culler, Jonathon. 1982. *On Deconstruction: Theory and Criticism after Structuralism*. Ithaca, NY: Cornell University Press.

Davies, Philip R., George J. Brooke, and Phillip R. Callaway. 2011. *The Dead Sea Scrolls*. Paperback ed. London: Thames & Hudson.

Deist, Ferdinand E. 2000. *The Material Culture of the Bible*. The Biblical Seminar 70. Sheffield: Sheffield Academic Press.

Delaney, Carol. 1987. "Seeds of Honor, Fields of Shame." Pages 35-48 in *Honor and Shame and the Unity of the Mediterranean* (see Gilmore).

Dell, Katharine J. 1991. *The Book of Job as Sceptical Literature.* Beihefte zur Zeitschrift für die alttestamentliche Wissenschaft 197. Berlin: de Gruyter.

_____. 2004. "'I Will Solve My Riddle to the Music of the Lyre' (Psalm LXIX 4 [5]); A Cultic Setting for Wisdom Psalms?" *Vetus Testamentum* 54:445-58.

Di Lella, Alexander A. 1992. "Wisdom of Ben-Sira." Pages 931-45 in vol. 6 of *Anchor Bible Dictionary.* Edited by David Noel Freedman. 6 vols. New York: Doubleday.

Dimant, Devorah. 2012. "Review of John Kampen, *Wisdom Literature* (Grand Rapids, MI: Eerdmans, 2011)." *Review of Biblical Literature.* Online at: http://www.bookreviews.org/pdf/7970_8717.pdf (accessed March 17, 2015).

Domeris, W. R. 1995. "Shame and Honour in Proverbs: Wise Women and Foolish Men." *Old Testament Essays* 8:86-128.

Dowd, Garin, Lesley Stevenson, and Jeremy Strong, eds. 2006. *Genre Matters: Essays in Theory and Criticism.* Bristol, UK: Intellect.

Duncan, Mike. 2012. "The Curious Silence of the Dog and Paul of Tarsus: Revisiting the Argument from Silence." *Informal Logic* 32:83-97.

Eagleton, Terry. *Ideology: An Introduction.* London: Verso.

Edelman, Diana. 2006. "The Iconography of Wisdom." Pages 149-53 in *Essays on Ancient Israel in Its Near Eastern Context: A Tribute to Nadav Na'aman.* Edited by Yairah Amit et al. Winona Lake, IN: Eisenbrauns.

Elliott, John H. 1991. "The Evil Eye in the First Testament: The Ecology and Culture of a Pervasive Belief." Pages 147-59 in *The Bible and the Politics of Exegesis: Essays in Honor of Norman K. Gottwald on His Sixty-Fifth Birthday.* Edited by David Jobling, Peggy L. Day, and Gerald T. Sheppard. Cleveland: Pilgrim.

Eshel, Esther, Amos Kloner and Emile Puech. 2007. "Aramaic Scribal Exercises of the Hellenistic Period from Maresha: Bowls A and B." *Bulletin of the American Schools of Oriental Research* 345:39-45.

Esler, Philip F. 2012. *Sex, Wives, and Warriors: Reading Old Testament Narrative with Its Ancient Audience.* Cambridge: James Clarke.

Faulkner, R. O. 1973a. "The Admonitions of an Egyptian Sage." Pages 210–29 in *The Literature of Ancient Egypt: An Anthology of Stories, Instructions, and Poetry.* New Edition. Edited by William Kelly Simpson. New Haven: Yale University Press.

————. 1973b. "The Maxims of Ptahhotpe." Pages 159–79 in *The Literature of Ancient Egypt: An Anthology of Stories, Instructions, and Poetry* (see Simpson).

Faust, Avraham. 2012. *The Archaeology of Israelite Society in Iron Age II.* Translated by Ruth Ludlum. Winona Lake, IN: Eisenbrauns.

Feder, Yitzhaq. 2011. *Blood Expiation in Hittite and Biblical Ritual: Origins, Context, and Meaning.* Writings from the Ancient World Supplement Series 2. Atlanta: SBL.

Fishbane, Michael. 1988. *Biblical Interpretation in Ancient Israel.* Oxford: Clarendon.

Floyd, Michael H. 2002. "The מַשָּׂא (*MAŚŚĀʾ*) as a Type of Prophetic Book." *JBL* 121:401–22.

Fontaine, Carol R. 1995. "The Social Roles of Women in the World of Wisdom." Pages 24–49 in *Feminist Companion to Wisdom Literature.* Edtied by Athalya Brenner. Sheffield: Sheffield Academic Press.

Foster, Benjamin R. 1995. "Humor and Wit in the Ancient Near East." Pages 2459–69 in vol. 4 of *Civilizations of the Ancient Near East* (see Sasson 1995).

Foucault, Michel. 1980. *Power/Knowledge: Selected Interview & Other Writings 1971–1977.* Edited by Colin Gordon. Translated by Colin Gordon et al. New York: Pantheon.

Fowler, Alastair. 1982. *Kinds of Literature: An Introduction to the Theory of Genres and Modes.* Cambridge, MA: Harvard University Press.

Fox, Michael V. 1977. "Frame-Narrative and Composition in the Book of Qohelet." *Hebrew Union College Annual* 48:83-106.

_____. 1986. "The Meaning of *Hebel* for Qohelet." *JBL* 105:409-27.

_____. 1996. "The Social Location of the Book of Proverbs." Pages 227-39 in *Texts, Temples, and Traditions: A Tribute to Menahem Haran.* Edited by Michael V. Fox et al. Winona Lake, IN: Eisenbrauns.

_____. 1999. *A Time to Tear Down and a Time to Build Up. A Rereading of Ecclesiastes.* Grand Rapids, MI: Eerdmans.

_____. 2000. *Proverbs 1-9.* Anchor Bible 18A. New York: Doubleday.

_____. 2004. "The Rhetoric of Disjointed Proverbs." *JSOT* 29:165-77.

_____. 2005. "Job the Pious." *Zeitschrift für die alttestamentliche Wissenschaft* 117:351-66.

_____. 2007a. "The Epistemology of the Book of Proverbs." *JBL* 126:669-84.

_____. 2007b. "Ethics and Wisdom in the Book of Proverbs." *Hebrew Studies* 48:75-88.

_____. 2009. *Proverbs 10-31: A New Translation with Introduction and Commentary.* Anchor Yale Bible 18B. New Haven: Yale University Press.

Frow, John. 2005. *Genre.* New Critical Idiom. London: Routledge.

Gammie, John, and Leo Perdue, eds. 1990. *The Sage in Israel and the Ancient Near East.* Winona Lake, IN: Eisenbrauns.

Gardiner, Alan H. 1947. *Ancient Egyptian Onomastica.* 3 vols. London: Oxford University Press.

Gardner, Gregg. 2007. "Jewish Leadership and Hellenistic Civic Benefaction in the Second Century B.C.E." *JBL* 126:327-43.

Gilmore, David D., ed. 1987. *Honor and Shame and the Unity of the Mediterranean.* Arlington: American Anthropological Association.

Giovannini, Maureen J. "Female Chastity Codes in the Circum-Mediterranean." Pages 61-74 in *Honor and Shame and the Unity of the Mediterranean* (see Gilmore).

Goff, Matthew J. 2013. *4QInstruction*. Wisdom Literature from the Ancient World. Atlanta: SBL.

Goodman, A. E. 1961. "The Words of Ahiqar." Pages 270-75 in *Documents from Old Testament Times*. Edited by D. Winton Thomas. Edinburgh: Thomas Nelson. Repr. from New York: Harper & Row.

Goldwasser, Orly. 2010. "How the Alphabet Was Born from Heiroglyphs." *Biblical Archaeology Review* 36:36-50.

Gordis, Robert. 1965. *The Book of God and Man: A Study of Job*. Chicago: University of Chicago.

_____. 1968. *Koheleth—The Man and His World: A Study of Ecclesiastes*. Third ed. New York: Schocken.

_____. 1971. "The Social Background of Wisdom Literature." Pages 160-97 in *Poets, Prophets, and Sages: Essays in Biblical Interpretation*. Edited by Robert Gordis. Bloomington: Indiana University Press. Repr. from *Hebrew Union College Annual* 18 (1943-44):77-118.

Gottwald, Norman K. 1985. *The Hebrew Bible: A Socio-Literary Introduction*. Philadelphia: Fortress.

_____. 1999. "The Expropriated and the Expropriators in Nehemiah 5." Pages 1-19 in *Concepts of Class in Ancient Israel*. Edited by Mark Sneed. South Florida Studies in the History of Judaism: The Hebrew Scriptures and Their World 201. Atlanta: SBL.

Grabbe, Lester L. 2010. "Wisdom of Solomon." Pages 1427-1455 in *The New Oxford Annotated Bible: New Revised Standard Version with the Apocrypha*. Fourth ed. Edited by Michael Coogan. Oxford: Oxford University Press.

Green, Ronald. 1987. "Theodicy." Pages 430-41 in vol. 14 of *The Encyclopedia of Religion*. Edited by M. Eliade. 16 vols. New York: Macmillan.

Gunkel, Hermann. 1967. *The Psalms*. Translated by Thomas M. Horner. Facet Books: Biblical Series 19. Philadelphia: Fortress.

Haidt, Jonathan. 2013. *The Righteous Mind: Why Good People Are Divided by Politics and Religion.* New York: Vintage Books.

Hamilton, Mark W. 2007. "Elite Lives: Job 29-31 and Traditional Authority." *JSOT* 32:69-89.

Hanson, K. C. 1994. "How Honorable! How Shameful! A Cultural Analysis of Matthew's Makarisms and Reproaches." *Semeia* 68:81-111.

Harris, Rivkah. 1990. "The Female 'Sage' in Mesopotamian Literature (with an Appendix on Egypt)." Pages 3-17 in *The Sage in Ancient Israel and the Ancient Near East* (see Gammie and Perdue).

Haviland, William A. 2002. *Cultural Anthropology.* Tenth ed. Fort Worth: Harcourt.

Heim, Knut Martin. 2013. *Poetic Imagination in Proverbs: Variant Repetitions and the Nature of Poetry.* Bulletin for Biblical Research Supplement 4. Winona Lake, IN: Eisenbrauns.

Hengel, Martin. 2003. *Judaism and Hellenism: Studies in Their Encounter in Palestine during the Early Hellenistic Period.* Translated by John Bowden. 2 vols. Eugene, OR: Wipf & Stock. Repr. from Philadelphia: Fortress, 1974.

Herzfeld, Michael. 1987. "'As in Your Own House': Hospitality, Ethnography, and the Stereotype of Mediterranean Society." Pages 75-89 in *Honor and Shame and the Unity of the Mediterranean* (see Gilmore).

Herzog, Ze'ev. 1992. "Administrative Structures in the Iron Age." Pages 223-30 in *The Architecture of Ancient Israel: From the Prehistoric to the Persian Periods.* Edited by Aharon Kempinski and Ronny Reich. Jerusalem: Israel Exploration Society.

Hick, John. 1978. *Evil and the God of Love.* Rev. ed. San Francisco: Harper & Row.

Hirsch, E. D., Jr. 1967. *Validity in Interpretation.* New Haven: Yale University Press.

Holmstedt, Robert D. 2009. "אני ולבי: The Syntactic Encoding of the Collaborative Nature of Qohelet's Experiment." *Journal of Hebrew*

Scriptures 9, article 19:1-27. Online at http://www.jhsonline.org/Articles/article_121.pdf (accessed August 19, 2014).

Hopkins, David C. 1985. *The Highlands of Canaan: Agricultural Life in the Early Iron Age*. The Social World of Biblical Antiquity 3. Sheffield: Almond.

Hurowitz, Victor Avigdor. 2013. "Unsavory Personalities in the Book of Proverbs in Light of Mesopotamian Writings." *Hebrew Studies* 54:93-106.

Izre'el, Shlomo. 1995. "The Amarna Letters from Canaan." Pages 2411-19 in vol. 4 of *Civilizations of the Ancient Near East* (see Sasson 1995).

Jameson, Fredric. 1981. *The Political Unconscious: Narrative as Socially Symbolic Act*. Ithaca, NY: Cornell University Press.

Jamieson-Drake, David. 1991. *Scribes and Schools in Monarchic Judah: A Socio-Archaeological Approach*. JSOT Supplement Series 109. Sheffield: Almond.

Jones, Scott C. 2006. "Qohelet's Courtly Wisdom: Ecclesiastes 8:1-9." *CBQ* 68:211-28.

————. 2014. "The Values and Limits of Qohelet's Sub-Celestial Economy." *Vetus Testamentum* 64:21-33.

Josephus. 1926-1965. Translated by H. St. J. Thackeray et al. 10 vols. Loeb Classical Library. Cambridge, MA: Harvard University Press.

Kahneman, Daniel. 2011. *Thinking, Fast and Slow*. New York: Farrar, Straus and Giroux.

Kampen, John. 2011. *Wisdom Literature*. Eerdman's Commentaries on the Dead Sea Scrolls. Grand Rapids, MI: Eerdmans.

Kessler, Rainer. 2008. *The Social History of Ancient Israel: An Introduction*. Translated by Linda M. Maloney. Minneapolis: Fortress.

Ki, Wing-Chi. 2006. "Gift Theory and the Book of Job." *Theological Studies* 67:723-49.

Kidner, Derek. 1964. *The Proverbs: An Introduction and Commentary*. Tyndale Old Testament Commentary. Leicester: InterVaristy.

King, Philip J. and Lawrence E. Stager. 2001. *Life in Biblical Israel.* Louisville, KY: Westminster John Knox.

Kitchen, Kenneth A. 1977. "Proverbs and Wisdom Books of the Ancient Near East: The Factual History of a Literary Genre." *Tyndale Bulletin* 28:69-114.

_____. 1998. "Biblical Instructional Wisdom: The Decisive Voice of the Ancient Near East." pages 346-63 in *Boundaries of the Ancient Near Eastern World: A Tribute to Cyrus H. Gordon.* JSOT Supplement Series 273. Sheffield: Sheffield Academic Press.

Kolarcik, Michael. 1997. "The Book of Wisdom: Introduction, Commentary, and Reflections." Pages 435-600 in *Introduction to Wisdom Literature; Proverbs; Ecclesiastes; Song of Songs; Book of Wisdom; Sirach.* Vol. 5 of *New Interpreter's Bible.* Edited by Leander E. Keck. Nashville, TN: Abingdon.

Kovacs, Brian. 1974. "Is There a Class-Ethic in Proverbs." Pages 173-89 in *Essays in Old Testament Ethics.* Edited by James L. Crenshaw and John T. Willis. New York: Ktav.

Kramer, Samuel Noah. 1990. "The Sage in Sumerian Literature: A Composite Protrait." Pages 31-44 in *The Sage in Israel and the Ancient Near East* (see Gammie and Perdue).

Kressel, Gideon M. 1994. "An Anthropological Response to the Use of Social Science Models in Biblical Studies." *Semeia* 68:153-61.

Krüger, Thomas. 2004. *Qohelet: A Commentary.* Translated by O. C. Dean Jr. Hermeneia. Minneapolis: Fortress.

Kuntz, Kenneth J. 2003. "Reclaiming Biblical Wisdom Psalms: A Response to Crenshaw." *Currents in Biblical Research* 1:145-54.

Lambert, W. G. 1996. *Babylonian Wisdom Literature.* Winona Lakes: Eisenbrauns. Repr. from Oxford: Oxford University Press, 1960.

Lang, Bernhard. 2004. "The Hebrew Wife and the Ottoman Wife: An Anthropological Essay on Proverbs 31:10-31." Pages 140-57 in

Anthropology and Biblical Studies: Avenues of Approach. Edited by Louise J. Lawrence and Mario I. Aguilar. Leiden: Deo.

Lauha, Aarre. 1981. "Kohelets Verhältnis zur Geschichte." Pages 393–401 in *Die Botschaft und die Boten: Festschrift für Hans Walter Wolff zum 70. Geburtstag.* Edited by Jörg Jeremias and Lothar Perlit. Neukirchen-Vluyn: Neukirchener Verlag.

Leithart, Peter J. 2013. "Solomon's Sexual Wisdom: Qohelet and the Song of Songs in the Postmodern Condition." Pages 445–64 in *The Words of the Wise Are like Goads: Engaging Qohelet in the 21st Century.* Edited by Mark J. Boda, Tremper Longman III, and Cristian G. Rata. Winona Lakes, IN: Eisenbrauns.

Lemaire, André. 1984. "Sagesse et ecoles." *Vetus Testamentum* 34:271–81.

Lemche, Niels-Peter. 1994. Kings and Clients: On Loyalty between the Ruler and the Ruled in Ancient 'Israel.'" *Semeia* 66:119–32.

———. 1995. "The History of Ancient Syria and Palestine: An Overview." Pages 1195–1218 in vol. 2 in *Civilizations of the Ancient Near East* (see Sasson 1995).

Lenski, Gerhard E. 1984. *Power and Privilege: A Theory of Social Stratification.* New York: McGraw-Hill, 1966. Repr., Chapel Hill: University of North Carolina.

Levine, Lee I. 1999. *Judaism and Hellenism in Antiquity: Conflict or Confluence?* Peabody, MA: Hendrickson. Repr. from Seattle: University of Washington, 1998.

Lichtheim, Miriam. 1975–1980. *Ancient Egyptian Literature.* 3 vols. Paperback ed. Berkeley: University of California Press.

———. 1997. *Moral Values in Ancient Egypt.* Orbis Biblicus et Orientalis 155. Fribourg, Switzerland and Göttingen: Fribourg University Press and Vandenhoeck & Ruprecht.

Lipiński, E. 1988. "Royal and State Scribes in Ancient Jerusalem." Pages 157–64 in *Congress Volume Jerusalem 1986.* Supplements to Vetus Testamentum 40. Leiden: Brill.

Liverani, Mario. 2001. *International Relations in the Ancient Near East, 1600–1100 B.C.* Studies in Diplomacy. Hampshire, England: Palgrave.

Loader, J. A. 1979. *Polar Structures in the Book of Qohelet.* Beihefte zur Zeitschrift für die alttestamentliche Wissenschaft 152. Berlin: de Gruyter.

Longman, Tremper, III. No Date. "Literary Approaches to Biblical Interpretation." Pages 95–192 in *Foundations of Contemporary Interpretation: Six Volumes in One.* Edited by Moisés Silva. Grand Rapids, MI: Zondervan.

_____. 1998. *The Book of Ecclesiastes.* New International Commentary on the Old Testament. Grand Rapids, MI: Eerdmans.

McCauley, Robert N. 2011. *Why Religion Is Natural and Science Is Not.* Oxford: Oxford University Press.

McCown, Chester Charlton. 1947. *Tell en-Nasbeh: Excavated under the Direction of the Late William Frederic Badé, Volume I: Archaeological and Historical Results.* Berkeley: Palestine Institute of Pacific School of Religion.

Machinist, Peter. 1995. "Fate, *miqreh*, and Reason: Some Reflections on Qohelet and Biblical Thought." Pages 159–75 in *Solving Riddles and Untying Knots: Biblical, Epigraphic, and Semitic Studies in Honor of Jonas C. Greenfield.* Edited by Ziony Zevit, Seymour Gitin, and Michael Sokoloff. Winona Lake, IN: Eisenbrauns.

Mack-Fisher, Loren R. 1990a. "A Survey and Reading Guide to the Didactic Literature of Ugarit: Prolegomenon to a Study on the Sage." Pages 67–80 in *The Sage in Israel and the Ancient Near East* (see Gammie and Perdue).

_____. 1990b. "The Scribe (and Sage) in the Royal Court at Ugarit." Pages 109–15 in *The Sage in Israel and the Ancient Near East* (see Gammie and Perdue).

Mannheim, Karl. 1936. *Ideology and Utopia: An Introduction to the Sociology of Knowledge.* New York: Harcourt Brace.

Matthews, Victor H. 1999. "The Unwanted Gift: Implications of Obligatory Gift Giving in Ancient Israel." *Semeia* 87:91–104.

————. 2000. *Old Testament Themes.* St. Louis: Chalice.

————. 2001. *Social World of the Hebrew Prophets.* Peabody, MA: Hendrickson.

Matthews, Victor H. and Don C. Benjamin. 2006. *Old Testament Parallels: Laws and Stories from the Ancient Near East.* Third ed. New York: Paulist Press.

Mattila, Sharon Lea. 2000. "Ben Sira and the Stoics: A Reexamination of the Evidence." *JBL* 119:473–501.

Meyers, Carol. 1997. "The Family in Early Israel." Pages 1–47 in *Families in Ancient Israel.* The Family, Religion, and Culture. Edited by Leo Perdue et al. Louisville, KY: Westminster John Knox.

————. 2013. *Rediscovering Eve: Ancient Israelite Women in Context.* Oxford: Oxford University Press.

————. 2014. "Was Ancient Israel a Patriarchal Society?" *JBL* 133:8–27.

Michalowski, Piotr. 1995. "Sumerian Literature: An Overview." Pages 2279–91 in vol. 4 of *Civilizations of the Ancient Near East* (see Sasson 1995).

Millard, Alan. 2011. "The Alphabet." Pages 14–27 in *Languages from the World of the Bible.* Berlin: de Gruyter.

Miller, Douglas B. 2000. "What the Preacher Forgot: The Rhetoric of Ecclesiastes." *CBQ* 62:215–35.

Miller, Peter. July 2007. "Swarm Theory." *National Geograhic.* Online: http://ngm.nationalgeographic.com/2007/07/swarms/miller-text (accessed March 17, 2015).

Mill, John Stuart. 1958. *Utilitarianism.* Edited by Oskar Piest. The Library of Liberal Arts. Indianapolis: Bobbs-Merrill.

Miller, Patrick D, Jr. 1986. *Interpreting the Psalms.* Philadelphia: Fortress.

Müller, Hans-Peter. 1980. "*Chākham.*" Pages 364–85 in vol. 4 of *Theological Dictionary of the Old Testament.* Edited by G. Johannes Botterweck and Helmer Ringgren. Translated by David E. Green. 15 vols. Grand Rapids, MI: Eerdmans, 1974–1995.

Murphy, Roland E. 1981. *Wisdom Literature: Job, Proverbs, Ruth, Canticles, Ecclesiastes, and Esther.* Forms of the Old Testament Literature 13. Grand Rapids, MI: Eerdmans.

_____. 1990. *The Tree of Life: An Exploration of Biblical Wisdom Literature.* Anchor Bible Reference Library. New York: Doubleday.

_____. 1998. *Proverbs.* Word Biblical Commentary 22. Nashville, TN: Thomas Nelson.

Nemat-Nejat, Karen R. 1995. "Systems for Learning Mathematics in Mesopotamian Scribal Schools." *Journal of Near Eastern Studies* 54:241–60.

Newsom, Carol A. 2003. *The Book of Job: A Context of Moral Imagination.* Oxford: Oxford University Press.

_____. 2007. "Spying Out the Land: A Report from Genology." Pages 19–30 in *Bakhtin and Genre Theory in Biblical Studies.* Edited by Roland Boer. Semeia Studies 63. Atlanta: SBL.

Neyrey, Jerome H. 1998. "Limited Good." Pages 122–27 in *Handbook of Biblical Social Values* (see Pilch and Malina).

Noll, K. L. 2013. *Canaan and Israel in Antiquity: A Textbook on History and Religion.* Second ed. London: Bloomsbury.

Parker, Simon B. 1995. "The Literatures of Canaan, Ancient Israel, and Phoenicia: An Overview." Pages 2399–2410 in vol. 4 of *Civilizations of the Ancient Near East* (see Sasson 1995).

Pearce, Laurie E. 1995. "The Scribes and Scholars of Ancient Mesopotamia." Pages 2265–78 in vol. 4 of *Civilizations of the Ancient Near East* (see Sasson 1995).

Pemberton, Glen D. 2005. "The Rhetoric of the Father in Proverbs 1–9." *JSOT* 30:63–82.

Penchansky, David. 2001. "Is Hokmah an Israelite Goddess, and What Should We Do about It?" Pages 81-92 in *Postmodern Interpretations of the Bible—A Reader*. Edited by A. K. A. Adam. St. Louis: Chalice.

Perdue, Leo G. 2008. *The Sword and the Stylus: An Introduction to Wisdom in the Age of Empires*. Grand Rapids, MI: Eerdmans.

Perelman, Chaïm and L. Olbrechts-Tyteca. 1971. *The New Rhetoric: A Treatise on Argumentation*. Paperback ed. Notre Dame, IN: University of Notre Dame.

Perry, T. A. 1993. *Wisdom Literature and the Structure of Proverbs*. University Park, PA: Pennsylvania State University.

Peristiany, J. G.,ed. 1974. *Honour and Shame: The Values of Mediterranean Society*. Chicago: University of Chicago Press. Repr. Midway.

_____. 1974. "Introduction." Pages 9-18 in *Honour and Shame*.

Petersen, David L. 1997. "Rethinking the Nature of Prophetic Literature." Pages 23-40 in *Prophecy and Prophets: The Diversity of Contemporary Issues in Scholarship*. Edited by Yehoshua Gitay. Semeia Studies. Atlanta: Scholars.

Petersen, David L. and Kent Harold Richards. 1992. *Interpreting Hebrew Poetry*. Guides to Biblical Scholarship Old Testament Series. Minneapolis: Fortress.

Pilch, John J. and Bruce J. Malina, eds. *Handbook of Biblical Social Values*. Peabody, MA: Hedrickson.

_____. "Introduction." Pages xv-xl in *Handbook of Biblical Social Values*.

Pitts-Rivers, Julian. 1974. "Honour and Social Status." Pages 19-77 in *Honour and Shame: The Values of Mediterranean Society* (see Peristiany).

Plevnik, Joseph. 1998. "Honor/Shame." Pages 106-115 in *Handbook of Biblical Social Values* (see Pilch and Malina).

Potts, Michael. 1995. "Hopkins and the Theory of Metaphor." *American Catholic Philosophical Quarterly* 68:502-13.

Poulantzas, Nicos. "On Social Classes." *New Left Review* 78:27-54.

Pritchard, James B., ed. 1969. *Ancient Near Eastern Texts Relating to the Old Testament.* Third ed. Princeton: Princeton University Press.

Rad, Gerhard von. 1972. *Wisdom in Israel.* Nashville, TN: Abingdon.

Rainey, Anson F. and Steven R. Notley. 2006. *The Sacred Bridge: Carta's Atlas of the Biblical World.* Jerusalem: Carta.

Redditt, Paul L. 1999. *Daniel.* Sheffield: Sheffield Academic Press.

Redford, Donald B. "Ancient Egyptian Literature: An Overview." Pages 2223-41 in vol. 4 of *Civilizations of the Ancient Near East* (see Sasson 1995).

Roberts, Adam. 2000. *Fredric Jameson.* Routledge Critical Thinkers. London: Routledge.

Rollston, Christopher A. 2010. *Writing and Literacy of Ancient Israel: Epigraphic Evidence from the Iron Age.* Archaeology and Biblical Studies 11. Atlanta: SBL.

Rose, Martin. 1999. "De la 'crise de la sagesse' à la 'sagesse de la crise.'" *Revue de théologie et de philosophie* 131:115-34.

Rudman, Dominic. 1999. "A Note on the Dating of Ecclesiastes." *CBQ* 61:47-52.

Ruffle, John. 1977. "The Teaching of Amenemope and Its Connection with the Book of Proverbs." *Tyndale Bulletin* 28:29-38.

Sadri, Ahmad. 1994. *Max Weber's Sociology of Intellectuals.* Paperback ed. New York: Oxford University Press.

Sanders, Jack T. 2001. "When Sacred Canopies Collide: The Reception of the Torah of Moses in the Wisdom Literature of the Second-Temple Period." *Journal for the Study of Judaism* 32:121-36.

Sanders, Seth L. 2004. "What Was the Alphabet for? The Rise of Written Vernaculars and the Making of Israelite National Literature." *Maarav* 11:25-56.

Sandoval, Timothy J. 2006. *The Discourse of Wealth and Poverty in the Book of Proverbs.* Leiden: Brill.

Sandy, D. Brent and Ronald L. Giese, Jr., eds. 1995. *Cracking Old Testament Codes: A Guide to Interpreting Literary Genres of the Old Testament*. Nashville, TN: Broadman & Holman.

Sasson, Jack M., ed. 1995. *Civilizations of the Ancient Near East*. 4 vols. New York: Charles Scriber's Sons.

————. 2002. "The Burden of Scribes." Pages 211-28 in *Riches Hidden in Secret Places: Ancient Near Eastern Studies in Memory of Thorkild Jacobsen*. Edited by Tzvi Abusch. Winona Lake, IN: Eisenbrauns.

Schellenberg, Annette. 2010. "A 'Lying Pen of the Scribes' (Jer. 8:8)? Orality and Writing in the Formation of the Prophetic Books." Pages 285-309 in *The Interface of Orality and Writing: Speaking, Seeing, Writing in the Shaping of New Genres*. Edited by Annette Weissenrieder and Robert B. Coote. Tübingen: Mohr Siebeck.

Schipper, Bernd U. 2013. "When Wisdom Is Not Enough! The Discourse on Wisdom and Torah and the Composition of the Book of Proverbs." Pages 55-79 in *Wisdom and Torah: The Reception of 'Torah' in the Wisdom Literature of the Second Temple Period*. Edited by Bernd U. Schipper and D. Andrew Teeter. Leiden: Brill.

Schniedewind, W. M. 2004. *How the Bible Became a Book: The Textualization of Ancient Israel*. Cambridge: Cambridge University Press.

Schwáb, Zoltán S. 2013. *Toward an Interpretation of the Book of Proverbs: Selfishness and Secularity Reconsidered*. Journal of Theological Interpretation Supplement 7. Winona Lake, IN: Eisenbrauns.

Seow, C. L. 1995. "Qohelet's Autobiography." Pages 275-87 in *Fortunate the Eyes That See: Essays in Honor of David Noel Freedman in Celebration of his Seventieth Birthday*. Edited by A. B. Beck et al. Grand Rapids, MI: Eerdmans.

————. 1996. "Linguistic Evidence and the Dating of Qohelet." *JBL* 115:643-66.

Wisdom

Index of Names and Subjects